# THE POLITICS OF INTEGRATION

# The POLITICS of INTEGRATION
## Caribbean Sovereignty Revisited

Terri-Ann Gilbert-Roberts

IAN RANDLE PUBLISHERS
*Kingston • Miami*

First published in Jamaica, 2013
by Ian Randle Publishers
11 Cunningham Avenue
Box 686
Kingston 6
www.ianrandlepublishers.com

NATIONAL LIBRARY OF JAMAICA CATALOGUING-IN-PUBLICATION DATA
Gilbert-Roberts, Terri-Ann
    The politics of integration : Caribbean sovereignty revisited /
Terri-Ann Gilbert-Roberts


        p. ; cm.
Bibliography : p. – Includes index
ISBN 978-976-637-622-2 (pbk)


1    Sovereignty    2. Caribbean Area - Politics and government
3.  Caribbean Area – Economic integration  4.  Caribbean cooperation
I.  Title


320.15    dc 22

Cover and Book Design by Ian Randle Publishers
Printed and Bound in United States of America

**To all Caribbean citizens** who retain faith and hope that their Community will eventually fully engage in a process of regional integration, enabled by an effective governance system, which reflects their common identity, connects them one to another, and helps them to meet their development aspirations.

# TABLE OF CONTENTS

List of Tables and Illustrations     ► viii

Acknowledgements     ► ix

Introduction     ► xi

Acronyms and Abbreviations     ► xviii

1 » Conceptualising the Problematic
of Sovereignty in Regionalism     ► 1

2 » Analysing Regional Governance
as an Institutional Imperative     ► 19

3 » West Indian Nationalism and
the Paradox of Sovereignty     ► 38

4 » The Caribbean Community (CARICOM)
as a Sovereignty Safeguard     ► 65

5 » Expert Recommendations on
Institutional Reform     ► 92

6 » First Generation Institutional Change     ► 119

7 » Shared Sovereignty and
Regional Governance Policy     ► 146

8 » Second Generation Institutional Change     ► 179

9 » The Eastern Caribbean
Subculture of Governance     ► 196

10 » Caribbean Sovereignty:
Legacy and Prospects     ► 226

Notes     ► 251

Select Bibliography     ► 287

Index     ► 313

# LIST OF TABLES AND ILLUSTRATIONS

Figure 1.1:   Unbundling Sovereignty ▶ 10

Figure 2.1:   The Sovereignty Bargains Cocktail ▶ 23

Figure 2.2:   Sovereignty Bargain Scenarios ▶ 25

Figure 2.3:   Framework for Regional Governance Analysis ▶ 36

Figure 3.1:   Contending Regionalist Perspectives ▶ 43

Figure 4.1:   Philosophies of Integration ▶ 66

Figure 5.1:   Interrelated Expert Analyses
of CARICOM Governance ▶ 96

Figure 5.2:   Proposals for a Community
of Sovereign States ▶ 105

Figure 5.3:   CARICOM Structures of Unity ▶ 107

Figure 6.1:   Organisational Structure of CARICOM ▶ 121

Figure 6.2:   Revamping the CRNM ▶ 135

Figure 7.1:   Rose Hall Pillars of Regional Governance ▶ 153

Figure 7.2:   Integration and Sovereignty ▶ 157

Figure 7.3:   The PMEGG's Pillars and Proposed Structure ▶ 163

Figure 7.4:   The TWG's Proposed Regional
Governance Framework ▶ 167

Figure 7.5:   Evolution of the Regional Governance
Reform Agenda ▶ 175

Figure 9.1:   The OECS Governance Framework ▶ 203

Figure 9.2:   Eastern Caribbean Path of
Governance and Integration ▶ 208

Figure 9.3:   Proposals for Governance Structure
of OECS Union (2006) ▶ 212

Figure 9.4:   Model 1 for Trinidad-OECS Economic Union ▶ 218

Figure 9.5:   Model 2 for Trinidad-OECS Political Union ▶ 221

Figure 10.1: Hierarchy of Attributes
in CARICOM Sovereignty ▶ 244

# Acknowledgements

I am grateful to several persons who have provided support in the preparation of this book. The manuscript emerged from a thesis developed during my three years of doctoral research at The University of Sheffield which could not have been undertaken without the generous scholarship awarded by the Commonwealth Scholarship Commission in the United Kingdom (CSCUK). Of course, I must express my gratitude to my thesis supervisors in the Department of Politics at the University of Sheffield for their guidance. Anthony Payne's detailed critique and thought-provoking annotations served as strong motivation during the research process and I also thank Jean Grugel for her advice.

This research on the politics of Caribbean integration has indubitably been enriched by the insightful thoughts shared with me by the various persons I interviewed during my visits to Barbados, Guyana, Jamaica and Trinidad and Tobago. In that regard, I make special mention of the staff of the CARICOM Secretariat, and in particular, former Secretary-General Edwin Carrington and Special Adviser Marilyne Trotz for being open to my critique of the existing framework. I am also grateful to former Assistant Secretary-General Edward Greene, and the 'youth' of the Human and Social Development Division for accommodating me and providing a space to work in the intervals between interviews. I was also deeply inspired and encouraged by my discussions with Denis Benn, Norman Girvan, Kenneth Hall and Vaughan Lewis; and I am grateful to Sir Alister McIntyre, Sir Shridath Ramphal, and Roderick Rainford for filling in so many historical gaps in such a stimulating but equally relaxed fashion. I also learnt immensely from the specialist legal tutorials given by Cuthbert Joseph and Duke Pollard; the views and experiences of Michele Lowe; and the up to date commentaries of David Jessop and Rickey Singh.

For their hospitality and demonstrations of Caribbean unity, I thank Emerson Bryan, Ryssa Brathwaite, Yldiz Beighle, Sherwin Bridgewater and Anthonette July.

Finally, my greatest debt of gratitude is to my mother, Marcia Gilbert-Roberts, whose searching questions, unwavering encouragement and enthusiastic monitoring of the work in progress provided stimulation to complete the study and have it published.

# INTRODUCTION

A critical three-tiered question lies at the heart of any discussion of politics and governance.

> *'Who governs whom...why (for what purpose)...and how (by what means?)'*

Accordingly, various theoretical traditions have made assumptions about the nature and role of leadership, about ideas and ideology and about governing institutions. In the context of Politics and International Relations scholarship, those assumptions have been confined to the conceptual parameters of a system of sovereign states. In that regard, the answers to the first two queries – *'Who governs whom...and why?'* – have been treated as axiomatic. States govern 'the people' through governmental representatives who are empowered to exercise political power on behalf of 'the people' in the pursuit of human and socio-economic development. State sovereignty has therefore, traditionally enjoyed an unopposed position as the dominant paradigm for governance. However, contemporary processes of globalisation and regionalisation have increasingly challenged the predominance of sovereignty, giving rise to a complex governance problematic.

Since the end of the Second World War in particular, scholars pursuing an answer to the third tranche of our question: essentially, *'How do states govern?'*, have been confronted with an arena for governance which extends beyond the territorial borders of the state. Firstly, the liberalisation of socio-economic activity worldwide, via processes of globalisation, has created an arena for international governance in which non-state actors also exercise political influence over the process of development, even without attaining sovereignty. In that regard, liberal theoretical traditions have continuously challenged the predominance of the realist state-centric paradigm, in light of the increased influence of transnational private and civil society interests in the governance process. Yet, both liberal traditions as well as neo-realist traditions, while acknowledging the role of other actors, continue to recognise the special role of the state in developing the regime of rules that govern the arena in which all the actors operate. Indeed, 'global governance', as a new area of enquiry, continues to investigate the role of states in intergovernmental organisations like the United Nations. In those settings, state sovereignty is not considered to be obscured by the agency of international organisations but rather, to be fully exercised within that collective framework.

At the same time, a second type of transnational activity has raised more serious challenges to sovereignty. The increased regionalisation of political activity, whether complementary to, or incongruous with the aforementioned global governance regimes, has given rise to the emergence of supranational actors that have, in many instances, assumed roles traditionally played by sovereign states. Although states ultimately retain responsibility for the creation of supranational capacity arising from intergovernmental regionalism, the emergent supranational institutions are empowered, on establishment, to operate autonomously of the state but also in cooperation with national governance institutions. The dynamics associated with the coexistence of intergovernmental, supranational and national spheres of power present a conceptual and institutional challenge to the 'state sovereignty' paradigm. That challenge is representative of a problematic relationship between sovereignty, on the one hand, and regional governance, on the other hand.

Certainly, a similar problematic has been explored in several other regions, particularly in Europe, Latin America and Southeast Asia and, to a lesser extent, in the Pacific and Southern Africa.[1] However, the experiences of smaller developing countries have hitherto received minimal attention. In that context, this book grapples with the dynamics of the problematic by way of an exploration of the experience of regional governance among the 15 developing states of the Caribbean Community (CARICOM), where a paradox of sovereignty is clearly evident.[2]

## THE PARADOX OF SOVEREIGNTY
## IN SMALL DEVELOPING STATES

Notwithstanding the acknowledgement of general 'paradoxes of state power' highlighted in the aforementioned literature on regionalism, a distinct nuance of 'paradox' emerges among certain categories of developing states. The special challenges associated with developing states such as those in the Caribbean include the fact that they are not only small, but that they are also relatively 'youthful'. In the first instance, consequent on their small size, CARICOM states face structural challenges related to limitations in natural, human and technical resources which suggest that a regional approach to governance holds greater potential to contribute to the attainment of their development goals than do exclusively statist strategies. In that regard, their small size has encouraged the pursuit of shared development strategies through regional integration. In the second instance, these states are further constrained in the implementation of regional integration by virtue of their limited historical experience of governance. The novelty of sovereignty – in a region where all but three of the member states gained sovereign independence less than 50 years ago – serves as an inducement to fragmentation and the emphasis on individual state projects of governance.[3] Together, those two characteristics – small size and youthfulness associated with limited sovereign experience – present the CARICOM region as a particularly interesting case for investigating the problematic relationship between sovereignty and regional governance. While the constraints of small size suggest that regional governance should be treated as an imperative for effective governance of the development process, the characteristic of 'youthfulness' undermines the process of addressing that imperative.

Accordingly, the concept of a paradox of sovereignty in the Caribbean provides a foundation to better contextualise the problematic analysed in these pages. The concept, first introduced by William Demas, and discussed more extensively in chapter 3, highlights the peculiar situation among small states in which, theoretically, the erosion of recently-attained sovereignty through the delegation of authority to regional institutions is, paradoxically, essential for the reinforcement of the sovereign capacity of the state. In effect, without collective action through transfers of authority to shared institutions, small states are constrained in the implementation of their development goals. In other words, Demas juxtaposed the erosion of formal state sovereignty with the potential for acheiving an effecive sovereignty at the regional level. However, the significance of contextualising the case within this paradox of sovereignty has less to do with the structural context of small size and more to do with the problematic that is presented to the leaders of *new* states, irrespective of their size. Fundamentally, the imperative of eroding sovereignty in order to reinforce it raises some interesting issues related to the value which political elites, that is, the leaders responsible for governance, place on sovereignty and the extent to which they display, at the same time, a level of willingness to compromise sovereignty in order to reap the benefits of regional governance. In effect, the central question raised by the Demasian paradox, which is the formative problem investigated in this study, is:

*How do the meaning attributed to and the value placed on sovereignty by political leaders, as well as their attendant interpretation of the imperative inherent in sovereignty paradox, constrain or catalyse the regional governance process?*

In that regard, the discussion in the following pages is concerned with the way in which political elites interpret sovereignty as well as the paradox of sovereignty. It is also concerned with the extent to which those interpretations have influenced the emergence, evolution and functioning of regional institutions, and ultimately, the extent to which they have determined the overall effectiveness of regional governance. The study assumes that the relationship between the theoretical implications of the Demasian paradox and the empirical manifestations (the institutional forms) will be influenced by and reflective of the historical, socio-cultural and broad political context from which they emerge.

Against the background of those assumptions, the following argument is proposed. In the context of new states, including those in the Caribbean, sovereignty has evolved in close association with movements for national independence and is reflective of emergent national identities. In that scenario, the legitimacy of the authority of political elites is firmly embedded within nationalist expectations of a responsibility to safeguard sovereignty. As a consequence, elites are likely to place a high value on the concept of sovereignty and be unwilling to compromise it in a regional context, since the maintenance of legitimate national authority will be contingent on their personal success in the guardianship of the concept. The hypothesis is further advanced to suggest that if elites embed an approach to safeguarding sovereignty within the regional governance framework, then, they will not have fulfilled the theoretical imperative of the paradox – the need to surrender sovereignty – and ultimately, regional governance institutions will be denied the capacity to govern the regional framework effectively.

In order to test this hypothesis, the study develops an understanding of the politics of integration, and more specifically the internal dynamics of CARICOM governance. The specific questions raised about CARICOM, which are refined further in chapter 2 relate to how sovereignty emerged in the region, how it was conceptualised, how political elites constructed interpretations of the paradox of sovereignty and how those interpretations have impinged on the institutional mode of governance. Those questions raised by the hypothesis provided the framework for the formulation of a historical and exploratory methodological approach to researching the CARICOM experience of regional governance.

The research which underpins this book was undertaken between 2007 and 2010 and has led to the formulation of a three-pronged review of the case. Firstly, the paradoxical relationship, established within the literature, between the concepts of sovereignty and regionalism – the one representing a traditional symbol of governance and the other a contemporary development strategy – is reviewed in the opening chapters in order to support the construction of a special framework for the definition and analysis of regional governance. Chapter 1 reviews the historical evolution of the concept of sovereignty, revealing its multi-dimensional character. It further discusses the role which regionalism plays in enhancing state capacity for governance and the implications which regionalism has had for the various dimensions of sovereignty. Finally, it uses the insights from those understandings of sovereignty and regionalism to define the concept of regional governance. Chapter 2 advances a three-tiered analytical framework which employs political context analysis, institutional analysis and sovereignty bargains analysis in order to contend with the central research questions on the relationship between the interpretations of sovereignty held by political elites and the strategies that they adopt to resolve the paradox of sovereignty.

The second part of the discussion presents an empirical review of the evolution and functioning of CARICOM and Eastern Caribbean regional institutions between 1947 and 2012 (chapters 3–9). The historical analysis compiles the results of document analysis and interviews with elites involved in regional and national decision-making at both personal and professional levels. The primary sources of documentation reviewed were official speeches, statements and agreements which reflect the analytical focus on the role of elites in framing the regional governance context and special attention has been given to analysis of the decisions emanating from the annual conferences of CARICOM Heads of Government which have been instrumental in the formation of a view on the meaning of sovereignty in a context of regional decision-making. Other secondary sources of academic literature assisted in the framing of the broader context of events, the assessment of the involvement of other state and non-state actors and the influence of ideologies and philosophies on the institution-building processes. As a complement to the document analysis, off-the-record interviews were conducted with the widest possible range of senior representatives of national governments, regional and national civil and public service, social scientists within academia, the private sector and civil society across the region. The findings from those interviews have been instrumental in reconstructing elite perspectives on CARICOM's history and the tradition of sovereignty. Respondents provided background information about the dynamics of high-level deliberations among leaders, technocrats and other stakeholders. As a consequence, those very instructive insights have been incorporated into the analysis without quoting or identifying individual informants.

Together, the findings highlight the way in which the interrelationships among the interpretations of political elites; the Caribbean political context and political culture; ideas and ideologies; and the institutional structures have affected the regional governance framework, with special reference to the efficiency and effectiveness of the decision-making and implementation processes. The chronological narrative culminates with an exploration of the potential and limitations inherent in the existence of a distinct Eastern Caribbean subculture of regional governance, having regard to the strengthening of the overarching CARICOM framework. In spite of the fact that the subregional framework is comfortably nested within the wider political context of CARICOM and the political elites share similar understandings of sovereignty, the historical evolution of the OECS has given rise to different institutional forms of governance which have been perceived to be more efficient. Chapter 9 explains the reasons for that distinction and its relationship to the CARICOM case.

Finally, the book presents some conclusions about the legacy of the regional tradition of sovereignty and discusses prospects for change. Therefore, chapter 10 concludes the entire investigation with a discussion on the influence of the CARICOM tradition of sovereignty on the effectiveness of the mode of regional governance and speculates on the prospects for reconstruction of new modes of regional governance. Specifically, by consolidating the empirical data on CARICOM and the assumptions of the conceptual and analytical frameworks, the study argues that the way in which the paradox of sovereignty has been construed and constructed by political elites has impinged negatively on the effectiveness of the CARICOM mode of governance. In essence, those elite interpretations have largely been responsible for the weaknesses widely acknowledged in the institutional framework.

Admittedly, limitations are inherent in analytical processes and there are two which are noted in respect of this investigation. The first is that in the context of this historical methodology, it has been difficult to interpret, with complete accuracy, the thoughts of elites. However, interviewees were particularly instrumental in providing insight into the ideational, philosophical and cultural views and beliefs which influenced the actions of key regional decision-makers. Where possible, close attention was paid to matching those insights to the written accounts of the decision-makers themselves. This generally revealed a strong commonality of themes in relation to identification of key factors that have influenced the governance process. In that context, the interpretations presented in this thesis can be considered as valid without intent of seeking to be clairvoyant. The second limitation is that the scope of the investigation is relatively wide and therefore the book does not claim to have accounted, at the time of writing, for every single contextual factor which could have impinged on regional governance between 1947 and 2012. Instead, the study focuses on significant events that have had a deep and lasting impact on the conceptualisation of sovereignty and the creation and modification of regional institutions. I trust that notwithstanding such limitations, the analysis will present an interesting and informative account of sovereignty within a regional framework and of the regional governance phenomenon which still requires new and effective strategies to reinforce its relevance to the development process. In pursuance of the research framework introduced here, we now turn to establishing the conceptual foundations of the study in chapter 1.

# ACRONYMS AND ABBREVIATIONS

| | |
|---|---|
| ACP | African, Caribbean and Pacific Group of States |
| ACCP | Assembly of Caribbean Community Parliamentarians |
| ACS | Association of Caribbean States |
| ALBA | Bolivarian Alternative for Latin America |
| ASEAN | Association of South East Asian Nations |
| APEC | Asia-Pacific Economic Cooperation |
| BLP | Barbados Labour Party |
| CAIC | Caribbean Association of Industry and Commerce |
| CARICOM | Caribbean Community |
| CARIFORUM | Caribbean Forum of ACP States |
| CARIFTA | Caribbean Free Trade Association |
| CCJ | Caribbean Court of Justice |
| CCL | Caribbean Congress of Labour |
| CDB | Caribbean Development Bank |
| CHOG | Conference of Heads of Government of the Caribbean Community |
| CLE | Council of Legal Education |
| CMC | Common Market Council |
| COFAP | Council on Finance and Planning |
| COFCOR | Council for Foreign and Community Relations |
| COHSOD | Council on Human and Social Development |
| CONSLE | Council for National Security and Law Enforcement |
| COTED | Council on Trade and Economic Development |
| CPDC | Caribbean Policy Development Centre |
| CRIP | Caribbean Regional Indicative Programme |
| CRNM | Caribbean Regional Negotiating Machinery |
| CSE | CARICOM Single Economy |
| CSM | CARICOM Single Market |
| CSME | CARICOM Single Market and Economy |
| CXC | Caribbean Examinations Council |
| ECB | European Central Bank |
| ECCA | Eastern Caribbean Currency Authority |
| ECCM | Eastern Caribbean Common Market |
| EEC | European Economic Community |
| EU | European Union |
| ECJ | European Court of Justice |
| ECSC | Eastern Caribbean Supreme Court |

| | |
|---|---|
| EPA | Economic Partnership Agreement |
| FLP | Federal Labour Party |
| FTAA | Free Trade Areas of the Americas |
| IDMAG | International Development Management Advisory Group |
| ISER | Institute of Social and Economic Research |
| JCC | Joint Consultative Committee |
| JCPC | Judicial Committee of the Privy Council |
| JLP | Jamaica Labour Party |
| JMA | Jamaica Manufacturer's Association |
| LDC | Less Developed Country |
| MDC | More Developed Country |
| MERCOSUR | Common Market of the South |
| PNP | People's National Party |
| NAFTA | North American Free Trade Area |
| NIEO | New International Economic Order |
| NWG | New World Group |
| OAU | Organisation of African Unity |
| OCC | Order of the Caribbean Community |
| OECS | Organisation of Eastern Caribbean States |
| OTN | Office of Trade Negotiations |
| PMEGG | Prime Ministerial Expert Group on Governance |
| PMSCEN | Prime Ministerial Subcommittee on External Negotiations |
| PNM | People's National Movement |
| RSS | Regional Security System |
| SCOPE | Standing Committee of Opposition Parties of Eastern Caribbean States |
| SCAC | Standing Closer Association Committee |
| SDV | Single Development Vision |
| SAP | Structural Adjustment Programme |
| SCMLA | Standing Committee of Ministers responsible for Legal Affairs |
| SCMFA | Standing Committee of Ministers of Foreign Affairs |
| SICA | Central American Integration System |
| TASU | Technical Assistance and Services Unit |
| TWG | Technical Working Group on Governance |
| UNASUR | Union of South American Nations |
| UG | University of Guyana |
| UWI | The University of the West Indies |
| WIC | West Indian Commission |
| WIF | West Indies Federation |
| WISA | West Indies Associated States |

# Conceptualising the Problematic of Sovereignty in Regionalism

Understanding the paradox of sovereignty is contingent on an appreciation of the political dynamics of regional governance. The central problematic presented by the latter phenomenon relates to an inherently contentious relationship between traditional nationalist paradigms of governance and contemporary strategies of regional integration. In that regard, this exploration of the problematic begins with a review of the history of sovereignty and its influence on the theory and practice of governance. Sovereignty is demystified and disaggregated so as to better associate it with regional integration as a strategy for enhancing governance capacity in small developing countries. That juxtaposition will facilitate a definition of regional governance which informs the remainder of the study.

## The History of Sovereignty

Sovereignty is firmly embedded within global political tradition. The utility of the concept in supporting the claims to power of political elites resulted in its modification and exploitation over several centuries pursuant to the leadership aspirations of those who have claimed it. FH Hinsley's astute analysis of the concept is instructive. He remarked:

> ...authority and power are facts as old and ubiquitous as society itself...[but] they have not everywhere and at all times enjoyed the support or suffered the restraints which sovereignty, a theory or assumption about political power, seeks to construct for them....It is a concept which men [sic] in certain circumstances have applied – a quality they have attributed or a claim they have counterposed – to political power which they or other men were exercising.[1]

Notably, prior to the emergence of a modern political discourse on sovereignty, the idea of a 'sovereign' was generally applied by the

*Republica Christiana* of Medieval Europe to a description of the unitary authority of God and, by extension, his papal representative. However, that religious authority came under threat of being overthrown by several kings who claimed the right to supersede the Pope's rule within their individual territories. Eventually, conflicts between Christian authority and the various territorial political authorities, particularly over freedom of religion, contributed to the crumbling of Medieval Christendom and the gradual emergence of a new 'societas' of states which accommodated and acknowledged the power of multiple authorities under a shared set of political rules and norms.[2] The modern conception of sovereignty emerges from this context as the patron of the 'societas', gaining in significance over four key stages of European and international political history which are highlighted here in order to explain the nexus between claims to sovereignty and the practice of governance.

The four stages in the history of sovereignty occur between the sixteenth century and middle of the twentieth century. First, the collapse of the Medieval Christian imperial authority in Europe left a power vacuum which fuelled religious disputes among the various constituent units of the former empire. During the period of conflict up to the mid-sixteenth century, French philosopher Jean Bodin, himself convinced that religion, in general, and Christianity, in particular, was a constraint on individual aspirations for peace and prosperity, argued for the lacuna to be filled with political rather than religious authority. As a consequence, in 1576, Bodin coined the term 'sovereignty' to describe an ideal political order in which absolute political authority would reside with the kings of Europe rather than the Pope.[3] This initial stage in the conception of sovereignty represented an *era of loyalty to king and country above the Church.* With further advances in European political philosophy into the seventeenth century, by theorists such as Grotius, Hobbes and Machiavelli, the concept was enhanced by its association with a geographically defined space for the exercise of monarchical power.[4] The conceptualisation of the 'territorial state' created a device for linking Bodin's concept of absolute monarchical authority to a fixed domain and population. Armed with this philosophical concept of the sovereign state, political leaders eventually won the battle against the Pope and gained the mutually recognised right, under the 1648 Treaty of Westphalia, to establish and then rule over individual kingdom states. Conventionally, that Treaty represents a watershed in Politics and International Relations because it introduced two new principles of political conduct which governed the relationships among leaders in the societas of states. Firstly, the principle of *cujos region ejus religio* removed the papal authority and permitted each monarch to determine the standards of religious conduct in the territory. Secondly, the principle of *Rex in regno suo est Imperator regni sui* established the king as the exclusive authority over his own state.[5] The significance of Westphalia to the history of sovereignty lies in its pluralisation of absolute authority and the subsequent confinement of each constituent authority to a given territory. After Westphalia, kings assumed direct responsibility for the enactment, application and enforcement of laws, used as instruments of control, and agreed not to intervene within the borders of any other state.

Westphalia was followed by further philosophical debate into the eighteenth century which heightened the significance of sovereignty by establishing a new relationship between the king (as state representative) and the society – two spheres which had previously remained separate. Classical theories of state sovereignty, including those of Bodin and Hobbes, had placed no responsibility on rulers to be accountable to 'the people' or to seek their consent to govern. In opposition to Bodin's original concept of unlimited state power, other theorists, particularly Locke and Rousseau, revised the concept of sovereignty and, arguably, adopted a morally-superior notion which acknowledged the need for a social contract between the state and the people, based on respect for the right of every individual to grant his or her consent to be governed and to be protected from unjust rule.[6] Thus, the second stage of conception, which we refer to as the *popularisation of sovereignty*, established a link between the will of the people and the legitimacy of state control. This new state-society association obliged European rulers to be accountable – an obligation which was increasingly delegated to elected government officials charged with maintaining order under a system of law developed in the interests of the people. In the same vein, Locke and Rousseau supported the separation of structures of government responsible for making legislation from those responsible for applying and enforcing the law, as one way of limiting opportunities for the abuse of power.[7]

The discussions on this new state-society relationship continued for some time – highlighting at some points, the role of the state in realising the 'common good' (Hegel); at other times, reconciling Hobbesian and Rousseauian models of authority under legal constitutionalism (Kant); and at yet others, challenging the ability of the state to represent popular interests over elite interests (Marx).[8] However, by the late eighteenth century the general notion of popular sovereignty, as exercised by states for the people as a collective, had been adopted as a hallmark of the French and American Revolutions and had become entrenched in the respective constitutional documents of those countries. For its part, the American Revolution (1775–83) rejected British imperial rule over a population not located within that state's defined territory and adopted a new set of laws suited to the interests of the American people. The French Revolution (1789–99), in opposing monarchical rule, highlighted a new civic duty to democratic and representative government as the appropriate framework for the exercise of sovereignty. These revolutionary legacies, buttressed thereafter by European colonial influence, facilitated almost worldwide adoption, between the nineteenth and twentieth centuries, of a dominant 'Western' model of representative government in a modern democratic state.

However, the advent of the modern state, supported by its democratic institutions of law and government, did not prevent political conflict. In fact, most European states continued to pursue imperialist foreign policies aimed at expanding their territory and authority across the globe. The conflict among European states soon erupted in a war which extended to their colonies on other continents. The human and infrastructural devastation of the First World War, waged between 1914 and 1918, was so extensive that states were compelled to attempt the creation of a new peaceful world order. This third stage, which we refer to as the *nationalisation of sovereignty*, was facilitated by the formation in the post-war period of the League of Nations, an intergovernmental organisation among some 42 countries. The League was intended to be a vehicle for the pursuit of collective security interests through the promotion of peaceful, diplomatic relationships among sovereign states. It reinforced the Westphalian origins of non-intervention, calling for respect of existing territorial borders. However, interestingly, the League also reinforced the popular sovereignty principle of 'rule by the people' by highlighting a contradiction between continued colonialism and the right of peoples to govern themselves. On the basis of a proposal by United States President Woodrow Wilson, the League of Nations adopted a declaration on the right of all peoples of the world to national self-determination as a universal, legal and constitutional aspect of sovereignty.[9]

In spite of the declaration, the practical application of the principle of national self-determination was problematic for two main reasons. Firstly, the League lacked the enforcement capacity to secure the cessation of European expansionism and colonisation of non-European nations.

Secondly, the declaration did not fully reconcile territorial sovereignty with an emerging alternative concept of national sovereignty. Nations, traditionally classified according to the common natural characteristics of a group of people, were rarely found within discrete territorial boundaries.[10] Indeed, in many parts of the world, colonial borders had been arbitrarily drawn across ethnic, racial and linguistic lines. The persistence of conflict between national culture and sovereign territory led, therefore, to the adoption, in these contexts, of a modern nationalism – a conscious political effort to fuse state and culture into the 'nation-state'. The concept of 'national sovereignty' was adopted in colonial territories as an alternative interpretation of the traditional European 'state sovereignty' and was used as a uniting force in the struggle for independence from colonial rule.

At the same time, in some European states and in some colonies, nationalism encouraged the rise of oppressive and elitist governments which exercised tight control over some racial and social groupings. Regrettably, in Europe, extreme nationalist movements, like Fascism and Nazism, operating under the cover of state sovereignty, emerged to launch new attempts at ideological and territorial expansion, culminating in a second world war. Sovereignty had been, undoubtedly, co-opted as justification of Nazi aspirations for power, prompting Germany's invasion of Poland in 1939. In retrospect, that eventuality reinforces the vulnerability of the sovereignty concept to manipulation by political elites. Notwithstanding the fact that the concept had been developed by Bodin, in the particular context of diffusing religious conflict; and despite its subsequent refinement, in another context, by a populism aimed at increasing its relevance to the needs of the people, it was later applied in a nationalist framework as a theoretical justification for war and a new imperialism, thereby denying some peoples the right to self-determination.

Fortunately, the failure of Germany to secure its imperial ambitions and the end of the Second World War in 1945 paved the way for yet another attempt to secure international peace and security. Sovereignty was once more re-embraced as a framework for enforcing the principles of territoriality, legitimate government and rights of citizenship. In the fourth stage of conception – *the international legalisation of sovereignty* – states secured a broader and more formal system for commanding respect for sovereignty. The formal institutionalisation of sovereignty was eventually achieved within the framework of the United Nations (UN), as successor to the League of Nations. In the aftermath of two destructive world wars and in the face of the League's failure to prevent the latter, the UN introduced principles of law to the international governance system, comparable to the legal system that had served as an instrument of control within state borders. The UN bestowed on each of its more than 50 founding Member States an 'international legal personality' created within a body of international law which upheld the principles of territorial integrity and non-intervention and recognised independent countries as equal participants in and beneficiaries of an international society of states. Sovereignty represented the essence of that personality and acquired a legal definition – one of the most widely used today – as all the international rights and duties of an independent territorial state as recognised by international law.[11] International law also acknowledged the rights of colonised people to self-determination, thereby setting an agenda for decolonisation and national independence. By instituting the principle of *uti possidetis juris* (respect for existing borders), the UN settled, to a certain extent, the residual tensions relating to multi-national territories which had been inherited from the League. It fixed the geographical framework in which modern nationalist strategies could be pursued, referring to independent countries as nation-states in which multi-ethnic communities of people maintained loyalty to nationalist leaders within inherited territorial borders. In an attempt to secure peace, the UN also encouraged the acceptance of pluralism in political systems and respect for diversity among the peoples of the world.[12]

By the end of the fourth stage in its incremental institutionalisation, the concept of sovereignty was treated as an absolute, indivisible, unitary, legal condition. As Robert Jackson argued, from a legal perspective, there could be no 'relative sovereignty'. A country became fully sovereign by virtue of its independence.[13] Sovereignty had evolved from a mere theoretical descriptor to a legal status to which nations could aspire. Countries which had not yet attained the right of self-government were keen, therefore, to achieve the status of national independent statehood, because of the benefits associated with participation in the international system. These included increased political influence for previously marginalised groups, recognition of the legitimacy and authority of their leaders, and access to a regulated regime of international aid and trade. For example, although all states were eligible for equal treatment in the international trading regime, irrespective of size or economic strength, the special challenges of small developing economies were specifically considered in the crafting of a temporary regime of preferential treatment. However, those rights and benefits were also explicitly linked to the state's responsibilities under international law. The legal criteria for sovereign statehood included the existence of a stable government which did not recognise any external authority; which exercised supreme rule in a territory with settled frontiers; and which had control over a defined population.[14] These criteria correspond to the responsibilities of the state with regard to the protection of human rights and ensuring the socio-economic welfare of its citizens. In that regard, the modern nation-state, unlike the Westphalian non-interventionist state, had become subject to UN intervention in cases where human rights, which were viewed as an element of sovereignty, were deemed to have been violated.[15] Based on that international legal framework, the modern state assumed responsibility for the development of institutional rules, norms and procedures of governance which would enable governments to meet the obligations of statehood.

Beyond the legal framework, statehood required governance capacity, that is, capacity to exercise political authority in order to produce a desired effect such as human welfare and development. Interestingly, in Europe, states had already begun to develop a level of capacity for this 'effect-producing' governance, over a period of several centuries involving the establishment, review and reform of various systems of government. From the period of Westphalia onwards, government agency had created institutions of law and democratic representation to support the state's claim to sovereignty. However, by the mid-century, two new trends in international affairs had emerged to challenge the capacity of even those state institutions to govern effectively.

First, the intensification of transnational processes associated with the globalisation phenomenon – including the internationalisation of trade and the spread of ecological and security problems – required institutional responses which defied traditional state boundaries and compensated for the incapacity of individual states to control global affairs.[16] States, therefore, sought to enhance their capacity for achieving peace, security and economic development through collective intergovernmental institutions like the United Nations. At the same time, non-state actors also sought to influence the intergovernmental arena, leading to further shifts in political analysis towards discussion of 'governance' instead of 'government' and thereby, acknowledging the diversity of actors involved in political and economic decision-making. A body of literature on 'global governance' emerged with a focus on examining the role of international legal regimes and security arrangements in exercising control over transnational problems. Although that literature acknowledged the coexistence of governance structures above and below the level of the state, and even as a wider range of non-state actors were included, the fundamental traditions of governance remain unchanged since states continued to dominate the global system.[17]

A second trend in the post-Second World War environment – a process of decolonisation – reinforced the significance of the widening range of actors and the intensification of globalisation. After 1945, some 100 new states asserted claims to sovereignty and, consequently, had the associated responsibilities of governance thrust upon them immediately.[18] Although the new states adopted European-style institutions, they were not as equipped as European states with the leadership experience or capacity to support them, in some instances, due to the limitations of small size.[19] These young states were neither able to effectively protect human rights and promote the socio-economic welfare of their peoples nor participate fully in the emerging international regimes. Notably, the majority of these states were located in the so-called Third World which was caught up in the Cold War ideological conflict between the democratic First World and communist Second World. Robert Jackson has offered a thought-provoking description of these new entities. He argued that they were, in effect, 'quasi-states' which held an internationally recognised claim to political authority but lacked the institutional tools to exercise it.

The point of Jackson's interesting argument, which he developed further over several years, is that sovereign authority in new states could be considered to be 'hollow' without the power of governance capacity.[20] As a result of the weaknesses of governance in those quasi-states, sovereignty adopted a significant developmental dimension. Having already become a symbol of nationalism, it came further to symbolise the aspirations of developing countries for the achievement of economic development and improved standards of living. The postcolonial quasi-states became increasingly dependent on international development assistance and preferential treatment in the international trading system in order to build their capacity for governance at the national level; while also seeking to participate in global governance regimes.[21] In that context, international institutions began to employ the concept of 'good governance' as a measure of state sovereignty and effectiveness, based on the achievement of principles of openness, transparency, integrity and accountability in government.[22] In some cases, based on good governance criteria, sovereignty was deemed to be fragile, problematic or non-existent in some developing countries.[23]

The coincidence of the two trends of globalisation and decolonisation encouraged academic enquiry into the capacity of states to regulate transnational issues, including questions as to whether states should seek to regulate them at all. Indeed, the fact that the authority structures established to address globalisation remained embedded within states was identified as a problem in itself.[24] The 'good governance' prescriptions of international organisations also suggested that the state needed to be 'rolled back' or reconstructed to facilitate increased developmental action by the private sector and civil society.[25] The relevance of sovereignty to the contemporary context was strongly questioned. For example, Beeson's analysis of the experience of globalisation in South East Asia, concluded that the concept of sovereignty had been so compromised by globalisation that its continued relevance to International Relations theory and practice was threatened.[26] The difficulty with Beeson's prediction of an end to sovereignty was that new and developing countries fiercely defended and protected their claims to sovereignty within the international system. Whether because of the novelty of the concept or because of its value in enabling them to access economic and financial benefits from the international system, developing countries adopted perspectives of sovereignty which were reminiscent of the absolute Westphalian notion which had driven the European tradition of state-building.

## UNBUNDLING SOVEREIGNTY

The preceding review of the history of sovereignty has revealed that it has held varying meanings and values in different contexts. It was liberally exercised in the collective context of the UN, but, at the same time, fiercely guarded in its purest sense by new states. Stephen Krasner argued that the differences in conception were part of an 'organised hypocrisy' among leaders who emphasised different attributes of state authority in their use of the construct, thereby violating or compromising the aggregate concept. Those attributes include territory and population, an effective domestic hierarchy of control, *de jure* constitutional independence, de facto absence of external authority, international recognition, and the ability to regulate trans-border flows.[27]

Krasner further argued, therefore, that in order to understand the way in which sovereignty is exercised, it had to be unbundled into four different political dimensions. Firstly, he highlighted the existence of *'international legal sovereignty'* which refers to the juridical state of independence based on mutual recognition among states. This dimension is most often associated with the legalisation of sovereign statehood after 1945. Secondly, *'Westphalian sovereignty'* represents an established international order of non-intervention of external actors within a given territory. This principle dates back to the seventeenth century origins of states and is the dimension of sovereignty which is most closely associated with the autonomy of states and governments. Thirdly, *'domestic sovereignty'* implies the 'formal organisation of political authority within the state and the ability of public authorities to exercise effective control within the borders of their own polity'. Autonomy in decision-making and legitimacy under 'popular sovereignty' are essential elements of this dimension of domestic control. Finally, *'interdependence sovereignty'* refers to 'the ability of public authorities to regulate the flow of information, ideas, goods, people, pollutants, or capital across the borders of the state'.[28] This aspect of control has arguably been most affected by globalisation.

The disaggregation of sovereignty into four dimensions is useful in highlighting the multidimensional nature of the concept. In figure 1.1, the dimensions have been juxtaposed with the historical periods from the review of sovereignty in order to highlight various attributes with which sovereignty is associated.

The first two of Krasner's dimensions may also be categorised as external aspects of governance; while the latter two correspond to the internal aspects of sovereignty. In essence, the external aspect relates to sovereignty when conceptualised as state authority recognised by other states in the international system. Alternatively, the internal aspects are related to the capacity of states to exercise control over their international and domestic affairs. Bearing in mind this distinction, the four dimensions of sovereignty are loosely related.

### Figure 1.1: Unbundling Sovereignty

| Historical Period | Sovereignty Dimension and Associated Attributes |
|---|---|
| Bodin to Treaty of Westphalia | *Westphalian*: autonomy<br>Territorial integrity; absolute (monarchical) authority; freedom from external interference |
| Towards Post World War Era | *International Legal*: authority and legitimacy<br>Popular sovereignty and legitimacy; de jure constitutional independence; mutual recognition |
| Post-Colonial Period | *Domestic*: control<br>Responsibility to effectively control domestic political and socio-economic affairs |
| Globalisation/Regionalisation | *Interdependence*: control<br>Ability to regulate and control flows across borders |

Krasner's unbundled framework usefully demonstrates that it is possible to exercise one dimension of sovereignty and not another. For example, possession of international legal sovereignty does not guarantee Westphalian sovereignty, nor is it automatically accompanied by capacity for domestic or interdependence sovereignty. Yet, the possession of one dimension and not the other does not make a state cease to be formally and legally sovereign. In that regard, in the exercise of sovereignty and in the governance process, states must seek to develop institutions which regulate more specific *attributes* of sovereignty. They must seek to create an appropriate balance amongst the attributes of authority, legitimacy, autonomy and control in governance. This implies a process of bargaining with the dimensions of sovereignty in order to enhance governance capacity vis-à-vis the regulation of transnational processes. It is in respect of regulating processes of regional integration that the rationale for such a bargain is most clearly evident. At the level of the region, there has been an observed tendency for sovereignty to be voluntarily ceded, pooled or shared with other states and sometimes surrendered to other actors in order to achieve this end.[29] Neither 'good governance' theories nor 'global governance' theories have been able to contend with this phenomenon. In that regard, it is worthwhile to explore the concept of regionalism at this juncture in order to facilitate an understanding of the principles of sovereignty which are applicable in a regional context.

## REGIONALISM AS A STRATEGY FOR ENHANCED GOVERNANCE

Regionalism is a deliberate strategy, conceived within the state sovereignty paradigm, by which states pursue a variety of activities across state boundaries aimed at reorganising the regional space along new economic and political parameters.[30] The increase in the number of regionalist structures, from fewer than five in 1960 to more than 64 some four decades later, suggests a greater level of state preoccupation with enhancing capacity for regulation of transnational processes.[31] The institutions established within these arrangements are particularly pertinent to our enquiry because they intrude on sovereignty in an unprecedented way by contributing to the 'denationalisation of normal government functions [as a result of] their delegation to regional decision-making units'.[32]

In the same way that we explored the history of sovereignty, we now turn to a brief review of phases of regionalism, including regional integration. The literature on regionalism highlights various approaches to regional institution-building, aligned with distinct historical phases. Louise Fawcett has provided a particularly succinct account of three main waves of regionalism which correspond to three types of regional institution-building.[33] Firstly, she highlights the emergence over a period of two decades (1945–65) of multi-purpose institutions endorsed by the UN, such as the Organisation of American States and the Organisation of African Union, which were established to enable the constituent members to wield greater collective influence over the multilateral agenda. In Europe, economic communities were formed in complement to the multilateral agenda for peace and economic reconstruction after the two world wars. These types of regional arrangements also supported the formation of regional security alliances in the context of the ideological Cold War between democratic and communist blocs of countries. In the Cold War era, regionalism served as an interim anti-Soviet strategy but was not necessarily viewed as the most desirable instrument of political order.[34]

Between 1965 and 1985, a second wave of regional arrangements emerged which also addressed some of the security concerns of the first wave, since the Cold War was ongoing. However, they were primarily focused on building the economic capacity of 'Third World' developing countries. After decolonisation, small developing states sought to emulate the European model and established similar frameworks for regional economic integration as a way of shielding themselves from the challenges of globalisation.[35]

Finally, a third wave, the 'new regionalism', emerged after 1985 with a focus on creating a diversity of regional communities aimed at facilitating the gradual and measured integration of states into the global political economy and the achievement of the goals of international organisations.[36] More recent analyses enhance this historical chronology by referring to three interrelated 'generations' of regionalism which are not mutually exclusive. In those conceptions of regionalism, a regional institution may demonstrate all the characteristics of a first generation economic movement; a second generation all-encompassing new regionalism; and a third generation regionalism aimed at global governance.[37]

In the early decades of the emergence of regionalism, a diversity of approaches to studying the phenomenon of economic integration as a form of regionalism emerged, including neofunctionalism, liberal intergovernmentalism, new institutionalism, network analysis and transactionalist analysis.[38] However, all of these economic integration frameworks had to contend with the political question of the impact of regionalism on sovereignty. Those queries were dominated by federalist, functionalist and neofunctionalist arguments about sovereignty. Federalism was the strongest opponent of nation-state sovereignty, prescribing a form of regionalism which merged territories by erasing their individual boundaries to create, in effect, another larger unified territorial sovereignty. With the exception of the enduring federations of territories in the United States, Canada, Australia and New Zealand, the approach was not very successful. In Europe, at least, there was no concurrence of views among political actors on pursuing a federalist strategy because the concept of the smaller territorial state had already been embedded within the political consciousness.

However, given a convergence of interest among trade unions and manufacturers in Europe with respect to non-political cooperation, a theory of functionalism emerged to suggest that the pursuit of technical and economic cooperation could contribute indirectly to peace and economic development. Rather than prescribing a particular institutional form, functionalism focused on avoiding cooperation at a political level because of the history of controversy and conflict associated with sovereignty in international relations. The formation of the European Coal and Steel Community (ECSC) in 1951 was an example of functionalism in practice. The Treaty of Paris established an intergovernmental 'High Authority' accountable to member states to govern a common market for coal and steel agreed between France, West Germany, Belgium, Luxembourg and the Netherlands. Arguably, the success of the ECSC generated increased interest among coal and steel producers in accessing wider political benefits, for example, in relation to formulation of common industrial development policies to support weak industries.

Recognising this, a neofunctionalist theoretical approach emerged which introduced the idea of 'spillover', defined as a process of deepening the integration process and increasingly ceding political functions to supranational institutions over time. Economic integration theory used the 'spillover effect' to predict the gradual transformation of a free trade area to a customs union, then a common market, followed by a deeper economic union and eventually a political union.[39] The absorption of the ECSC into the European Economic Community (EEC) in 1957 and eventually the European Union (EU) in 1993 can be seen as a reflection of this neofunctionalist logic. So, regional integration, as a distinct field of study, emerged from the European context and sought to contend with the question of 'how and why states cease to be wholly sovereign'.[40] It explored the ways in which states could 'pool' their sovereignty in support of existing multilateral arrangements for liberalised trade. Yet, regional integration studies rarely advanced understanding of the internal dynamics of regions themselves.[41] There was limited attention to the role played by domestic politics and political leaders in the construction of regions and a sense of regional identity or 'regionness'.[42] In addition, the studies largely ignored the evolution of the second phase of regional integration among developing countries. These weaknesses, coupled with stagnation in European integration and the failure of several attempts at federation and functional cooperation among developing countries, led Ernst Haas to declare by 1975 that regional integration theory was obsolete.[43]

The defunct integration studies gave way to the emergence of new approaches to analysing the link between regional activities and globalisation. Analysts began to focus on assessing a 'new regionalism'. It was assessed as both an endogenous search for 'regionness', perhaps in opposition to dominant Western political ideology, as well as an exogenously-derived phenomenon aimed at countering the challenges of globalisation.[44] In the first sense, the literature focused on analysing the internal dynamics of regions as communities which were constantly being constructed, deconstructed and reconstructed by various political actors, including civil society.[45] In the second sense, the literature focused on the mediatory role played by regions in managing the effects of globalisation on states.[46] Overall, the new regionalism literature placed political, rather than economic, considerations at the centre of the regional integration process, which had hitherto been dominated by an economic discourse. It focused on the role of various actors, levels and dimensions of political action and even acknowledged the region itself as an international legal personality. It further acknowledged the existence of several types and models of regionalism, including sub-regionalisms, conducting comparative studies across these models in both developed and developing countries.[47] In essence, not unlike sovereignty, the new regionalism was multi-dimensional, involving a variety of actors and operating at several levels. Regional integration also began to be analysed for the first time in the broader context of 'regional governance'.

Interestingly, a debate ensued between two schools of thought within the new regionalism as to whether the region should be conceptualised as a utilitarian space aimed at enhancing state participation in the international system, or as a conception of identity created to represent the national, cultural and political distinctiveness of the participating states. Fawcett cautioned against attributing too much credence to the 'identity argument' since regionalism was primarily a strategy for state bargaining in the international system.[48] Others, however, have emphasised the potential of the region to have a primary role in enriching cultural identity.[49] The new regionalist approach, however, was able to contend with the coexistence of both scenarios on either side of the identity-utility debate. The duality of purpose was reflected in the fact that regionalism aimed to enhance state participation in the global governance while simultaneously strengthening internal regional 'polities' and identities.[50] The new regionalism also acknowledged regional institution-building as a paradoxical waning of individual state power as a result of globalisation accompanied by a reinforcement of collective state power in global affairs.[51]

While much of the new regionalism literature continued to focus on Europe as a distinct area of enquiry, some scholars also began to explore non-European regional movements and the aspirations of developing states to pursue cooperative development.[52] The paradoxical nature of the process of regional institution-building was particularly evident in former colonial developing countries since, in many cases, the creation of national identity, regionalism and membership of the international states system emerged simultaneously. In that regard, the paradox of sovereignty was manifest in an ongoing conceptual and philosophical tug of war between the retention of sovereignty as a symbol of a new national identity and the desire to capitalise on the opportunities presented by regionalism for overcoming the feature of quasi-state incapacity. That paradox therefore illustrated the challenges inherent in surrendering a recently-attained sovereignty, in order to facilitate a more effective regional governance process. That has been the crux of the regional governance problematic.

## THE REGIONAL GOVERNANCE PROBLEMATIC

Explicit references to regionalism as a governance project are relatively recent.[53] The concept of regional governance has, hitherto, been defined by Fredrik Söderbaum as a broad process which encapsulates 'spheres of authority at the regional level of human activity that amount to systems of rules – formal or informal, private or public – in which goods [or benefits] are pursued through the exercise of control'.[54] Notably, however, the definition does not identify the need for a regional governance framework to be supported by a distinctive set of institutions, values and norms. Kanishka Jayasuriya, however, has been one of the first to highlight the fact that normative and ideational constructs as well as a regional identity are key elements of a regional governance project.[55] In light of that, it seems that the regional governance process should not be described generically as a system of rules, in the way in which the multilateral system has been described. Each region's mode of governance emerges from a particular cultural, political and socio-economic context in relation to the particular mix of various elements of the political economy. Based on that understanding, the ambivalence of regional governance, in light of the sovereignty paradox, can, arguably, be resolved if forms of regional governance are viewed as more than the collective actions of states but also as a medium through which states define an identity which they portray to the world.[56] The institutions that emerge from that identity-formation process – including the roles ascribed to states and other actors and the relationships between them – are the reflection of the regional governance identity or the mode of governance.

The functionalist debates about regional integration, as already noted, have long acknowledged a distinction between intergovernmentalist and supranationalist institutional models of governance. These two institutional models represent the problematic of the paradox because each is expected to either erode or uphold sovereignty.[57] Intergovernmentalism supported the complete preservation of state sovereignty, while supranationalism seemed to require some surrendering of sovereignty by ceding it to supranational institutions, thereby generating a rethinking of traditional conceptions of sovereignty. However, as Liesbet Hooghe and Gary Marks have argued, the experience in Europe revealed that governments did not choose between one or other of those institutional models but sought to create regional 'communities of sovereign states' comprising both intergovernmentalist and supranational arrangements.[58] In that sense, the intergovernmentalist-supranationalist debate, on its own, made limited contribution to exploring the paradox of sovereignty, since it skewed the analysis away from the intricacies of the European governance framework – that is, the way it actually evolved, changed and functioned.[59] Interestingly, however, recent discussions within the sovereignty discourse provide some insight into the way in which this paradox might actually be analysed within regional communities. While it is assumed that states will either seek to retain full sovereignty or else surrender or pool it, in reality, they conclude a range of 'sovereignty bargains' which will be discussed further in chapter 2.

The discussion thus far has suggested that regional governance is a conceptual and practical challenge emerging from the paradoxical relationship between sovereignty and regionalism. While governance, in general, has always posed a challenge at state level, governments have benefited from a set of fixed parameters (conceptual, territorial, and cultural) for governance which limit the variables to be considered in the formulation of strategy. In contrast, conceptually, regions are constantly undergoing change, embracing, all at once, several levels of action associated with multiple centres of power and authority; multiple actors interacting at different levels; and multiple interests. All these levels contend in the pursuit of an overall purpose of the regional movement, whether it is to uphold sovereignty, facilitate technical cooperation and international participation, or contribute to development. The interaction amongst these institutional levels and amongst different actors is a part of the dynamism of the governance process and the regional environment – a dynamism which creates a special challenge for understanding and determining *who holds power, over whom, for what purpose and in what way.*

As we have argued, Söderbaum's earlier rules-based definition of regional governance, although useful, does not fully embrace this dynamism. It does not take into consideration the interaction between levels and actors, nor the context of ideas and interests which shape regional institutions. It does not highlight the roles of state elites in crafting the governance structures which influence the actions of others. Furthermore, it has not acknowledged the significance of development to the relationship between regionalism and governance. Rather than focusing on a system of rules, there is need for a broader focus on the preferences of leaders, their choices of institutional framework and institutions and the relationship of those preferences and choices to the political context. Taking all of those variables into consideration, we have adopted a working definition of 'regional governance' in small developing countries as:

> ...a process of transforming the political context for national development into shared development outcomes, which reflects the identity and aspirations of the people. It involves the regulation of power by the state within a multi-level institutional system, via a process of bargaining with attributes of sovereignty, in order to achieve an optimum balance between national authority and legitimacy, on the one hand, and effective autonomy and control, on the other, in the pursuit of defined national and regional development goals.

That definition raises three broad areas for analysis in relation to the problematic of regional governance. Firstly, there is need for identification of the actors who influence the emergence of regional institutions and an explanation of how their interpretations of sovereignty in the context of decision-making are shaped and affect the institution-building process. Secondly, there is need for analysis of the broader historical, socio-cultural and ideational or ideological factors which impinge on the whole process of institution-building. Finally, an assessment of the effect of those actors and factors on the functioning of regional institutions is essential. Those three broad areas require a comprehensive analytical framework, able to contend with the broad contextual issues which impinge on the process of the institutionalisation of the regional governance process. Such an analytical framework is proposed in chapter 2 on the institutional imperative which must be addressed via processes of sovereignty bargaining and institution-building.

# Analysing Regional Governance as an Institutional Imperative

Our introduction to the relationship between sovereignty and regionalism concluded that the classical institutional debate per se between neofunctional supranationalism and intergovernmentalism does not provide a comprehensive overview of the internal dynamics of regional institution-building. The dichotomy presented by those two theoretical approaches does not adequately explain the phenomenon by which states can increase their sovereignty while simultaneously ceding it. There is need, therefore, for greater clarity in the analysis of sovereignty in regional governance. In that regard, this chapter outlines an approach to analysing the institutionalisation of regional governance, using a multi-tiered framework for 'regional governance analysis' which facilitates the investigation of the emergence, evolution and functioning of regional governance institutions. Firstly, the chapter demonstrates the value of sovereignty bargains analysis to the advancement of an understanding of the factors which influence the emergence of regional institutions. Secondly, it discusses the influence of bargain outcomes and other factors of political context on the form and functions of regional institutions. Finally, it concludes by consolidating the elements of an analytical framework which will subsequently be applied to a historical review of the politics of integration in the Caribbean Community (CARICOM).

## Sovereignty Bargains

The literature on political bargaining makes a significant contribution to promoting a deeper understanding of the paradox of sovereignty. While the traditional debate between neofunctional supranationalists and intergovernmentalists assumed that states either seek to retain full sovereignty or else surrender or pool it, scholars have argued more recently that, in effect, states undertake a range of 'sovereignty bargains' which result in an array of potential institutional outcomes.[1]

These bargaining arrangements do not involve the ceding of sovereignty as an aggregate concept but, rather, the reconfiguration of its various dimensions which were highlighted in chapter 1. More specifically, the attributes of state autonomy, authority, legitimacy and control are traded off for the benefits of membership in regional economic communities. In forming such communities, states limit one or more attributes of sovereignty in the interest of some developmental benefit.

The concept of sovereignty bargains was introduced to International Relations within the literature on the regulation of transnational ecological problems. Scholars of ecological politics were engaged, during the 1980s and 1990s, in analysing of the way in which sovereignty was modified by international agreements so as to enable geographically-bound states to manage transnational resources and resolve transnational problems. Bruce Byers was amongst the first to use the concept, having drawn on Djuva Nincic's work on sovereignty in the UN.[2] Nincic had recognised in 1970 that membership in the UN implied state acceptance of what we have termed the paradox of sovereignty. Nincic argued at that time that, participation in an international organisation was likely to increase the 'effectiveness' of sovereignty despite the fact that membership would curtail some aspects of sovereignty.[3] The synergy between this idea and William Demas's juxtaposition of formal and effective sovereignty will not have escaped the reader's attention. Byers referred to the paradoxical process identified by Nincic as a 'sovereignty bargain' in which a state would cede control of some level of control of eco-regions and peoples within its territory in order to increase the overall effectiveness of state sovereignty. He argued that, based on those bargains, states voluntarily limited their autonomy in policymaking by developing international agreements on the protection of eco-regions within their territory or eco-regions shared with other states and also relinquished some level of control over the activities in those eco-regions by allowing international agencies or indigenous groups to monitor preservation activities.[4] An interesting contribution of Byers' analysis was the suggestion that the newly acquired sovereign effectiveness was potentially two dimensional – measurable by better external relations with other states and or better internal relationships with the people within the territory over which the state had authority.

It is in relation to this matter of effectiveness that Karen Litfin – the eco-politics scholar most associated with sovereignty bargains – makes a useful contribution to the literature. Litfin complemented the autonomy and control attributes highlighted by Byers, with the concept of legitimacy as a third bargained attribute.[5] Effectiveness was inextricably linked to legitimacy – the latter defined as either external recognition of state authority by other states or as internal recognition of state authority by domestic citizens. Having explicitly identified three elements of the bargain, Litfin presented a more nuanced definition of sovereignty bargaining as a process in which states 'voluntarily accept some limitations in exchange for certain benefits. The cumulative effect of these trade-offs...alter[s] the norms and practices of sovereignty by reconfiguring expectations regarding state autonomy, control and legitimacy'.[6] In essence, control was defined as the ability to produce a certain effect; autonomy as a level of independence in policymaking; and legitimacy as the recognised right to make decisions and implement them. This tripartite disaggregation of sovereignty was then applied by other scholars, in conjunction with Stephen Krasner's dimensional typology, to specific cases of international and regional bargaining. Two examples of its application are highlighted below in order to demonstrate the potential of sovereignty bargains analysis.

One of the earliest studies to apply the sovereignty bargains model to regionalism was Walter Mattli's review of the implications for state sovereignty of membership in the European Community.[7] Membership in the regional group implied a loss of autonomy in policymaking – a consequence which most state representatives intuitively resisted. However, Mattli's findings showed that, particularly in times of economic hardship, where states were experiencing difficulties in meeting their obligations to provide for the economic welfare of the people, the loss of autonomy was viewed to be marginal in comparison to the potential benefit to be had from regional economic cooperation. He noted that 18 out of the 20 membership applications made by Western European countries in the early years of the European Union were submitted in times of sustained economic difficulty.[8] Later, during the process of EU expansion to the East, beginning in the late 1990s, candidate states opted to abide by the strict membership criteria, including a set of Copenhagen conditions, covering practically every aspect of economic, political, social and cultural life, since the benefits of participation in the EU far outweighed the loss of autonomy in policymaking. Furthermore, the international legitimacy to be gained by association with other 'democratic' states, as well as the tangible financial and technical assistance they would receive for institutional modernisation, was expected to facilitate greater domestic legitimacy and economic control. Mattli's discussion highlighted a distinct trade-off between autonomy and control.

A second example of the application of Litfin's model to regionalism highlights a different configuration of attributes. Christopher Rudolph focused on the fact that European arrangements on migration involved the limiting of interdependence sovereignty (state control over migration flows) as a way of preserving the value of the territorial boundary associated with Westphalian sovereignty (authority within borders and autonomy from external interference).[9] Although the decision to permit freedom of movement within the Schengen zone eliminated the borders between participating states, the 1985 agreement also created a substitute boundary which drew a wider and stronger border around the Schengen zone as a whole, thereby preserving a sense of distinction from third parties. In Rudolph's discussion, state control over migration flows is bargained away in order to preserve and strengthen European authority and autonomy vis-à-vis the rest of the world.

These two examples provide a basis for asserting that sovereignty bargains do not diminish sovereignty but, rather, reconfigure its attributes. By way of analogy, the negotiation of a sovereignty bargain could be compared to the mixing of a cocktail comprising various ingredients (see figure 2.1). Different combinations of the ingredients produce varying levels of consistency, concentration, acidity or sweetness, without compromising the overall integrity of the cocktail. In theory, the challenge lies, therefore, in creating a cocktail which satisfies the tastes (aspirations) of the people. The resulting state cocktail should suggest to the people that sovereignty has been enhanced, whether or not larger or smaller measures of each attribute have been retained in the mixture. However, if the analogy is to be appropriately applied to regional governance systems, then Litfin's tripartite disaggregation must be expanded to include a fourth attribute – authority. Furthermore, the relationship among all four attributes – authority, legitimacy, control and autonomy – must be fully explained.

Figure 2.1 includes 'authority' as a fourth bargained attribute. Litfin's model had implied that legitimacy was a proxy for authority, given the special relationship between the two concepts by virtue of their association with popular sovereignty. Indeed, state authority is only achieved by legitimate recognition by external or internal actors. However, given this two-dimensional nature of legitimacy, it is also possible for authority to be separated into internal and external dimensions. The implication of this is that states can voluntarily relinquish their external legitimacy and recognition of authority in order to maximise an internal legitimacy and

Figure 2.1: The Sovereignty Bargains Cocktail

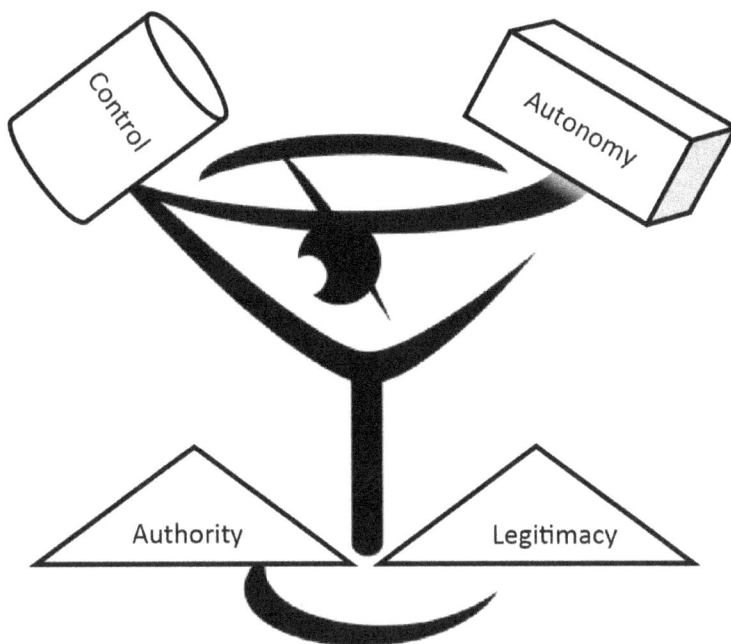

recognition of authority. For example, the state can limit its externally recognised authority to rule in its territory by allowing any particular ethnic or religious group to develop autonomous systems of internal community rule within the country's borders. Although the state will have lost authority over a part of its territory, it will, at the same time, have gained legitimacy in the eyes of a segment of society. In another example, a state may relinquish its internal legitimacy and authority by allowing external actors to operate autonomously within Economic Export Zones (EEZs), which are legitimated by some international actors, in order to attract investment for domestic production. Admittedly, other international actors may not view this as legitimate, given the labour exploitation often associated with these zones. The point of these examples, however, is that both authority and legitimacy can be further disaggregated and therefore they are included here, as separate elements of the bargain, so that the intrinsic relationship between the two enriches the analysis. Another reason for the disaggregation is that, in governance, other actors may come to exercise authority. The literature highlights a diversity of authority structures which function in their own space – whether religious leaders exercising authorities over believers, doctors over patients and parents over children.[10] In the context of regional integration, a sovereignty bargain could result in the establishment of a supranational authority. Such distinct supranational authority could, in turn, be involved in subsequent bargains, alongside state authority, which determine the evolution of the regional arrangement.

Based on this understanding of authority and legitimacy, both concepts are placed as parallel foundation elements in the sovereignty bargains 'cocktail' analogy in figure 2.1. While they can be manipulated, as we have illustrated in the preceding discussion, in many cases, they are the dependent variables affected by the bargaining process. The other two ingredients – autonomy and control – which are placed at the top of the cocktail, represent the attributes which are most involved in the bargaining process. For example, Mattli's study, referred to earlier, focused on the relationship between the two within an autonomy-prosperity cost-benefit analysis of the European Union. In that context, reduced autonomy was accepted in order to enhance control.[11] His discussion of the value of control is interesting and relevant for two reasons. Firstly, he observed that several different bargains were made by each country based on their different conceptions of the meaning of control in relation to their domestic context. Control could be about political, social or economic progress vis-à-vis trade, technical assistance or a place at the decision-making table. For example, he argued that the UK's decision to join the EC was not only about economic prosperity but, also about having a voice in European decision-making. Secondly, Mattli highlighted the way in which control influenced the extent of sovereign authority and legitimacy given the nature of electoral politics. Without relatively high levels of economic growth, as a symbol of capacity to control the domestic economic environment, leaders were likely to be ousted by the forces of internal legitimacy (democratic elections) and, therefore, lose their authority.[12]

Elsewhere, the literature also bears out a special hierarchical relationship between autonomy and control. Shaun Narine's discussion of the importance of control (domestic sovereignty) over and above autonomy (Westphalian and international legal sovereignty) in the South East Asian context is interesting.[13] States, from his account, seem to be most concerned with maintaining control over the domestic climate, given the ethnic, religious and linguistic diversity of the countries in the region and the resulting potential for conflict in the context of poor economic conditions. While the Association of South East Asian Nations (ASEAN) states formally reject the notion of 'pooling' of sovereignty within their association, they, in fact, engage in external bargaining arrangements which permit external powers and authorities (often associated with more developed countries) to operate within special economic zones or triangles which contribute to economic development. In this case, they have compromised Westphalian sovereignty (autonomy and freedom from external authority) as a means of exercising greater control over the economic situation within the country.

*Figure 2.2: Sovereignty Bargain Scenarios*

| Maximised Attribute | Impact on other Attributes |
|---|---|
| Control | Autonomy is readily limited in the interest of enhancing domestic sovereignty.<br>Legitimacy and Authority may also be enhanced internally and externally.<br>However, if Control is conceptualised as power of individual leaders, then the state loses its Legitimacy since internal Authority is questioned by citizens. |
| Formal Authority | Enhanced Legitimacy at the national level is implied since ceding Authority to external actors could weaken internal legitimacy.<br>However, if formal national Authority is not accompanied by effective Control, Legitimacy may be lost. |
| Legitimacy | Full internal Authority is preserved since it is tied to internal Legitimacy via the process of democratic elections and external Legitimacy via international recognition of the state; or,<br>Autonomy is readily limited and Authority ceded to an external actor but via a process of development partnership where the people are able to influence and have access to the supranational institutions. |
| Autonomy | Internal Authority and Legitimacy may be retained.<br>However, if the state is unable to exert effective Control, both internal and external Authority and Legitimacy are lost. |

These discussions on the most dynamic attributes of sovereignty, control and autonomy, suggest that other contextual factors are likely to determine the way in which each is understood and the expectations of each. In the Western, more developed European context, preservation of Westphalian authority vis-à-vis borders has been important, while, in developing country contexts, control over the economic development environment has been the single most important attribute states are unwilling to bargain away. In that regard, this analytical framework acknowledges that historical and cultural influences on political norms, including the interpretations by political elites of sovereignty and its paradox, as well as changes in the external international environment affect the bargaining process. It is therefore, difficult to provide detailed scenarios of sovereignty bargain outcomes. However, figure 2.2 summarises a simplified typology of potential bargain outcomes which might emerge from the process.[14]

These scenarios of individual state outcomes, alone, do not help us, however, to understand the institutional outcomes of an overall interstate bargain which is reached at the conclusion of the process. It is here that we can usefully juxtapose the analysis of sovereignty bargains with the study of regional institutions in order to develop an understanding of the different types of institutions – whether intergovernmental, supranational or other – which are associated with sovereignty bargains.[15]

## INSTITUTIONS AS OUTCOMES OF SOVEREIGNTY BARGAINS

Regional institutions, as outcomes of sovereignty bargains, provide mechanisms for enforcement. Without adherence to agreements, states cheat by gaining external legitimacy from participation in the international or regional agreement without having to make any real concessions.[16] However, ultimately the state could lose its internal and external legitimacy by reneging on its agreement. Therefore, having reached an inter-state bargain, there is need for some compliance mechanism to ensure implementation of the benefits expected to accrue from the sovereignty bargain.[17] These institutional control mechanisms reflect the complexities of the interaction between the international and national contextual factors, such as political norms, ideas and culture and the material aspects of the bargains in relation to power, territory and sovereignty.[18]

No detailed review of the various models of regionalism and modes of regional governance which exist throughout the international system is undertaken here, since other studies have provided in-depth discussions of those models – in Europe, Latin America, South-east Asia and Africa.[19]

Rather, the focus is on explaining the types of governance institutions which have been developed to support modes of regional governance in relation to the demands of sovereignty bargains. In that regard, the literature has pointed to the emergence of a range of institutional frameworks which either represent the extreme archetypes of supranationalism or intergovernmentalism, or represent hybrid frameworks which include elements of both. For example, Alex Warleigh-Lack's typology of regionalisation has been useful in distinguishing between, for example, the highly centralised regional centres of power (structured regionalisation) associated with the EU and the decentralised national centres of power (network regionalisation) associated with regional groups of developing countries.[20] Similarly, Jonas Tallberg presents a trichotomy of purist nationalist, intergovernmental and supranational structures for to addressing development concerns.[21]

Based on that understanding, this section briefly explores the possible outcomes of sovereignty bargains in regional contexts by reference to the institutional frameworks developed in various regions of the world. There are three types of compliance institutions discussed – legislative institutions; deliberative institutions, including mechanisms for consultation; and executive institutions, including administrative mechanisms. Although they are discussed separately here, it is worth noting that the institutional outcomes which emerge in each area influence the options available and choices made in other institutional areas and reinforce the overall nature of the institutional framework.

One of the first steps towards the establishment of compliance institutions is the formulation of common legislative arrangements to support implementation by each party to the bargain. Indeed, any resulting regional agreement or treaty signed by the parties often constitutes the primary legislative instrument. Subsequently, states may proceed to make decisions and issue declarations, regulations or recommendations, which are considered as a body of secondary legislation, to support the bargain. There are two initial observations which should be made with regard to the distinction between primary and secondary law. The first is that there is a division between grand bargains which result in the treaties from which the regional arrangement emanates and consequential commonplace bargains which arise in the decision-making process and involve relatively fewer and smaller transfers of sovereignty.[22] The second observation is that the regional legislative framework will remain in a state of continuous evolution as new bargains are created and influence change in legislation.[23] These grand bargains and commonplace bargains will also dictate the position to be accorded to the regional legal order vis-à-vis the pre-existing laws made by national legislatures and those enshrined in the Constitutions of each member state.

Patricia Luíza Kegel and Mohammed Amal  have provided, via their comparative study of the European Union (EU) and the Common Market of the South (MERCOSUR), a particularly useful typology of options for institutionalisation of regional legislative capacity.[24] Theoretically, they argue that states can pursue three types of legislative framework. Firstly, in a supranational system, the body of regional law is treated as superior to national constitutions and other legislation and, in that context, no regional treaty or regional decision can be modified by national legislatures. Secondly, in a supralegal system, the body of regional law is also superior to national legislation but not the national constitution. In that regard, if national legislatures deem the regional law to be unconstitutional, it cannot be implemented in the member state. Notwithstanding, if regional law is deemed to be consistent with the national constitution it can be implemented at the national level and cannot be repealed by national law, save by a constitutional amendment. Thirdly, in a purely legal system, the regional law is not given a defined position. In fact, it is not perceived to bear any relationship to the national legal order. If regional treaties and decisions are to be incorporated at the national level they must follow the legislative procedures in each member state and can, consequently, also be altered and modified by national law. The EU and MERCOSUR regional arrangements represent interesting cases of the adoption of the two extremes of the bargain typology cited above.

There is no gainsaying the fact that the EU, comprising 27 states, has been widely regarded as the archetypical model of regional governance. The supranational legal system which has developed over more than five decades of both deepening and widening regional integration is considered to be one of the most effective regional legislative systems, in large part, because the regional law has immediate and direct effect at the national level. In fact, European Community Law, comprising the various treaties negotiated up to 2009 and now superseded by the Treaty of Lisbon, as well as secondary law created from the directives and regulations passed collectively by member states in other regional institutions, is considered to be a distinct body of international law which is superior to national law. This supranational legal order is clearly representative of a sovereignty bargain in which each member agreed, albeit perhaps reluctantly in some cases, to transfer their legislative authority over matters concerning the European Single Market and monetary union to the European Community and lose their legislative autonomy in these areas.[25] In some cases, EU states were obliged to undertake constitutional amendments to facilitate this delegation of legislative authority and the adoption of a monist legal tradition which permits the immediate reception of international law in national legislation.[26] The bargain also resulted in the development of an independent regional judiciary – the European Court of Justice (ECJ) – charged with interpreting European Community Law and enforcing its implementation. Furthermore, all institutions of the state, that is, national courts and legislatures, are compelled to play a complementary role to the ECJ in applying regional norms and not national ones to the implementation process. Theoretically, this supranationalism could potentially be regarded as illegitimate since authority is delegated and autonomy relinquished to institutions which are neither directly elected by the people nor directly managed by elected politicians.[27] However, the EU supranational legal order is even more interesting in this respect since the legitimacy of European Community Law is preserved and a link to popular sovereignty maintained, whereby, EU citizens have the right to invoke EU legislation in national courts. In that regard, the regional law becomes enmeshed with national institutions and identities.[28]

In contrast to the EU, the members of MERCOSUR, created by the Treaty of Asunción in 1991, have adopted a purely intergovernmental framework supported by a simple legal system based essentially on the principles of equality among member states and non-interference in domestic affairs. Consequently, the Treaty of Asunción had to be ratified by each of the member states in order to give effect to its provisions in relation to the harmonisation of policy for supporting a common market. In this case, the outcome of the sovereignty bargain has been that national agencies retain full authority, autonomy and control over legislative matters. The states prescribe to dualist systems of law in which international treaties must go through internal legislative processes in order to be incorporated.[29] The implications of this system are two-fold. Firstly, the process of incorporation is lengthy and complex. The Treaty and each piece of secondary regional legislation must be first transposed into a form which is consistent with each national legal tradition; then the MERCOSUR Secretary-General must await notification of ratification in all four states before the legislation can be published and accepted as a framework for compliance. The second implication is that each member state can potentially hold different perspectives on the hierarchy which should be applied to the regional framework. In fact, amongst the four members, Argentina is deemed to favour a broad supralegal system, while Paraguay favours an even more limited supralegal system, and Brazil and Uruguay prefer a basic legal system. These differences in interpretation retard the process of ratification as it is constrained by the resistant legislative processes in Brazil and Uruguay. In sum, the model of the legal system adopted by MERCOSUR is deemed to be less effective in securing compliance with the sovereignty bargain than a supranational system, such as that of the EU, since there is potential for non-incorporation of regional laws by those states operating under a legal system. If the system is to be more effective, other non-legislative instruments must be employed to support the expediting of the process of ratification and the consistent and uniformed application of the law across the four jurisdictions.

A preference for intergovernmental legal frameworks has been observed among most developing countries. That inclination towards limited supranational institutionalisation provides a protective mechanism against exploitation of smaller countries by larger more developed countries. In that context, a greater degree of sovereignty is retained within the state, rather than delegated to an external institution which could potentially be controlled by more powerful states. This intergovernmental trend has been observed in the context of international treaties; in the 'hub and spoke' model of regionalism of the US-dominated North American Free Trade Area (NAFTA); and in the Asia-Pacific Economic Cooperation (APEC), which unites small developing Asia-Pacific states with large developed states like the United States, Canada, Australia and New Zealand.[30]

The second area for the institutionalisation of sovereignty bargains is in the convening of fora for decision-making and consultation. Not surprisingly, given the leadership role played by states in initiating regionalist strategies, these frameworks tend to be representative of member governments, that is intergovernmental in structure. However, there remain a variety of available options in relation to the development of decision-making procedures, including informal consensus-building and majority voting, as well as unanimity voting.

In Europe, decision-making has been undertaken by a European Council, comprising Heads of State and Government, and a subsidiary Council of Ministers comprising other governmental representatives, both charged with guiding the decision-making process so as to ensure that any resulting legislation takes account of the interests of states. Prior to the adoption of the Treaty of Lisbon in December 2009, the chairmanship of these councils was based on a rotational formula by which each Head of State and Government assumed the Presidency of the EU for six-month periods at a time, thereby, allowing each state to influence the policymaking agenda. With the advent of the Treaty of Lisbon, a full-time President of the European Council has been appointed by the Council to advance the regional agenda in an independent fashion over a two-year term. Traditionally, with regard to the cooperative decision-making, the unanimity rule has been viewed as one of the most effective ways of coordinating the actions of parties toward common objectives.[31] However the disadvantage is that decisions can only be reached if all members register an affirmative vote. The EU began with such a system of unanimous voting, designed to protect the sovereignty of each state by maximising their control over regional decision-making, but has evolved to a system of qualified majority voting ushered in by the 1986 Single Europe Act. In addition, the decision-making processes are supported by a European Parliament which evolved from a deliberative forum without the power to make decisions into a directly-elected legislative body which supports the role of the European Council. Since 1979 when the first direct election took place, the Parliament has assumed a more autonomous role from the Council and has increased its powers to influence the decision-making process while still operating within the overall government-led framework.[32]

In other regions, the deliberative functions are supported by intergovernmental institutions similar to those in the EU (and generally modelled on them), but which have had much less influence on the national political agenda or are considered to be informal. In MERCOSUR, for example, the policymaking agenda is supported by a Common Market Council of Ministers of foreign and economic affairs presided over by a semi-annual rotating chair; a Common Market Group of other governmental and central bank representatives; trade and parliamentary commissions; and a technical consultative forum. The primary decision-making principle is 'consensus', requiring unanimous agreement. However, despite the highly institutionalised system for decision-making, decisions do not have legislative effect.[33] In another Latin American case, the Central American Integration System (SICA) is similarly institutionalised and without legislative effect, even those structures accorded a level of autonomy from state structures, such as the Central American Court of Justice, have not been able to exercise their functions because the agreements have not been ratified by some states.[34]

Similarly, ASEAN is well-known for the informality of its arrangements. Each state seeks to maximise its autonomy while participating in intergovernmental meetings of Heads of Government, ministers and senior officials, aimed at supporting a consensus-building decision-making process in which members are not obliged to take decisions that contravene national interest.[35] The bargain amongst Indonesia, Malaysia, Philippines, Singapore and Thailand, giving rise to the 1967 Bangkok Declaration, established a certain diplomatic style of deliberation, often referred to as the 'ASEAN Way', which promotes 'perpetual peace, everlasting amity and cooperation, establishing three basic principles: respect for state sovereignty, non-intervention and renouncing the threat or use of force'.[36]

The regional governance arrangements in the South Pacific are even more informal, given the haphazard and overlapping pattern of regionalism which has resulted in the development of several under institutionalised groups which are supported, moreso, by national rather than regional structures.[37] Finally, in the Middle East, the League of Arab States was formed by a pact among six states in 1945 to cooperate on the safeguarding of sovereignty through a Council of Ministers supported by functional committees of officials.[38] Decisions of the League are not considered binding on states, *ipso facto*, unless any given state accepts them as such.

In light of these examples, it is apparent that, outside Europe, regional arrangements rely heavily on consensus-building and unanimous decision-making procedures, which, effectively, give each Member State, the power of veto. The preference for these approaches has been a reflection of a desire to protect newly-acquired sovereignty from former colonial powers and more dominant states. The treaty establishing the 1963 Organisation of African Unity (OAU) clearly highlighted the protection of sovereignty as a key objective. Equally, Etel Solingen shows that the informal, sovereignty-oriented structures of the League of Arab States were created for the specific purpose of defending all aspects of national sovereignty from Britain's plans to unify the individual territories in a federal arrangement.[39] In another case, Narine notes that, at the time of ASEAN's formation, member states were in the early stages of state-building. In that context, states needed to assert their autonomy within the regional group, as a symbol of the legitimacy of their governments which were faced, in the domestic context, with societies divided along ethnic, religious and political lines.[40] In other words, the reluctance to concede aspects of sovereignty to external actors, and the consequent ineffectiveness of regional decision-making, was directly related to the imperative of asserting and protecting a fragile sovereignty. In all these cases, the sovereignty-protecting institutions also helped states to deflect the interests and influence of more powerful Western states.[41]

At the same time, these informal institutions have also been associated with small but dominant political elite systems, which, in order to secure their power at the national level, distribute the benefits of the bargain among the members of their national support groups.[42] Amitav Acharya notes, for example, the prevalence of government-sponsored think tanks in the South East Asian regional consultative arrangements, rather than greater involvement of non-partisan civil society representatives.[43] Söderbaum identifies a similar role of elites in Southern African political and economic regional arrangements, where regional governance has been used to boost the status of officials and their governments.[44] Non-governmental groups are therefore marginalised from the consultative process in many developing country regions because sovereignty is associated more with the power of the elites than with a notion of a social contract. Greater involvement of the people in regional decision-making has become a recent new objective of several regional movements, including ASEAN, and critics have suggested that ruling elites will need to develop a more relaxed view of state sovereignty and loosen their control over the decision-making process, if truly participatory regionalism is to be achieved.[45]

In addition to the creation of legislation and deliberative fora, bargain compliance requires the development of political and administrative executive structures charged with implementation and enforcement of programmes. In Europe, the executive and administrative institutions adopt a supranational character. For example, a European Central Bank (ECB) was established when the EU decided to pursue a monetary union in 1999. As in the case of the European Court of Justice, national financial institutions are subordinate to regional ones and accordingly, national central banks must comply with the ECB's decisions, since states have ceded authority over monetary policy to the regional body.[46] The decisions of the ECB override whatever alternative strategies state institutions may prefer to pursue in respect of, for example, the national context of inflation. The EU has also been equipped with an executive European Commission which is empowered to take decisions on behalf of the 27 member states on matters including trade, the internal single market, customs, competition and fisheries and to implement them.[47] The full extent of the Commission's role, beyond its implementation mandate, has been debated in the literature – at certain times suggesting that the Commission deliberately influences the outcome of the bargain process to suit its own collective integrationist agenda; and at other times, suggesting that it is, principally, a champion for integration, which operates according to the letter of its mandate and according to the interests of the Councils, Parliament and national institutions.[48] In fact, there are enough examples of the role played by the Commission to suggest that both approaches occur concurrently, to varying degrees. However, the Commission is generally viewed as a tool which has enhanced the effectiveness of the integration implementation process.

The absence of those kinds of executive structures in other regions has been the subject of significant discussion. For example, Benny Teh Cheng Guan has argued that, despite the strength of the ASEAN diplomatic culture, member states are not equipped to actually implement the establishment of an economic community.[49] Similarly, in Africa, it is argued that too much focus is placed on decision-making and not enough on policy implementation.[50] In general, developing country groups rely on minimally staffed administrative secretariats to fulfil the executive functions.[51] These secretariats are charged with coordinating the meetings of the intergovernmental bodies and following up on the implementation. However, since decisions have no binding effect, the secretariats are not legally empowered to advance the implementation process. Consequently, responsibilities for implementation are delegated to national-level technocrats.[52] These public servants tend to waver between an incapacity for action, as a result of the lack of direction from the political leadership, and a lack of incentive to implement, given greater national priorities. This latter discussion of the executive institutions highlights the particular significance of legislative capacity to enabling other institutional mechanisms to secure the implementation of agreed objectives.

The preceding review of the variety of options available for the institutionalisation of the legislative, deliberative and executive aspects of regional governance has been interesting in two respects. Firstly, it has highlighted the fact that, at the end of the bargaining process, a new regional concept of sovereignty is derived from a re-aggregation of the attributes of sovereignty. The 're-aggregated' concept is assigned a new meaning, in light of the regional arrangement, which is used by both national and regional elites to define, catalyse or constrain the role of regional institutions in the governance process. Secondly, it has shown that other contextual factors, outside the bargaining process among member states, impinge on the construction of that new meaning of sovereignty and the adoption of various institutional forms. In that regard, we have also noted, within the discussion, that historical, socio-cultural and political factors influence the way in which elites interpret the desire for control (whether as an economic or political construct) and also influence the choice of intergovernmental or supranational structures. In developing countries, we have seen that elites have considered, for example, the existence of the EU model as well as the novelty and fragility of sovereignty in the domestic context of their countries, as factors which influence the choice of legislative, deliberative and executive institutions. The literature has suggested therefore, that these elements of the political context are essential to an understanding of the meaning(s) which elites attribute to sovereignty both before the bargain and after the institutionalisation process. It is argued here, therefore, that the best approach to defining and analysing modes of regional governance is to formulate a multi-level analytical framework which draws on sovereignty bargaining, institutionalism and political contextual analysis. The analytical framework is set out in the final section of this chapter.

## FRAMEWORK FOR REGIONAL GOVERNANCE ANALYSIS

An innovative approach to regional governance analysis which explains the internal dynamics of regional governance is advanced here. The concentric multi-tiered framework, represented in figure 2.3, is comprised of three interrelated elements of an overall approach to regional governance analysis. Firstly, the sovereignty bargain element is employed as a tool to explain the inception of regionalism and the trade-offs involved in decision-making, based on an understanding of a bargaining process among political elites. It allows the revisiting of the four key attributes of sovereignty in the historical review. Secondly, institutional analysis is employed to review the evolution and functioning of governance structures which allows for an analysis of the characteristics of institutions and the changes observed over time. Traditionally, institutionalism has focused on the procedures, routines and conventions embedded in an organisational structure, but has had to incorporate wider political and economic forces which influence institutions, including those mentioned in this chapter.[53] It is in this regard that the framework also adopts a third approach – an analysis of the political contextual factors – which complements the sovereignty bargains and institutional analyses. It outlines the norms, values, ideas and wider events in the national, regional and international political context which affect bargaining and institution-building. This third level of political context analysis forms the foundation and outer

*Figure 2.3: Framework for Regional Governance Analysis*

| Concentric Circles of Analysis | Levels | Application |
|---|---|---|
| 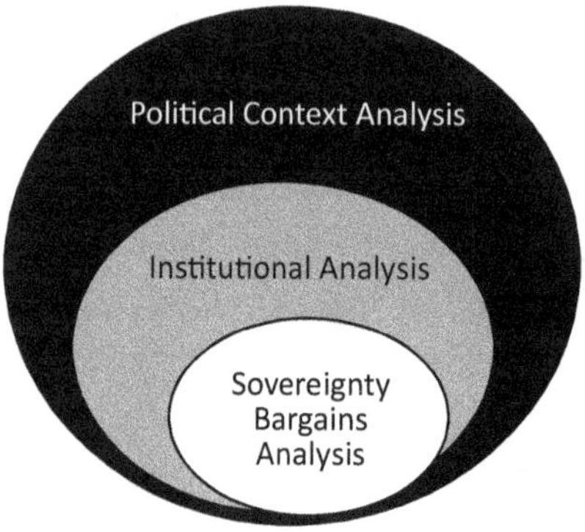 | Political Context Analysis | Understanding of the broad historical, socio-cultural and political contextual factors which underpin the other two levels of analysis and sustain the mode of regional governance. |
| | Institutional Analysis | Understanding of the evolution and functioning of the legislative, deliberative, consultative and executive structures and procedures which reflect the outcomes of the bargains in order to ensure compliance with the expected benefits. |
| | Sovereignty Bargains Analysis | Understanding of the power trade-offs which determine the genesis of regional institution-building. |

parameters of the framework. It is important to note, however, that when applied to the discussion of the CARICOM case, reference is made, via other literature, to significant events and influences in international affairs and changes in the international political economy which have impinged on the dynamics of regional governance, these references are made as an acknowledgement of the overarching structural context of Caribbean openness and vulnerability, which has at times influenced the decision-making process. Notwithstanding those references, the principal contribution here resides in the revelation of the internal dynamics of the political process in CARICOM, which have often been neglected or relegated to a level of insignificance in the grand analyses of, for example, the influence of external forces of globalisation and global economic changes on Caribbean regionalism and governance.[54] The challenges of governance are revealed here, through an emphasis on Caribbean political history, culture and traditions which impinge on the processes of sovereignty bargaining and institutionalisation of those bargains, rather than on the external economic factors which have and continue to shape the context of Caribbean political economy.

In sum, the sovereignty bargains analysis and the institutional analysis are contextualised within the broader political context and, therefore, the three elements are presented in figure 2.3 as concentric circles of analysis. Taken together, the three levels – broadly defined as 'regional governance analysis' – provide an excellent framework for building a holistic perspective on the broad questions of 'who, why and how' in the dynamics of CARICOM governance. More specifically, it links the role played by political elites in generating particular outcomes via the process of sovereignty bargains (who); to the influence of history, culture, traditions, values, ideas, including political ideologies, on the decision-making process (why); to the role that formal regional institutions play in the governance process (how).

Against the background of that broad agenda for analysis, the ensuing chapters present a chronological study of the different phases of CARICOM governance, including the relevant aspects of subregional governance. It enquires into the role played by political elites and political ideas in the establishment and evolution of CARICOM and the effect those influences have had on the efficiency and effectiveness of the institutional framework for regional governance. The investigation of the CARICOM case begins with a discussion of the Caribbean region's first experiences with sovereignty and regionalism.

# WEST INDIAN NATIONALISM AND THE PARADOX OF SOVEREIGNTY

The events that led to the pursuit of sovereign independence of the British West Indies colonies have been a compelling aspect of Caribbean political history. That quest for independence, although initiated by aspirations for political autonomy in the individual territories, was in fact undertaken within a regional framework, thereby instituting a paradoxical association between regional governance, on the one hand, and the attainment of sovereignty, on the other hand. Ten of those colonies first became eligible for sovereign independence within the West Indies Federation (WIF) established in 1958.[1] However, the legacy of the Federation's collapse in 1962 has been the adoption of a nationalist interpretation of sovereignty under the framework of independent statehood and the adoption of a minimalist approach to regional governance in the independent Commonwealth Caribbean. Against that background, this chapter introduces the historical developments, which occurred between 1947 and 1971, and which have influenced the way in which regional governance institutions were conceived and functioned in the Caribbean region.

Firstly, the chapter introduces the ideological foundation of regional governance, emanating from the nationalist campaigns for increased autonomy from Britain and full political control over territorial socio-economic affairs. Secondly, it reviews the process of negotiation, establishment and collapse of the WIF and the adoption of a purist conception of Westphalian national sovereignty on the attainment of independent statehood in each of the territories from 1962 onwards. Thirdly, it discusses the way in which the paradox of sovereignty became evident in the independence period, prompting a renewal of regional economic cooperation, through the 1968 Caribbean Free Trade Association (CARIFTA). Finally, it concludes with a brief discussion of the overall legacy of this period of regional political history in relation to the tradition of sovereignty and interpretation of the paradox which has impinged on the evolution of successive institutions of regional governance.

## THE NATIONALIST FOUNDATIONS OF REGIONAL GOVERNANCE

The people of the West Indies were subject to colonial administration for several hundred years, including over 200 years of British rule aimed at sustaining a West Indian political economy, based on agricultural production by enslaved and indentured labour from Africa and Asia, and the subjugation of the local population to external political rule.[2] Even after the abolition of the slave trade and the emancipation of West Indian slaves by 1838, the British Government continued to impose upon the people a system of governance which excluded them from participation in the management of their own political, social and economic affairs. In particular, the Crown Colony system of government instituted in the late nineteenth century was generally criticised by local merchants and workers alike for its maintenance of British power at the expense of progress for the local black and Indian populations.[3] The beginnings of a nationalist movement emerged from several decades of petitioning the British Government to modify the system to permit elected representation. The movement adopted an increasingly violent form in the twentieth century as the people revolted against increasing levels of unemployment and poverty which they perceived to be a direct result of the unjust system of governance. In that context, several leaders who represented the disenfranchised working population, including A.A. Cipriani in Trinidad and Tobago, Albert T. Marryshow in Grenada and Cecil Rawle in Dominica, became the champions of an anti-colonial movement towards legitimate and elective governance institutions. That cadre of labour leaders was of the view that self-government, based on full adult suffrage, including the poor, unemployed, black segments of the population, was the only way to achieve socio-economic progress for the people in their respective territories.[4] In that regard, the nationalist movement was initially confined to the territorial boundaries of each colony.

Although the colonies were collectively regarded by the British as a single administrative region, they had at various times each maintained separate political governance arrangements. Indeed, the region was further predisposed to political separation since it covered some 8,000 square miles spread from British Honduras in Central America, through Jamaica and the Leeward Islands to the Windward Islands, Barbados, Trinidad and Tobago and finally British Guiana on the north coast of the South American continent. Half of the regional population – estimated to be about only three million people in the mid-twentieth century – was located on a single island, Jamaica, which is situated some 1,000 miles to the north west of the others, whilst British Guiana, situated at the extreme south of the West Indies, accounted for the vast majority of the total landmass. In the south eastern part of the region, Trinidad commanded a majority share of the population there and accounted for most of the economic activity; while Barbados represented one-third of the remaining population in the eastern part of the region.[5] Although there was some level of inter-island communication and travel, especially in the east where the islands were in relatively close proximity, most West Indians knew very little about one another. Due to the difficulties of intra-regional travel before the advent of commercial air transportation after the First World War, Jamaicans, in particular, rarely came into contact with other West Indians except when they met them in North America or Europe.[6] This geographical and administrative polarisation, occasioned by distance and the natural barrier of the Caribbean Sea, therefore fostered the development of a psycho-social construct of insularity or 'islandness' in the West Indian psyche, which in turn encouraged the evolution of distinct island administrative structures under separate British governors.

Notwithstanding, taking account of the commonalities among the individual movements for self-government, nationalists could not deny the extent to which shared history and experience pointed to common interests. Each nationalist movement shared the desire for increased autonomy, legitimate authority and local control of West Indian affairs. Consequently, in spite of the tenacity of the fragmented structures and the polarized environment, the nationalist movement began to assume a regional character after the First World War. West Indian labour leaders began to identify strongly with a sense of unity and their ideas converged around the concept of regional integration as an alternative and superior path to the achievement of the sovereign autonomy which they so strongly desired. That common vision encouraged the convening of a conference of West Indian labour leaders in Georgetown, Guyana in 1926. During that meeting and in subsequent sittings, the nationalists discussed their common political aspirations and developed proposals for addressing the worsening socio-economic conditions in each of their territories. By 1938 the group, which had evolved into a Congress of Labour Leaders, reached the conclusion that their shared nationalist ideology should be channelled into a demand for elected self-government in the form of a West Indian federation.[7] For these leaders, both insular territorial nationalism and regionalism were representative of the popular desire for local control. So, there emerged from this period a unique ideology of 'West Indian Nationalism' which became the philosophical foundation for the involvement of a group of emerging political party leaders in the negotiation of the West Indies Federation. However, differences in interpretation of the ideology among politicians would later lead to increasing divergence between the two strands of the ideology with regard to the institutionalisation of the federal powers.

## THE HISTORY OF THE WEST INDIES FEDERATION

The West Indian Nationalist consensus on federation coincided with an emerging British interest in relinquishing its responsibilities for the colonies. The British Government had a favourable attitude towards federation as a model of granting sovereign independence, having pursued two sub-regional federations in the eighteenth and nineteenth centuries among the Windward and Leeward Islands of the West Indies. Furthermore, Britain had successfully transferred power, within a federal framework, to the Canadian Federation in 1867, and to Australia, New Zealand and South Africa in the early 1900s. Coincident on the resolution of the Congress of labour leaders, it was agreed that federal union was the best available solution to addressing the smallness and poverty of the Caribbean territories.

Parallel to labour advocacy for federation and British favourable disposition to the idea, a Westminster-style framework for partisan politics was emerging in each of the territories. Many of the prominent labour leaders were also budding politicians who founded, after the Second World War, local political parties to provide leadership in the negotiation of the federation. The dynamics of the debate and negotiations among politicians were significantly indicative of the fact that the apparent consensus among labour leaders on West Indian nationalism, would eventually give way to a level of ambivalence in the political arena over the course of the 15 years of deliberations and negotiations on the federal institutional structure between 1947 and 1962. In other words, the politicians' interpretations of West Indian nationalism became increasingly divergent, polarizing the discussions between contending approaches to the creation of federal institutions.

One of the most prominent among the politicians involved in the negotiation process was Norman Manley, who founded the People's National Party (PNP) in Jamaica in 1936 around the concept of 'nationhood'. Although he viewed the region's common cultural history and traditions as the 'soul and life' of the nationhood he advocated, his political priority was to unite the segments of an intensely class-stratified and racially-divided Jamaican society.[8] Consequently, Manley placed great emphasis on using the struggle for self-government as a way of consolidating a common Jamaican national identity. Notwithstanding, he joined the ranks of those pursuing regional federation, perhaps not out of absolute conviction that it was an ideal model of governance, but in recognition of its value to the quest for self-government.

While Norman Manley's brand of politics embraced much of the territorial dimensions of nationalism, elsewhere in the region, politicians were more closely aligned to the regional dimension. For example, in Trinidad – an even more racially-polarised society – the emerging political leader, Eric Williams believed that regional integration held great potential for creating a pan-ethnic regional identity around which both Afro and Indo-Trinidadians could converge. He incorporated the spirit of West Indian nationalism in the 1955 People's Charter of the People's National Movement (PNM) which he founded and called explicitly for self-government for Trinidad within a Caribbean Federation. Politicians in the Barbados Labour Party (BLP), including Grantley Adams and Errol Barrow, were equally attracted to the potential of the federal model to provide sovereign autonomy. The political leaders from these three larger West Indian territories featured prominently in the negotiations of the institutional architecture.

The backdrop against which the Federal negotiations were initiated by the British Government is instructive. Britain's economy had declined significantly after the Second World War and its capacity to support its overseas territories had diminished. Therefore, the Colonial Secretary proposed in 1945 the convening of a conference to discuss closer union among the West Indian territories. He was of the view that an appropriate form of union could be achieved by gradually building on the existing colonial institutional arrangements. For example, the (British) Development and Welfare Committee and the Anglo-American Caribbean Commission had both served the region as fora for research, discussion and development of joint action on common social and economic development issues. In addition, a range of common functional entities, including the University College of the West Indies, the West Indies Shipping Service and a Meteorological Committee, had also been in operation. Cooperation among the territories was achieved largely through the convening of several conferences of officials and resulted in the formulation of recommendations for joint action on issues related to labour and immigration, customs procedures, education, health, communications and air transport. This conference methodology had fostered increased communication, familiarisation and a spirit of cooperation and friendliness among the leaders of the territories. In that regard, Jessie Harris Proctor argued that the Colonial Office had intended for the West Indies to employ a neo-functionalist approach to the achievement of closer union by way of gradual spillover from technical cooperation into deeper forms of economic and political union.[9]

Jamaica, British Honduras (now Belize) and British Guiana (now Guyana) – all of which were somewhat geographically isolated from the rest of the region – were in favour of this neo-functionalist approach because it emphasised non-political steps towards federation. At the same time, the other closely-knit territories in the eastern subregion, which had prior experiences of colonial federal administration, recognised a weakness in the existing functional framework – the lack of a central political authority to ensure implementation by the institutions.[10] In essence, the existing institutions were largely advisory bodies without the authority to implement development strategies. Previous subregional federations had been dissolved precisely because a lack of central authority had rendered them ineffective.[11] Those territories in the east, therefore, adopted a contending federalist approach and called for the immediate establishment of a federal union with strong central governmental machinery, empowered to exercise supranational authority over the various functional institutions.

It was against the background of these opposing positions to union, represented in figure 3.1, that the September 1947 Conference on Closer Association of the British West Indies Colonies brought labour, political and community development leaders together in Montego Bay, Jamaica, to develop a constitutional framework for the Federation.

*Figure 3.1: Contending Regionalist Perspectives*

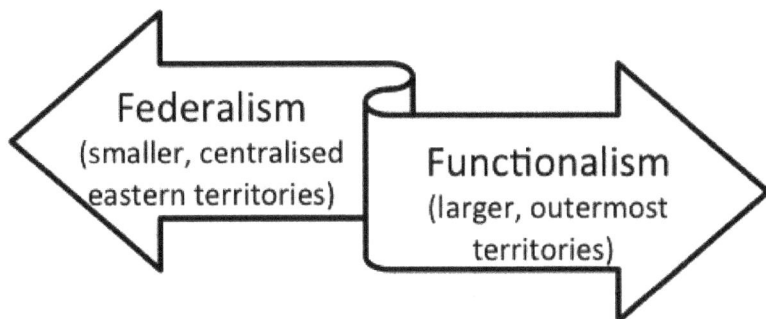

Federalism
(smaller, centralised eastern territories)

Functionalism
(larger, outermost territories)

Interestingly, while the conference considered international models of federation, including the Australian and Canadian models, it largely ignored the democratic approaches to public consultation and education used in those cases.[12] The ordinary West Indian people were largely ignorant of all that was happening in Montego Bay. During the conference, the Jamaican, British Guianese and British representatives recommended that the question of regional integration be confined to the unification of services and that the discussion on federation be postponed. At the other extreme of views, Albert Gomes, a labour representative from Trinidad and an ardent federalist, recommended that the region proceed with an immediate federation, even if it meant proceeding without Jamaica. Heated exchanges ensued between Gomes and Alexander Bustamante, Jamaica's Chief Minister and official representative to the conference. Differences also emerged between Bustamante, as leader of the Jamaica Labour Party (JLP), and his cousin Norman Manley, leader of Jamaica's Peoples National Party (PNP). During the conference, Manley expounded on the rationale for immediate federation:

> Here are we all on a sea of world conditions, stormy and hazardous in the extreme, each huddled in some little craft of our own. Some hardly have oars and only a few have accomplished a rudimentary sail to take them along. And here offered us is a boat substantial, capable of being made seaworthy and ready to be manned by our own captains and our own crew. If we won't leave our little boats and get into the larger vessel which is able to carry us to the goal of our ambitions then I say, without hesitation, that we are damned and purblind and history will condemn us.[13]

On the other hand, Bustamante declared:

> Whilst some people say we of the West Indies are all the same, I am not going to follow that trend of thought, for although we of the West Indies are all alike, to me Jamaica and Jamaica's interests come first. It must be so.[14]

His principal concern was about the extent of power the federal government would have over each of the territorial units. He continued:

> I fear, that someone should stay over in St. Kitts or Grenada or British Guiana and direct us in our country as to what we should do and what is good for us here. We must know what power, what

authority the federal government would have over the West Indies. I understand the federal government would sit over there and tell people what to do here. Not so long as I live that won't happen.[15]

Those sympathetic to Bustamante's views were cognisant of the fact that the proposed centralised federal government had potential to evolve into a neo-colonial structure – not a British, but a West Indian impediment to Jamaica's achievement of full self-determination. Eric Williams' contribution to the 1947 conference underscored his concern that economic progress was unlikely outside the context of a federation. Williams had noted emerging international trends towards the transformation of limited economic capacity within small territories into large-scale production capabilities, under larger units of government facilitated by improvements in transportation and communication. He appealed to the participants:

> Look around the world today and try to find a community of 700,000 people of the size of Trinidad and Tobago playing an important part in world affairs. There is none. There can be none. The units of government are getting larger and larger. Whether federation is more costly or less costly, whether federation is more efficient or less efficient, federation is inescapable if the British Caribbean territories are to cease to parade themselves to the twentieth-century world as eighteenth-century anachronisms.[16]

The Resolution which eventually emerged from the Montego Bay discussions suggested a consensus on the principle of pursuing a federation. However, the decision to 'proceed concurrently with both the preparation of a federal constitution and the unification of services, the establishment of a customs union, the creation of a uniform currency and various other types of regional economic cooperation' certainly implied a lack of consensus on the approach to regional governance.[17] The Standing Closer Association Committee (SCAC), which was established to implement the Conference's recommendations, found itself employing, concurrently, federalist and functionalist approaches. For, as various subcommittees and working parties of the SCAC considered the functionalist approach to the unification of public services, the development of a customs union and a common currency *inter alia,* they also recognised the need for a federal executive authority to coordinate those arrangements.[18]

It is not surprising, therefore, that the resulting draft constitution did not reflect the preferences of either poles of the West Indian debate. In fact, the official negotiations, which began in 1953 between the British colonial administration and West Indian political leaders, started with consultation of a text which favoured continued control by the British. The outcome of the negotiations did not alter this situation. In 1956, the British Caribbean Federation Act was passed, paving the way for the legal establishment of a political union among ten islands in January 1958 known as the West Indies Federation (WIF). The members of the Federation were Antigua and Barbuda, Barbados, Dominica, Grenada, Jamaica, Montserrat, St Kitts-Nevis-Anguilla, St Lucia, St Vincent and Trinidad and Tobago. By this point, both British Honduras and British Guiana had opted out of participation in the Federation to pursue opportunities for closer association with territories on their respective mainlands of Central and South America. Moreover, the East Indian population in British Guiana (like that in Trinidad) was less enthusiastic about joining what they perceived to be a majority Afro-West Indian Federation.[19] We have already noted that, in contrast, the leadership in Trinidad – a territory with a similarly divided ethnic population – focused on the potential for the Federation to overcome the challenges of the multi-ethnic national context.

The 1958 Federal Constitution did not reflect the features of independent sovereignty to which West Indians aspired. The institutional structure outlined within it was very colonial. The Federation was led by a British Governor-General, Lord Hailes, who held special discretionary powers, including referring decisions for review by the Government in London. The Governor-General appointed most of the public servants, including the Federal Supreme Court Justices, members of the Public Service Commission and the 19 members of the Senate – the upper House of the Legislature. The lower House of Representatives was composed of 45 elected West Indian representatives according to the proportions of their populations. The principal decision-making body was the Council of States which played an advisory role to the office of the Governor-General. The Council comprised 14 members – six directly appointed by Hailes himself from the civil service and the Senate; and eight 'democratically' appointed. The West Indian Prime Minister, Grantley Adams, was elected from the ruling Federal Labour Party (FLP) and served on the Council, appointing the remaining seven West Indian members.

The West Indian political leaders were undoubtedly dissatisfied with the structure since it did not reflect a progression in political status, given the limitations on elective representation. Most of the senior officials of the Federation were non-West Indians. In spite of the fact that, eventually, the

Council of States was abolished in 1960 to make way for a full Cabinet-style government, the limitations of the initial structure was likely to have been responsible for discouraging the most influential political leaders, Norman Manley and Eric Williams, from running for seats in the House of Representatives. It is likely that they preferred to pursue opportunities for a greater political profile at the national level. However, there was generally low voter turnout in the federal elections in all the territories and the FLP lost in both Jamaica and Trinidad and Tobago.[20] Indeed, Manley's absence from the federal ballot in Jamaica was disastrous for the ruling FLP with which his national PNP was affiliated. The PNP won only five of the 17 seats allocated to Jamaica, thereby weakening the position of the Federal ruling party vis-à-vis the Federal Opposition party which, by coincidence, was led by Bustamante, the leader of the JLP. John Mordecai has argued persuasively that, because both of the Federal Parties were led by Jamaican politicians already engaged in political contest at the national level, the other leaders in the region felt that Manley and Bustamante's positions on federal issues were incidental to their tactical positioning with regard to Jamaican politics.[21] Undoubtedly, the increased partisan politicisation of Federation in Jamaica would eventually contribute significantly to its ultimate demise.

In spite of its legal establishment in 1958, the institutions of the Federation had not been finalised and so the negotiations on the constitution continued into the early 1960s. The post-establishment federal-functionalist debate centred on the fact that Jamaica and Trinidad had opposing views on the role and powers of the Federal government.[22] The Federal Government was, in fact, embroiled in internal conflict between Manley and Williams. Eric Williams adopted an almost fanatical radicalism, given a strong dissatisfaction with the initial constitution which he referred to as 'weak and anaemic' since it did not possess a strong central government with powers over economic development in the constituent units.[23] He advocated that the Trinidad legislature support the establishment of a strong federal government with powers of taxation and which would have the final word in legislation on all matters of economic planning and development in order to have complete control of all the resources needed to build the regional economy. In one of the papers his government commissioned in 1959, 'The Economics of Nationhood', Williams argued the indispensability of a regional executive authority:

> These islands have a long history of insularity, even of isolation,
> rooted in the historical development of their economy and trade

and the difficulties of communications for centuries. No amount of subjective, that is to say historical, cultural or other activity of the time can be expected to overcome this heritage. Only a powerful and centrally directed economic co-ordination and interdependence can create the true foundations of a nation. Barbados will not unify with St Kitts, or Trinidad with British Guiana, or Jamaica with Antigua. They will be knit together only through their common allegiance to a Central Government. Anything else will discredit the conception of Federation, and in the end leave the islands more divided than before.[24]

In the interim, however, Manley had become the Premier of Jamaica and having been confronted with the practicalities of the operationalisation of the Federation, he considered it necessary to adopt a more moderate federalism and evidently found Williams' radicalism unpalatable. He advocated therefore a more flexible form of cooperation, recognising that the creation of central governance mechanisms with strong powers would require substantial sums of money, and that Jamaica was likely to be required to pay the greatest portion. Furthermore, Jamaica received most of its revenue from its high tariffs, thereby making the idea of a customs union with lower rates of duty less appealing.[25] Jamaica and Trinidad thereafter argued about the Federation's powers of taxation. Trinidad further quarrelled with Jamaica about the latter's decision to build an oil refinery which would reduce Trinidad's competitive advantage in that area. Jamaica then squabbled with Trinidad over the location of the Federal capital in Chaguaramas, Trinidad, because it was a symbol of power and sovereignty. Interestingly, others suggest that whatever the political conflicts, private sector elites were not keen on the strengthening of the Federal Government. In the interest of maintaining control over their own commercial affairs, they were likely to have dissuaded both sides from continued commitment to the Federation.[26]

Those political conflicts ensued through an 'open diplomacy', via radio and press, which weakened the popular view of Federation, particularly in Jamaica where the extent of its isolation – both geographically and ideologically – from the rest of the region had reinforced the lack of knowledge among ordinary Jamaicans about federal affairs. As early as 1952, Norman Manley's son, Michael, who was a journalist and trade unionist in Jamaica, argued that the remoteness of Federation from the Jamaican consciousness had rendered it either meaningless or akin to an experimental 'alliance with aliens'.[27] Some Jamaicans were, therefore, sceptical of allowing their government to cede any of their already limited political power to the Federal Government. As territorial nationalism strengthened in Jamaica, the nationalist movement became more antagonistic towards regionalism. Then a significant event in international affairs created an alternative opportunity for self-government. In August 1960, a small island in the Mediterranean achieved full independence, becoming the Republic of Cyprus. The advent of that independent small island state influenced Manley and the Jamaican people's view of the limitations of federation. There was now potential for each West Indian leader to command full authority, control and autonomy in a legitimate framework – that is, to command the dimensions of sovereignty not available under the British-controlled Federation. Although Manley remained an ardent supporter of West Indian cooperation, he took the initiative to approach the Colonial Office to enquire about the possibility of Jamaica achieving independence as an entity separate from the Federation. The British Colonial Secretary, Iain Macleod, indicated his support for this option.

The escalating public squabbles between leaders over operationalisation of the Federation provided an opportunity for Jamaica's Opposition leader, Bustamante, to exploit the internal political climate against the background of public 'ignorance' of the implications of the Federal negotiations. He proposed that the question of Federation be put to a referendum of the people and Premier Manley agreed. Bustamante, capitalising on the public disagreements between Manley's PNP Government and the Trinidadian Government, advanced the argument that the Federation would not benefit Jamaica.[28] He succeeded in convincing a slight majority of Jamaicans to vote in the September 1961 referendum against participation in the Federation, on the grounds that it would place a financial burden on Jamaica and lead to re-colonisation of the country (possibly by Trinidad). The anti-Federalists held fast to the conviction that, with its larger size and relatively better economic position, including the increased significance of bauxite in the global political economy, Jamaica did not need the Federation. The outcome of the referendum was not necessarily a surprise to other leaders in the region. A Trinidadian member of the ruling FLP, A.N.R. Robinson, had predicted the outcome based on the phrasing of the referendum question. From his perspective, since the referendum question asked whether Jamaica should *remain in* the Federation, Jamaicans were never afforded the opportunity of dialogue on their preferred form of federation.[29]

The referendum result led to Jamaica's withdrawal from the ten-member Federation and its transition to national independence in August 1962, under a Bustamante-led government. Eric Williams, acknowledging that without Jamaica's financial and political support, the Federation would not survive, summed up his view of the impossibility of the situation by way of the well-known analogy of an equation, 'Ten minus One equals Zero (10–1=0)', and immediately withdrew from the Federation to negotiate Trinidad and Tobago's national independence less than a month later. The Federation had, in effect, almost fully collapsed by 1962 and a new conception of sovereignty was beginning to take hold in the region. As each of the West Indian territories attained their independence, they became incorporated as members of the Commonwealth of Nations in their own right, resulting ultimately in the emergence of the Commonwealth Caribbean.

## THE PARADOX OF SOVEREIGNTY IN THE COMMONWEALTH CARIBBEAN

The body of literature on the WIF generally excludes an explicit discussion of the linkages between the Federal institutions, the West Indian nationalist ideology underpinning the negotiation process and the nature of the regional institutional framework which evolved after 1962.[30] The legacy of the Federal experience was the ushering of absolute 'state sovereignty' into a prominent position in national political discourse and political culture. There was an ideological shift from the West Indian nationalist ideals of socio-cultural homogeneity to the more practical preoccupation with the economic viability of small states.

In the immediate aftermath of the independence of Jamaica and Trinidad and Tobago, and the consequential federal deflation, there was little or no formal discussion among the leaders about regional affairs. It was only among the remaining non-sovereign members of the Federation, dubbed 'the little Eight', that efforts continued towards political union. However, even in that case, squabbles over aid provisions and the powers of the federal government under a subsequent 1962 Constitution, led to the abandonment of that pursuit in 1965 since those states had, by then, also begun to pursue independent statehood.[31]

The attainment of independence marked a watershed for the Jamaican and Trinidadian Governments, which were able for the first time to exercise full political authority and control within their territories. These aspects of sovereignty became closely associated with the island nationalism which was being solidified, as symbolised by the independence flags and anthems. Beyond the consolidation of nationalism, the states attended to the pressing duties of joining international organisations, establishing defence and constabulary forces and diplomatic missions overseas, and electing or appointing ministers to replace the colonial officials. As such, the meaning of sovereignty adopted a purist and absolutist conception, reminiscent of the early beginnings of the concept in Westphalian Europe. Leaders adopted personal responsibility for safeguarding territorial integrity, autonomy from external interference, their own political authority and governmental control over their new nations.

However, even as the new sovereign governments enthusiastically built their national governance apparatus, the economic position of their countries began to decline. In the early period of independence, the inextricable link between political and economic sovereignty was revealed, with the recognition that the breakdown of the colonial political system had not ameliorated the fundamentally inefficient socio-economic structure of the former colonies.[32] The economies were still as weakly structured, undiversified, and uncompetitive as they had previously been. They had started out at a disadvantage because of the false sense of security they had under British 'protection'. The new states were obliged to acknowledge that statehood and nationhood did not guarantee economic viability within a competitive environment of international trade and economic relations. The value of cooperation with other states in the region therefore soon resumed significance in the political discourse.

Notwithstanding the residual awkwardness and distrust among leaders, on the initiative of Eric Williams, a regionalist spirit was renewed under a new economic and non-political rationale. Williams, who had remained in power in Trinidad as prime minister, began to revamp his regionalist vision to focus on the creation of a Caribbean Economic Community. His approach had become notably more measured, given his newly acquired appreciation of the sanctity of national sovereignty. He would most certainly have reflected on the Federal experience and come to the conclusion that he had to adopt, henceforth, a gradual approach to union, which focused essentially on the economic imperatives of the time and built on the few remaining elements of the common institutional framework, without posing a challenge to the political authority of individual states or interfering in their domestic affairs. In this regard, the relative success of the conference methodology employed in the pre-independence period led Williams to propose a conference to discuss the management of the surviving common services, such as the Shipping Service, Meteorological Office and the University of the West Indies. Accordingly, the beginning of a primitive post-colonial regional governance structure began to take shape with the convening, in 1963, of the first in a series of Conferences of Heads of Government of Commonwealth Caribbean Countries. Between 1963 and 1971, the Heads of Government – the truly Caribbean political directorate – negotiated a new institutional architecture for regional governance. Our ensuing discussion of the deliberations and outcomes of those Conferences are particularly instructive, providing insights into the emerging post-Federal cooperative philosophy as well as the full extent of the federal legacy.

The first Heads of Government Conference, convened in July 1963 in Port of Spain, Trinidad, was intentionally limited to the participation of the four leading West Indian economies. Jamaica and Trinidad were the only two independent states and the strongest economies, while also representing the majority of the regional population. Barbados was the largest and strongest of the remaining 'Little Eight' economies from the former Federation and acted as a link to the other seven eastern Caribbean states. Those three were joined at the meeting by British Guiana, whose participation was perhaps most significant by virtue of its lack of involvement in the Federal disputes. It has been suggested that the 'Big Four' were strategically selected because of their level of autonomy from Britain – as Barbados and Guyana were already well advanced in their own negotiations for independence – since the meeting was intended to be a forum which represented the vision of a fully decolonised regional framework.[33] It was perhaps equally strategic to exclude the rest of the eastern Caribbean, in the expectation that Barbados would act as their intermediary, since the other 'little' seven were still involved in the pursuit of an alternative political union and were likely to raise the issue of federation in this new forum.

While Williams had hoped for some discussion of options for regional economic integration, the conference focused on the administrative issues related to the maintenance of common services. However, in their opening addresses the leaders of the four acknowledged the need for broader regional cooperation. Cheddi Jagan, the Premier of British Guiana, advocated the development of a broad agenda for social change in the region, warning that small size and economic strength should not be the only factors for consideration in regional cooperation since the uniting of 'pygmies' could, in his view, also provide greater opportunity for further colonial exploitation.[34] A significant inhibiting factor in the realisation of a new postcolonial regional initiative was the continued colonial administration of the majority of the territories in the region. Williams's vision of a Caribbean Economic Community had been modelled on the Organisation of African Unity (OAU) which had been set up just months before the Caribbean meeting to champion the interests of independent African states, while advocating the elimination of colonialism in the others.[35] In that regard, in his address, Williams expressed his hope that the new community would reverse the 'centuries of subordination to outside control...[and the perception of the Caribbean]...as hewers of wood and drawers of water for other people'.[36] The discussions also reflected uncertainties about the approach to be adopted, given the failure of the federal model. Errol Barrow, the new Premier of Barbados, noted that, despite the potential benefits of economic cooperation, the Eastern Caribbean territories were likely to be suspicious of attempts at economic integration without the benefit of a political union as a safeguard against the exploitation of their limited resources by the larger territories. However, Jamaica's new Prime Minister, Bustamante, was very clear that any hopes of renewing the Federation was, from his perspective, 'stone cold dead'.[37]

A second meeting of Heads of Government was convened in Jamaica in January 1964 but also made limited progress towards consensus on the approach to regional integration. However, the Heads issued a joint foreign policy statement which reflected the high value which they placed on sovereignty. The Heads emphasised 'the right of all nations, small as well as large, to respect for their territorial integrity and their sovereign status' and agreed to pursue cooperative relations with other states against colonialism and discrimination.[38] In spite of the lack of progress on regional governance in general, the first two meetings served to ease the tensions among leaders occasioned by the Federal debacle and years of fragmentation. Leaders viewed the conference methodology 'not only as an instrument for unity but as a means for consolidating the sovereignty they had won'.[39] Relationships had improved so much that in 1964 Bustamante affirmed:

> It might have been thought that when we crawled...out of Federation it was because we were against you; it is not so...I can give you this assurance, that my government and my people are very friendly towards the...British West Indies.[40]

A third meeting of the Conference, convened in Georgetown in 1965, by the new Premier of British Guiana, Forbes Burnham, was better positioned to produce proposals on developing a governance structure. However, although the 1965 meeting was described as having been 'marked by a most cordial atmosphere', there was a level of tension over the role to be played by Burnham.[41] His colleagues had some misgivings about his pro-socialist politics, so much so that neither Bustamante nor Williams attended the conference. Their representatives, conscious of the fragile geopolitical position of the Caribbean within a Cold War context, were keen to assert their preference for democratic political stability in all areas of the region, especially British Guiana.[42] However, the conference provided an opportunity for Burnham to assert the legitimacy of his newly-won authority via membership in a regional grouping which included two independent states. Whatever his national politics, Burnham's regionalist vision was not tainted by the Federal experience. Unfettered by past conflicts, and perhaps influenced by pro-federalist governmental advisors like Shridath Ramphal, the former Federal Assistant Attorney-General, Burnham was free to dream of a new Caribbean entity which could reflect the people's aspirations for regional unity.

Burnham, therefore, proposed the establishment of a permanent Secretariat to service the Conference and ensure implementation of its decisions. The proposal was rejected by the other Heads and was deferred for future consideration, possibly because Jamaica was wary of the proposal being a covert attempt at reviving political union. Obviously dissatisfied with the level of progress made during these early meetings of Heads of Government, Burnham initiated informal discussions with his Barbadian and Antiguan colleagues in July 1965 on an experiment to deepen the trade linkages between those countries. Burnham perhaps chose to engage Antigua's Premier,Vere Bird, in order to include a member of the smaller eastern Caribbean group of countries which were favourable towards deeper integration, even while they moved towards Associated Statehood – a precursor to full independence. Bird would have then engaged his friend, Premier Errol Barrow who also had not played a significant role in the Federation squabbles.

Those tripartite discussions were supported by an emerging academic consensus on the desirability of economic integration. Indeed, the observation of increasing regionalisation around the world, especially in Europe, had encouraged various studies of new strategies for national economic development. States were experiencing a period of economic instability, which eventually culminated in a series of commodity price decreases accompanied by oil price increases in the mid 1970s. During the mid-1960s, Jamaica began to experience declining bauxite prices and eventually other Caribbean countries began to feel the unpleasant effects of what Anthony Payne refers to as 'the cold draught of self-government', heightening their awareness of the challenges of steering the development of very small, though politically autonomous, economies within a much larger and intimidating international system of liberalised trade.[43]

The convergence of opinions emanating from various pieces of research by Caribbean economists thus led to the evolution of a strong economic rationale for regional economic integration. In particular, the coincident findings and conclusions of research undertaken by Grenadian economist Alister McIntyre and Trinidadian political economist William Demas strongly supported the strategy. Between 1963 and 1964, McIntyre was involved in research on decolonisation and trade at Columbia University, while Demas, working at McGill University, explored the case for regional economic integration as a means to economic viability and competitiveness for small vulnerable Caribbean economies. In 1964, McIntyre prepared a paper which suggested great opportunities for development of coordinated production strategies within a regional economy to enhance competitiveness.[44] Demas used McIntyre's paper as a basis for convening a Seminar on Regional Integration at the Institute of Social and Economic Research (ISER) at the University of the West Indies. The other participating economists also expounded on the potential of regional integration to move the territories in the region out of a perpetual mode of dependence on international aid and preferential trading arrangements with Britain – the latter privilege, by then, on the verge of erosion in the wake of the United Kingdom's application to join the European Economic Community (EEC). The group agreed that the region needed to widen its markets, pool and combine natural resources under regionally-programmed economic activities and strengthen their collective bargaining power in the international trading markets. In addition to the strong economic rationale, Demas's own research contained an important political or governance-related element. He emphasised a difference between the 'formal' sovereignty exercised by the individual countries of the region and the 'effective' sovereignty which could be derived from their collective strength. Demas had argued that:

> A greater degree of economic independence for each country can, paradoxically, be achieved only through meaningful economic integration in the region. This is the 'paradox of sovereignty'. A greater degree of effective sovereignty is attainable by each Caribbean

country only through some surrender to the regional collectivity of some of its formal sovereignty.[45]

Demas further revealed a special distinction between the roles of the two dimensions of sovereignty. A state could, in essence, exercise formal sovereignty, that is, its internationally and legally recognised political authority, as freely and fully as desired without ever attaining effective sovereignty. However, effective sovereignty represented a level of capacity to assume the responsibilities of statehood, which the Caribbean states so eagerly desired – that is, the capacity to maintain political authority in the state; while also maintaining governmental control of domestic affairs and international relations; and ensuring political and economic independence and viability. It was the strength of Demas's political argument that this could be achieved by surrendering formal sovereignty, that convinced Heads of Government to put their past political differences behind them in an attempt to embark on a new integration experiment.

## THE NEGOTIATION OF THE CARIBBEAN FREE TRADE ASSOCIATION (CARIFTA)

On July 6, 1965, Premiers Errol Barrow, Forbes Burnham and Vere Bird announced the imminent formation of a small free trade area among their countries, known as the Caribbean Free Trade Association (CARIFTA). Although Barbados and Antigua were both still involved in negotiating a Federation amongst the 'little Eight', those discussions were at the point of breakdown and the two were intrigued by the possibility of widening their trading markets via the proposed association with British Guiana. In December 1965, the three non-independent territories signed the Dickenson Bay Agreement establishing CARIFTA in which they agreed to limit state authority over setting import restrictions and duties within the free trade area. The formal announcement of the new regional Association included an open invitation for other territories to join.

Some of the scholars who had participated in the ISER Seminar – most notably, Alister McIntyre, George Beckford, Havelock Brewster, Clive Thomas and Norman Girvan – who were affiliated with an academic group called the New World Group, used the opportunity of Dickenson Bay to outline policy prescriptions for addressing Demas's paradox. The Group argued that free trade alone would not contribute to development, without the integration of structures of production. Their proposals hinted at the nationalisation of foreign investment entities and implied the breaching of sovereign territorial borders in order to achieve a system of rationalised production. The three Heads of Government were wary of the highly political tone of those proposals, and rejected them for fear that their adoption would dissuade other territories from participating in CARIFTA. Whilst this academic advice was not politically convincing, a 1966 mission of the Incorporated Commonwealth Caribbean Chambers of Industry and Commerce was able to use the strength of their business influence to persuade other territories of the benefits of customs union and free trade. Subsequently, Trinidad and the Associated States expressed their intention to join the CARIFTA and later the Jamaica Manufacturer's Association (JMA) convinced the Jamaican Government to participate.[46]

This emerging intellectual consensus and political interest in regionalism led to the convening of a fourth Conference of Heads in Bridgetown, Barbados in October 1967. In the interim, Barbados and Guyana had achieved independence in 1966 and the Eastern Caribbean states had achieved Associated Statehood status with the United Kingdom. The Heads of Government agreed to use the existing Dickenson Bay Agreement and the proposals emanating from a set of the integration studies as a point of departure for negotiating a new institutional architecture for a widened CARIFTA. It is significant that the meeting was the first to involve the participation of all the Commonwealth Caribbean territories, regardless of their political or constitutional status. Burnham summed up the awesome sense of responsibility which accompanied the agenda: 'If this conference fails we perish, if this conference succeeds we survive'.[47]

The three main studies, considered by Heads, were completed in 1967 and reflected the ideas of the New World Group. One was the 'Possibility for Rationalising Production and Trade in the West Indies' by Alister McIntyre, Norman Girvan, George Beckford and Eric Armstrong; another was the 'Problems of Caribbean Air Transport Industry' by Steve DeCastro; and most significantly, the third was the 'Dynamics of West Indian Economic Integration' by Havelock Brewster and Clive Thomas. Brewster and Thomas's central thesis was that production integration was needed in order to maximise the economic gains from free trade and customs union.[48] They argued that integration in the region should go well beyond the trade in goods to encompass the integrated production of those goods. They also recognised that the realisation of their vision of economic integration was directly linked to the 'institutional form and quality of potential decision-making' and the development of appropriate institutions for regional governance.[49] They recommended, as a first priority, the establishment of a Regional Commission for Economic Integration of the Caribbean. The proposed Commission would be responsible for administering the integration activities and bringing proposals into effect. The study further recommended the establishment of a regional development bank and the creation of other institutions to manage deeper forms of integration, including the movement of labour.

The first outcome of the Conference was the agreement to introduce free trade across the region by May 1, 1968, under an amended CARIFTA agreement, as the first step in realising a deeper form of integration. The delegation of greater levels of authority as prescribed by the recommendations of the integration studies was deferred. In that regard, the Heads passed a Resolution on Regional Integration which highlighted a wide range of long-term objectives related to the development of regionally integrated industries, the rationalisation of agriculture, the imposition of a common external tariff and the harmonisation of fiscal incentives for economic investment. Secondly, the conference decided on the establishment of some central governance machinery to support the association. Thirdly, it agreed to establish other institutions and common services to support the functional needs of the various territories and promote 'regional thinking and awareness...[as an] essential basis for the effective working of regional institutions'.[50] Consequently, CARIFTA came into effect on May 1, 1968 with a phasing-in of membership, eventually leading to a full complement of 11 members including independent Jamaica, Trinidad, Barbados and Guyana; and the seven non-independent West Indies Associated States.[51]

## THE CARIFTA INSTITUTIONAL FRAMEWORK

The final CARIFTA Agreement highlighted that the primary objective of the Association was to increase and diversify intra-regional trade through removal of tariff and quota restrictions as a means of meeting the region's aspirations for full employment, the optimal use of resources and improved living standards.[52] With respect to the central governance mechanisms, Article 29 established a Council of Ministers as a sub-committee of the Conference of Heads of Government with general responsibility for the establishment of the free trade area; administration of a secretariat and a regional budget. The Commonwealth Caribbean Regional Secretariat (a revised form of the Burnham proposal which had been rejected in 1965) was established to coordinate regional technical assistance and William Demas was appointed as the Secretary-General. Jamaica entered a reservation on both the establishment of the Secretariat and its location in Guyana; while Barbados entered a reservation on the location and budget. The Bahamas, which participated in the Conference, agreed to contribute to the budget of the Regional Secretariat, although it did not join CARIFTA. These structures represented the first formal institutions of regional governance. However, the hierarchy of the structure reveals several interesting issues in relation to the protection of national sovereignty.

These governance mechanisms were all made subordinate to the Conference of Heads of Government, although there was no legal basis for the Conference within the Dickenson Bay Agreement. By making them subject to the authority of the informal grouping of Heads, the drafters hoped to avoid debate about the powers of the central administration. Instead, all authority remained squarely within national territories. The agreement itself did not come into effect until it had been ratified by national legislatures (Article 31(1)). Although the decisions of the Council of Ministers were regarded as binding under Article 35, the agreement stipulated that all such decisions had to be reached by unanimous vote with each territory commanding one equal vote (Article 28 (4),(5)). That voting arrangement provided the sovereign states with some protection from the influence or interference of other states in their domestic policy. In addition, the respect for sovereignty was further entrenched in Article 32(3), which acknowledged the special status of sovereign states within the Association. The Agreement also provided for certain exceptions which enabled territories to disregard provisions of CARIFTA based on their national interests (Articles 15 and 16) and also provided for the amendment of the agreement in cases where territories were unable to abide by its provisions (Article 31 (2)).

The 1967 conference had discussed the possibility of establishing other regional institutions to support cooperation on external representation, regulation of a common external tariff, common tourism services, applied development technology, regional air transport and a regional news service. The most significant of the proposals for further institution-building was, however, for the establishment of a Caribbean Development Bank (CDB), which was expected to play a key role in achieving the objectives of equitable development between the more developed countries (MDCs) and  the less developed ones (LDCs) in the Association. The concept of the CDB had its genesis in initiatives spearheaded by the United States, Canada and United Kingdom shortly after the collapse of the Federation, to leverage development funds for the Caribbean islands, so as to avert potential socialist and communist revolutions, as had occurred in Cuba in 1959. A recommendation emerged from the 1966 Canada-Commonwealth Caribbean Conference for the creation of a regional financial institution and was later refined by a UNDP group of experts which called for the establishment of a development bank to be funded primarily by the UK and Canada with US support. Caribbean Heads accepted those proposals in 1967 and appointed an Inter-Governmental Committee to draft a constitution by February 1968.

It was clear that the Bank, although not a primary institution of the Association, was intended to play an important part in the attainment of the goals of CARIFTA. The CDB Agreement thus 'recognise[d] the resolve of these States and Territories to intensify economic cooperation and promote economic integration in the Caribbean'.[53] It served to protect the interests of the LDCs within CARIFTA and also acted as a bridging mechanism between the CARIFTA territories and other British dependent territories which joined as borrowing members. The date of establishment of the CDB was initially set to coincide with the inauguration of CARIFTA on May 1, 1968; however, the agreement was not signed until October 1969 in Jamaica and came into force in January 1970. The Bank was governed by an independent, though nationally-representative, Board of Governors and Board of Directors. In spite of the potential of these common institutions to facilitate the realisation of even closer regional cooperation, a spirit of rivalry persisted among the territories, manifesting itself in disagreements over the location of the Bank which was eventually decided by the Board to be Barbados. Indeed, the CDB was a development bank and not an 'integration bank' charged with resolving the political disputes over regionalism.

Almost immediately upon the establishment of CARIFTA, some 90 per cent of manufacturered goods no longer had trade restrictions and there was growth in regional trade from EC\$95.7 million in 1968 to EC\$298 million in 1973.[54] However, the implementation of the other provisions of the agreement which extended beyond the market-led aspects of trade was slow. Payne argues that this may have been due simply to the inter-island competitiveness which prevailed.[55] However, the inefficiencies in implementation were fundamentally related to the fact that the Heads had opted for a very weak framework which was readily amended to protect national industries, thereby fuelling the rivalry. Moreover, due to the delayed establishment of the CDB, the Association lacked the internal machinery to ensure equity in relation to the development interests of the LDCs.

Nonetheless, the fifth Conference of Heads convened in 1969 opened on an optimistic note. Williams contrasted the bright mood with that of the first meeting of Heads in 1963 which 'took place under the shadow of the frustration and suspicion brought about by the break-up of the Federation'.[56] He refered to the 'godfather' role Trinidad and Tobago had played in fostering closer collaboration in air transport, technical assistance and financing, and lauded the contribution of the private sector to the success of CARIFTA in spite of persistent reservations in some quarters. In response, Jamaica's Robert Lightbourne pledged that country's unstinting commitment to regional cooperation. Guyana continued to promote the idea of building a West Indian Nation and Vere Bird spoke to the significance of the common interests among the countries. At the same time, Eric Gairy of Grenada, Chair of the Council of Associated States, announced that the Associated States intended to consolidate their own economic cooperation with the establishment of an Eastern Caribbean Common Market (ECCM).[57] There is no doubt that the announcement of the ECCM was an expression of dissatisfaction with the CARIFTA framework, given the fact that the CDB was still a work in progress.

By the time the April 1970 Meeting of Heads of Government was convened in Jamaica, the 11 members of CARIFTA were gradually coming to the realisation that the new regional initiative, though entirely of their own making, had by and large not been any more successful in meeting their needs than the Federation. A special meeting of the CARIFTA Council, which preceded the Heads of Government meeting, had considered the implications of the UK's announcement of its intention to join the EEC – an event which would affect Caribbean trading preferences. That meeting concluded with a "Resolution on the Challenge of Change in the Seventies" which reiterated the need for greater opportunities for the LDCs and mandated the formation of Joint Consultative Committees (involving the private sector and labour unions) to examine issues of interest to the people of the Commonwealth Caribbean which had not hitherto been addressed. It also broadened the remit of the Secretariat, mandating it to administer the common services which fell outside the CARIFTA framework. The Jamaican delegation's proposal for the establishment of a Regional Court of Appeal to replace the UK Privy Council was also accepted.[58] Nevertheless, the disappointment with CARIFTA was so great that, in the following year, the Heads of some of the member territories met in Grenada to discuss options for the creation of a new West Indian State as an alternative to CARIFTA.[59] The subsequent 1972 meeting of all the CARIFTA Heads agreed to embark on an upgraded regional framework which will be discussed in the next chapter.

## THE LEGACY OF THE WEST INDIES

The period following the collapse of the West Indies Federation in 1962 and leading up to the establishment of the CARIFTA in 1968 reveals layers of political complexity in the emergence of a Caribbean regional governance system. The Federal legacy significantly influenced the tone of the ensuing negotiations and ideologies which ultimately gave way to the CARIFTA as a loose arrangement for economic cooperation, rather than as a political framework for an integrated region. The relationship between the two regional governance experiments is evident in, first, the interwoven elements of philosophy which guided the respective negotiation processes and, second, the structures which emerged as institutional expressions of those philosophies.

Firstly, the West Indian Nationalist ideology, driven by the concepts of 'West Indiannesss' and 'Islandness', was replete with ambivalence, having regard to both fragmentary and integrative trends – isolation, on the one hand, and connectivity as island states, on the other hand. The desire for political autonomy was juxtaposed with the recognition of the need for economic development cooperation. However, in the post-1962 period, the ideology was abandoned, save in the eastern Caribbean, with the strengthening of territorial nationalist movements in Jamaica and Trinidad, where all aspects of sovereignty were invested in the governments of the independent nation-state. The paradox of sovereignty, identified by Demas, was most evident in this post-1962 period. The imperative of negotiating a regional governance structure, by compromising political authority and control in order to attain effective national sovereignty, was no doubt viewed by new political leaders as unfair. Indeed, European states had enjoyed the privilege of sovereignty within nation-states for centuries, before they began to pursue the benefits of regional integration. However, recognising the dynamic relationship between the political and economic aspects of sovereignty, a new philosophy of regional economic cooperation emerged to assume predominance over that of West Indian political union.

Since the new regionalism adopted an economic focus, federalism was irretrievably discredited as an appropriate model of governance for the region. Furthermore, the potential for questions of political unity to be politicised in the context of partisan competition also led to the process of CARIFTA negotiations being largely devoid of participation by ordinary people. In this regard, only a few private sector leaders were marginally involved, given their particular stake in ensuring its functioning. The negotiating process emphasised the inordinately powerful role of Heads of Government in protecting national sovereignty and also reflected their general reluctance to involve the people of the region in both the national and regional decision-making processes, for fear that their 'ignorance' or the opportunistic nature of national opposition movements would derail the project. Unfortunately, the lack of a participatory approach may have contributed to the relative irrelevance of CARIFTA institutions to the human and social development needs within each of the territories.

Secondly, as a result of the constraints of small size and islandness, the paradox of sovereignty which appeared very pronounced in the context of independence, affected the nature of the institutional framework. The small islands continued to demonstrate dual tendencies towards a fear of separateness and isolation from the world, on one hand – a trend which encourages international cooperation; and on the other hand, tendencies towards the preservation and celebration of territorial boundaries – a trend which increases scepticism of integrative experiments. While the literature indicates that there are special features of island development, the constraints of size and vulnerability inherent in islandness are arguably no more significant than those faced by small countries more generally.[60] In that regard, it is argued that the factor which was most influential to the nature of the 1968 Caribbean institutional framework, was the emergence of a paradox in the context of a failed West Indian nationalism, rather than issues of size or islandness per se. The West Indian predisposition to preserve national authority and political control within territorial boundaries, while at the same time, preserving connections with the extra-regional or international environment as a means of enhancing legitimacy, is a key component of that legacy. In that sense, CARIFTA, though essentially an economic arrangement, made a tacit political statement. As a reflection of both a colonial and federal legacy, CARIFTA helped to define modern Caribbean political culture. The prominent role played by Heads of Government in the emergent regional governance structure and the loophole provisions within agreements were all reflective of an embedded West Indian cum Caribbean psyche which emphasised economic cooperation as a means of enhancing national political sovereignty, but rejected regional political integration as a symbol of the colonial past.

In conclusion, it is argued that this foundation period in the emergence of Caribbean sovereignty and regionalism revealed two distinct approaches. Prior to 1962, the region boasted an ideologically-grounded approach to political integration. However, in the post-1962 period the approach became more tentative. Although there seemed to be initial consensus on a gradual approach towards the development of a regional economic community, focus was placed instead on facilitating a free trade regime which eschewed the elements of a deeper integration which the West Indian nationalist ideology required. Consequently, the actual structures which evolved remained rather minimalist, with limited political or social impact. The regional governance framework reflected a level of uncertainty about how best to assert principles of 'effective sovereignty' within a framework of emerging and competing 'formal sovereignties'. All authority over the regional agenda was formally invested within national legislatures. However, the challenges inherent in that approach were as evident as they had also been in the Federal context. Without the authority of an independent regional entity, the application and implementation of the CARIFTA provisions in relation to regional development programmes remained a challenge. Within four years of establishing CARIFTA, the Heads of Government acknowledged an urgent need to confront the paradox by establishing an improved governance structure for regional integration.

# THE CARIBBEAN COMMUNITY (CARICOM) AS A SOVEREIGNTY SAFEGUARD

The sovereignty paradox became more pronounced during the politically and economically turbulent decades of the 1970s and 1980s. Even though Commonwealth Caribbean countries were being gradually integrated into the international community of states, their prospects for achieving effective sovereignty were steadily declining, in spite of the CARIFTA facility. Given the failure of that free trade framework to deliver on key development goals, the deepening of regional cooperation emerged in 1972 as an urgent imperative of Heads of Government in an effort to liberate their fragile countries from economic dependence. Against the background of that particular agenda, this chapter examines the establishment of the Caribbean Community and Common Market (CARICOM) as an alternative institution for safeguarding national sovereignty. Firstly, the chapter introduces the elements of an emergent philosophy of integration which sought to reconcile the desirability of West Indian nationalism with imperatives of achieving economic independence – a key dimension of effective sovereignty. Secondly, it describes how that philosophy influenced the transformation of CARIFTA into a uniquely designed CARICOM in 1973. The third section highlights the embeddedness of national sovereignty in the institutional framework, while the fourth section highlights the weaknesses in the framework, revealed between 1974 and 1988, with regard to efficiency and effectiveness of regional governance. The chapter concludes with a summary of four sets of governance challenges faced by CARICOM in that period.

## TOWARDS A PHILOSOPHY OF CARIBBEAN INTEGRATION

Even after four years of its existence, most of the proposals contained in the 1967 Heads of Government resolution on deepening the CARIFTA framework for regional integration had not been realised. The Secretariat was still in the process of studying the feasibility of proposals for, *inter alia,* integrated production and investment. The Secretariat staff, led by William Demas, recognised that those objectives could only be practically achieved if the existing framework for regional cooperation was upgraded to a more advanced framework for regional integration. They also acknowledged that such a process would require the development of some consensus among the political directorate on the role regionalism should play in the national development process. In 1971, differences in opinion still abounded among leaders as to whether the movement should be viewed as either an 'end' in its expression of West Indian unity or as a 'means' to national economic development (see figure 4.1). The 'end' rationale suggested a willingness to relinquish some aspects of sovereignty to an independent authority within a deeply integrated governance framework, given the presumption of a West Indian identity capable of representing all national interests. Conversely, the 'means' rationale, which had been the dominant rationale of CARIFTA, was less favourable to any institutional reform which would require concessions of state control over domestic economic affairs and it proposed instead the widening of the existing arena for free trade to include other Caribbean countries.

However, a third rationale emerged from an interchange of ideas among four concurrent discussions on the foundations of Caribbean development and came to challenge the false dichotomy presented by the debate among the politicians. That third rationale proposed the reconciliation of the political and economic dimensions of regionalism through a focus on the ultimate goal of effective sovereignty. The ideas emerging from four sets of discussions and their contribution to the development of that third rationale – an ideology of regional integration and effective sovereignty – are the focus of this section of the chapter.

The first discussion emerged from the context of a 1971 initiative, spearheaded by Guyana, to create a unitary West Indian state among six territories.[1]

*Figure 4.1: Philosophies of Integration*

| Desired Outcome | Philosophy of Regionalism | Governance Implication |
|---|---|---|
| West Indian Unity ⟶ | Political End ⟶ | Deeper Integration |
| National Economic Development ⟶ | Economic Means ⟶ | Wider Cooperation |

One of the advocates of the initiative, Shridath Ramphal, who had become Guyana's Minister of External Affairs, was very vocal about the need for deeper integration to be extended beyond free trade in order to embrace a quest for collective strength, based on the principles of nationalism, brotherhood and unity.[2] He was aware that commitment to these principles was not yet strong enough across the region to encourage participation of other territories in the West Indian state initiative and recognised, therefore, the need to concentrate on enhancing CARIFTA. While he acknowledged the value of maintaining strong relationships with countries in the wider Caribbean, he argued that the premature widening of CARIFTA would threaten the intimacy of the grouping by introducing new political and socio-cultural influences that would complicate the consensus-building process. Interestingly, however, Ramphal avoided making any proposals on the adoption of a specific institutional structure – no doubt fully cognisant of the outcome of past misunderstandings over the association of the concept of West Indian unity with the instruments of political union. Instead, he urged the development of a normative framework, characterised by some form of indigenous ideology of regional economic integration, which could also accommodate a political commitment to West Indian kinship.[3]

Although the quest to preserve West Indian identity persisted, even as island nationalisms strengthened in the four independent states and independence movements were mounted in the remaining West Indian territories, those kinship sentiments were often overshadowed by the imperatives of national economic survival. A second set of discussions, based on scholarship associated with the New World Group (NWG), revealed the alarming extent to which Caribbean territories were economically dependent on the outside world and thus vulnerable to the changing dynamics of international relations. During the latter part of the 1960s and into the early 1970s, Jamaica and Guyana's economies had been severely weakened by decreasing prices of their major commodity exports, which coincided with increases in the prices of manufactured imports on which the countries relied. In addition, control over the extraction and exploitation of the mineral resources in most Caribbean territories remained firmly in the hands of multinational and foreign private companies. Furthermore, the intensification of a multilateral agenda on the 'liberalisation' of international trade threatened to erode the preferential trading agreements from which the small Caribbean economies had hitherto benefitted. These compounded factors highlighted a state of 'dependent underdevelopment', arising from inequitable relationships between developed and developing countries. The prescriptions recommended to address this dependence implied the need for increased governmental control over economic activities at both national and regional levels – economic independence.[4] Political leaders associated the regional strategies proposed by the discussants for achieving that level of regulatory control, with a return to regional political union. Interestingly, however, the various dimensions of NWG scholarship emphasised the role of the state in the exercise of power and the maintenance of sovereign autonomy, authority and control, even in a regional context. For example, Norman Girvan focused on increasing state autonomy from colonial powers and state control over natural resources, while Clive Thomas emphasised maximising state control over means of production and George Beckford gave priority to the role of the state in broadening popular participation in governance and economic development.[5] The sovereignty of the state was therefore expected to play an important role in regional strategies. The overall contribution of this discussion was the identification of economic independence, via regional coordination of state power, as an important aspect of any meaningful ideology of integration.

That discussion of the exercise of state sovereignty evolved parallel to a wider 'Third World' political movement against dependency and underdevelopment, in which newly decolonised states were increasingly challenging the international trade regime established by 'older' states. 'Third World' states, because of their majority membership in the United Nations, their geopolitical significance in relation to the democracy-communism debate of the Cold War, and the relative dependence of developed countries on their natural resources, began advancing an argument for the establishment of a New International Economic Order (NIEO), 'based on equity, sovereign equality, interdependence, common interest and cooperation among all States irrespective of their economic and social systems'.[6] The philosophy of collective self-reliance inherent in that emerging campaign – based on the combination of resources without disrupting the state sovereign control over those resources – resonated with Caribbean aspirations and inspired the quest for an ideology consistent with the other two themes. This was particularly so since leading Caribbean political figures, including Guyana's Forbes Burnham and Jamaica's then Leader of the Opposition, Michael Manley, were principal proponents of this 'Third World' initiative. This third set of ideas emphasised 'Third World' solidarity as a foundation for development.

William Demas, who was strategically positioned within the CARIFTA Secretariat to monitor the preceding discussions, was also engaged in 1971 in preparing his own contribution to the quest for an ideology of integration. In a series of essays – constituting the fourth set of discussions – he explored the interconnectedness of West Indian nationhood and Caribbean integration.[7] This supplemented the ongoing dialogue in two ways. Firstly, Demas offered a definition of development which embraced the assertion and promotion of a West Indian identity. This sort of philosophy served to bridge the apparent gulf between West Indian nationalism and the emerging focus on achieving economic independence by demonstrating the applicability of the former ideology to the contemporary institutional needs of the region. He argued that West Indian unity would provide a strong foundation for Caribbean people to pursue their relationships in the international system without fear of economic, political and cultural 'subjugation' in such relationships'.[8] Secondly, he linked his concept of effective sovereignty to the concept of legitimate governance which he defined as a process of providing opportunities for citizens to participate in governance and economic development at the national and regional levels in order to make state authority more accountable.[9] Demas's contribution to the discussion is particularly interesting because this conception of legitimacy had been omitted from the early campaigns for sovereignty. In the early independence period, the attributes of governmental control, authority and autonomy had been emphasised. For the first time, sovereignty and the dimension of authority in particular, was associated with processes of accountability to citizens and responsibility for social change, and not just the maintenance of the power of the political directorate.

In summary, the four ideological discussions on West Indian unity, economic independence, Third World solidarity and legitimate governance contributed three important ideas about the way in which an effective sovereignty could underpin a potential ideology of Caribbean integration. Firstly, they emphasised the maintenance of both political and economic independence – that is, autonomy from Britain and other states, full authority within states, and control over economic potential, including human, financial and natural resources. Secondly, they embraced a populist vision of sovereignty based on legitimate and accountable governance. Finally, recognising the imperatives raised by the paradox of sovereignty in small developing states, the ideology called for the exploitation of the concept of West Indian unity in order to develop a collective approach to the exercise of sovereignty, while respecting the equality of states.

The challenge, therefore, was to translate these three dimensions into a programme of action which could inspire Heads of Government to create an appropriate governance framework to give effect to the ideology.

## THE COMMUNITY APPROACH TO EFFECTIVE SOVEREIGNTY

In May 1972, Demas spearheaded the preparation of a Secretariat paper which proposed the establishment of an economic community in order to advance an 'indigenous West Indian ideology of development and social change'.[10] Consequently, great weight was placed on political commitment at the national level, including a responsibility for maintaining accountability to the citizenry as a part of the new approach to regional economic integration. The paper entitled, 'From CARIFTA to Caribbean Community', proposed the establishment of two distinct institutional pillars. Firstly, the paper suggested that existing CARIFTA instruments should be developed to accommodate the objectives of integrated production within the framework of a common market – an institutional modality which implied greater economic policy coordination beyond trade issues. Secondly, the paper proposed the consolidation of continued functional cooperation in education, health, communications, public administration and law and the development of common foreign economic policies, all under the banner of a Caribbean community. This latter institutional pillar was perhaps inspired by Eric Williams's 1963 vision, but was also induced by the institutional precedent of the 1957 European Economic Community (EEC). The Secretariat argued that an overarching community framework would contribute to greater coherence among the existing instruments of regional cooperation and enhance the efficiency and effectiveness of the movement. In order to secure the agreement of the political directorate, the Secretariat proposed that the Community be founded on the basis of an intergovernmental treaty, which it argued, would facilitate the collective pursuit of the three objectives (economic integration, functional cooperation and foreign policy coordination) without requiring the surrender of any formal sovereignty.[11] In that respect, the community would be governed by the Conference of Heads of Government, legally formalised within the treaty, with responsibility for safeguarding the sovereign authority of each territory. In effect, the proposal emphasised the institutionalisation of existing structures to which leaders had already agreed rather than the creation of new instruments which would potentially threaten national sovereignty. Later, Demas would explain that the Community proposal was intended moreso to coordinate national economic development than to create an integrated regional framework.[12] That measured focus on coordination was interesting in the context of Demas's prior argument that the paradox compelled the surrender of formal sovereignty in order to achieve effective sovereignty. Yet, the 1972 Secretariat paper suggested that an intergovernmental structure which sought to safeguard all aspects of formal sovereignty could equally facilitate the achievement of 'effective community sovereignty'. Perhaps, the shift in argument came about as a result of Demas's awareness of the fact that Heads were likely to reject the entire proposal if it made an explicit recommendation on surrendering sovereignty. The modification of the argument was intended, therefore, to open the door to the consideration of and perhaps the eventual acceptance of the imperatives of bargaining with formal sovereignty.

When Heads of Government returned to the regional conference table in October 1972 to consider the Secretariat's proposals, the discussions revealed that, from the perspectives of the leaders, even the diluted proposals for the achievement of a 'community sovereignty' made too many demands on formal sovereignty. For example, the proposed common market called for the removal of restrictions on the movement of all factors of production – including labour. However, the movement of people across national borders presented a threat to the Westphalian, domestic and interdependence dimensions of sovereignty – that is, state control over immigration flows across territorial borders. It was not surprising, therefore, that Heads merely mandated the CARIFTA Committee of Ministers to examine the feasibility of implementing this aspect of the common market rather than agreeing to its merits outright.

Other aspects of the common market were equally controversial. The smaller countries in the Eastern Caribbean were not in favour of conceding any autonomy in decision-making with respect to the negotiation of a common external tariff. The group had already negotiated a much lower common import duty within their sub-regional common market (ECCM) and the effect of a wider Caribbean tariff would have been increased costs of living in their countries. Interestingly, Guyana, Trinidad and Tobago, and Barbados favoured the development of the common tariff as well as a framework of fiscal incentives, since the overall outcome of the requisite concession of autonomy in decision-making was likely to be very beneficial to the manufacturing industries in their territories. Jamaica's new Prime Minister, Michael Manley, elected in February 1972, was also favourable to the common market proposal. It was perhaps fortuitous for Demas and the CARICOM advocates that Manley had risen to power, since the previous administration led by Hugh Shearer had been disinclined to concede any further elements of autonomy in decision-making and preferred to widen the existing tariff-free zone to include the Spanish, French and Dutch-speaking Caribbean territories. In contrast, during the 1972 Heads of Government meeting, Manley expressed his conviction that deeper integration, as opposed to wider cooperation, would improve Jamaica's position with external partners.

Notwithstanding the uncertainties about the common market in some quarters, the deliberations on the community pillar of the proposal revealed in many ways a common desire among Heads to safeguard national sovereignty. Heads expressed their support for the securing of all dimensions of formal sovereignty by the still non-independent countries and acknowledged the potential of the community – as a political institution – to facilitate advocacy in this area.[13] Barbados' Prime Minister, Errol Barrow, emphasised the potential for the consolidation of a unique West Indian cultural identity; while Williams and Burnham emphasised the defence of the territorial integrity of each state, perhaps unsurprisingly, given the former's suspicion of Venezuela's political dominance in the region and the latter's involvement in a border dispute with the Venezuelan Government. On the whole, the proposed community was viewed as a valuable construct for shielding the region from vulnerability and dependence and for the assertion of the right to command full sovereignty. However, only one of the Heads spoke of the community as a sphere for joint policymaking. Manley explicitly embraced the implication of compromise in shared decision-making as a means to shared strength, self-reliance, social justice, decreased dependence on the metropolis and a reinforcement of West Indian identity.[14]

Interestingly, one proposal related to governance within the proposed community, having regard to sovereign control over judicial affairs, elicited an unusual response from the Heads. The Secretariat had reiterated a proposal made during the April 1970 Meeting of Heads of Government for the creation of a regional court of appeal. In spite of the potential benefits to be derived from shared judicial administration at the regional level, the Heads, in typical fashion, declined to transfer any aspect of final appellate jurisdiction to a regional body – even one emanating from their own formulations. However, atypically, they agreed to maintain a system which effectively surrendered that final authority to an extra-regional entity – the United Kingdom's Judicial Committee of the Privy Council (JCPC). Demas's team had attempted to grapple with this anomaly in their paper by proposing that Heads adopt a regional court with dual jurisdiction – the first related to the settlement of disputes arising within the proposed common market and the second related to final appeals for constitutional, civil and criminal cases.[15] This division of competencies would have facilitated the immediate creation of a dispute settlement mechanism for the common market, while leaving room for reconsideration in due course, of state positions with regard to the delegation of authority in other judicial matters. However, the matter received no further attention until the late 1980s and the anomaly, which is discussed further in chapter 8, remains unresolved in most member states.

At the end of their 1972 meeting, Heads agreed to the transformation of the CARIFTA into a Caribbean Common Market by the fifth anniversary of CARIFTA on May 1, 1974, but agreed only 'in principle' to the creation of a Caribbean Community – requesting further examination of the legal implications by a Committee of Attorneys-General of the CARIFTA and The Bahamas.[16] That Committee eventually decided that the maintenance of a legal distinction between the two institutions was potentially useful, given the special position of The Bahamas within the movement. The Bahamas, which had not joined CARIFTA but had participated in Heads of Government meetings and functional cooperation arrangements and also contributed to the Secretariat's budget, expressed a desire to continue its functional relationship within the proposed Community, without participating in the common market dimension. At the same time, such a distinction was also potentially risky, since Jamaica's interest in the common market was accompanied by warnings from the national political Opposition about the community dimension being a symbol of an emerging conspiracy towards political union and a consequent threat to Jamaica's sovereignty.

Notwithstanding Manley's support for the community and his willingness to compromise, the Committee, cognisant of the federal legacy, feared he might buckle under those domestic pressures and agree only to Jamaica's membership in the common market but not the community, thereby limiting the legitimacy and viability of the whole framework. Therefore, in order to secure Jamaica's participation, the Committee drafted a legal instrument, considered to be a juridical hybrid, which created two distinct legal personalities within a single organisation, by linking the two personalities both to a single governance body – the Conference of Heads of Government. The effect of this mechanism was to make participation in the common market conditional on participation in the community without requiring the converse. The Bahamas could therefore, participate in the community without joining the common market. However, the Conference was not invested with any supranational decision-making authority or independence from national legislatures – a provision that was necessary to secure Jamaica's agreement.

Having reviewed the draft treaty, the Heads of Government met in Georgetown in April 1973 and formally agreed, on the basis of a Georgetown Accord, to establish the Caribbean Community and Common Market (CARICOM) as a reflection of a 'common determination to fulfil, within the shortest possible time, the hopes and aspirations of the people of the Caribbean territories for industrial and agricultural development, full employment and improved standards of living'.[17] The Accord reflected a desire for the new arrangements to support equitable development among the larger and smaller territories – agreeing in that regard to allow the existing lower tariffs within the ECCM to apply in the CARICOM Common Market; to support increased functional cooperation; to enhance bargaining power in relation to third parties; and to enhance economic, social and cultural development. The CARIFTA Secretariat was slated for transformation into the Caribbean Community Secretariat. The meeting also discussed the institution of an annual Caribbean Day and the establishment of a joint diplomatic mission in Japan.[18] Having reached this accord, the four independent states agreed to found CARICOM in July 1973, with the expectation that the other territories would join within a year.

## THE INSTITUTIONALISATION OF CARICOM'S SOVEREIGNTY SAFEGUARDS

On July 4, 1973, a special and final meeting of Heads of Government of Commonwealth Caribbean Countries was convened in Chaguaramas, Trinidad for the signing of the Treaty of Chaguaramas which included a Common Market Annex. The date was a symbolic tribute to the birth of Norman Manley and also, according to Burnham, to the anniversary of the commencement of informal talks between Premiers Barrow, Bird and Burnham in 1965, which had led to the Dickenson Bay Agreement. Michael Manley's remarks at the ceremony suggested that the treaty represented a new meaningful relationship – a compromise forged out of the separate postures of each country's sovereignty.[19] In a sense, he was perhaps hinting at the fact that, on the one hand, Jamaica had conceded to participation in a Community which demanded joint decision-making in areas beyond free trade cooperation, given the shift to a guiding philosophy of economic integration and the addition of a new objective of foreign policy coordination, which was traditionally associated with the exclusive sovereign authority of states. On the other hand, other members of the Community had agreed to a governance framework based on loose confederation which was devoid, perhaps disappointingly so, of any independent regional authority. The lack of supranationality has, consequently, often been associated with Jamaica's role in the negotiations. However, viewed from a broader perspective, the aversion to supranational authority was not a unique feature of Jamaica's nationalism, but was rather a characteristic of broader West Indian and 'Third World' political culture during the 1970s, born out of the novelty of sovereign statehood. Indeed, Duke Pollard later suggested that such preferences emerged from developing country observation of the tendency for larger and more powerful states to control the executive functions of multilateral institutions.[20] In that regard, it can be argued that although the confederal principle had indeed worked to encourage Jamaica's participation, the entrenchment of sovereignty within the treaty provisions, through, for example, unanimous voting procedures, was also potentially beneficial to all the territories since it limited the extent to which the 'Big Four', individually or en bloc, could seek a privileged position in the regional decision-making process.

Accordingly, the legal framework was linked to the principle of respect for sovereign equality among members.[21] Pursuant to that framework, the provisions of the treaty did not have direct effect in the national law, since all the states subscribed to dualist legal traditions. Therefore, under Article 240 (1), the provisions of the treaty and all decisions made by CARICOM were subject to separate national constitutional procedures before they became legally binding.

Interestingly, Article 4 also called for equity in the distribution of benefits among members. It is arguable that the bestowing of equal voting rights on all members (Articles 9 and 13 of Treaty and Article 8 of Annex) might have reasonably raised an expectation of equity in the decision-making process. However, the principles of equality and equity in decision-making appear somewhat discordant. In other words, equal treatment of members still under British administration posed a direct risk to the full assertion by the four independent states of their rights to the international legal and Westphalian dimensions of sovereignty – in particular, their rights to autonomy from external colonial influences. Consequently, greater weight was placed on the votes of the more developed independent countries than on the votes of the non-independent countries. Therefore, the two principal 'equity' mechanisms enshrined in the legal framework – a distinction between Less Developed Countries (LDCs) and More Developed Countries (MDCs) in Article 3, and a Special Regime for Less Developed Countries in chapter 7 of the Treaty – remained mechanisms of economic equity which did not in fact render the LDCs eligible for completely equal political status in decision-making, until they had assumed independent statehood.

These principles were embedded within the procedures of the main institutional mechanisms identified in chapter 2 of the Treaty. The Treaty outlined two types of mechanisms – those involved in the decision-making process and those involved in the implementation process. The decision-making mechanisms were two-tiered: Principal Organs and Institutions. Although it was apparently unusual for regional integration movements to make a distinction between organs and institutions, the distinction facilitated the placing of emphasis on the high levels of political authority invested in the Organs and the consequent subordination of Institutions to which limited formal authority was delegated. The Principal Organs of the Community were the Conference of Heads of Government (CHOG) and the Common Market Council (CMC) which governed the two separate entities within CARICOM (Articles 20 of Treaty and Article 63 of Annex).

The Treaty endowed the CHOG with statutory authority and legal responsibility for the supervision of the entire regional movement, including the determination of policy, creation of new institutions, direction of Organs and Institutions, conclusion of treaties with other states, financial decision-making and establishment of consultative arrangements (Article 8). The procedural requirement for an affirmative vote from each member state in order to effect both decisions and recommendations was an important device for safeguarding sovereignty in the CHOG (Article 9). The affirmative vote rule in effect made the decision-making process rely on unanimity in decision-making. Any negative vote would defeat the proposal and too many abstentions, especially from MDCs, would perhaps call into question the legitimacy of decisions. In that regard, no more than a quarter of the members, including no more than two MDCs, could abstain if a decision was to be passed. The eventual achievement of independence in the LDCs led to the removal of the weighting in favour of the MDCs and the achievement of full equity and equality in decision-making.

The CMC, comprising Ministers of government with responsibility for economic or foreign affairs, was also invested with high levels of authority over the Common Market (Articles 7 and 8 of the Annex) and, consequently, unanimous affirmative voting was also entrenched within its rules of procedure. It was also delegated responsibility for convening ad hoc informal arrangements for the settlement of disputes in relation to the functioning of the Common Market.

The second tier of deliberative mechanisms was a set of Community Institutions (Article 10). The Conference of Health Ministers and Standing Committees of Ministers responsible for labour, foreign affairs, finance, agriculture, mining, industry, and transportation were invested with authority to make decisions by unanimous affirmative vote and pass recommendations by a two-thirds majority, including at least two MDCs. Here again, the bias towards the independent MDCs presented itself. However, the relaxing of the unanimity rule with respect to the making of recommendations facilitated the process of approving non-binding proposals at this level, even if they were ultimately subject to the unanimous authority of the two Principal Organs. The Institutions played an important role in the consultative process since they were permitted to admit observers to their deliberations and appoint and convene sub-committees and working groups, including non-governmental representatives to consider various policy matters (Article 12). The Joint Consultative Committee (JCC), which had served the CARIFTA Council of Ministers, continued to function with regard to the CMC. No further consultative mechanisms were explicitly identified within the Treaty, even though the Conference had the authority to form such machinery (Article 8 (7)).

With regard to the implementation of Community decisions, no central executive mechanism was created to act separately from implementing agencies within member states. The Community executive was therefore, based on national governance and not regional governance. The general undertaking for implementation enshrined in Article 5 was the responsibility of ministries within member states. However, several other mechanisms which exercised functions independently of the Community were also acknowledged within the Treaty. The Associate Institutions (Article 14) were governed by separate legal arrangements but were involved in the implementation of technical initiatives closely associated with CARICOM's strategic objectives. The most prominent of the Associate Institutions was the Caribbean Development Bank (CDB), which held a principal role in the financing and administration of initiatives related to the fulfilment of the Common Market obligations and the Special Regime for LDCs. The Council of Legal Education (CLE), the Universities of the West Indies (UWI) and of

Guyana (UG), the Shipping Council, the Caribbean Examinations Council (CXC) and the governance mechanisms of the sub-regional movement – the West Indies Associate States Council of Ministers and the Eastern Caribbean Common Market Council of Ministers – were also among those so recognised. However, the treaty failed to specify the relationship between these Associate Institutions and the governmental Institutions and Organs of the Community.[22]

The other mechanism which contributed to the implementation process was the CARICOM Secretariat – an administrative organ mandated to follow up on the decisions of the Organs and Institutions, conduct research and provide services at the request of member states (Articles 15 and 16). It was headed by a Secretary-General appointed as an independent officer of the Community (Article 15 (4). Demas continued in the post for the first few months after the inauguration of the Community. The Secretariat was therefore, the only truly regional institution amongst the governance mechanisms outlined in the treaty, since its staff served the interests of the Community as a whole, rather than individual national administrations. At the same time, Heads were careful to limit the responsibilities of the Secretariat to administrative services so as not to create the profile of a regional political authority. Interestingly, however, over time, the Secretariat grew to wield significant, though informal, influence over the regional decision-making process. Anthony Payne argues that this was due partly to the fact that its small but competent and industrious staff gained the confidence of member states and partly to the mediating role played by Demas, as Secretary-General, given his close personal relationships with some Heads of Government.[23] Indeed, that informal influence prompted Jamaica's Opposition Leader, Donald Sangster, to suggest in 1973 that the Community had been devised as a strategy to transfer Jamaica's decision-making authority to the Secretariat in Guyana. It may well have been the case, as some interviewed elites have suggested, that some Heads of Government also feared that the Secretary-General occasionally came too close to playing the role of a 'super-Prime Minister' – which was potentially an even greater threat to national sovereignty than any material supranational.

Overall, the CARICOM governance framework, although more elaborate than CARIFTA, was quite modest since the Treaty provided for only a few central institutions – excluding a supranational executive body, a court or parliament. The simplicity of CARICOM's initial form held potential for the gradual building of regional governance capacity over time and the measured evolution of a more sophisticated structure in due course. However, even in its initial form, the CARICOM framework failed to make the appropriate functional and authoritative links between the associate implementing agencies and the regional authority of the CHOG. There was no reference to the relationships between associate institutions, ministerial Organs, Institutions and national departments. In other words, the rudimentary governance framework failed to make an effective link between the sovereign authority of Heads and delegated executive authority; and therefore, between central decision-making and decentralised implementation. As a consequence, even when several of the Associate Institutions – the Caribbean Examinations Council and the Council of Legal Education being good examples – began to make steady progress in their respective areas of functional cooperation, and in so doing, directly affected the lives of the Caribbean people, their successes were rarely associated by the public with CARICOM. Conversely, the lack of progress made by ministerial departments in respect of the regional agenda was readily associated with CARICOM's inefficiency. The framework had therefore failed to create synergy between the aspects of authority, control and legitimacy, which the ideology of integration had highlighted. Within a few months of the inauguration of CARICOM, these and other weaknesses of the governance framework were revealed against the background of a changing international environment for development.

## CARICOM's Performance

The performance of the CARICOM governance framework between 1974 and 1988, particularly in the areas of economic integration and foreign policy coordination, was disappointing. It failed to develop a level of efficiency in decision-making or secure effective implementation. Efficiency in decision-making refers to the extent to which the deliberative and consultative processes resulted in the making of binding decisions reflective of CARICOM's strategic direction. On the other hand, effectiveness refers to the extent to which those decisions resulted in action towards the desired objective. Against the background of periods of economic crisis in the 1970s and structural adjustment in the 1980s, this penultimate section of the chapter reviews the flaws revealed in the institutional framework and shows how they affected CARICOM's capacity to function efficiently and effectively in relation to its three main pillars of integration.

The 1970s was a period of intense conflict in Caribbean politics. CARICOM entered a period of interconnected economic, political and interpersonal disagreements almost immediately after the signing of the Treaty of Chaguaramas. The First Meeting of the Conference of Heads of Government of the Caribbean Community (CHOG), which was convened in Barbados in January 1974, was dominated by discussions of the negative effect of an energy crisis on the balance of payments and foreign exchange reserves in member states, excluding oil-producing Trinidad. The significant increase in oil prices in 1973 was also accompanied by an introduction of flexible interest rates (which had the effect of decreasing the purchasing power of local currencies vis-à-vis the US dollar), and increased instability in commodity prices, particularly that of bauxite, on which Jamaica and Guyana depended heavily. Moreover, the United Kingdom's announcement of its application to join the EEC suggested a threat to the preferential trading relationship from which Caribbean territories benefitted.[24] All these events challenged the functioning of the instruments of economic integration and institutions for foreign policy coordination – inducing member states to disregard certain provisions of the treaty in an effort to protect their economies. The MDCs applied quantitative import restrictions which, although allowed under Article 28 of the Common Market Annex, were instituted without consultation with members through the Principal Organs. The authority of the regional Organs was obviously not compelling enough to oblige states to account for their actions. The imposition of import restrictions in MDCs had the effect of contracting intra-regional trade, negatively affecting the economies of the LDCs in particular. Such action refuelled hitherto dormant tensions among Heads of Government over the distribution of benefits within the regional space. In spite of proposals made during the second CHOG convened in December 1975 in Basseterre, St Kitts for the creation of a financial safety net for the LDCs, the Eastern Caribbean states remained unconvinced of the potential benefits of the Common Market without a strengthened sub-regional framework. Their concerns eventually culminated in the establishment of an alternative framework – the Organisation of Eastern Caribbean States (OECS) in 1981.[25]

The 1970s was also a period of political conflict occasioned by the adoption of divergent ideological stances among CARICOM politicians. Although the CHOG had been able to reach consensus on uncontroversial foreign policy positions, including the independence of the Associated States from Britain and opposition to apartheid in South Africa, other issues, such as an emerging threat to the Grenadian government by a socialist revolutionary movement, frustrated the foreign policy coordination process. Against the background of the Cold War, differences between democratic and socialist governments intensified to the extent that, after the 1975 meeting, the Heads of Government did not meet in conference for another seven years. The ideological differences fuelled interpersonal conflicts among political leaders. One conflict erupted between Barbados' Prime Minister, Tom Adams (son of the Federation Prime Minister, Grantley Adams) and Grenada's Prime Minister, Maurice Bishop, over the latter's espousing of socialist philosophy. In 1973 Bishop publicly criticised Adams, using particularly derogatory language, and Adams reportedly retaliated by harassing Grenadian officials visiting Barbados.[26]

Another prominent conflict, emerging between 1974 and 1975, resulted in the breakdown of the relationship between Michael Manley and Eric Williams over the abandonment of a proposal for a joint aluminium smelter which would have combined Trinidad's oil with bauxite from Jamaica and Guyana.[27] An agreement for Jamaica's participation in the initiative had initially been reached during an informal telephone conversation between Williams and Manley. It was perhaps this preference for informality among leaders which contributed to the misunderstandings and, ultimately, to the failure of the initiative. Manley was presumably of the view that the agreement was not yet official and therefore continued to pursue alternative options for exploiting Jamaica's bauxite deposits, pursuant to Jamaica's sovereign rights, under his democratic socialist government. In 1974, the media reported that Manley was to sign an agreement with Mexico and Venezuela for a similar initiative. Burnham and Williams allegedly learnt about Manley's decision through the media. Later, Manley explained that the talks with Mexico and Venezuela were related to increasing Jamaica's alumina production and not for the establishment of an aluminium smelter.[28] Williams, nevertheless, viewed Manley's unilateral initiative as a personal betrayal of great proportion – comparing himself to Caesar being betrayed by Brutus (Manley) – perhaps not least because of his concerns about an expansionist tenor in Venezuela's involvement in the region. This interpersonal conflict, in particular, frustrated the attempts of the new Secretary-General, Alister McIntyre, to convene further meetings of Heads after 1975.

Against the background of these disagreements, Williams reportedly became increasingly resentful of the fact that Trinidad had made greater financial and political commitments to CARICOM than other member states. Trinidad was, at that time, relatively economically prosperous, having benefitted from the rise in oil prices, and had provided significant amounts of financial assistance to other MDCs and the Eastern Caribbean territories.[29] To make matters worse, while its imports from other CARICOM countries had increased between 1973 and 1978, Trinidadian exports to the rest of CARICOM began to decline after 1976. Williams's expression of resentment led to a view among other Caribbean officials, especially Jamaicans, that Trinidad viewed the rest of the region with a certain level of disdain – fuelled by Williams's tendency to speak publicly of Trinidad as the 'godfather of the Caribbean'. Williams's posturing encouraged ordinary Trinidadians to blame their country's eventual economic decline in the 1980s on the fact that money was being given away to the Caribbean, particularly to Jamaica.[30]

Unfortunately, given the sensationalism of these types of public disputes, the people of the region gained a very negative perception of CARICOM from the media. The quarrels among the Heads of Government encouraged the insular jealousies and negative stereotyping which had persisted since the Federal negotiations. On account of his or her exclusion from the formal governance processes, the ordinary Caribbean citizen's experience of CARICOM – though not the same as their experience of informal patterns of regional social integration[31] – was lived largely through the negative commentary of newspaper columnists. In addition, academic critics began forecasting the failure of the entire regional movement.[32] Shridath Ramphal, then the Commonwealth Secretary-General, aptly portrayed the sentiments of the times in a speech to CARICOM officials in July 1975:

> ...just as a house does not a family make, but the quality of relationships under the roof that gives it the character of a home – so a Treaty does not a Community make, but the quality of the relationships between its Member States that give life and constant freshness to the formal ageing parchment....In the busy rush for development, in the consciousness of our own commitment to regional goals, we sometimes forget to pause, to inform, to consult, to reassure, to coordinate with our Community colleagues. There is no malice in the omission; but in these formative years – as in early love – even innocent thoughtlessness can be a major offence.[33]

The economic and political conflicts had in fact occasioned a serious governance problem; for none of the institutions which had been created in and around the Community were equipped to resolve either the economic challenges or to smooth the political and personal tensions. In a 1977 article in Caribbean Contact, Clive Thomas argued that the CARICOM framework was no more than a 'paper tiger' – an organisation legally constituted by the treaty but without the requisite institutional teeth required to address the development challenges of member states.[34] In the following year, Andrew Axline argued that CARICOM had placed too much emphasis on the potential trade benefits of CARICOM and not enough on developing the appropriate mechanisms for governance. He predicted that CARICOM would stagnate without mechanisms for strong political cooperation, once trade benefits declined within a context of economic polarization and dependent underdevelopment.[35]

Although the Common Market Council, Institutions and Secretariat continued to meet and function between 1975 and 1982, without the full authority of the CHOG, few decisions could be reached with respect to economic and foreign policy. The CMC and Institutions had come to function instead as fora for the venting of frustrations over the slow progress of the movement.[36] Ministers were often unwilling to refer matters to the attention of Heads of Government for fear of worsening already tense relationships. In the area of foreign policy cooperation, the movement had only been able to produce symbolic statements on issues of international significance, but none of importance to the region's economic challenges. Most importantly, members struggled to coordinate their positions on an issue of such great substance as the negotiations of the first Lomé Agreement on preferential trade with Europe.[37]

Earlier, a joint report presented by CARICOM Secretary-General, Alister McIntyre, and CDB President, William Demas, to the tenth Meeting of the CMC in January 1977 revealed the extent of CARICOM's disappointing record. McIntyre and Demas noted a 'general display of negative attitudes towards regional institutions and the regional movement in public statements by some government representatives'. The report showed how the weaknesses of the Treaty framework had permitted Guyana and Jamaica's restriction of CARICOM imports, and how the Community still lacked instruments for policy coordination, industrial programming, financing of intra-regional trade, an external tariff and protective policy, common fiscal incentives and a double taxation regime. The report further demonstrated that the Special Regime had failed to improve the position of the LDCs in the Common Market – their exports had fallen between 1967 and 1974 by three per cent.[38] Other criticisms levelled at the movement included the lack of consensus on the meaning of development in a context of ideological and political pluralism; the lack of regional dispute settlement mechanisms, such as a regional court and insufficient involvement of the people. Responsibility for these failures was levelled at national administrations which had failed to demonstrate the political commitment to West Indian unity over and above national interest and the imperatives of economic survival.[39] However, the apportioning of blame may not have been justified, since national departments had not been involved in setting up the system or developing the ideology of integration, which depended on them. These challenges of governance continued into the 1980s.

Demas had anticipated that the formal sovereignty to which Caribbean states clung would become increasingly subject to 'influence, manipulation and even domination by other states, groups of states or powerful external private entities – principally foreign investors, foreign suppliers of technology and MNCs'.[40] The extent of that external influence became apparent in the 1980s, as new international prescriptions for structural adjustment impinged on the indigenous ideology of development. Although much of the adjustment regime included prescriptions for 'good governance' in national public administration, their external imposition did not foster the development of Caribbean approaches to building national capacity. In fact, the underlying neoliberal ideology underpinning the internationally-accepted formula for structural adjustment programmes (SAPs) was intended to minimise the role of the state in economic development.[41] The programmes therefore contradicted the Caribbean ideology of integration which had advocated a role for strong state regulation. The dominance of the United States in the region and the austerity of structural adjustment programmes had effectively weakened member states' control over their domestic affairs. Consequently, the assertion of sovereignty in the CHOG before 1975 was merely symbolic and made no real contribution to preparing states to counter the gradual erosion of sovereignty by SAPs.

It is the weaknesses inherent in the CARICOM framework which had, in some measure, contributed to the process of erosion in the 1980s, by granting national administrations full autonomy from the regional system. Consequent on the insubstantial regional executive authority and member states' preoccupation with meeting their individual obligations to international financial institutions, national ministries were free to disregard the few decisions and agreements of the CARICOM Organs and Institutions which could have potentially contributed to the achievement of effective sovereignty. This disconnectedness between national and regional governance was highlighted in a report on the prospects for Caribbean development in the 1980s, prepared by a Group of Experts, called the 'Wise Men' – including highly regarded scholars and officials such as Demas, McIntyre and Ramphal. They argued that the shortcomings in implementation were directly related to the lack of political commitment, particularly by Heads, to the integration process. Acknowledging the way in which ideological conflict had affected the functioning of the CHOG, they encouraged the adoption of 'ideological pluralism' as a principle which would ensure that differences in political philosophy would not be used as a 'sword against solidarity'.[42]

Changes of governments and leadership in several countries perhaps provided an opportunity for Heads to demonstrate their commitment to the regional movement by resuming the meetings of the Conference. The first meeting in seven years was convened in November 1982 in Ocho Rios, Jamaica under the Chairmanship of Jamaica's new Prime Minister, Edward Seaga. There were also eight other newly-elected Heads of Government participating, as the Community celebrated the independence of Dominica, St Lucia, St Vincent and the Grenadines, and Antigua and Barbuda in the intervening years. The resulting Ocho Rios Declaration expressed a commitment to regional integration as the only viable option for survival (perhaps given the emerging weaknesses of SAPs models of national development) and reinforced the Community's position on the sanctity of sovereignty, especially with regard to the right to self-determination, freedom from external interference, and respect for borders and jurisdictional delimitations.[43] However, CARICOM's tenth anniversary was fast approaching and there was a sense, even among the politicians, that the Community's progress on its objectives of production integration, industrial development, functional cooperation and involvement of the people was still too slow.[44] Unfortunately, interstate rivalry and interpersonal conflict persisted without effective mediation by regional mechanisms.[45] In addition, a conflict among MDCs over restriction of imports had erupted in 1983, occasioning the convening of an informal meeting among the Heads of the MDCs in Bridgetown. Furthermore, Nevis's attempt to seek independence separately from St Kitts risked greater fragmentation and polarisation in the region.[46] Growing differences among states led to the convening of a Special CHOG Summit on Grenada in September 1983 – during which several Heads of Government called for Grenada's expulsion from the Community. The summit was clearly not an effective framework for building consensus or influencing the actions of other governments and therefore, member states were not able to reach and apply a consensus on 'ideological pluralism' to their conflict, as had been recommended by the 1981 Group of Experts. One month later, some members of the Community found themselves complicit in the US-led invasion of Grenada. The incident was a particularly serious indictment of CARICOM's rhetoric of 'community sovereignty' since the framework had explicitly failed to safeguard the Westphalian rights, including the territorial integrity, of one of its members.

Even beyond those high-profile conflicts, the routine functions of CARICOM continued to demonstrate weaknesses. CARICOM had by this time developed a reputation for very lengthy meetings on trivial issues, without achieving any useful outcome. In particular, the agendas of the CMC and CHOG were extensive and inclusive of technical matters which could have been more appropriately addressed by subordinate institutions and committees, if these latter mechanisms had been empowered to exercise full authority in making binding decisions. Communiqués from the CHOG often made reference to statements made by Heads on many issues, but without firm decisions or timetables for action. Heads relied heavily on the recommendations of several standing committees or working groups of experts, to which they would agree 'in principle' but without assigning responsibility for execution at national level.

It was not until the fourth meeting of the CHOG in Port of Spain in July 1983 that Heads explicitly addressed the problems of decision-making and implementation. Edward Seaga suggested that the ineffectiveness of the movement and slowness of implementation was related to an improper focus on the institutional architecture of CARICOM, instead of on its processes of governance – in other words, the efficiency of interactions among institutions and their decision-making procedures.[47] At his prompting, Heads called for an elaboration, by the Secretariat, of the relationships among the Institutions of CARICOM and between CARICOM and the Associate Institutions. The following year, during the fifth Conference in Nassau, Bahamas in July 1984 at which the independence of St Kitts and Nevis was celebrated, Heads further mandated the new Secretary-General, Roderick Rainford, to conduct a study on decision-making under the Treaty of Chaguaramas 'with a view to identifying areas in which consideration should be given to other than unanimous voting procedures'.[48] Legal expert, Duke Pollard, was commissioned to undertake the study which was completed in 1985 and is discussed further, in relation to other expert studies, in chapter 5. However, even before the commissioning of that study, the Secretariat had hinted at the challenges of the unanimity rule of decision-making, in an issue of the magazine *CARICOM Perspective*:

> ...the principle, while it ensures the broadest possible agreement, has the effect of placing Community decision-making in a straight-jacket, since no decision is legally binding unless it has the approval of all the Member States of the Community, unless of course a Member State chooses to abstain....Any state can paralyse Community action and programmes by entering a reservation or by absenteeism.[49]

Rainford also offered another assessment of the decision-making process. In addition to the 'straightjacketing' effect of the unanimity rule, he argued that the whole system was challenged by a lack of capacity for regulation of the implementation process. He concluded that, in practice, the institutions functioned between two extremes. On the one hand, some decisions were made by a fairly smooth process in the central machinery but without provisions for implementation or regulation of national responsibilities by sanction. On the other hand, associate institutions were able to expedite the implementation of their programmes, given their autonomy from the sovereignty-bound mechanisms, but there was no capacity for regulation to ensure coherence of their actions with the Community's strategic objectives.[50] Rainford realised, therefore, that there was a need for closer relationships among the various levels and categories of institutions.

The 1984 CHOG also raised concerns about the financial sustainability of the system, given the proliferation of new institutions which included a statistics bureau and a customs commission. Barbados Prime Minister, Tom Adams, proposed a system of automaticity of financing for the Secretariat based on contributions of a proportion of stamp duties on imports collected at the national level.[51] Such a system would have ensured that those territories most able to support the regional movement would assume the financial responsibility. However, this proposal was not accepted by Heads, since duties were an important source of funding for national administrations and Heads were unwilling to cede control over their national income.

Interestingly, the same Conference adopted a consensus which merged national commitments to ongoing structural adjustment programmes with their commitment to the economic integration process. Heads signed the Nassau Understanding on Structural Adjustment for Accelerated Development and Integration in the Caribbean, which included reference to moving beyond reliance on market forces to building national and regional institutional capacity.[52] Whatever the substance of the Understanding, one politician's comments on it are noteworthy in relation to the weaknesses of the CARICOM framework. Trinidad and Tobago's Prime Minister reportedly remarked after signing, that he had no intention of implementing the Nassau Understanding because he was displeased with the terms of trade between his country and other members. Interestingly, he admitted that he had only agreed to sign because of the unanimity rule.[53] A negative vote from him would have prevented the passing of the agreement and it is perhaps likely that his colleagues would have placed significant pressure on him to agree. The significance of this anecdote lies in its revelation of the inefficiency of the decision-making process and the irrelevance of the regional agenda during this period, even to the policymakers themselves. Furthermore, the commissioning of expert studies on regional integration and development only served to provide opportunities for repetition of previous advice on the need to improve CARICOM's institutional arrangements. The 1988 Bourne report on the prospects for Caribbean development, commissioned by the Heads in 1986, was no different from the 1981 Expert report in flagging the priorities of institutional reform in CARICOM and national governance.[54]

Towards the end of the 1980s, the irrelevance of the CARICOM sovereignty safeguards were highlighted. States still accorded authority for judicial appeal to the Privy Council in the UK. CARICOM had also failed to make progress on those aspects of integration from which the Caribbean people could benefit – such as free movement of labour. By 1987, St Lucia's Prime Minister, John Compton, concluded that CARICOM was an 'unsatisfactory substitute to West Indian Nationhood' because it had added little to the economic and social well-being of the people; while Dominica's Prime Minister, Eugenia Charles, suggested that her colleagues would be forced to abandon the movement if it was not made meaningful to the lives of the Caribbean people by instituting sanctions for non-implementation of the Treaty provisions.[55] In the same 1987 meeting, Barbados' new prime minister, Erskine Sandiford, argued that the framework lacked an appropriate assembly of parliamentarians to link the people and their representatives to the regional administration.[56] Against the background of those criticisms, the 1988 meeting of the CHOG in Deep Bay, Antigua commissioned a further full-scale review of the functioning of regional programmes and institutions of the community in order to develop a new strategic direction for reviving the movement.[57]

## CARICOM's Governance Challenges

It is fair to conclude that the first 15 years of CARICOM were marked by a record of general failure to translate the potential inherent in political independence into effective sovereignty. In a 1986 lecture Demas noted that:

> The thinking West Indian is acutely aware that something is missing, that we almost have been cheated by independence in that our freedom of action falls far short of what we and our forefathers anticipated. There is perhaps a general feeling of anti-climax combined with a certain degree of disillusionment and even battle-weariness arising from the constant fight to keep our economies afloat and our self-respect (where it still exists) intact.[58]

The Caribbean Community had been intended to provide an arena in which this trend of sovereignty erosion could have been reversed. In fact, the relatively quick transformation from CARIFTA to CARICOM was perhaps achieved not least, because of the intensification of global forces which threatened the economic stability within small economies. However, the institutional framework which was established within the Community only served to reinforce aspects of formal state sovereignty in a symbolic way, without contributing to the attainment of 'effective community sovereignty' as had been intended. In fact, by the end of the 1980s, CARICOM had been faced with four specific challenges of governance, which encapsulate the instances of inefficiency and ineffectiveness reviewed in this chapter.

First, there was the challenge of regional political authority. The embedding of a conception of pure state sovereignty within the legal framework cemented the authority of national representatives and prevented the creation of a truly regional governance architecture. The consequent elevation of the CHOG and of individual Heads of Government to the status of absolute authority, compounded by an overriding reliance on the informality of the relationships among leaders, provided an unstable foundation for the movement. The competencies of regional technocrats, for example those in the Secretariat, were overshadowed by the pre-eminence of those Heads who retained their prerogative to demonstrate enthusiasm or disdain for the movement according to their feelings, given the absence of a supranational authority to which they would have to be accountable.[59] Once relationships among leaders deteriorated, the decision-making process slowed down and the implementation process came to a halt. Furthermore, the structure did nothing to compensate for weaknesses in national public administrations which were largely incapable of facilitating the full realisation of regional decisions.

Consequently, there was a second challenge of implementation and regulation. CARICOM relied on the 'good faith and morality of Member States for the implementation of the Treaty'.[60] Given the absence of independent executive authority at the regional level, the decisions of the Community were rendered irrelevant or inapplicable to the national policy agenda. Although Article 9 (3) of the Treaty indicated that decisions were binding, the frequent derogation from Treaty provisions suggested that the decisions, though politically compelling, were not legally binding since, in many cases, they had not been entrenched in national law.[61] The lack of a regulatory framework for sanctions only increased the irrelevance of the movement.

These weaknesses of regulation were related to a third challenge of conflict resolution and dispute settlement. Without provisions for a legal dispute settlement mechanism, there was no basis for the imposition of sanctions. Furthermore, there was no effective instrument for mediation among the various postures of national sovereignty with respect to the economic, political and personal differences of opinion which emerged in a complex period of global economic turmoil. The preference for informal ad hoc arbitration and caucuses among leaders was only marginally useful, since it did not contribute to the permanent resolution of conflicts. In fact, in one prominent case – the Grenada Invasion – the special Summit of Heads may even have served to fuel the conflict.

Finally, the irrelevance of the structure was cemented by a fourth challenge of legitimacy and public confidence. The resistance to the full involvement of the Caribbean people in the decision-making process was maintained from the Federal and CARIFTA experiences. The absence of CARICOM debates from national parliaments, the marginalisation of the Joint Consultative Committee, the failure to make progress towards freedom of movement, or towards the development of a regional court of appeal or a regional parliament, effectively locked the people out of the governance process. The alienation of the Caribbean people from the new structure only served to make it unpopular among public servants, thereby reinforcing the cycle of slow decision-making, non-implementation and conflict.

It is significant, albeit surprising, that CARICOM survived these challenges unaltered. In spite of a series of ministerial meetings on the weaknesses of institutional structure and expert studies on enhancing it, there had been no steps taken to reform the structure. In his recollections of his time in office as Secretary-General, Roderick Rainford made an insightful comment about why there had not perhaps been greater expediency in addressing the problems. He recalled: 'Rightly or wrongly, there was an apprehension that trying to force the pace of things prematurely could unravel the still embryonic and brittle machinery that was being constituted to serve the people's sense of affinity and [could] thus be counterproductive in the long run'.[62] In light of that observation, the purpose of the actions of the political directorate in this period of safeguarding sovereignty was to embed the CARICOM institution within the political culture – as a symbolic tradition of sovereignty and independence – before seeking to advance the integration process itself. With regard to its symbolism, the political directorate was reluctant to abandon the CARICOM tradition but, perhaps, remained uncertain about how to rescue it from its own weaknesses. Therefore, at their meeting at Grande Anse in 1989, the Heads of Government finally took stock of the lack of progress made in regional integration and decided to move towards more expedient implementation by correcting the deficits of decision-making, implementation, conflict resolution and participation, associated with the CARICOM of the 1970s and 1980s.

# EXPERT RECOMMENDATIONS ON INSTITUTIONAL REFORM

The governance challenges that had gripped CARICOM by the end of the 1980s overshadowed the potential implied by the Community's status at that time as one of the oldest movements of economic integration among developing countries. Even the political directorate seemed aware of the presumption that, relative to other movements, CARICOM could have advanced beyond the institutional framework of a common market. In an effort to reverse the effects of the pressures of the preceding period, the Conference of the Heads of Government (CHOG) agreed in 1989 to upgrade the Common Market to a single market and economy, complemented by new mechanisms for more efficient, effective and legitimate governance. Against the background of that decision, this chapter discusses the outcome of the interplay between expert recommendations on improving governance and the political deliberations between 1989 and 1996 on the creation of the CARICOM Single Market and Economy (CSME). The role of the Grande Anse Declaration in catalysing the governance reform process is analysed along with the recommendations for institutional reform proposed by three important expert reviews – the 1985 Pollard report on decision-making, the 1990 Mills report on institutional functioning and the 1992 report of the West Indian Commission – which recommended a new model of governance. Finally an explanation is offered as to why the experts failed to convince Heads of Government to reform the fundamental ethos of the Community and the way in which Heads responded with an unyielding defence of the CHOG's absolute sovereign leadership of the movement. At the same time, it highlights the contribution made by some initial adjustments to the institutional framework, with a view to resolving the governance challenge is highlighted.

## GRANDE ANSE AS CATALYST FOR REFORM

Certainly, by 1989, the irrelevance of the Common Market model to the development profile of Caribbean economies had become evident.

In one respect, CARICOM had not enabled its members to participate effectively in an emerging globalised system of transnational production, since arrangements for increased diversification and integration of production had not been implemented.[1] In another respect, the institutions of the Common Market had ignored the informal patterns of transnational economic activity in which Caribbean people were engaged. In particular, the failure to facilitate the movement of people for employment within the Common Market underscored the irrelevance of the formal institutions to the aspirations of the people.[2] These weaknesses highlighted the urgency of upgrading the regionalist framework.

During the tenth meeting of the CHOG in July 1989 at Grande Anse in Grenada, the imperative of transformation was discussed. Trinidad's Prime Minister, A.N.R. Robinson, presented a paper entitled 'The West Indies Beyond 1992', which summarised the context of changes in the global political economy that impinged on the Caribbean development process. The dissolution of the Soviet Union and end of the Cold War; the establishment of a US-Canada Free Trade Area and discussions of a possible wider hemispheric trading arrangement, as well as the imminent emergence of a Single European Market by 1992, had all diminished the significance and favourable geopolitical position of individual Caribbean states. Robinson argued that the common market model of integration, which was associated with a protectionist philosophy of economic development, was no longer appropriate to a context in which most other regions were embracing a model of 'open regionalism' based on global export-oriented growth patterns. These trends of intensified globalisation and regionalisation reinforced the strategic imperative of deepening regional economic integration for Caribbean survival. Grenada's Prime Minister and Chairman of the CHOG, Herbert Blaize made the dramatic observation that the countries were faced with two options – either collective prosperity through collaboration or individual destruction through confrontation.[3] He also acknowledged that the 1970s political foundations of Caribbean regionalism, which were embedded in norms of exclusive nationalism, were no longer appropriate to the contemporary context and therefore argued that a transformation of the normative and political framework for cooperation would be required.

In that regard, Guyana's President, Desmond Hoyte, made an interesting contribution to the Conference. He argued that the movement required not only economic and political change but also psychological transformation of the West Indian psyche of individuality into one of community. Perhaps this represented an acknowledgement of the fact that CARICOM had not fully embraced the elements of the 1970s ideology which had called for broad-based unity and solidarity, since the movement had focused extensively on safeguarding the sovereignty of the political directorate. Hoyte asserted: 'We have to learn to see CARICOM as an integrated entity in which we live and move and have our being as a Caribbean people, bound together by a common culture, common values, common objectives and enjoyment of common opportunities'.[4] The Conference embraced this theme of strengthening the bonds among Caribbean people in order to create an association between the formal institutional framework and an authentic Caribbean personality and identity. On that basis, the Heads indicated their support for the development of institutions for recognition of the people, including a system of regional honours for outstanding achievement and a parliamentary assembly. The latter proposal, initiated by Barbados' Prime Minister, Erskine Sandiford, certainly held potential, not only for greater involvement of the people through their parliamentary representatives, but also for involving members of Opposition parties in order to minimise what A.N.R. Robinson had described as the 'partisan rancour' which had been an enduring feature of the movement's historical legacy.[5] The CHOG stressed however, that any such assembly would not be accorded any legislative powers which could potentially impinge on the sovereignty and constitutional independence of member states.[6] In addition to these proposals for addressing the crisis of legitimacy and public confidence, other Heads, particularly A.N.R. Robinson and Michael Manley (the latter having returned to power in Jamaica), suggested that the movement needed to embrace a stronger framework for developing strategic targets and benchmarks in order to monitor the implementation and regulation process.[7]

It was thus at Grande Anse that CARICOM reform – including the transformation of its economic integration model, its ideological foundations, its socio-cultural and psychological substructure and its institutional procedures and processes – became the priority of the next phase of its evolution. The resulting *Grande Anse Declaration* affirmed the commitment of the Heads of Government to the establishment of a CARICOM Single Market and Economy (CSME) 'in the shortest time possible'.[8] It was accompanied by a 13-point *Work Programme for the Advancement of the Integration Movement* which, in a manner notably atypical of the CHOG, included specific targets and timelines for implementation. The goals included: the fulfilment of all obligations under the Treaty of Chaguaramas by July 4, 1993; the free movement of skilled and professional personnel by January 1991; the elimination of passport controls for intra-regional travel for CARICOM nationals by December 1990; and the convening of a tripartite Caribbean economic conference involving government, labour and private sector leaders. Heads also agreed to convene a ministerial group to consider the establishment of a CARICOM Assembly; to draft an intergovernmental treaty for an Order of the Caribbean Community as a regional honours system; and to prepare another intergovernmental treaty for the establishment of a regional Court of Appeal and Judicial Services Commission. In keeping with a more 'open' ideology of integration, Heads also discussed widening of the movement, including the admission of Suriname as the first non-Anglophone member.

Heads decided, however, that those specific objectives had not captured *per se* the essence of the overarching ideological framework which was required to guide the transformation process. Therefore, based on the proposal of A.N.R. Robinson, the Declaration also established another group of experts – an independent West Indian Commission (WIC) – with a mandate to recommend a framework for advancing the goals of the Treaty of Chaguaramas.[9] The denomination of the Commission as 'West Indian' was perhaps deliberate, since in spite of the rhetoric on open regionalism, some Heads, like Robinson, maintained a philosophical stance on protecting the historical and cultural identity of the West Indies within a wider arena of Caribbean cooperation. In that regard, the appointment of Shridath Ramphal as the Chairman of the WIC, given his role in advancing West Indian Nationalism in the 1970s and his familiarity with the political directorate, was strategically appropriate. Former Secretary-General Alister McIntyre was appointed Deputy Chairman and other members of the established CARICOM 'technostructure', like William Demas and Roderick Rainford, also joined the 15-member Commission. The extensive scope of the WIC's Terms of Reference, including an expectation of the widest possible level of public consultation, inevitably called for a lengthy period of study. It is conceivable therefore, that the CHOG used the high profile appointments as a distraction from its deferral of action on the 13 objectives until the completion of the WIC's assessment, three years later.

The Heads had commissioned two other studies on specific aspects of the governance process, which had been overshadowed by the appointment of the WIC. The Heads had neither discussed nor commented on either the study on decision-making commissioned in 1984 nor the study on the functioning of CARICOM programmes and institutions

*Figure 5.1: Interrelated Expert Analyses of CARICOM Governance*

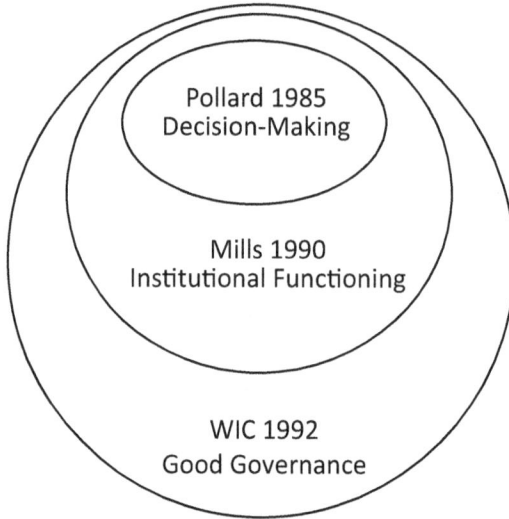

commissioned in 1988. The WIC was therefore also mandated to consider the recommendations of those two reports. The relationship between the three studies is represented in figure 5.1.

The key recommendations from those reports are highlighted here as they have not been given much attention in the CARICOM literature and because they also provide insight into some of the specific challenges associated with CARICOM's functioning, which were lost in the wider philosophical review of the WIC report.

## THE POLLARD ASSESSMENT OF UNANIMITY IN DECISION-MAKING

Duke Pollard, an international law expert from Guyana, who participated in drafting the Treaty of Chaguaramas, was engaged by the Secretariat in 1984, on a mandate from the Heads, to conduct an analysis of the Treaty and make recommendations on the feasibility of relaxing the unanimity rule. His 1985 report further outlined a broader profile of inefficiency in the regional decision-making process. Pollard identified five interrelated manifestations of an impaired CARICOM decision-making process.[10] Firstly, he noted that the internal processes and procedures of the CARICOM Organs and Institutions were not conducive to informed and effective decision-making, often producing uncertainty among national representatives about decisions. Frequently, representatives were not afforded adequate time or supporting documentation to develop their positions on various issues. That situation created a secondary problem of ambivalence among officials about the extent to which their governments were legally bound by the decisions emanating from Community fora. That ambivalence further resulted in a third problem of low levels of national compliance with decisions, facilitated by an absence of monitoring and evaluation mechanisms. Fourthly, the absence of a dispute settlement mechanism made the effective interpretation of the Treaty and decisions troublesome, thereby highlighting a fifth weakness – the lack of punitive sanctions for non-compliance. Overall, in Pollard's view, all of these shortcomings contributed to the inefficiency of the decision-making process and the irrelevance of decisions to the environment for implementation in member states. Against the background of that overarching profile, Pollard made two principal contributions which are particularly useful to this chapter's discussion of institutional reform. Firstly, Pollard acknowledged the inappropriateness of the indiscriminate application of the unanimity rule. Secondly, he commented on the confusion over the role of the Secretariat in the decision-making process.

In the first instance, Pollard argued that, at the time of the Community's emergence in 1973, the adoption of the unanimity rule as a safeguard for sovereignty had served a useful purpose. This form of sovereignty safeguard was typical of developing country approaches to protecting their autonomy from the influence of more powerful states. However, Pollard argued that the founding members of the Community had anticipated the deepening of the integration process over time and also progressively greater transfers of autonomy in decision-making. However, in practice, CARICOM continued to apply the unanimity rule indiscriminately to every aspect of the decision-making process. So, even in 1985, substantive matters related to functional, economic and foreign policies were subject to the rule, as were simple administrative or procedural matters. Binding decisions and guiding recommendations were also equally subject to the rule, even though each type of decision implied different levels of compliance. Pollard conceded that the complete removal of the unanimity rule from the Treaty was unlikely to be accepted by the Heads, given the embeddedness of the sovereignty tradition in their political interpretation of the integration process. However, he recommended, as a first course of action, that the Treaty be amended to make a distinction between the different types of issues subject to decision-making and between the expected levels of compliance, as a means to developing criteria for application or non-application of the unanimity rule.

Pollard proposed that simple administrative or procedural matters considered by CARICOM institutions should proceed by a process of a simple majority vote. In addition, matters related to functional cooperation should be decided by a similar majority process which would allow like-minded member states to proceed on an initiative while allowing other states to enter reservations on that particular course of action. The decision would then only become binding on those states which had agreed to proceed.

In contrast, Pollard suggested that the unanimity rule be maintained in the Conference and the Standing Committee of Ministers of Foreign Affairs (SCMFA), since those fora typically considered matters of great national importance, such as foreign economic policy, in which member states had developed, since independence, vastly different national positions. He argued that the CHOG and SCMFA should be allowed to negotiate a consensus which would be subject to the unanimity rule and, thus, any resulting decision would become legally binding on all members. Those recommendations on the unanimity rule suggested a strategy for expediting the decision-making process in subsidiary Organs and Institutions, while preserving the traditional authority of the CHOG.[11]

The second of Pollard's specific observations related to the role of the Secretariat in the decision-making process. His analysis revealed that the Secretariat, despite its denomination under the Treaty, as a non-executive, administrative institution, held tremendous influence and control over the decision-making process. Its lack of *de jure* executive authority (outside of the limited authority of the post of the Secretary-General) was compensated by a de facto assertion of authority over internal procedures. The Secretariat had been able to capitalise on weaknesses in member states' capacity in order to increase its own authority in three principal ways. Firstly, given its mandate, under Article 16c of the Treaty, to initiate and carry out studies on economic and functional cooperation issues, the Secretariat often determined the agenda of meetings of Institutions. The Secretariat staff further controlled the direction of the discussions, since member state representatives were often ill-prepared to lead discussions, whether by virtue of a lack of capacity for preparation or the non-timely dissemination of documentation by the Secretariat. Secondly, by controlling the schedule and protocol of regional meetings, the Secretariat often determined the pace of the decision-making process. For example, Pollard found in his investigation that member state representatives were often dissatisfied with the time provided by the Secretariat, for instance between technical and ministerial meetings, to allow for proper briefing, reflection, discussion and preparation of national positions on the decision-making agenda. Thirdly, the Secretariat's role in recording decisions and, by extension, its interpretation of the outcomes of discussions in the consensus-building process, had also elicited complaints from government representatives about the 'creation' of decisions with which member states were ultimately reluctant to comply.[12]

While there is no evidence of misconduct on the part of Secretariat staff, the persistence of an organisational culture of tacit persuasion and creative documentation engendered by the Secretariat does exist. While there is no reason to doubt staff commitment to furtherance of the regional integration process for the common good, the official records often left participants with a sense of uncertainty about what had, in fact, been agreed in meetings. The relevance of this point, which has largely been ignored in the wider CARICOM literature, is that the perception of misconduct by the Secretariat, then and now, has emanated from a lack of separation of administrative and executive competence. That confusion resulted from the fact that gaps were left in the Treaty with respect to regional executive authority (as a means of safeguarding sovereignty) which encouraged the emergence of proxy institutions to fill those gaps but without the appropriate authority and capacity for execution. In this case, the Secretariat staff, who attempted to provide technical as well as political guidance towards optimum solutions for regional problems, found that their efforts were deemed to be illegitimate because they were not formally empowered to play that role. The effect of this was that member states took advantage of the ambivalence to excuse their non-implementation of decisions at the national level.

## The Mills Review of Institutional Functioning

Those two issues highlighted by Pollard were also noted by the Mills Review of Regional Programmes and Organisations which was completed while the West Indian Commission's (WIC's) assessment was underway.[13] Gladstone Mills et al. endorsed Pollard's recommendations on relaxing the unanimity rule in specific instances and also proposed a strategy for filling the *de jure* institutional gap in executive authority cited in Pollard's discussion of the Secretariat. The team, which was led by Jamaican government official and public administration expert, Gladstone Mills, and included three other senior civil servants from Barbados, Dominica, and Trinidad, highlighted an extensive list of administrative weaknesses in its comprehensive audit of all the programmes and institutions of the Community. It identified weaknesses related to a lack of civil society participation, public management capacity for implementation, unsustainability in financing of institutions and a lack of mechanisms for dispute settlement, monitoring and evaluation – all of which, it argued, had hampered the effective functioning of a viable regional institutional framework. The report contextualised these weaknesses in relation to an observed disjointedness between the Caribbean people and their leaders with respect to the role and pace of the integration movement. The preface to the report implied a disconnected dialogue between the leaders and their constituents. On the one hand, the politicians indicated a desire to proceed slowly on the road to integration based on an assumption that the people were not ready. On the other hand, the people indicated a lack of confidence in their leaders who failed to consult them and were holding them back from the unity they most desired.

At the same time, this state of detachment and frustration among the people was also being observed by the West Indian Commission, which had begun the first of its public hearings in Guyana and Trinidad.[14] Beyond the issue of the need for greater legitimacy, the Mills team made two other contributions to the agenda for reform. Firstly, with regard to Pollard's observation about the role of the Secretariat, the Mills team proposed the granting of legitimacy to the influence which the Secretariat had exercised informally. The team recommended that the Secretary-General be empowered to 'formulate recommendations or deliver opinions on matters dealt with in the Treaty whenever he wished to do so', in order to establish the office of the Secretary-General as the 'rallying-point' for the taking and implementing of Community decisions.[15] That recommendation is interesting because it sought to increase the authority of an existing institution rather than propose the development of a new supranational competence which may have been viewed as a threat to the sovereignty of the political directorate. The team acknowledged, however, that if the Secretariat were to play a more authoritative role in the movement, its internal procedures, including those related to the timely dissemination of documentation, would have to be improved and its management capacity enhanced. In a related observation, the team suggested that the location of the Secretariat in Guyana – one of the member states with the least advanced public infrastructure – should be reviewed since it had stifled operations. It noted that the inadequacy of physical working conditions for Secretariat staff had hampered the effective recruitment of experienced personnel.[16]

The second contribution made by the Mills team was to highlight the need for greater financial independence of Community institutions, particularly the Secretariat and the Associate Institutions. The financial position of several institutions was described as precarious, given the limited contributions from member states and the declining availability of foreign aid. The challenge of financing was compounded by the fact that the report revealed a lack of coherence among the many programmes and institutions being administered by the Secretariat and being funded by member states. This pointed to areas of duplicated activity and suggested the need for a full revision of the Treaty to create machinery for the monitoring and evaluation of programmes and for the development of a system of sustainable and automatic financing.

The Mills report was not discussed by the political directorate but forwarded to the WIC for consideration in its ongoing assessment. In the interim, the deliberations among Heads at the beginning of the 1990s became transformed into a discourse on popular participation. In fact, the CHOG, which convened in Jamaica in July 1990 in the wake of an attempted coup against the government of Trinidad and Tobago, focused on opportunities for increased participation of Caribbean people in governance. Acting Prime Minister of Jamaica, P.J. Patterson, called for special attention to be paid to the preservation of the Caribbean democratic tradition and the creation of opportunities for greater involvement of citizens as a shield against threats to security and democracy.[17] The resulting *Kingston Declaration* called for the 'full involvement of all...citizens in the governance of their affairs...towards a truly authentic Caribbean personality'.[18] This emerging discourse on popular participation recalls the element of the 1970s ideology of integration which called for legitimate governance. Indeed, the concept of empowering a new 'Caribbean Man' had been also raised among the Heads in 1974 by the Premier of St Kitts-Nevis-Anguilla, Robert Bradshaw, who had perhaps been inspired by William Demas's 1970 paper which had envisioned a future Caribbean citizen who would drive the process of creating a distinctive Caribbean society truly independent of colonial and neocolonial influences.[19] Bradshaw believed that CARICOM would provide the vehicle which would propel the Caribbean man.[20] Sixteen years later, as Heads discussed the need to transform CARICOM, the 1990 Kingston Declaration called for greater attention to the development of human resources as well as the creation of an Assembly of Caribbean Community Parliamentarians (ACCP). It became the first regional statement which explicitly acknowledged the rights of the Caribbean citizen in the CARICOM framework.

Interestingly, in the following year, during the February 1991 Intersessional meeting of the CHOG, Heads acknowledged the fact that, while awaiting the WIC's report, they had, in the interim, made limited progress towards the single market and economy since the 1989 Declaration. In that regard, Heads agreed, on Trinidad's proposal, to appoint by the end of that year a CARICOM Commissioner who would 'work closely with individual member states and the CARICOM Secretariat in ensuring the effective and urgent implementation of all the measures agreed within the timetable set at Grande Anse in 1989 and at Kingston in 1990. That proposal, which was never fulfilled, may have been the inspiration for the most significant recommendation of the WIC report which is the subject of the remainder of the discussion in this section.

## TIME FOR ACTION: THE REPORT OF THE WEST INDIAN COMMISSION

It took the WIC three years to complete its assessment. Cognisant of the time lag, Ramphal had submitted an interim report in the second year of its review during the twelfth meeting of the CHOG convened in July 1991 in Basseterre, St Kitts. The central message emerging from the interim assessment was that implementation was the crux of the governance challenge. Ramphal warned the Heads that 'the West Indies [could not] afford the luxury of marking time, mistaking it for progress'.[21] He painted a picture, based on the WIC's consultations, of a regional constituency concerned about the freeness and fairness of the democratic process, the freedom of press, women's and children's rights, corruption and public accountability and transparency in member states. These aspects of good governance required the immediate attention of the political directorate. The WIC also benefitted from a range of written submissions on various issues of governance. Outgoing Secretary-General Roderick Rainford submitted a discussion of the "Shortcomings of CARICOM" which highlighted the inadequate involvement of social partners in regional decision making.[22] A *Port of Spain Consensus* reached at the end of the tripartite Regional Economic Conference held in Trinidad in February 1991 (one of the few Grande Anse targets attained) which had brought public, private, labour, NGO, academic and financial stakeholders together with nine of the thirteen Heads of Government, also emphasised the importance of developing systematic arrangements for the participation of social partners in the regional framework. It further recognised that the resolution of the implementation problem would 'inevitably entail the surrendering of some degree of national sovereignty but [that] the potential benefits...[would] more than compensate'.[23] The WIC was therefore forming an understanding of the fact that the governance crisis was directly related to the protection of sovereignty in the CARICOM framework. Sovereignty had been conceived as a symbol of the power of individual Heads of Government and therefore Prime-Ministerial/Presidential structures had been positioned to safeguard against executive competences for other mechanisms. One of the most interesting submissions to the WIC was a paper prepared by one of the Commission's members, Vaughan Lewis, on the *Compulsions of Integration*. Lewis argued that the time had come for

> ...CARICOM to ask itself whether the institutions and mechanisms appropriate to the tasks and objectives identified for the future [were] now in place, and if not, whether some further sublimation of personal (national) sovereignty [was] required through new collective arrangements in order to ensure effective economic integration... and the realisation of a more effective regional sovereignty.[24]

The significant phrase in Lewis's assessment is personal (national) sovereignty. Lewis had, whether deliberately or inadvertently, pinpointed the issue of an interesting interpretation of sovereignty in the CARICOM political culture.

Based on those submissions and the rest of its assessment, the WIC proposed in its preliminary report that Heads give immediate attention to six areas in which they could advance good governance as the 'ethical basis of 'community' in the Caribbean'.[25] The WIC recommended that Heads take concrete steps towards instituting freedom of leisure travel within the region, free movement of skilled workers, a common currency, coordinated mobilisation of investment, the single market and joint mobilisation for international negotiations. These recommendations elicited an interesting response from Heads of Government. On the proposal of Barbados' Prime Minister, Erskine Sandiford, Heads agreed to assign responsibility for each of the six areas to a lead Head of Government.[26] This decision served to apply a governmental principle – that of a cabinet-style portfolio allocation to regional issues – thereby establishing a closer link between regional programmes and national authority. At the same time, by reinforcing the link between national authority and individual Heads of Government, the proposal also attached a sense of personal responsibility for the success or failure of proposed initiatives. Heads were expected to be accountable to each other, even if not to their constituencies.[27]

In the interim, the expectation of accountability fostered greater activity in the succeeding months. By the time of their third Intersessional meeting in February 1992, most of the Heads reported some progress, achieved by their unilateral interventions, in relation to their respective portfolios. With regard to freedom and ease of intra-regional travel, Grenada indicated that five member states had put in place legislation for a common queue at immigration points for national and CARICOM citizens. With regard to free movement of skills, Guyana reported that it had enacted legislation effective March 1992 to allow free movement of UWI graduates to Guyana and that it had secured commitment from other states to do likewise. Trinidad reported on the commissioning of studies related to the development of a common currency and the scheduling of a seminar for March 1992 to discuss the achievement of monetary union by 2000. Jamaica, in its capacity as lead for investment mobilisation and external negotiations, had developed a proposal for the formation of a Caribbean Investment Fund to enlarge investment prospects and reported satisfactory progress in joint negotiations of trade and investment agreements with Venezuela and the United States. Barbados reported on the adoption of a timetable for the establishment of the single market (CSM).

In addition, Barbados (via Sandiford) and Guyana (via Hoyte) signed the agreement for the establishment of the Assembly of Caribbean Community Parliamentarians (ACCP) and Heads decided to appoint Edwin Carrington – a former Secretary-General of the ACP Secretariat – to the post of CARICOM Secretary-General effective from August 1992.[28] It is conceivable that all this initial frenzy of activity was due to the novelty of the new portfolio system and the desire to demonstrate to the public some semblance of progress, during the period when the WIC's final report was being prepared. However, implementation soon lost momentum, perhaps as the demands of the regional office began to weigh on the Heads of Government who had taken on so much personal responsibility. It would take several years for the ACCP and the CSM to finally come into effect.

The final WIC report, entitled 'Time for Action', was discussed at a Special Session of the CHOG convened in October 1992. The report proposed the model of a 'Community of Sovereign States' as a framework for encouraging the sharing of formal sovereignty. During the special meeting, newly-appointed Jamaican Prime Minister, P.J. Patterson, suggested that there was need for 'psychological adaptation' to the model, which is discussed below and represented in figure 5.2.[29]

The scope of the more than 200 recommendations of the WIC contained in 12 chapters was far-reaching, covering politics, culture,

human resources and development, popular participation including the
Caribbean Diaspora, environmental protection, gender, trade and finance.
However, the recommendations related to the new model of governance
had three elements. The first was the WIC's vision of a strong community
equipped to compete in an increasingly regionalised world (see third
column of figure 5.2). The recommendations contained in Chapter XII,
entitled 'Defining a Strong Community', were intended to encourage
the leaders to 'pursue initiatives, conclude agreements and establish
institutions of implementation with a sense of such urgency that, by the
end of the decade of the 1990s the West Indies, by whatever name – but
still with some six million people – [would be] near enough an integrated
union of states'.[30] In order to achieve that vision, the Commission argued
that an indigenous model of integration would have to be developed,
based on West Indian values, including the special reverence for national
sovereignty. Those values, in which the institutional structures would be
grounded, represented the second element of the model (see first column
of figure 5.2).

**Figure 5.2: Proposals for a Community of Sovereign States**

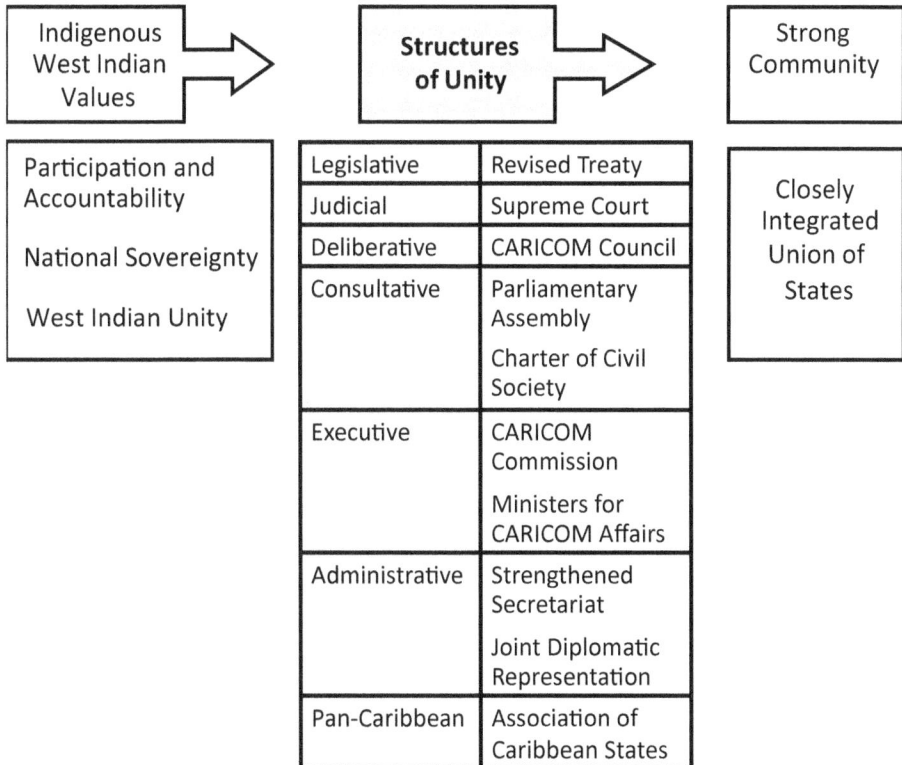

| Indigenous West Indian Values | Structures of Unity | | Strong Community |
|---|---|---|---|
| Participation and Accountability | Legislative | Revised Treaty | Closely Integrated Union of States |
| | Judicial | Supreme Court | |
| National Sovereignty | Deliberative | CARICOM Council | |
| | Consultative | Parliamentary Assembly | |
| West Indian Unity | | Charter of Civil Society | |
| | Executive | CARICOM Commission | |
| | | Ministers for CARICOM Affairs | |
| | Administrative | Strengthened Secretariat | |
| | | Joint Diplomatic Representation | |
| | Pan-Caribbean | Association of Caribbean States | |

## WEST INDIAN POLITICAL VALUES

Having conducted extensive consultation with a wide cross section of the citizenry, it was natural that the WIC proposed the adoption of a concept of popular sovereignty to create the 'normative moorings' for the regional movement. It emphasised the fact that the sense of community could only be sustained where institutions afforded the West Indian people opportunities to participate in decision-making and ensured greater political accountability of leaders . In its assessment of CARICOM's record in Chapter II, the WIC outlined the people's view of the disconnection with the regional movement which the Mills report had also identified:

> In the end the people's instinct has been right. In the senses of achieving an integration which deeply matters in their lives which allows their children more ample prospects, which gives the lands in which they live greater stature and a safer niche in a world of turmoil, the real balance sheet, the true bottom line, shows us falling well short of potential.[31]

The WIC therefore proposed that unity – among the West Indian people – be used as a guiding principle for operationalising the vision of a strong community. However, the Commission assumed that the Heads of Government would not agree to any form of political union or political federation – even though they acknowledged that many people were in favour of such a strategy. In that regard, it suggested that unity could be achieved through the limited pooling of sovereignty and the collective exercise of authority in very specific areas of regional cooperation through institutions of governance appropriately situated within the intergovernmental structure which respected the role of Heads of Government. These institutions of governance, viewed by the Commission as 'Structures of Unity', made up the third element of the model and the core of their recommendations for institutional reform (represented in the centre column of figure 5.2).

The structures of unity, some of which are further delineated in figure 5.3 were proposed as mechanisms which would address the movement's 'Achilles' Heel' of non-implementation. The details of the six most significant proposals demand our attention. Firstly, the WIC proposed that the CARICOM Heads, in keeping with their endorsement of open regionalism, initiate a proposal to neighbouring countries for the creation of an Association of Caribbean States (ACS) as a forum for small states cooperation. This recommendation was perhaps intended to position

CARICOM to play a leadership role in the emerging scheme of wider Caribbean integration and hemispheric cooperation through the proposed Free Trade Areas of the Americas (FTAA).

Secondly, in respect of institutions for increased participation and accountability, the WIC endorsed the decision to establish the ACCP, but urged the admission of social partners to its deliberations. The WIC's concept of an Assembly was that of an assembly of CARICOM people which would include representatives of young people, farmers, religious groups, women, labour and business. It also proposed the admission of observers to the Assembly and the convening of joint meetings with other government assemblies. It further criticised the provision within the existing agreement under consideration which prohibited the discussion of matters which fell exclusively within domestic jurisdiction. The WIC felt that it would be more useful for the Assembly to shed light on all issues and weaknesses at national and regional levels towards the formulation of effective solutions.[32]

The third recommendation, also in relation to increasing participation and accountability, was to formulate a Charter of Civil Society which would codify the norms of governance to which the Community aspired. The WIC had carefully noted the political discourse of the 1990 Kingston Declaration in which the rights of citizens were acknowledged. The Charter was expected to become the 'soul' of the Community and would accommodate a system of participatory monitoring of compliance, even though the legal

## Figure 5.3: CARICOM Structures of Unity

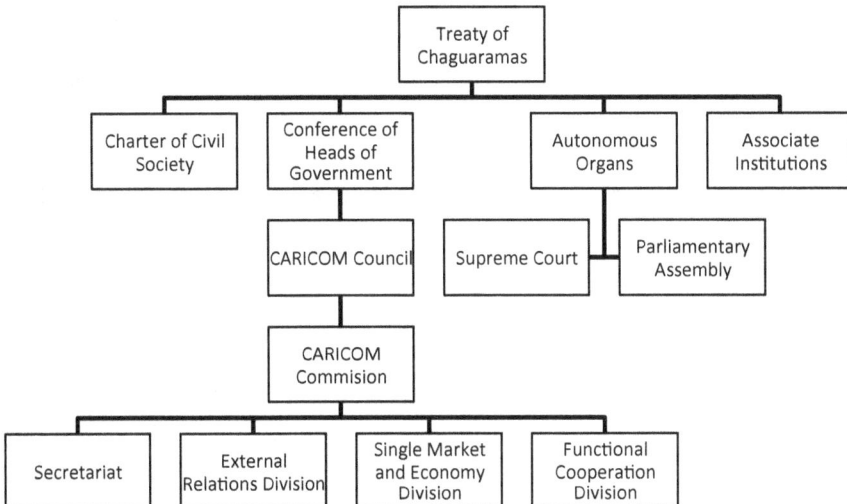

enforceability of such an instrument seemed unlikely. Notwithstanding, the Commission foresaw a role for a CARICOM Supreme Court – a fourth recommendation – to issue judicial advisories on compliance with the Charter's provisions as a part of its original jurisdiction in interpreting the provisions of a Revised Treaty of Chaguaramas, which would highlight the new goal of establishing the CSME. The Supreme Court would also have an appellate jurisdiction for civil and criminal cases and could, therefore, potentially have reversed the anomaly of sovereignty over judicial affairs.

The fifth recommendation of the Commission was the modernisation of the regional public service. In that regard, it supported proposals for the strengthening and restructuring of the Secretariat, including the measures which had been outlined by the Mills report, as well as the appointment of national Ministers of CARICOM Affairs to take responsibility for implementation at the state level with the support of well-resourced technical departments. It further proposed that a system of joint international representation – a regional foreign service of sorts – be arranged.

Finally, in relation to maximising political authority at the regional level, the WIC proposed that the Common Market Council be replaced by a CARICOM Council with a broader jurisdiction for all three pillars of the movement and empowered to relieve the Conference of some of the items on the agenda of the annual summits. The strengthened decision-making machinery would be complemented by an implementation mechanism – a CARICOM Commission – which would act as a central directorate of authority delegated from national governments. The CARICOM Commission would comprise a President and two Commissioners appointed by the Heads of Government 'from among persons with high-level public and political experience in the Region' and would additionally include the Secretary-General, acting in an ex-officio capacity. The Commission would be mandated to further the process of integration by creating 'instruments of implementation' which would be given the immediate force of law in member states once approved by the CARICOM Council and the Heads. The WIC called for the Commission to be established, as a priority, within a year of its recommendations. Mindful that the cost of establishing the Commission would be a cause for concern and aware of the precarious financial position of existing institutions as highlighted by Mills et al., the WIC proposed that the Commission be funded by a system of automatic transfers from member states, similar to the proposal put forward by Tom Adams in 1984.

There are two interesting issues emanating from this final proposal from the WIC. The first is that, while proposing the strengthening of the Secretariat, the WIC did not envision its greater empowerment as the Mills team had, but rather emphasised the maintenance of its administrative role. The Secretariat would service the proposed CARICOM Commission and the Secretary-General would act as a 'high-level' bridge between the two entities. The WIC argued that, since the Secretariat had not even been able to secure the implementation of the six areas outlined in the WIC's 1991 interim report, 'to imply that the way forward lies in the 'strengthening [of] the Secretariat' [would be] disingenuous'.[33] Indeed, the progress made on the interim issues had been presumed to be the result of the unilateral efforts of individual Heads of Government according to their portfolios and not by the Secretariat. The second issue is that the proposed Commission was situated within the intergovernmental framework, not as an autonomous institution like the Supreme Court or the ACCP, but as a direct subordinate to both the Conference and the Council of Ministers. The WIC had expressed the view that, notwithstanding the need to reform the unanimity rule as Pollard and Mills had identified, the process of decision-making via consensus within the Conference was, in fact, effective. The CARICOM Commission was not proposed as a supranational autonomous institution but rather as an executive mechanism which would be subject to the authority of Heads and Ministers, as reflected in figure 5.3 above. In effect, this was intended to ensure that the proposed model of a 'Community of Sovereign States' respected the Heads of Government tradition, while giving the overall CARICOM system the requisite regional authority to implement the kind of integrated strategies demanded by the CSME.

The Commission's report was generally viewed by the political directorate and academic commentators as a significant achievement and its members were commended for their in-depth discussion of the philosophical foundation for good governance in the Community. Moreover, many commentators were appreciative of the wide consultative process undertaken and the extent to which the analysis suggested a holistic view of development that went beyond the economic, to embrace the integration of other social, cultural and political aspects of regionalism.[34] At the same time, other critiques challenged the validity of the Commission's 'independence', the feasibility of its proposals, and the persuasiveness of its arguments. Some analysts perceived a conflict of interest, inherent in the appointment of members of the WIC who had been responsible, along with the presiding political directorate, for the evolution of CARICOM – the same structure that they were charged with critiquing. In that context, some had anticipated that the WIC would not propose initiatives which would have challenged the fundamental traditions of the Community too strongly.[35] Havelock Brewster was not particularly convinced of the feasibility of the proposals as he thought that the broad scope of the new Council was likely to be too demanding on Ministers and that the responsibilities of the Commission for implementation were too vaguely outlined. He was also disappointed by the fact that the Commission had lost an opportunity to propose a radical shift in the political philosophy of regionalism in the Caribbean.

The crux of the matter was that the WIC members were particularly sensitive (perhaps overly sensitive) to the wishes of political leaders and therefore avoided giving the transfer of sovereignty a higher level of priority in the proposals, opting instead to emphasise procedural weaknesses which could be remedied by a reorganisation of the institutional framework. In fact, Fauzya Moore proffered the view that the Commission's proposal was 'a watered down version of the European Community's central structures without much acknowledgement of the need to ensure transfer of authority to regional institutions'.[36] These critiques were plausible to the extent that they identified a level of common interest between the Commission and political leaders, a lack of detail in the proposals and a minimisation of the issue of sovereignty-transfer. However, as much as one could be independent in a small society, the Commission had attempted to be creative in the presentation of a proposal for a European-style Commission which, nevertheless, adopted a West Indian approach of non-supranational, intergovernmental mediation. If the feasibility of such a structure posed challenges, it did not negate the validity of the intention of the proposals. In reality, the failure of the Commission was not so much in the nature of its proposals but in its failure to be adequately convincing in presenting its arguments to Heads. Ultimately, even the highly acclaimed WIC had not solved what had been the recurring problem since the days of the Federation, specifically, 'the vexed question of the distribution of power between central authorities and member states, whether in a political or an economic association'.[37] Ramphal himself was skeptical regarding the likely reaction of Heads. Reflecting on the report in a Special Edition of the *Caribbean Quarterly*, he proffered the view that the people would 'not be surprised if in [that]time for action [Heads did] not act, if at [that] moment of decision [they would] differ and defer'.[38] Ramphal knew many of the

Heads well and, understandably, was not so naive as to expect an easy acceptance of the proposals. The WIC was not able to secure the relatively swift and smooth transformation which had accompanied the move from CARIFTA to CARICOM, under Demas's initiative.

## THE POLITICAL DEFENCE OF SOVEREIGN LEADERSHIP

Although the Chairman of the 1992 Special CHOG, Trinidadian Prime Minister, Patrick Manning, described the WIC report as a seminal work, at the end of their extensive discussions of the principal recommendations, the Heads had agreed to make six principal concessions with regard to reforming the CARICOM governance framework.[39] Firstly, they signalled an acceptance of the fact that there was a greater need for the insertion of executive authority at the regional level to ensure implementation. However, they did not agree that a CARICOM Commission, as proposed by the WIC, was the most appropriate modality for the delegation of that authority. Instead, Heads decided that political authority should remain invested within Heads of national governments, but that each would take greater responsibility for the oversight of the implementation process. At Prime Minister Patterson's prompting, Heads agreed to establish a Bureau composed of the current, outgoing and incoming Chairmen of the Conference, and the Secretary-General in an ex-officio capacity, which would rotate on a six-monthly schedule. The Bureau would be charged with the initiation of proposals for institutional development, supporting the consensus-building process, mobilising action in member states and therefore securing implementation of CARICOM decisions in an expeditious manner. The concept of the Bureau was an adaptation of the traditional principle of pooling sovereignty proposed by the WIC. It is not clear whether Heads had any intention of discussing or considering the establishment of an executive Commission and whether Patterson therefore arrived at the Special Meeting already armed with the alternative proposal of the Bureau – his own model for shared sovereignty. It is conceivable that the close interpersonal relationships among the new cadre of Heads – tensions having eased dramatically since the period of turmoil in the 1970s – was a facilitating factor which supported the concept of delegating to colleague Heads, rather than to external non-elected and potentially antagonistic agents. Heads, accordingly, agreed that the Bureau should be established by January 1993 and that Manning would assume immediate chairmanship. The Bureau is discussed further in chapter 6.

The official arguments for rejection of the WIC's Commission proposal – based on brief national parliamentary debates in Jamaica and Barbados, initially – was that the proposed Commission lacked mechanisms for democratic legitimisation and would have been prohibitively expensive. Indeed, the Terms of Reference discussed by Heads in caucus at the Special Meeting in 1992 proposed a salary for the President which was in excess of that of any of the Heads of State and Government and also called for a seven-year term in office – well beyond the norm for political representatives in Westminster democracies. In that context, taking account of the fact that sovereignty was so intertwined with the personal power of Heads of Government, it is not surprising that there was a perceived personal dimension to the rejection of the proposal. The threat of such a cadre of very highly-paid regional officials was further compounded by a popular perception that the mechanism had been proposed by the WIC as a means of securing permanent new posts for some of its members, particularly Ramphal. Heads of Government were also not keen on the possibility of having retired politicians – perhaps Michael Manley or A.N.R. Robinson – interfering in or limiting the sphere of their personal sovereignty.[40]

Other explanations of the rejection suggest that the Secretariat, especially the new Secretary-General, Edwin Carrington, may have had reason to 'kill' the proposal, perhaps because of disappointment at the diminished role accorded to the Secretariat vis-à-vis the proposed Commission in the new institutional framework. In its review of the proposals, the Secretariat staff had certainly disagreed with the design of the Commission model. Secretary-General Carrington claimed, however, that the Heads had almost unanimously rejected the idea in their caucus even before the Secretariat's opinion was solicited. The Secretary-General also proffered a view that the weaknesses of the proposal may have been compounded by the fact that Ramphal's rather lengthy presentation – as had become the well-observed practice associated with the intellectual and political profile of the former Commonwealth Secretary-General – had annoyed several of the Heads, who felt as if he had upstaged them in some way. It was perhaps also likely that, whatever his own views on the CARICOM Commission model, Carrington would have been wary of the fact that, as the 'new boy on the block', an open disagreement with Heads at his very first CHOG, would not have been a wise course of action. His support of their views perhaps earned him their trust and confidence and honorary membership of the 'boys club' which the Conference represents.

Carrington went on to become the longest serving Secretary-General in the movement's history to date.

The second point to which Heads agreed was the strengthening of the Secretariat. Again, they disagreed with the WIC and adopted the Mills solution which accorded the Secretary-General a level of executive authority to secure the management of Community affairs. Interestingly, the Heads left it to Carrington to propose how the Secretariat should be restructured and requested that he submit his proposals to the Fourth Intersessional in 1993. This further revealed the extent of the trust which they had vested in Carrington. The third concession signalled a significant departure from tradition. Heads agreed to appoint Ministers with responsibility for CARICOM Affairs who would form the upgraded CARICOM Council to replace the CMC. This decision was significant since regional affairs were, traditionally, intended to 'have little or no direct impact on the internal administrative structure of government'.[41] Up to this point, most member states had resisted the establishment of ministerial departments to support CARICOM since the competence of what was perceived as a 'super-department' was expected to be challenged by other technically specialised line ministries and departments. Brewster was of the view that the Council should rather have been convened with varying national representatives, taking account of the particular technical issues to be addressed.[42] Whatever would have been the most useful configuration, the acceptance of responsibility for CARICOM at the national level was a positive step. Unfortunately, these portfolios were later assigned to Ministers of Foreign Affairs, thereby maintaining the ideological perception of CARICOM as a forum for international relations and not an instrument of regional integration.

The fourth concession made by Heads was an agreement to pursue joint representation and collective approaches to international issues. The renewed focus on joint representation belied a history of failed attempts in that regard. As early as March 1976, the SCMFA had discussed the establishment of a single CARICOM mission in Brussels but eventually decided that such a course of action would not be feasible.[43] That position was upheld by the CMC in 1978 and 1979, again, by the SCMFA in 1985, and once more, by a 1990 'Think Tank' on Joint Representation.[44] The Community seemed to have adopted a consensus that, since individual states had already established their own missions, they should seek only to enhance cooperation among their representatives. The decision taken at the 1992 Special CHOG was therefore not strictly a revival of previous proposals for joint diplomatic or consular representation, but rather, the adoption of a simplified approach which emphasised the maximisation of cooperation among existing national missions in London, New York, Washington and Ottawa.

The fifth concession made by the Heads was an agreement to foster institutions of popular sovereignty to increase the involvement of the citizenry. They reaffirmed their commitment to the establishment of the ACCP and also agreed to adopt a Charter of Civil Society. Finally, Heads conceded the need to improve the dispute settlement capacity of CARICOM and agreed to establish a regional court with an original jurisdiction for interpretation of a revised Treaty which would outline the new goals towards a CARICOM Single Market and Economy (CSME). They did not focus on the appellate jurisdiction. At the end of the Special Session, Heads issued the *Protocol of Port of Spain* which appointed the Secretary-General as Chair of an Inter-Governmental Task Force which would revise the Treaty of Chaguaramas and draft the Charter of Civil Society to reflect the agreements taken there.[45]

## INITIAL ADJUSTMENTS TO THE CARICOM STRUCTURE

In the four years following the 1992 Special CHOG, there appeared to be some progress on institutional reform. In 1993, Heads reorganised the Organs of the Community, under the direction of the Bureau and Ministers of CARICOM Affairs and agreed to the implementation of a monetary union and a Caribbean Investment Fund. In the following year, as they reached a landmark agreement to admit Suriname as the first non-West Indian member of CARICOM, two other significant contributions to institutional development occurred. Firstly, Heads moved closer to the goal of the establishment of the ACCP. Secondly, they agreed to the execution of a new plan for the restructuring of the Secretariat.[46]

By August 1994, the ACCP had come into effect as the first of the CARICOM consultative and deliberative mechanisms which introduced an element of accountability to the governance structure.[47]

The ACCP was certainly one of the most significant institutional evolutions in the history of the movement. Its institutional profile and stated objectives were a radical departure from the traditions that had been operational since 1973. Article 4 of the Agreement set out the objectives of involving the people and their representatives, including those in Opposition, in discussions of regional affairs and in encouraging

Member State adoption of coordinated foreign policies and common economic, social, cultural scientific and legal policies.[48] These objectives implied a potential for the reversal of some aspects of the Federal legacy. Yet, however laudable the objectives, the subsequent article (Article 5, paragraph 4) forbade the discussion of any matter which fell 'exclusively within the domestic jurisdiction' of a Member State or Associate Member State.[49] Consequently, shortly after its establishment, critics began to refer to the ACCP as a 'talk shop'. The greatest weakness was perhaps the lack of any binding commitment to its principles and lack of credible machinery for monitoring or enforcement.[50]

Its inaugural meeting was held in Barbados in May 1996, during which Guyana proposed a motion on the admission of NGO representatives as observers to the Assembly, as had been proposed by the WIC. After spirited discussions on the proposal, and having realised the implications of amendment of the Agreement, as well as the strong positions held by some member representatives about the dilution of the Assembly with non-elected representatives, the Assembly decided not to grant this status but to allow the Assembly time to develop and mature before reconsidering such action.[51] It was unfortunate that they missed an opportunity for greater involvement of civil society, especially since the Agreement only accorded observers the right to speak but not to vote in the Assembly (Article 6 (7)). Furthermore, since the capacity of regional NGOs to mobilise public opinion and disseminate information generally far exceeded the capacity of government machinery, the admittance of NGO observers could have played a useful role in public education and sensitisation. Admittedly, several NGOs were already organised in regional alliances.[52] At the same time, those associations suggested a threat of potential NGO-opposition alliances which could perhaps have furthered the partisan politicisation of the movement in the national sphere. It was this fear which had prompted Dame Eugenia Charles's statement in 1992, made on the occasion of the opening of the ACCP agreement for signature, that her government would not be willing to fund the participation of the Opposition in any regional agenda.[53]

Interestingly, however, at the end of the 1994 CHOG Summit in Barbados, the social partners involved in the Joint Consultative Committee (JCC) were afforded the opportunity of interacting directly with the Heads of Government – compensating for their exclusion from the ACCP. Unfortunately, that exchange was limited to brief presentations from a narrow range of organisations (the Caribbean Association of Industry and Commerce [CAIC], the Caribbean Congress of Labour [CCL] and a representative of the Convention on Biodiversity), thereby limiting the concept of social dialogue. In the following year, Heads agreed to allow broader NGO participation in the JCC along with the CAIC and CCL. It was agreed that the Caribbean Policy Development Centre (CPDC) should act as the representative body.[51]

Although the agreement stipulated that the Assembly should meet at least once per year (Article 6 (1)), the ACCP did not meet again until October 1999 in Grenada at which time it passed, inter alia, a resolution on the establishment of the Caribbean Court of Justice (CCJ) as a symbol of the 'inalienable right [of every state] to establish a judicial system which is responsive and sensitive to the culture and traditions of its citizens while upholding the rule of law, preserving democratic principles and protecting the constitution'.[55] The extent to which CARICOM citizens had become aware of those deliberations is not clear. Even more significantly, uncertainty remains about the extent to which those endorsements by the peoples' representatives had any influence at all in the principal Organs and Institutions of the Community.

The ACCP met again in November 2000 in Belize, at which time it discussed a variety of issues and reissued a commitment on behalf of their countries to the CSME and the CCJ and greater involvement of Opposition representatives.[56] It was never convened again. The infrequency of meetings was attributed not to the lack of usefulness of the meetings per se but to the logistical challenges posed by the coordination of 12 parliamentary schedules with the regional one, since the speakers and clerks of each national assembly were representatives to the regional body.

The process of restructuring the Secretariat was also initiated in 1994. The Secretariat had received advice on institutional strengthening from a management consultancy firm which suggested that neither Member States nor the Secretariat had succeeded in 'developing and supporting, in a...comprehensive manner, an environment...conducive to effective implementation'.[57] Specifically, the consultants proposed the establishment of new machinery within member states for improved and more frequent consultation between governments, social partners and other interest groups and for the dissemination of public information and education. The consultants also proposed the strengthening of the Secretariat's capacity for the preparation and dissemination of documentation in support of the decision-making process, for improved communication with member states, for strategic planning and resource mobilisation, and for monitoring and evaluation as well as the establishment of an improved senior and middle management system. By 1995, three Assistant Secretaries-General and a General Legal Council had been appointed as part of a new core management system at the Secretariat. They were charged with responsibilities for oversight of a streamlined work programme and budget organised under a trimmed schema of thematic priorities. They reported to the General Management Committee, a Committee for Programme Review and Evaluation and one for Organisational Development. The Technical Assistance and Services Unit (TASU) was also established to coordinate inputs. Farier has suggested, however, that this restructuring was hampered by the fact that budget contributions for the Secretariat often fell within foreign affairs budget allocations and therefore had, sometimes, to compete with more sensational, if not more influential, international priorities.[58] This meant that the restructuring process slowed down and the Secretariat was not able to attract the calibre of staff needed to ensure implementation of its core services.

The year 1996 marked the end of a significant period in the history of CARICOM. Although the Community was by no means at a stage of full recovery, it undertook some level of institutional reform, manifested largely in two primary adjustments which emanated from the discussions at Grande Anse. Firstly, it was the period in which the movement embarked on the most innovative of its institutional proposals, notably the creation of a Bureau of Heads of Government and a wider portfolio system of responsibility. These mechanisms played an integral role in defending the sovereign leadership of the Heads of Government. The expert studies, which had diplomatically hinted at the necessity of reconfiguring sovereignty by establishing a supranational executive mechanism in order to support a single market and economy, had posed a threat to that leadership. Those studies had also shown that, in the absence of such machinery, control of the movement could be usurped by inappropriate proxy institutions. Committed to the deepening process, but wary of the delegation of authority to other agencies, the Heads developed their own model of 'shared sovereignty'. Their choice of instruments – the Bureau and cabinet-style mechanism – reflected an attempt by Heads to exert greater individual influence over those aspects of the movement which most interested them, on behalf of their colleagues. In other words, they sought to avoid the challenges of collective exercise of sovereignty by instituting a process of 'sharing' sovereignty on a rotational basis, in the case of the Bureau, and on a unilateral basis, in respect of the portfolio system. However, in 1995, several member states were still in default on their obligations with respect to the CSME.[59] The model had not yielded the gains that had been expected. In that regard, a particularly interesting development occurred during the 1996 CHOG. An offer made by the governments of Antigua and Barbuda and Trinidad and Tobago to prepare a joint paper for the next Intersessional Meeting of Heads with regard to a proposal for the establishment of a CARICOM Commission to strengthen implementation. During his opening address, the Prime Minister of Antigua and Barbuda, Lester Bird, argued for a

> ...return to the concept of a Caribbean Commission as proposed by the West Indian Commission....The work of such a Commission would greatly enhance the decision-making process in CARICOM and considerably aid Heads of Government to focus on issues which require[d] their specific attention to move the integration movement forward, and by doing so, improve the prospect of a better life for the Caribbean people.[60]

The paper was submitted to Heads in 1997 but, even at that point, it was clear that the initiative was an admission of the ineffectiveness of the alternative Bureau and portfolio allocation structures previously adopted by the Heads. The Bureau had, in effect, presented too heavy a work load for Heads of Government.[61]

The second adjustment related to the rejection of the aspect of the federal legacy which excluded the Caribbean people from the integration process. For the first time, CARICOM acknowledged the rights and role of Caribbean citizens in the integration process, providing a place for their representatives in the ACCP; expanding the JCC to include NGOs and protecting their rights by drafting a Charter of Civil Society. Although the fundamental philosophy of regionalism had remained the same, an emerging popular character was slowly driving the process of reform. Notwithstanding those positive trends, CARICOM had still not fully resolved its problems related to political authority, implementation, regulation and dispute settlement. In that regard, the ensuing chapter discusses the evolution of more substantial changes in the CARICOM institutional framework as well as the extent of their contribution to moving the Community closer to an appropriate framework for implementation of a CARICOM Single Market and Economy (CSME).

# FIRST GENERATION
# INSTITUTIONAL CHANGE

In spite of the initial adjustments in institutional capacity for participatory governance in the preceding period, CARICOM's core weakness – its limited capacity for implementation of the CARICOM Single Market and Economy (CSME) – remained. Consequently, between 1997 and 2002, CARICOM underwent a period of fundamental institutional change marked by experimentation with new institutional models of governance. This chapter reviews that first period of significant change, beginning with an analysis of the new decision-making and administrative framework which emerged from a revised Treaty of Chaguaramas. Secondly, it discusses, against the background of intergovernmental and academic discourses on governance, the evolution of three models of executive governance – the Head of Government model used in the creation of the Bureau and Quasi-Cabinet; the Project model used in the creation of the Caribbean Regional Negotiating Machinery (CRNM); and the Supranational model used in creation of the Caribbean Court of Justice (CCJ). The chapter concludes with a discussion of further alternatives proposed by Heads and by an institutional review completed in 2002, and offers an analysis of the lessons emerging from the institution-building exercise.

## REVISING THE TREATY OF CHAGUARAMAS

The decision to implement the CSME called for the revision of the Treaty of Chaguaramas to reflect the new goals of a regional economic space and new institutional arrangements for its regulation. The Intergovernmental Task Force, which had been established in 1992, drafted a series of nine legal protocols outlining the elements of the CSME which were later incorporated into a Revised Treaty.[1] The most important of these protocols, in respect of this account of regional governance, was the Protocol Amending the Treaty Establishing the Caribbean Community (referred to as Protocol I) which outlined new institutional arrangements for CARICOM. It was approved in January

1997 by the Standing Committee of Ministers responsible for Legal Affairs (SCMLA), along with a final draft of the Charter of Civil Society.[2] The following month the CHOG signed Protocol I and the Charter during the eighth Intersessional Meeting, as a sign of its commitment to 'structures of unity and governance' (different interpretations of the WIC vision) which significantly modified the decision-making procedures and administrative arrangements of CARICOM.[3] The following sections discuss, first, the structural changes contained in the Protocol and, secondly, the new consultative arrangements outlined in the Protocol and the Charter.

Protocol I fundamentally altered CARICOM's decision-making processes and administrative arrangements.[4] While the 1973 organisation had been explicitly bifurcated, under the new dispensation, the single market and economy was integrated within CARICOM as a development instrument of the Community. Thus, the new arrangement referred to the Caribbean Community *including* the Caribbean Single Market and Economy (CSME) (Article I of Protocol).[5] Duke Pollard, a member of the Task Force, who had been involved in the drafting of the original 1973 treaty, has drawn a metaphoric allusion to the difference between a woman and child – referring to the 1973 Community and the Common Market; and a woman with child – referring to the Community from 1997 onwards.[6] The most obvious implication of this modification is the consolidation of the political and economic aspects of Caribbean integration for the first time since the Federation. That process of integration pointed to further implications for the participation of special members in the decision-making process and for the overall voting procedures.

The amalgamation of the political and economic aspects of integration implied the need for a special legislative arrangement to accommodate parties not intending to join the CSME. The Bahamas had signed Protocol I in 1997, but maintained its reservation about participation in the CSME – a situation which raised questions about the legal appropriateness of its participation in fora in which matters pertaining to the CSME were discussed. In practice, under the 1973 treaty, The Bahamas had participated in meetings of the Community without entering a vote or statement on matters related to the Common Market. It contributed to the CARICOM budget and maintained macroeconomic policies which were not in conflict with the common market policy framework. The Bahamas was viewed by other member states as a valuable partner and therefore retained its status as a full member of the Community.[7] However, The Bahamas did not sign the Revised Treaty in 2001 once all nine protocols had been completed, since the treaty carried an expectation that members would honour obligations in respect of the CSME or be held in breach of the legislation. Later in 2006, in order to allow the Single Market to come into effect without its signature, The Bahamas signed an agreement with CARICOM to legitimise the informal relationship which had hitherto existed.[8] Accordingly, The Bahamas continued to participate in the structures established under Protocol I but not in relation to decisions on the CSME. Although the informal arrangement made for an unusual decision-making environment, it does not seem to have had any adverse effect on the decision-making process itself.

The new integrated organisational structure outlined in Protocol I (see representation in figure 6.1) was complemented by relaxed decision-making procedures. The unanimity voting rule was only retained at the level of the Conference Heads of Government (CHOG) which remained the supreme Organ of the Community. The functions of the CHOG were unaltered (Article 7); however, the Bureau structure which had come into effect in 1993 was explicitly defined as a Committee of the CHOG (Article 7(a) subparagraph 11). Its executive responsibilities for the initiation of proposals, updating of the consensus among member states, facilitation of implementation at regional and national levels and provision of policy guidance to the Secretariat were highlighted.

### Figure 6.1: Organisational Structure of CARICOM

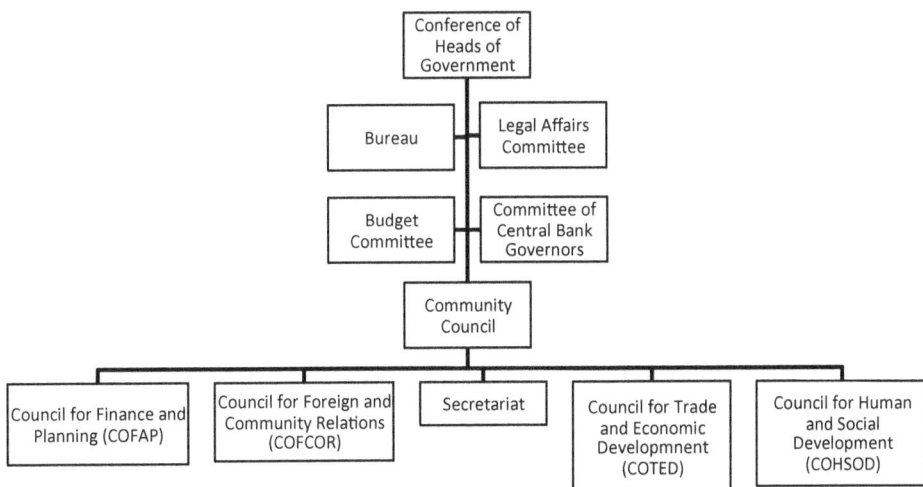

More significant changes were made to the functional procedures of subsidiary structures. First, the Common Market Council (CMC) was replaced by a Community Council of Ministers (referred to as the Council). The new nomenclature in itself alone reflected the absorption of the economic instrument of integration into the Community. The Council, as the second highest Organ, had responsibility for community strategic planning and for co-ordination of all three pillars of economic integration, functional cooperation and external relations (Article 8(2)). It had authority to approve programmes and budgets, monitor implementation and resolve internal disputes between subsidiary structures. Significantly, the affirmative voting procedure was abolished in the Council in favour of majority formulae. As such, the Council was empowered to make binding decisions on procedural matters by a simple majority; on more substantive policy issues by a qualified majority vote of three-quarters of the membership; and on non-binding recommendations by a two-thirds simple majority. That change paved the way for a more expeditious and efficient decision-making process.

The Standing Committees identified in the previous treaty as Community Institutions were replaced by four ministerial Councils which were upgraded to the status of Community Organs. The Council for Trade and Economic Development (COTED), the Council for Foreign and Community Relations (COFCOR), the Council for Human and Social Development (COHSOD) and the Council for Finance and Planning (COFAP) were mandated to make decisions with respect to the three pillars of the Community and overall financial management. The COFAP worked towards the harmonisation of foreign investment policy, fiscal and monetary cooperation and capital integration and also supervised the Committee of Central Bank Governors. The COTED, a key CSME Organ, was responsible for the oversight of all elements of policy related to the full integration of national economies, including the movement of factors of production to facilitate integrated production and the management of production quality, marketing and environmental protection. The COTED was expected to have a close working relationship with the COFCOR in relation to external economic and trade relations, given the latter's remit for intra-regional, inter-regional and international relations. The COFCOR, in turn, was expected to promote friendly relations among member states and coordinate foreign policies, including overseas representation and candidatures in inter-governmental fora. Finally, the COHSOD was given responsibility for the coordination of all the areas of functional cooperation managed by associate and other institutions in relation to health, education, youth, women, labour, culture, sports and the environment.

Article 10 of the Protocol intended that there be maximum levels of cooperation among these four Councils which would submit their decisions and recommendations to the Community Council. Furthermore, as had occurred in the Community Council, these subsidiary Organs were empowered to make binding decisions by a three-quarters majority vote and pass non-binding recommendations by a two-thirds majority. The removal of the unanimity rule in these arenas also suggested a more efficient and faster-paced process of decision-making which had perhaps been designed specifically, as per Pollard's recommendations, to prevent abstentions or vetoes at lower levels of the structure from stalling the approval and progression of projects and programmes.

A further innovation of Protocol I was the creation of three Subsidiary Bodies: the Legal Affairs Committee, the Budget Committee, and the Committee of Central Bank Governors (Articles 9 and 10). The three Bodies were distinct from the Organs since they did not command policy mandates but served technical functions and were, consequently, composed of senior civil servants who operated within their professional rather than political capacities. These civil servants assumed responsibility for the administrative issues which had previously crowded the agendas of the superior Organs.

Finally, consequent on the conversion of the ministerial structures into Organs, the term Institutions was employed to refer to specific technical bodies which had been created by the CHOG to carry out functions in disaster management, health, agriculture, meteorology, education, food and nutrition and development administration. The Assembly of Caribbean Community Parliamentarians (ACCP) was also included in this category. The list of Associate Institutions was significantly reduced in the Protocol to exclude defunct entities such as the Shipping Council. They, henceforth, included the Caribbean Development Bank (CDB), University of Guyana (UG), University of the West Indies (UWI) and the Caribbean Law Institute (Article 12). Interestingly, the institutions of the Eastern Caribbean integration movement were excluded from the list under the Protocol; however the Secretariat of the Organisation of Eastern Caribbean States (OECS) was included among the list of Associate Institutions in the eventual 2001 Revised Treaty.

With respect to Community administration, Protocol I further amended the provisions related to the role of the Secretariat. Although the

Secretariat was essentially accorded the same administrative position as it had in the original treaty, there was increased emphasis in Article 13 on the maintenance of the highest standards of efficiency, competence, integrity and considerations of geographical distribution in staffing in direct response to the recommendations of the Pollard and Mills reports. In addition, Article 14 outlined a new role for the Secretary-General, who was now dubbed the Chief Executive Officer (CEO), appointed for a renewable five-year term and invested with authority to initiate proposals, implement and monitor national and regional projects and programmes – in keeping with the role of the Bureau of which he was a member. Notwithstanding this new executive function, there remained two principal caveats on the implementation aspect of the mandate. Firstly, implementation at the regional level generally referred to the administration of Community meetings. The Secretary-General could not facilitate policy implementation at national level without the consent of individual member states. Where consent was granted, he could not act in respect of those matters which required legislative or administrative action by national authorities. Certainly, it must have been difficult to isolate many objectives of the Community or CSME which would not have required legislative or administrative action by national authorities, given the lack of regional executive structures. The second caveat was that the Secretary-General continued to rely on the support of administrative and not executive machinery. The authority of the 'executive' Secretary-General was, therefore, limited and was, in fact, impugned by a lack of technical capacity for implementation. The executive implant – a reinterpretation of the West Indian Commission (WIC) proposal for a CARICOM Commission – was certainly an incomplete solution to the implementation deficit.

Protocol I also defined a strategy for increased consultation in the decision-making process. The Community Council and the Secretary-General were charged under Article 16 with ensuring that all Community deliberations were informed by appropriate consultations with governmental and non-governmental stakeholders. In addition, the subsidiary Organs and the Legal Affairs Committee were expected to include these stakeholders in their deliberations. Thus, there evolved within the CARICOM framework an appreciation of the relationship between consultation and decision-making at national and regional levels. This was reinforced by the provisions of a Charter of Civil Society.

The principles outlined in the 27 articles of the Charter covered a wide range of issues including good governance, human rights and respect for cultural and religious diversity.[9] However, the purpose of the discussion here is not to critique the content of the Charter but to highlight its place within the institutional structure. The Charter intimated a framework for social partnership which would complement the consultative processes outlined in Protocol I. The Charter began with the phrase: 'We, the People of the Caribbean Community, acting through the assembled representatives of our Governments', which suggested the acceptance of the principles of participation and accountability in governance, as conceptualised in Kingston in 1990 and elaborated by the WIC in 1992. The new social partnership was expected, on the one hand, to 'enhance public confidence in governance, thereby reinforcing the loyalty of the people', perhaps to their leaders and to the regional movement. On the other hand, it was expected to secure governmental commitment to 'respect and strengthen the fundamental elements of a civil society'.[10] The Charter called for the institutionalisation of interaction between the CHOG and other Community Organs with the social partners who were identified as those government employers, workers and other non-governmental associations recognised by member states. That call led to the convening of direct consultations between the Joint Consultative Committee (JCC) and the CHOG on an annual basis and to the convening of a broader regional consultative forum in 2002 called 'Forward Together'.

However, the Charter's potential role in regional governance was limited by the inadequacy of the provisions for its implementation. The implementation of the Charter – a document which was not legally binding – was based solely on member states' 'resolve to pay due regard to the provisions' (Article XXVI). In addition, the vague provisions for reporting on the progress of implementation were not accompanied by any enforcement mechanisms (Article XXV). At the end of the 'Forward Together' Forum involving over 150 civil society representatives and eleven Heads of Government, a Liliendaal Statement was issued which called for a commitment on the part of the Heads of Government to the institutionalisation of dialogue as a part of the CARICOM decision-making processes and for the establishment of a Task Force to carry forward the recommendations.[11] Eventually, rather than an intensification of the social partnership at the highest levels, the annual 'exchange of views' with the three principal social partners of the JCC, which had become an informal tradition of the CHOG, was suspended because the interaction with NGOs, in particular, was viewed by the Heads as being overly antagonistic and argumentative. Following the suspension of these initiatives, the Secretariat encouraged greater consultation at the national level and in the ministerial Councils so as to avoid the annual interaction with the Heads.

Consequent on the revision of the legislative framework, via Protocol I and the Charter of Civil Society, more efficient and participatory institutions for regulation of the CSME evolved, at least on paper. However, the implementation of the various policies on single market and economy still required mechanisms which could effectively mediate among the fourteen individual sovereignties participating in the intergovernmental framework. During this phase of institutional change, three distinct models were employed to address the implementation weakness.

The reorganisation of the regional institutional structure in a revised legislative framework represented an attempt to develop new methods of sharing or pooling sovereignty towards a more democratic and consultative decision-making process. However, the upgraded legal foundation had not provided for supranational modalities for implementation and enforcement which would make the regional framework work better and secure effective sovereignty.[12] The mechanisms for executive authority outlined in the new legislative framework – that is, the Bureau of the CHOG and the offices of the Secretary-General – did not appear to be effectively complemented by technical capacity for implementation. With a dawning realisation of the need to improve the functioning of these mechanisms, the Heads of Government embarked on a somewhat unmethodical process of modifying or creating institutions to fill the gaps in central executive authority, trade negotiation capacity and dispute settlement capacity. The subsequent subsections will discuss, against the background of Heads of Government deliberations and other stakeholder commentary, the emergence of the Bureau and Quasi-Cabinet, the Caribbean Regional Negotiating Machinery (CRNM) and the Caribbean Court of Justice (CCJ) – which represent three different models of delegating executive authority and bargaining with formal sovereignty.

## THE HEAD OF GOVERNMENT EXECUTIVE MODEL

Weaknesses in central executive capacity were placed at the top of the agenda in 1997. During the February Intersessional Meeting of the CHOG, Chairman Lester Bird of Antigua reiterated his 1996 proposal for the creation of more effective machinery for implementation. Bird's Government and the Government of Trinidad and Tobago had submitted to this meeting the promised paper on transforming the Bureau into a structure similar to the CARICOM Commission proposed by the WIC. Bird's presentation to the Conference included a confession of the ineffectiveness of the Bureau up to this point in relation to sharing sovereignty in an effective way. He said:

> My own experience of serving on the Bureau of Heads of Government as a member and chairman has not dissuaded me from the views that the Bureau is inadequate to carry out the very functions which the Heads of Government set for it....Without doubt, the Bureau has been of assistance in strengthening institutional arrangements. However, it has not done so adequately, nor can it do so with national responsibilities which become more complex every day. Heads of Government simply do not have the time to dedicate to tasks of the Bureau. Both those tasks and their own day-to-day responsibilities urgently require 24-hours-a-day attention. They simply do not have the time.[13]

Bird was convinced that there was a need to revisit the concept of a CARICOM Commission in order to help Heads of Government focus on those issues which required their specific attention to move the integration process forward. One side of Bird's argument called for a permanent repository of shared sovereignty – machinery empowered to initiate, update, implement and guide, as was the mandate of the Bureau, but on a full-time basis. However, another side of his argument suggested that the political directorate, as opposed to technocrats, should play a significant role in oversight of the Commission. Heads could not reach a consensus on whether to abandon the Bureau and adopt a new mechanism. Rather, the Bureau structure was replicated at lower levels of the policy framework. As Community Organs developed their rules of procedure, they created substructures – either intersessional committees or advisory councils – to which they delegated executive responsibilities to the current, past and future ministerial chairmen of the Councils.

There were, in fact, two generally positive trends which emerged from this governance-by-committee framework. The first is that these substructures had the effect of inserting a level of coherence across the regional system of governance. The coincidence of Chairmanships in the ministerial councils with the CHOG chairmanship held potential for improved and seamless communication in the hiatus between meetings since the principal actors were located within the same country and government. The second observation is that these subcommittees provided fora for the participation of non-governmental stakeholders, thereby further suggesting adherence to a commitment to consultation in decision-making. However, like the Bureau, these structures only added value to the decision-making process and made no impact on the environment for implementation. Like Heads of Government, Ministers rarely had time to dedicate to monitoring their colleagues' actions in relation to implementation. More significantly, although they acted as representatives in deliberative fora, none had the authority to enforce implementation in another member state.

Later, against the background of the 1999 CHOG meeting in Paramaribo, Suriname where the Community's 'dynamic inertia' and unsustainable gap in regional executive authority were acknowledged, the Heads attempted to compensate for the weaknesses by expanding the portfolio system they had adopted following the acceptance of the WIC report.[14] That portfolio system had led to some modest progress – all but two protocols had been concluded in relation to the process of revising the treaty, the Agreement Establishing the Caribbean Court of Justice (CCJ) was approved, and some member states had enacted legislation to facilitate free movement of some skilled nationals.[15] However, at a special meeting in Trinidad in October 1999, Heads adopted the Consensus of Chaguaramas which outlined an agreement on the 'Governance of Regional Institutions' and agreed to broaden the existing portfolio system to include new areas of responsibility, as a complement to the Bureau. Lead Heads were already in place since 1993 for the CSME and Monetary Union (Barbados), External Negotiations (Jamaica), Science and Technology (Grenada) and Labour Mobility (Dominica). To those responsibilities Heads assigned additional portfolios, which were later refined as follows: Services (Antigua and Barbuda), Environment/ Sustainable Development (Belize), Human Resource Development/Health (St Kitts and Nevis), Information Technology and Telecommunications, Justice and Governance (St Lucia), Sports and Culture (Suriname), Agriculture (Guyana) (St Vincent and the Grenadines) and Tourism (The Bahamas).[16]

In subsequent years the Quasi-Cabinet was shuffled to adjust to changes in leadership and government so as to better align Head of Government interest and expertise with portfolio subject matter. In 2000, St Vincent and the Grenadines adopted a special portfolio for bananas; Haiti adopted the portfolio for transport and Trinidad and Tobago the portfolio for security. The effectiveness of the system had been noticeably enhanced in cases where the lead Head held a special interest in his portfolio and was supported by a well-equipped technical and administrative arm to further implementation. In that regard, the relative success of the portfolios for External Negotiations and CSME were largely attributed to the existence of support from the Prime Ministerial Subcommittee on External Negotiations (PMSCEN) and CRNM, in the case of the former, and the CSME Unit established in Barbados in October 2002, in the case of the latter.

The 1999 Consensus reflected two other key commitments to governance. First, Heads agreed to forge closer consultative links with political Opposition groups. That commitment was operationalised by an agreement in March 2000 that the Secretary-General should brief Opposition groups on developments in the integration process whenever he visited member states; and also by a reaffirmation of the role of the ACCP in updating both sides of national parliaments.[17] In due course, members of Opposition were afforded the opportunity to engage directly with the CHOG in June 2006. However, as a result of the tense debates between the two sides, the engagement was never repeated. Secondly, Heads agreed in 1999 that the Bureau should 'review the structure and functioning of the institutions of the Community, including its Secretariat, with a view to better equip them with the necessary authority and capacity to discharge their responsibilities, [and] accelerate decision-making and implementation in the regional integration process'. Heads set a deadline of making a definitive decision on governance by January 2001. The resulting study joined the ranks of the Mills and WIC reports as one of the seminal studies of CARICOM governance and is the first in a series of post-millennium studies which effectively legitimised the conclusions of the WIC – that Heads needed to agree to a reconfiguration of their sovereignty in order to facilitate the delegation of authority to a regional executive.

## Foreign Policy Coordination and the Project Model

Another area in which the Community lacked regional mechanisms for implementation was in foreign policy coordination. In particular, Heads raised concerns at the end of the 1990s about CARICOM's lack of preparedness for three major international trade negotiations – a Free Trade Area of the Americas (FTAA), a post-Lomé framework for EU-ACP preferential trade relations, and the negotiation of the international rules of trade liberalisation in the World Trade Organization (WTO).[18] These simultaneous negotiations were significant to the maintenance of special trade preferences for small developing states which were considered indispensable to strategies towards effective sovereignty. However, Heads acknowledged that these negotiations were likely to tax the limited capacity of individual CARICOM States and therefore there was need to pool resources in order to develop a central technical entity empowered to further the negotiation process.

Prior to 1997, the Secretariat held responsibility for coordinating negotiations by assisting a special Committee of the Common Market Council in the development of a detailed negotiating position based on a broad strategy outlined by the CHOG. PMSCEN, chaired by the Prime Minister of Jamaica, had emerged, in 1993, from the process of allocation of portfolios to individual Heads of Government. The PMSCEN, which was supported by an advisory group of experts, spearheaded the development of the CHOG's broad strategy. However, the process was inefficient in three main ways. First, former Secretary-General Alister McIntyre, a member of the advisory group to the PMSCEN, noted a tendency for Heads of Government to exert too much control over the process, becoming involved too early in the negotiation process so as to eclipse the role of officials and technocrats operating at lower levels of political intervention. Secondly, he noted that the negotiating teams convened by member states, via the Secretariat, did not always include the appropriate technical, networking and communications skills required to prepare for international negotiations.[19] Additionally, there was also a third problem related to frequent misunderstandings between the Secretariat and member states resulting from the tardy exchange of information between the two spheres of action and the consequent preparation, by the Secretariat, of positions viewed to be contrary to national positions. Consequent on those weaknesses, McIntyre himself proposed that the Secretariat develop a proposal for creation of an 'interpositioning' authority which would act as the central technical machinery for the coordination of foreign negotiations.[20]

According to Cedric Grant's account, Secretary-General Edwin Carrington presented his proposal in a memo to the CHOG in July 1996 entitled, 'Measures to Enhance the Coordination and Execution of External Negotiations'.[21] In the memo, he proposed that the PMSCEN and the Secretariat continue to function as the political and administrative components of the negotiating machinery but that a separate technical arm be established as a temporary project to facilitate the mobilisation of additional funding and technical expertise to improve negotiating capacity. It was thought that, by the end of the period of intense negotiations, estimated at that time to be no longer than seven years from 1997, the project would be dissolved and the Secretariat would have built up its capacity. The Secretariat assumed, therefore, that the project would be placed under the direct oversight of the Assistant Secretary-General for regional trade and economic integration. However, when the proposal was discussed during the 1997 Intersessional Meeting, the Heads requested that the Secretariat make two changes to the proposal. Firstly, Heads requested that social partners be accorded greater involvement in the decision-making process. In response, the Secretariat conceptualised an advisory group for the PMSCEN which would comprise of civil society and private sector representatives. Secondly, Heads requested a greater role for 'political actors'. Their fundamental concern was that the structure would require strong political competence at its highest level, rather than mere technical expertise, if the engagement with international representatives was to be effective. Heads therefore suggested the mobilisation of a small group of people exclusively responsible for driving the negotiation process. In response, the Secretariat conceptualised a role for a full-time Chief Negotiator, at ambassadorial rank, supported by a Chief Coordinator and a Technical Advisor, to which the Heads agreed.

It is interesting that this call for greater political competence emanated from the discussions among Heads who had previously rejected a proposal for similar competence as a part of a CARICOM Commission. The threat of being dictated to by former politicians perhaps paled in significance to the deteriorating environment of external relations. Initially, former Prime Minister of Barbados, Bernard St John (a trade lawyer), was nominated by the Secretariat for the position of Chief Negotiator. However, in the final stages of establishment, that nomination was rejected by member states, and P.J. Patterson, as Chair of the PMSCEN took the initiative to offer the position to Shridath Ramphal – who had strong credentials in international negotiations as well as a close personal and professional relationship with Patterson, since their involvement in the negotiation of the first Lomé Agreement in 1975. Ramphal, however, had two main conditions for accepting the post. First, he indicated that he would only accept if he was accorded ministerial and not ambassadorial status. Secondly, he requested that he be permitted to report directly to Heads of Government and specifically to Patterson. The Secretariat's initial proposals for appointment of a Chief Negotiator outlined a line of reporting to the PMSCEN, through the Secretary-General. It is conceivable, therefore, that Ramphal's conditions, in addition to being related to his distinguished status, were perhaps also an expression of his disinclination to work closely with, and most certainly not under, the supervision of the Secretary-General.

Perhaps because of their confidence in Patterson's recommendation, or because of the desperation of the external relations situation, or even because of a lack of other suitably qualified candidates, the Heads agreed to Ramphal's conditions and established the Caribbean Regional Negotiating Machinery (CRNM) under his leadership in April 1997. The CRNM was mandated to develop, coordinate and execute a negotiating strategy for the three principal arenas of international negotiations. It was established as a project unit of the Secretariat, but was based in London where Ramphal resided at the time. Although it was not fully independent of national actors or the intergovernmental structures, because it did not have a legal status or position in the hierarchy of CARICOM Organs and Institutions under the Treaty, the CRNM attained increasing levels of autonomy over time. Grant argued that the CRNM was CARICOM's first experiment in supranational governance.[22] However, it is considered, as a quasi-supranational authority, given its legal dependence on governments. Interestingly, it was perhaps the imperatives of mobilising additional financing to support this technical unit which was the determining factor for its establishment as an independent project, rather than as a new Community Institution or Associate Institution under the treaty.

In an awkward turn of events, since the Secretariat had anticipated the appointment of Bernard St John, it had proceeded to hire two Barbados-based experts to support the Chief Negotiator. Bishnodat Persaud, an international economic development specialist, was engaged as the Chief Coordinator and Arnold McIntyre, an economist, as the Technical Adviser. Another technical official, Maurice Odle, was engaged to support the CRNM from the Secretariat in Guyana. The result of the eventual appointment of Ramphal, in London, constituted an unfortunate geographical spread of the institution, which not only tugged at CARICOM's purse strings, but also created complications for administrative processes. When Ramphal was appointed, the Chief Coordinator, Persaud, who had also been a former colleague of Ramphal at the Commonwealth Secretariat, was moved to London. The Technical Advisor, Arnold McIntyre, remained in Barbados to supervise the small technical and administrative unit there. Subsequently, Patterson, to whom the CRNM reported, felt he needed to have a direct link to the institution and so Alister McIntyre, an advisor to the PMSCEN, was appointed as Chief Technical Advisor within the CRNM and installed in an office in Jamaica. Fortunately, the fact that Sir Alister was father of Arnold McIntyre does not appear to have worsened the already clumsy and somewhat incestuous evolution of the new framework.

Later, the CRNM's geographical representation was extended to offices in Geneva and Brussels in order to monitor developments in the WTO and the ACP respectively.

This geographical spread as well as the high profile of its top officials led to the de facto removal of the CRNM from the supervision of the Secretariat and the development of independent administrative machinery to support it. The fact that the CRNM's emerging autonomy and quasi-supranational authority emerged under the leadership of the principal authors of the WIC report (Chairman Ramphal and Deputy Chairman McIntyre) is an irony which cannot be ignored. Grant was certainly correct in arguing that, following the modification of the Secretariat's initial proposals, the CRNM became 'the embodiment of the proposed [CARICOM] Commission' and, in so doing, 'disrupted the equilibrium that existed between sovereignty and regionalism' within Caribbean governance.[23] The evolution of this commission-type structure was allowed by Heads perhaps because the CRNM was expected to be a temporary project. However, given the complexities of international negotiations, the matters under consideration were not concluded swiftly and in fact, the CRNM's tenure extended over a 12-year period towards the end of which the challenges of its unusual evolution were further.

During its first four years, the CRNM and its staff developed a good professional reputation among regional leaders, donors and the international and local media. The working relationships between the CRNM and the PMSCEN functioned smoothly. The negotiation strategies developed by Ramphal's team in 1997 gained ready acceptance by Patterson's PMSCEN.[24] The CRNM was, according to Patterson, a model for developing countries for the management of external economic negotiations.[25] However, the COTED and the COFCOR were completely bypassed in the process of review and approval of strategies. In spite of its technical merits, the withdrawal of the CRNM from the broader regional framework raised specific administrative, jurisdictional and interpersonal problems which led to its eventual restructuring. Firstly, because it was a project, the CRNM lacked independent legal status, thereby hindering its administrative functioning. The Government of Barbados had to assume special fiduciary responsibility for the CRNM, concluding agreements with donors on its behalf.[26] However, this financial arrangement created bureaucratic layers which posed severe problems related to the timely transfer of funds between the Government of Barbados, the CRNM (in all its locations) and the Secretariat for the execution of programmes. At the same time the Secretariat maintained responsibility for issuing the employment contracts for the staff of the CRNM.

The second problem that arose was a confusion of delegated competence between the Secretariat and the CRNM, which catalysed an institutional rivalry over jurisdiction. The CRNM's mandate had been specifically limited to three multilateral negotiating arenas, with the Secretariat retaining responsibility for bilateral negotiations. However, in July 1999, the Heads of Government decided that the CRNM should assist the Secretariat with the CARICOM-Dominican Republic Free Trade Area which they adjudged was progressing unsatisfactorily under the management of CARICOM's administrative machinery. Subsequently, and perhaps as a consequence of the perceived poor performance of the Secretariat, the CRNM was granted sole responsibility for concluding another bilateral agreement – between CARICOM and Cuba – even though the Secretariat retained responsibility for similar negotiations with Costa Rica. These successes drew attention to the CRNM and boosted its reputation.

However, much of the media was drawn to the activities and statements of its high-profile Chief Negotiator, leading to the third problem of interpersonal conflict. This extraordinary recognition was a source of irritation to several senior officials, particularly national ministers serving on the COTED who felt that Sir Shridath Ramphal's persona (and perhaps to a lesser degree Sir Alister McIntyre's) had eclipsed their own contributions to the negotiation process. These tensions reached their climax in 2001 when a few ministers openly voiced their disapproval of what they viewed to be Ramphal's illegitimate assumption of the role of 'minister' at the negotiation table. As a result of deteriorating relationships, Ramphal announced his intention to leave the CRNM before the end of the year. McIntyre had also unexpectedly submitted his resignation as Chief Technical Advisor earlier in the year, perhaps to avoid the foreseen conflict. It was probable that these interpersonal rivalries, more than any other factor, revealed to Heads just how autonomous the structure had become and the extent to which it had evolved out of their direct control. Taking advantage of the opportunity provided by the changes in leadership, the Heads of Government, likely on the prompting of Ministers of Trade and Secretariat officials, mandated the Chair of the PMSCEN to undertake a review of the CRNM. This was the opportunity to restore the balance between sovereignty and regionalism mentioned earlier.

Patterson presented his review to the members of the CHOG in September 2001. It contained four important recommendations for creating greater accountability of the CRNM vis-à-vis Community Organs and for achieving greater efficiency in its internal procedures.[27] Firstly, it proposed the forging of a closer working relationship between the CRNM and the COTED via three Ministerial Spokespersons appointed for each of the three major negotiating arenas. The PMSCEN would consult with the Spokespersons in making decisions only on those proposals received directly from the COTED. Second, it encouraged the strengthening of the CRNM's relationship with the Secretariat to ensure the effective utilisation of resources via the establishment of a tripartite Committee comprising a CRNM Chief Technical Spokesperson, the Secretary-General and the Director-General of the OECS, to coordinate the activities of the three entities. Thirdly, it recommended the adoption of a consultative approach which maximised the involvement of the national stakeholders through Technical Working Groups (TWGs) involving member state, private sector, civil society, academic and Secretariat representatives. Fourth, it proposed that, since the cost of maintaining the structure had evolved to surpass the capacity of member state contributions, the CRNM should be conceptualised as a 'compact entity, well defined and simply structured'.[28] The changes emanating from Patterson's report are represented in figure 6.2.

Patterson also recommended that the posts of Chief Negotiator and Chief Technical Advisor be merged into a single position of a Director-General, who would play a politico-functional role – a political profile with technical negotiating expertise – and be based in Jamaica along with the Chair of the PMSCEN. The office in Kingston became the Headquarters of the CRNM. The Director-General was supported by three Senior Directors

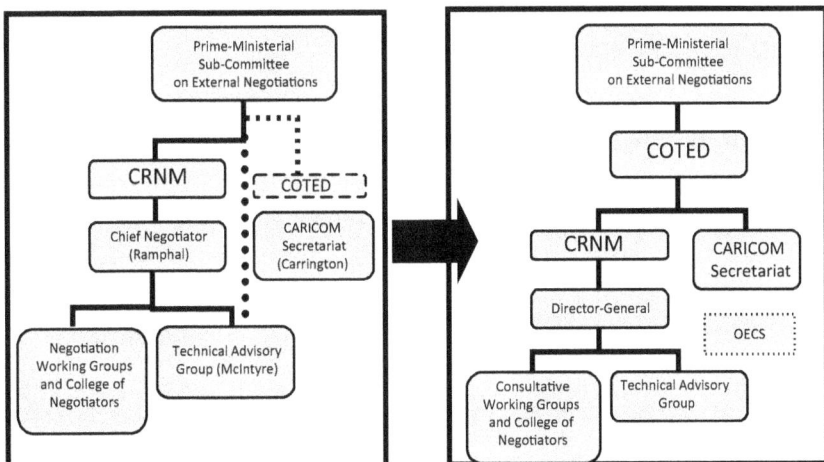

Figure 6.2: Revamping the CRNM

based in Barbados who supervised the three arenas of negotiations under the RNM mandate. The London office was dissolved, but representation was maintained in Washington, Geneva and Brussels pending the completion of various bilateral and multilateral negotiations in those arenas.

So, in essence, Patterson managed to create a simplified and rationalised structural arrangement for the CRNM, while maintaining a certain level of autonomy from the Secretariat with respect to its day-to-day functioning. Following Ramphal's departure in November 2001, Heads appointed Richard Bernal, a former Jamaican Ambassador, to the post of Director-General. After the restructuring, there were fewer meetings of the PMSCEN since all reports went to special sessions of the COTED dedicated to negotiation issues. In effect, Heads had corrected what they perhaps perceived to be an 'error of judgement' on their part, namely, the creation of a quasi-supranational authority which was only marginally connected to the rest of the governance framework. Analytically, the evolution of the CRNM begs the question as to whether experimentation with new models of regional executive authority, including supranationality, had occurred in this period because of changes in leadership occurring in the region. We have already seen the way in which Patterson's thinking influenced the emergence of the CRNM and the Bureau structures.

While Patterson was Chairman of the Conference in 1997, he welcomed two other new Heads of Government – Samuel Hinds of Guyana and Kenny Anthony of St Lucia. The latter's contribution to the opening ceremony suggested a serious approach to resolving issues of governance. Anthony called for a more sincere style of leadership at the regional level: 'a new style of governance in CARICOM requires that we make decisions that are capable of implementation, that we argue and negotiate differences so that the final accord represents not a false, facile concession, but a genuine digestion of division that ultimately produces a decision that envelopes our hopes and dreams'.[29] He continued to reflect on his personal commitment to the integration process, having been an official of the CARICOM Secretariat, and he advocated for better governance when he assumed Chairmanship of the CHOG during CARICOM's 25th Anniversary in 1998.[30] It was also under his Chairmanship that Heads agreed, in principle, to the establishment of the Caribbean Court of Justice (CCJ) – the first fully supranational structure in the regional framework.

## THE CARIBBEAN COURT OF JUSTICE AND
## THE SUPRANATIONAL MODEL

Ten Heads of Government signed the agreement establishing the Caribbean Court of Justice at their Intersessional Meeting in February 2001 in Bridgetown.[31] The signing represented a milestone in two main respects, given the dual jurisdiction of the Court (Article III). The Court represented the first independent dispute settlement mechanism for adjudication of matters relating to the existing Common Market and the proposed CSME. Secondly, it acted as a symbol of the assertion of the Westphalian aspects of national sovereignty by creating an appellate court of last resort for civil and criminal cases, as an alternative to the United Kingdom Judicial Committee of the Privy Council (JCPC). This model of supranational institution-building accorded the CCJ full independence of funding and staffing. Of course, the fact that the CCJ was accorded this level of supranational autonomy is closely linked to the expectations of judicial independence which formed a part of the norms of Caribbean democracy.

A Trust Fund of US$100 million was established, through the channels of the CDB, in order to ensure the Court's independence and sustainability of funding.[32] This financial autonomy was complemented by the establishment of an independent Judicial and Legal Services Commission (Article V of the Agreement) which was responsible for the appointment of up to nine judges. A President of the Court was appointed by Heads. Finally, the Agreement outlined expectations for national compliance with the final decision of the court (Article XV), even though the Revised Treaty of Chaguaramas, which had by that time been completed, identified alternative methods of dispute settlement, including the mediatory role of the Conference, informal ad hoc conciliation committees and adjudication tribunals.[33] Unfortunately, implementation was slow and the Court was not inaugurated for another four years. The adoption of the appellate jurisdiction of the Court was subject to controversial partisan competition, especially in Jamaica and Trinidad and Tobago, and was eventually dropped by most members just before the inauguration of the Court in 2005. Chapter 8 will present the controversy in greater detail – one which demonstrates a failure on the part of Heads of Government to capitalise on the opportunity presented by the creation of a regional court to fully assert national sovereignty.

## LESSONS IN INSTITUTION-BUILDING

CARICOM's experience with institution-building up to 2002 suggested that, outside of the context of the CCJ, a more effective method of delegating authority had not yet been conceived. There were two different explanations offered by politicians, academics and experts for the failure in this area. The first explanation emanated from statements made by the Prime Minister of St Vincent and the Grenadines, Ralph Gonsalves, and corroborated by academics, related to the lack of a value-based ideology to support better governance. It was during the regular meeting of the CHOG in July 2001 in The Bahamas, that Gonsalves posited his views about the kind of values which should underpin the regional integration project. He suggested that the region be conceptualised not as a place for the contestation of sovereignty but as a unique civilisation of people.[34] In essence, Gonsalves seemed to view the debate on delegation of sovereignty in regional governance as premature, given the fact that the fundamental normative issues related to the forging of a common identity had not been settled. His thinking was grounded in a view that, the psychological and personal aspects of the political relationships among Heads had constrained the evolution of good governance practices and that, consequently, the movement needed to be grounded in more progressive ideas. The point of Gonsalves' exposition of the need for a people-based value system – or an ideology of civilisation – was to support his call for the development of a confederal political arrangement between member states in CARICOM, which he felt was the most appropriate institutional modality for supporting the development of a common regional identity among Caribbean people. In the following year, during the 2002 Mona Academic Conference, discussions on governance at the regional level endorsed the concept of a value-based integration process in order to achieve better governance. In particular, Havelock Brewster suggested that 'the poor record of implementation [could not] be wholly due to the inadequate institutional capacity'; rather the problem was that there was 'nothing in the Treaty...that commits states to the essential values of the Caribbean Community'.[35]

The fundamental question raised by these discussions is whether the influence of the political directorate had, by focusing solely on the implications of regionalism for their political power and sovereignty, failed to foster a set of more progressive and regionalist political values which would have supported the development of more effective central machinery for regional regulation. The experiences of institution-building with the

Bureau, Quasi-Cabinet and CRNM in particular give credibility to the view that the process, thus far, had been more about defending national sovereignty rather than defending a regional identity or civilisation.

The second explanation for CARICOM's failure to develop the appropriate method of delegating sovereignty emanated from the completed review which had been commissioned under the 1999 Consensus of Chaguaramas. Submitted in January 2002, The Archer-Gomes Report, like the other studies which had preceded it, provided a historical perspective on the institutional position of the Community.[36] It was frank about the weaknesses in the Secretariat and in member states and about the centrality of the sovereignty paradox to any question of institutional reform in the Community. In its discussion of the Community's institutional arrangements, its decision-making processes and its strategic planning capacity, the reader is struck by the extent to which all the recommendations were hinged on and buttressed by statements which called for the reconceptualisation of the way in which the Community could be empowered with executive authority at the regional level and improved administrative capacity at national levels. The team recognised that, without some indication of the extent to which Heads were amenable to the delegation of meaningful authority to a regional entity, 'the implementation of critical decisions [would] remain haphazard and entirely subject to the favourable and opportune disposition of individual Heads of Government of Member States'.[37] It further noted that:

> ...every decision of Conference is dependent on thirteen independent sovereign decisions in the Member States, and the fact that some Member States act as if the Conference decisions do not obligate them to act nationally is partly responsible for the reality that Conference decisions are rarely implemented in a timely manner.[38]

The analysis was completely accurate. Consequently, the team proposed the 'devolution of executive authority to the appropriate regional body/institution or office without violating principles of sovereignty'.[39] The report, having taken stock of CARICOM's previous experiments in executive institution-building, made two observations about the appropriateness of regional institutions. Firstly, on the one hand, it noted that the structures created by Heads in 1992 – the Bureau and what evolved into the Quasi-Cabinet – were not the appropriate mechanisms. According to the 2002 review, the Bureau placed too much control in the hands of a minority of leaders. Furthermore, the role of the Quasi-Cabinet could not always be substantiated, save within the context of the PMSCEN and in relation to the CSME, which were both appropriately supported by technical arms. In the other areas, the lead Heads had made negligible contributions to the advancement of the aspects of regionalism falling within their portfolio. In that regard, the team proposed that these structures be replaced by specialised Working Groups, involving a broader base of stakeholders, convened on an ad hoc basis to support the implementation process. Secondly, on the other hand, the review team was of the view, like the Gladstone Mills team, that the Secretariat was the most appropriate mechanism for the delegation of executive authority. Eschewing the WIC's proposal for a new Commission, they suggested that since the Secretary-General had already been accorded executive authority under the Revised Treaty, he was already positioned to play the role. However, the team also acknowledged that the treaty had positioned the Secretariat as an Administrative Organ. The contradiction of these provisions signalled a level of determination that the Secretariat remained a non-sovereignty-violating entity. In fact, the exercise of the Secretary-General's executive authority was 'dependent on the consent of Member states, which effectively neutralise[d] the executive power accorded to the Office of the Secretary General in the Protocol'.[40] This created a level of ambivalence about the *de jure* administrative-executive authority of the Secretary-General but de facto absolute authority of Heads of Government.

In that regard, the Archer-Gomes team argued that the Secretariat should be restyled as the principal Administrative and Implementation Support Organ of the Community and that a Secretariat Executive Council (SEC) be established as the mechanism to exercise the authority for implementation delegated from Heads. The SEC would be composed of the Secretary-General, Deputy Secretary-General and four Assistant Secretaries-General and the General Counsel, all having ambassadorial rank, who would advance implementation by instituting, pending the establishment of the CCJ, fines for non-compliance; and by facilitating the harmonisation of national policies, the abolition of internal tariff barriers, state subsidies and other restrictive measures which would hamper the CSME. The most interesting aspect of the proposal for the SEC was the team's assertion that it would exercise a 'regional governance' function. The insertion of this term for the first time in the Community's official vocabulary signalled, if not least from the perspective of the consultants, a need for a paradigm shift from intergovernmental cooperation to the full governance of a regional integration entity. The SEC would be supported by an administrative arm, the Senior Management Committee (SMC), which would be chaired by the Deputy Secretary-General and include Directors appointed as heads of the six directorates within the Secretariat and responsible for the administrative management of the Community's work programme. The SEC would therefore operate at a political level and the SMC at an administrative level.

Those proposals were hinged on the need for appropriate physical accommodations for the Secretariat, including a significantly enhanced communication technology capacity which would enable closer working relationships with other regional and sub-regional structures. Interestingly, although Heads had cautioned in March 2000 that no relocation of the Secretariat would be considered, the team recommended the decentralisation of some Secretariat operations in order to promote a measure of national ownership of regional processes. They were keen to ensure, however, that any such decentralisation would not follow the same confusing path experienced by the CRNM.

Another imperative for change at the regional level identified by the team was for improvement in the decision-making processes of the Community. It identified a need for the insertion of concepts of participation and partnership in the decision-making process. In that regard, it proposed an enlarged role for the ACCP – manifested by more frequent meetings on issues of Community relevance and informed by properly researched papers and national level Parliamentary discussions. In addition, it proposed the formation of a Consultative Committee on Civil Society as a part of the COHSOD and supported by the Directorate for Human and Social Development which would also feed into the ACCP. The team further argued for increased decision-making by ministerial Councils and the suspension of the practice of deferring decisions in order to refer matters to the attention of the CHOG. It concurred with the weaknesses identified by Pollard in 1985 and suggested that the decision-making and implementation processes would benefit from a more strategic approach to planning and the determination of priorities which would be best served by a greater level of collaboration between the CCS and other regional institutions, including the OECS.

The team also proposed that the Community seek to develop the appropriate mechanisms at the national level to support the implementation process. It noted that Jamaica had set an example with the appointment of a Technical Director and the establishment of business and labour consultative mechanisms to support the Minister with responsibility for CARICOM Affairs. However, the fact that the designated Minister for CARICOM Affairs was also the Minister of Foreign Affairs brought its own challenges in relation to the preference for prioritisation of international over regional matters.

In sum, the two explanations for the continued gap in central executive authority – the politically-charged values-based argument and the technical assessment of weak regional governance institutions – are not mutually exclusive. In fact, they both highlighted two sides of the central challenge in CARICOM governance. The framework had suffered not simply from a lack of ideology but from the fact that one ideational principle – sovereignty – was so highly valued and closely associated with the power of the leaders that it had stifled the development of effective institutions for regional governance. So both were right in acknowledging that the movement needed to shift to a people-based understanding of sovereignty and consequently accept the need to bargain with it in order to develop the appropriate institutional expressions.

Between 1997 and 2002, CARICOM made several attempts to prepare a suitable governance framework for implementation of the CSME. The legislative framework for regional integration was revised, the delegation of executive authority was attempted in three different ways, and arrangements for increased consultation in decision-making were strengthened. It would be fair to say that, at the end of 2002 CARICOM's capacity for decision-making had significantly improved but, not adequately to have secured implementation of the new objective.

That period of institution-building reveals some interesting implications for governance and for sovereignty within a CSME framework. Firstly, with respect to decision-making, the significance of strengthening consultation in order to ensure that decisions taken at the regional level were truly reflective of a consensus borne out of consideration of the diversity of views of various actors in the 15 member states. Pollard identified an important link between implementation and consultation as a feature of effective governance. He noted that: 'more often than not, implementation paralysis is a function of inadequate consultations prior to the taking of determinations resulting in uninformed and oftentimes unimplementable [sic] decisions'.[41] The Treaty provisions on the Consultative Process, the Charter of Civil Society and the Forward Together process represented important attempts to forge that better balance between efficient decision-making and effective implementation. Unfortunately, the lack of enforcement mechanisms did not result in the full operationalisation of the consultative framework.

Secondly, with respect to implementation capacity, it was important, especially to the political directorate, to maintian as much control as possible over institutions and the maintenance of an acceptable equilibrium between sovereignty and regionalism. This did not work. The Prime-Ministerial/Presidential models of executive representation did not delegate effective authority for implementation. Delegated authority at the level of the regional deliberative fora did not extend to intervention within member states. These Head of Government structures suffered as a result of this and also because representatives were often not supported by full-time staff dedicated to execution. The perpetuation of this model over the years – from the Bureau in 1993 to an enhanced Quasi-Cabinet model in 2000 – rather that their transformation into truly executive structures, also demonstrates the control complex over regional decision-making as typical of the 'commandist' style of statehood.[42] Edwin Jones's summation of governance in CARICOM was that of a system based on the 'delimitation on decisional authority, a political style reliant on symbolism and ambivalence, slowness to move on 'agreement in principle' to action'.[43]

On the other hand, the imperative of effectiveness in a technical capacity was sufficient to secure agreement among the leadership to experiment with delegation of actual authority for implementation, though intended to be on a temporary basis. The CRNM, as the first quasi-supranational structure in CARICOM, held significant potential for transforming the regional architecture. Its autonomy facilitated its effectiveness in many instances, particularly in its ability to draw on independent technical expertise to fulfil its mandate. However, the lack of coherence between this new structure and existing structures created a measure of instability in the regional system. The need for appropriate oversight of regional executive bodies has been a key lesson from that experience.

Thirdly, the creation of a supranational structure for dispute settlement was an indispensable element of CSME regulation. The emergence of the CCJ as a truly supranational (fully independent and autonomous) entity was a milestone in the history of CARICOM institutional development. The development of an independent and sustainable source of financing for the structure was an important lesson from that experience. At the same time, its evolution seems atypical, given the lack of governmental control over the entity. We have already established the necessity of independence in the judiciary as a principle of governance, but the extent of its autonomy is unusual. However, given the fact that the CSM would not be inaugurated for another five years, the Court posed no immediate threat to national sovereignty, since there were no treaty disputes to adjudicate. The more threatening role of the Court, that is, its appellate jurisdiction, was effectively dissolved by national partisan wrangling which prevented member states from fully asserting a fundamental principle of Westphalian sovereignty.

Finally, throughout our discussion of the evolution of the structures of governance, we have seen that other circumstantial factors related to the broader political context have impinged on the emergence of an effective institutional framework. In particular, the prominent influence of individual leaders on the direction of the movement has been notable. In many cases, Heads of Government and regional technocrats have left their personal stamp on the regional framework. Indeed, this is in keeping with the definition of sovereignty – as a personal sovereignty – which has been emerging from this discussion thus far. Changes in the global political economy also precipitated change in the case of the CRNM. The effective functioning of institutions has often been affected by the extent to which their purpose is fully appreciated by all those they serve. In that sense, all the institutions created for the CSME were predicated on the assumption of some level of commitment, on behalf of the Caribbean citizen, to the preservation of a common CARICOM identity and the attendant desire to sustain the regional movement. The relevance of the sovereignty paradox – the tug of war between national control and regional action – is hinged on the extent to which the regional project reflected a popular solution to the region's development challenges. A modest postgraduate study at the UWI, in fact, indicated a difference between older and younger Caribbean people in their views of integration – the older having largely positive attitudes but the youth being largely apathetic and having stronger attachments to national identities. However, more educated respondents, irrespective of nationality and age, seemed to have greater support for integration.[44] An apparent loss of faith in the CARICOM regional integration process has from time to time been evident in the intermittent calls for other regional cooperative arrangements, whether a Barbados-OECS confederation (à la Owen Arthur), a wider Caribbean political confederation (à la Gonsalves) or even the full political union which Havelock Brewster continued to advocate.[45] Although Heads met in 2002, against the background of a widened Community with admittance of Haiti as the second non-Anglophone and first Francophone member, a Revised Treaty, a Charter of Civil Society and an agreement for a CCJ, fundamental concerns remained about the extent to which the institutional framework reflected a commitment to regional integration and to CARICOM as the appropriate vehicle for that process.[46] Both Prime Minister Patrick Manning of Trinidad and Tobago and President Bharat Jagdeo of Guyana were concerned about the financing and human resource servicing of regional institutions.[47] As Chairman of the CHOG, Jagdeo was troubled by the costs of erratic institution-building: 'Far too often we create institutions that become self-perpetuating although they have lost their effectiveness. Our fiscal situation does not permit institutional luxuries. We must therefore rationalise these bodies, and by doing so, we may locate the resources to support those that serve us well'[48].

In the new millennium, it was becoming apparent, not least to the academic community, that in the context of global trends, less emphasis was being placed on formal sovereignty and greater emphasis on enhancing sovereignty through developing greater capacity development action. [49] The experiments with delegating authority in the preceding period and the consequent implications for the sovereignty paradox precipitated a further series of Caribbean studies, specifically focused on 'regional governance' as a political concept, in an attempt to outline new options for sharing sovereignty in a regional framework. Those quests to understand sovereignty and the implications for regional governance gave rise to proposals for the development of a regional policy on the exercise of sovereignty and the reform of the governance framework.

# SHARED SOVEREIGNTY AND REGIONAL GOVERNANCE POLICY

The milestone celebration of CARICOM's thirtieth Anniversary, held in 2003 under the theme 'Integration: Our Key to Prosperity', was tempered by the worrying levels of institutional dysfunctionality which remained unresolved by the first generation change to the legislative and institutional framework. That context stimulated a process of re-evaluation of the relationship between state sovereignty and regional integration in pursuit of innovative modalities of 'regional governance', appropriate to the goals of a 30-year-old movement. Consequently, over a six-year period between 2003 and 2009, an agenda for governance reform emerged as the focal point of the discourse on Caribbean regionalism. That policy agenda is analysed here as an introduction to a complementary discussion in chapter 8 of a second generation of change during the same period. This chapter, therefore, examines the evolution of new interpretations of sovereignty, beginning with the emergence of the concept of 'shared sovereignty' emanating from official and academic contributions to the regionalism discourse. It further explains how the concept guided the process of setting an agenda for reform, through the formulation of further 'expert' recommendations for a more effective policy and institutional framework for CARICOM. The chapter concludes with a brief commentary on the potential for implementation of a new policy on regional governance reform.

## INTRODUCING 'REGIONAL GOVERNANCE' THREE DECADES LATER

After the introduction of the concept of 'regional governance' in the 2002 Archer-Gomes report, a debate was formally introduced within the Caribbean regionalism discourse via three principal channels. Firstly, a series of seven distinguished lectures presented the goal of advancing a civilization of Caribbean people as the ideological basis for regional governance. Secondly, various members of the academic community discussed the influence of the prevailing sovereignty tradition to the process of institutional advancement and the achievement of development goals. Thirdly, a consultation between CARICOM governments and regional social partners discussed the future direction of CARICOM governance. The contributions made by each of those three discussions to the redefinition of the sovereignty-regionalism nexus, inherent in the emerging concept of 'regional governance', are reviewed in this section.

The thirtieth anniversary lecture, delivered in February 2003 by Ralph Gonsalves, Prime Minister of St Vincent and the Grenadines and Chairman of the OECS, set the framework for the entire reinterpretation exercise. Gonsalves used the opportunity to urge the adoption of his previously highlighted concept of 'Caribbean Civilisation' as the ideological framework for deepening the integration process. Consequently, he argued for the establishment of political, rather than merely economic or functional, institutions to sustain it:

> It makes little sense for us to...dump into CARICOM and the OECS Secretariats a host of additional functional cooperation tasks without the means or the political superstructure to match. Integration has never been, and will never be, a series of technical functions. It is a profoundly political exercise. It is escapism and irresponsibility not to so acknowledge this in practice. It is for this reason basically, [that] the CSME and other regional initiatives or mechanisms are faltering.[1]

However, his remarks also implied an appreciation of the fact that a full re-engagement with the politics of regionalism demanded sovereignty concessions in relation to state authority and control. In that regard, he argued that, although the majority of his fellow colleague Heads of Government were committed regionalists, they were in fact imprisoned by the 'ghosts of the past' (which may very well be interpreted as a reference to the Federal legacy) and by electoral imperatives which drew them away from making the requisite sovereignty bargains and towards territorial nationalism instead. Gonsalves therefore proposed the adoption of a flexible approach to developing political institutions which would accommodate varying types and levels of regionalism within a unified Caribbean civilisation. Accordingly, some states, most specifically Trinidad and Tobago and the members of the OECS, which were prepared to make greater concessions, could consider moving towards deeper models of political integration, while still maintaining economic and functional relationships with other CARICOM states.[2]

Gonsalves' proposal for a new political and ideological foundation for integration resonated with the other six distinguished lecturers who emphasised the roles of a new generation of political institutions in advancing the cultural and human developmental aspects of a Caribbean civilisation. Compton Bourne suggested that institutions extend beyond the functional, economic and foreign policy objectives of the Community to embrace the preservation of regional kinship and unity. In a similar vein, the then University of the West Indies (UWI) Vice-Chancellor, Rex Nettleford, and Jamaica's Minister of Education, Youth and Culture, Maxine Henry-Wilson, argued that regional institutions should promote the bonds of that unity – the region's culture and human resources. As another lecturer, Pro-Vice Chancellor and Principal of the UWI St Augustine Campus, Bhoendradatt Tewarie, argued, it was only in such a context, that CARICOM states would be able to achieve international competitiveness.[3] Those ideas certainly recall the advocacies of the New World Group members, particularly William Demas and Lloyd Best, in relation to the education and empowerment of the Caribbean citizen.[4] The lectures also outlined a role for integrative institutions in encouraging participatory governance at the national level while also fostering coherence among governance mechanisms at the regional level.[5]

However, it was perhaps the seventh and final lecture, delivered by P.J. Patterson to members of the Caribbean Diaspora in New York in October 2003, which best consolidated the themes of the entire lecture series. In his presentation, entitled 'Towards the Further Enhancement of Caribbean Civilisation', Patterson minimised the significance of territorial borders in relation to the emerging transnational space for development. He asserted: 'The 'people' boundaries of CARICOM are not confined to the physical boundaries of our regional homelands. The living boundaries of CARICOM are to be found wherever CARICOM nationals or their progeny reside and work'.[6] Beyond the obvious affirmation of the significance of the Diaspora to Caribbean development, Patterson's remarks also reflected a subtle politico-intellectual shift in thinking about the parameters for development. In fact, his observations seemed to challenge the relevance of holding unswervingly to Westphalian notions of sovereignty within a context of globalised development. Conceivably, hidden within his remarks was an understanding that, since the raison d'être of the CARICOM Single market and Economy (CSME) was based on processes of globalisation and regionalisation which encouraged intra and extra-regional migration of

Caribbean people and the harnessing of their transnational skills in the development process, then, the establishment of transnational regulatory capacity, via better regional institutions, would have to become a priority.

Fortuitously, in the same year, this theme of transnational boundaries was similarly reflected in the work of UWI academics on the Cave Hill campus who were exploring the future of sovereignty and self-determination within the context of globalisation. Cynthia Barrow-Giles and Don Marshall argued that the reconfiguration of the attributes of sovereignty was an imperative for regional development.[7] A warning delivered by Barrow-Giles in a speech on the occasion of St Lucia's twentieth independence anniversary in February 2003 is noteworthy. She argued that 'the idea and practice of absolute sovereignty', – interpreted as the traditional conception of sovereignty, – based on complete state authority, were 'even more tattered, more bruised, more bloodied than a decade ago and a lot more tarnished than in the decade of the 1970s'.[8] That fact had not escaped the attention of other thinkers. Compton Bourne postulated that sovereignty, beyond its limited juridical meaning, was a mere illusion for small Caribbean states within the era of globalisation.[9] Therefore, as Havelock Brewster again argued, in remarks which coincided with the Gonsalves lecture, the CSME required more than mere institutional strengthening, but rather political conviction about the need to move beyond intergovernmental cooperation and towards the delegation of authority to supranational actors, based on a reconfiguration of sovereignty.[10] Accordingly, Barrow-Giles proposed an interesting contextual framework from which such conviction might arise. She advised that 'Caribbean states [should] respond, not by compressing the idea of the nation-state, but by adopting a more flexible, far broader approach to nationalism, in the direction of the regional. Regional nationalism is preferable to subjugation and re-colonisation'.[11] That assertion, in early 2003, evoked the same logic of West Indian Nationalism which had prompted leaders such as Marryshow and Cipriani initially, followed by Manley and Williams, and then Demas, Ramphal and McIntyre, and to some extent Gonsalves, to make the case for exercising nationalism and sovereignty within a regional institutional framework – whether, in the form of federation, free trade area or economic community. Barrow-Giles developed the point further:

> National identity, then, is capable of being manifested in different
> political clothing at different historical moments....Identity politics
> can be used and manipulated as a vehicle for the expressed purpose

of achieving national consciousness and sovereignty....Regionalism must be seen as perhaps a last bid attempt to preserve what little sovereignty is left of nation-states like ours.[12]

The foregoing lectures, studies and reflective remarks thus presented political leaders with an opportunity in 2003 to develop a form of regional identity politics capable of fostering a new conception of sovereignty which accommodated both the national and regional consciousness of a Caribbean civilisation. Against that background, Heads of Government engaged in a special consultation with social partners on specific institutional options for regional governance reform.

That consultation, hosted by Trinidad and Tobago's Prime Minister, Patrick Manning, was convened in February 2003 ahead of the Intersessional Meeting of the CHOG. In order to stimulate the discussion, Manning presented a paper, prepared with advisory support from the UWI St Augustine entitled: 'Options and Strategies for CARICOM in the Area of Governance for Caribbean Regional Integration'; while the Prime Minister of Barbados, Owen Arthur, presented another analysis entitled: 'Shifting the Rubicon: New Governance and the CARICOM Single Market and Economy', prepared in consultation with the Cave Hill campus. Interestingly, the two papers offered divergent views about the pace at which the integration movement should proceed and on the extent of ambition which should be ascribed to institutional development. Manning's paper suggested that the CSME could be implemented within a year by investing the requisite enforcement and executive authority in the Secretariat. In contrast, Arthur's discourse suggested that a Commission structure, as proposed by the WIC in 1992, was the preferred modality which should be complemented by national representation to CARICOM Councils. It is likely that the discussions of these proposals was as challenging as had been the discussion of the divergent proposals put forward by Mills et al., by the WIC and by Archer, Gomes et al. Some of the social partners urged the acceptance of Arthur's proposal for a Commission; while some Heads rallied around Manning's more moderate proposal for empowerment of the Secretariat; and the rest remained wary of the implications of both options for their sovereignty. Ultimately, no agreement was reached on the proposals and consequently, when the matter was further discussed at the Fourteenth Intersessional Meeting of the CHOG, the Heads of Government found themselves re-engaging in a protracted debate on whether to pursue full-scale political integration or to focus on strengthening existing instruments of economic integration.[13] The failure to reach consensus on the divergent options before them prompted the CHOG, almost automatically and quite predictably, to establish yet another group of experts – on this occasion, a Prime-Ministerial Expert Group on Governance (PMEGG) chaired by Gonsalves – to consider the proposals from the consultation and the Intersessional meeting. The Prime Ministers of Antigua and Barbuda, Barbados, Jamaica and Trinidad and Tobago as well as experts, including Shridath Ramphal, were co-opted to support Gonsalves. The Group was mandated to examine options for institutional strengthening and for pursuing alternative modes of governance, including political integration. The decision to form a Prime-Ministerial group, rather than a group of technocrats, as had hitherto been the custom, is particularly interesting since it buttressed the tradition of direct Head of Government control which had been evident in other areas of decision-making. At the same time, it also created an opportunity for the formulation of a policy framework for governance reform to guide any eventual strategy for institutional improvements that might be developed by technical experts. In that regard, the nomination of Gonsalves as Chair of the PMEGG, in lieu of Kenny Anthony in his capacity as Quasi-Cabinet lead on governance, was more likely influenced by Gonsalves' novel approach to the governance problematic enunciated in his lecture on Caribbean civilisation – an approach which would have inspired elder statesmen like Manning, Arthur and Patterson, to endorse the appointment in view of their desire for resolution of the debate.

## The Political Agenda for Governance Reform

The PMEGG benefitted from a continuation of the debate amongst the Heads of Government at their 23rd Conference at Rose Hall, Montego Bay, Jamaica. The resulting declaration outlined the conceptual framework for a policy on reform which was subject to comprehensive academic analysis in the ensuing months. The PMEGG then sought to interpret and consolidate the official and academic contributions into an agenda for governance reform. These three commentaries on sovereignty and governance – that is, the Rose Hall Declaration, the academic analyses and the recommendations of the PMEGG – are discussed below.

The passing of the chairmanship baton from Prime Minister Pierre Charles of Dominica to Prime Minister P.J. Patterson at the Rose Hall Conference in July 2003 facilitated the presentation of a third Prime-Ministerial paper on the future of the movement. Patterson solicited the advice of experts, particularly Professor Denis Benn of UWI Mona and Roderick Rainford, in the preparation of a 'Chairman's Perspective' on the future of the integration movement. Although Patterson was reluctant to duplicate the work entrusted to the PMEGG, of which he was a member, he evidently felt compelled, in light of the rather conflicting contributions made by Manning and Arthur earlier in the year, to exert his influence on the emerging agenda. The 'Chairman's Perspective' argued for a distinction to be made between matters 'crystallised into regional consciousness which [could] be fast-tracked to implementation and those that require[d] a consciousness-raising initiative'.[14] He argued that the inauguration of the Caribbean Court of Justice (CCJ), in both its original and appellate jurisdictions, should be fast-tracked as a matter of self-respect and judicial sovereignty. At the same time, he viewed political union as a longer-term initiative which required greater levels of public sensitisation.

In the interim, Patterson proposed that 'the leadership and people of the region should explicitly accept that for the foreseeable future the Community [would] operate as an association of states exercising sovereignty individually and collectively and without prejudice to sub-groupings of the membership entering into political integration or other forms of closer association among themselves if they so desire'.[15] That statement reflected a level of firm support for the kind of flexibility proposed in the Gonsalves lecture. In the context of Patterson's proposed arrangement, national sovereignty as an expression of political authority and regionalism as a development strategy were not treated as mutually exclusive, since the former had the potential to be exercised both collectively and individually within the regional arena. Against the background of Patterson's contextual proposal, the PMEGG presented to the Rose Hall Summit an initial opinion that the development of a supranational Commission, rather than an enhanced Secretariat, was the best option for future governance.[16] Patterson cautioned, however, that careful consideration should be given to the explicit definition of relationships between such a commission and existing intergovernmental CARICOM structures – a lesson he had undoubtedly learned from the challenges of incoherence which had arisen from the informal emergence of the Caribbean Regional Negotiating Machinery (CRNM) in 1997.[17]

The Chairman's intervention and the opinion of the PMEGG prompted the Conference's adoption of the Rose Hall Declaration on Regional Governance and Integrated Development, which signalled an intention to develop a system of regional governance, supported by institutions vested with executive authority to implement the goals of an integrated regional economy.[18] The integrated development policy framework outlined in the latter part of the Rose Hall Declaration included commitments to the involvement of the social partners in regional development processes. However, the spirit of commitment to developing political authority beyond the nation-state, via the concept of the collective exercise of sovereignty, was drastically altered in the provisions recorded in the Declaration itself. The Declaration affirmed that regional integration would continue to proceed within the political and juridical context of a 'Community of Sovereign States'. This elevation of the sovereign state to the position of raison d'être of the Community, without qualifying its role as one of exercising sovereignty both collectively and individually, in fact undermined the ensuing four 'agreements in principle' to institutional reform summarised in figure 7.1.

The first agreement was to develop a legislative framework for 'mature regionalism' in which decisions at the regional level assumed the force of law in each member state. Although the provision was primarily intended to recognise the authority of the CCJ to enforce the rules of the single market and economy, the sovereign state clause curtailed the judicial authority of the CCJ by prohibiting judgments which could be perceived to be in conflict with national constitutional provisions. The terminology was broad enough to allow for the widest possible interpretation of constitutional conflict. The second agreement 'in principle' was to extend executive competency to a regional mechanism, perhaps to be called a CARICOM Commission, to exercise full-time responsibility for implementation of decisions on the CSME. As obtained with the CCJ, the guiding principle of state sovereignty dictated that this new mechanism would have to be directly accountable to each member state, via the Conference and ministerial Organs. Evidently, it was intended that the regional executive should remain within an intergovernmental framework since there was no reference to supranationality. Thirdly, the Conference agreed 'in principle' to develop mechanisms for the automatic transfer of financial resources from member states to support new regional governance mechanisms,

**Figure 7.1: Rose Hall Pillars of Regional Governance**

| Legislative | Executive | Administrative | Deliberative |
|---|---|---|---|
| Regional Decisions Enforced at National Level | Regional Mechanism for Implementation of Decisions | Adequate Financing of Institutions | Improved Parliamentary Representation |

including the executive body and a reformed Secretariat. It is remarkable that Heads arrived at this decision to intrude on national budgets, given their longstanding assertion of state sovereignty. However, to have omitted a proposal on the sustainability of financing would not only have signalled a complete disregard of expert opinions on the matter (from Mills et al. onwards) but would also have rendered the maintenance of a Commission unfeasible. Finally, the Conference agreed, equally 'in principle', to strengthen the role of the Assembly of Caribbean Community Parliamentarians (ACCP) in the regional decision-making process, though again, only in relation to matters outside national jurisdiction. The Declaration acknowledged that the four proposed changes would necessitate the rationalisation of existing Organs and Institutions to achieve the requisite level of systematic coherence for governance of a 'mature regionalism' and therefore called for a further review of the functions of existing functional Institutions, which was completed in 2006 and is discussed in chapter 8, as a part of the discussions on institutional change.

In light of the aforementioned issues, the assertion of a 'Community of (absolutely) Sovereign States', on the one hand, and the agreement to the four proposed institutional innovations and particularly the regional Commission, on the other hand, appear incongruous. Fortunately, the unravelling and resolution of the contradictions was facilitated by the Declaration's appointment of three technical sub-groups of the PMEGG to develop specific modalities for, firstly, revision of the legislative framework and establishment of a Commission; secondly, the strengthening of the ACCP; and thirdly, the financing of regional institutions. Stalwarts of the regional integration process re-emerged to design yet another proposal for institutional reform. Shridath Ramphal chaired the sub-group on the Commission which also included former Secretary-General and WIC member, Roderick Rainford, and legal expert Cuthbert Joseph. Denis Benn, who had participated in other groups of experts, chaired the sub-group on strengthening the ACCP. Finally, another former Secretary-General and Deputy Chairman of the WIC, Alister McIntyre, joined the sub-group on automaticity of financing which was chaired by CDB President Compton Bourne, who had also chaired the 1988 group of experts that prepared the report on Caribbean development up to the new millennium. The Rose Hall Declaration and the ongoing work of these three technical sub-groups sustained the emerging academic interest in the concept of 'regional governance' and its relevance to the CARICOM context, thereby creating a common agenda among official and academic stakeholders in developing the agenda for reform.

## ACADEMIC ANALYSIS OF SOVEREIGNTY AND REGIONALISM

In the weeks following the adoption of the Rose Hall Declaration, Havelock Brewster reviewed its provisions, concluding that, while the Declaration implied a willingness on the part of Heads of Government to move beyond a purely intergovernmental governance framework, the principle of a 'Community of Sovereign States' was inappropriate and redundant. In that regard, he argued that the absence of such terminology from the Revised Treaty of Chaguaramas constituted proof that 'pure sovereignty' had not been intended as the only political and juridical context in which the CSME should proceed. Rather, returning to the concept developed by Patterson, he felt that other contexts for implementation of the CSME could include 'the deliberate exercise of sovereignty collectively, when so desired by the member states for specific purposes; and the incremental acquisition of supranational qualities through a variety of means'. For Brewster, 'integration among States [was] better represented as a continuum along a path of intergovernmentalism and supranationalism. Progression along that path [was] not necessarily, and always by means of premeditated acts of suppressing national sovereignty'.[19]

The value of Brewster's reflection on the relationship between deepening integration and more advanced governance lies in its explicit association of supranationalist forms of governance with the collective exercise of sovereignty, rather than the complete suppression of sovereignty. Therefore, in a mature system of governance states would use an intergovernmental decision-making process to exercise sovereignty as a collective, by defining the parameters for some supranational mechanism to exercise authority legitimately in execution of the CSME strategy. At the same time, individual states would maintain control over matters not central to the regional agenda. Brewster was concerned that without such a framework, an executive Commission, placed within an intergovernmental framework, that is, under the unqualified authority of the Conference, would not function effectively. Indeed, there had been no precedent of the Conference delegating full authority to a regional mechanism – save temporarily to the CRNM and in theory to the CCJ. Furthermore, existing Organs, to which the Commission would be expected to respond, often did not exercise the authority accorded to them under the treaty, preferring to refer matters to the CHOG, where the unanimous voting procedures ultimately rendered the framework vulnerable to stalemate. In the context of that eventuality, Brewster argued, prophetically, that implementation of automatic financing, on which the Commission would be dependent, was unlikely to materialise.[20]

The discussion of the relationship between sovereignty and supranationalism continued at a UWI Conference at Mona on Regional Governance and Integrated Development held in October 2003.[21] The anniversary colloquium, held over 12 days, provided a wide range of perspectives on three aspects of the regional governance problematic. Firstly, there was discussion of the influence of sovereignty on traditional Caribbean understandings of regional governance. Secondly, the participants deliberated on the national political foundations of CARICOM. Thirdly, they debated proposals for reforming the regional institutional framework. The principal ideas emerging from the conference in relation to these three themes are discussed here only briefly.

First, the academic symposium grappled with the meaning of sovereignty and regional governance. The traditional political discourse had suggested, up to that point, that sovereignty and supranationalism were completely irreconcilable. Since the emergence of regionalism in the West Indies, integration had been maintained on the basis of a minimalist pattern of governance, marked by a 'conscious avoidance of the derogation of sovereignty and the reining of the concept of supra-national governance' in an attempt to retain 'a balance between sovereignty and integration'.[22] It is against the background of that legacy that Assistant Secretary-General Edward Greene, a former political scientist at UWI, sought to develop a new language for Caribbean regional governance. Instead of using language associated with the surrender or transfer of sovereignty and the establishment of supranational authority, Greene spoke explicitly to the reconfiguration of sovereignty. With the exception of a federation, which Greene correctly excluded as a viable option for the foreseeable future, the traditional jargon of supranationality was replaced by references to 'pooled sovereignty' in a common market model and 'shared sovereignty' in the multinational model that Greene associated with the CSME. This 'shared sovereignty' concept later became the guiding framework for the agenda on governance reform. Essentially, Greene's argument accommodated the Chairman's Perspective which had suggested that a deeper (multinationalist) integration process should not preclude the existence of a 'community of [juridically] sovereign states', but would require the sharing of some elements of state sovereignty with regional institutions. This 'shared sovereignty' solution to the paradox would allow states to maintain authority through the Organs, to choose the most appropriate means of implementation – whether national or regional (based on the principle of subsidiarity) and to retain freedom from excessive or unnecessary intervention from regional authority (based on the principle of proportionality) – the latter two principles having emerged from the European experience.[23] However, regional institutions would not be constrained in the exercise of the authority mandated to them under a regional legal framework. A summary of Greene's approach to linking models of integration with different sovereignty configurations is reflected in table 7.2.[24] It is interesting that Greene's proposed institutions of shared sovereignty were in fact akin to supranational institutions and could easily have been nominated as such in a different political context. Notwithstanding the semantics, Greene's contribution to the discussion on reconfiguring sovereignty into a shared framework provided a good basis for the conference to discuss the weaknesses inherent in the national foundations of CARCIOM, which had also impeded its effectiveness.

### Figure 7.2: Integration and Sovereignty

| Type of Integration | Type of Sovereignty |
| --- | --- |
| Federalist (Political Union) | Supranationality: Vertical transfer of sovereignty from constituent states to central sovereign state. |
| Functional (CARIFTA) | Community of Sovereign States: Limited sovereign rights from constituent member states to a regional authority for specific social and economic activities. National sovereignty remains intact. |
| Transactional (Common Market) | Pooled Sovereignty in specific areas: delegation of state sovereignty in economic and social areas to regional institutions for implementing a common agenda. Maintaining the principle of a Community of Sovereign States but striving towards integration of structures. |
| Multinational (CSME) | Shared Sovereignty: A fusion of functional and transactional types of integration (with optional inclusion of political union) operating on the basis of Community Law under the original jurisdiction of the CCJ. Sovereignty exercised individually and collectively. |

The second theme addressed by the UWI Conference was the national foundations of CARICOM politics and governance. Political scientist Trevor Munroe warned that any institutional innovations proposed under the emerging reform agenda would rest on 'foundations of sand unless the pace, the breadth and the depth of transformation of governance at the national level [was] accelerated, consolidated and linked in positive ways with rationalisation [of regional institutions]'.[25] Improvements were necessary in partnership-building and power-sharing; enhancement of national integrity systems, particularly in criminal justice; transparency and accountability; and renewal of national and regional identity. Munroe concluded:

> 'Reconceptualise the Region' we must, but simultaneously let us transform the national systems of governance, so our people can develop the levels of satisfaction that allow them at the same time to go to the next tier – regionalism, so that they can remove themselves from levels of dissatisfaction which encourage them to view the regional projects with scepticism, cynicism and indeed, in pockets, with hostility.[26]

The latter assessment of the popular view of integration highlighted the fact that the national foundations of CARICOM were essentially the human foundations of CARICOM. In that regard, sociologist Ian Boxill explained that Caribbean people viewed regional structures as direct reflections of ineffective national structures of governance. By way of example, he argued that Jamaican opposition to the CCJ's appellate jurisdiction (an issue discussed in chapter 8) did not emerge from an unqualified dislike of regional structures but out of an expectation that it was likely to become a supranational extension of unjust national politics.[27] In that regard, regional institutions were viewed as symbols of poor national governance which shrouded the few national successes (for example, in music and sports), for which Caribbean people, and not just their governments, had received international acclaim.

In fact, a small study on Jamaican perceptions of the CSME conducted by the Sir Arthur Lewis Istitute of Social and Economic Studies (SALISES), Mona corroborated the statements on the lack of public confidence in formal institutions of governance, showing very low levels of public identification with the formal institutions of integration including the CSME, CRNM, CCJ and ACCP. At the same time, however, the respondents showed significant support for characteristics of regional integration such as free movement of skilled persons and a single currency.[28] These preceding observations by Munroe, Boxill and SALISES suggest that the reconfiguration of the concept of sovereignty becomes relevant only in light of its value, in practical terms, to the ordinary Caribbean citizen. Whatever new understanding is developed must ensure a practical application to popular aspirations for the achievement of socio-economic development. Having explored the national context of governance, the Mona conference turned finally to specific proposals for institutional change in the Community.

Thirdly, the conference provided an opportunity for members of the PMEGG to outline their initial recommendations for preventing, as some members perceived it, a level of regression in the regional movement.[29] Cuthbert Joseph outlined a proposal for bridging the divide between national and regional levels of governance by way of developing a system of 'Community Law'. This 'Community Law' would ensure the operation of individual and collective sovereignty in tandem, so that CARICOM would not be reliant solely on regional executive action but also on enforcement authority.[30] A body of Primary Law, in essence a further revised treaty, would be incorporated into national law via the exercise of individual national sovereignty. The revised treaty would provide for a regional Commission to prepare legal interpretations of the decisions of the Principal Organs (Secondary Law), also for incorporation into national legislation. Finally, the CCJ would act as a mechanism of collective sovereignty by enforcing the law.

Shridath Ramphal expounded on the role of the Commission in facilitating the adoption of Community Law through the development of 'draft instruments of implementation' – a tool which we recall Ramphal had proposed through the WIC.[31] Those *sui generis* instruments would not have immediate statutory effect unless complemented by the enforcement authority of the CCJ to issue 'orders of implementation'. On that basis, according to Ramphal, national governments would remain the final arbiters of Community Law which would not rest on a pillar of supranationality but rather on one of national sovereignty exercised collectively.[32] It appears that the arguments made by Ramphal and Joseph were intended to quell the perceived threat of supranationalism notwithstanding the fact that, supranationalism was embedded within the proposals. Although they may have, understandably, argued that the proposed facilitative authority of the executive Commission would reflect the intergovernmental exercise of collective sovereignty (despite the Commission's additional role in initiating proposals), the type of authority ascribed to the CCJ, that is, to order implementation, could not be considered anything other than supranational – albeit a supranational expression of the collective exercise of sovereignty.

Other participants commented on the aspects of the PMEGG's proposals related to financing and parliamentary representation, Havelock Brewster proposed the direct participation of individual CARICOM citizens in the financing of regional institutions, perhaps through some form of taxation. He further argued that the ACCP should play a greater role in building trust among the people, especially since the sustainability of new institutions depended on the support and confidence of the people.[33] The issue of sustainability had attained even greater relevance in the context of calls for rationalisation of regional institutions, including the transformation of the CRNM's temporary ad hoc delegated negotiation authority into a permanent institution acknowledged within the treaty.[34]

Interestingly, despite the prominent place of the four-pronged Rose Hall agenda in the conference discussions, alternatives to the Commission were also considered. The 2002 Archer-Gomes assessment had recommended that the Secretariat play the role of an executive authority. Patrick Gomes reiterated this proposal during the UWI conference, questioning the extent to which an additional bureaucratic layer of governance, such as the Commission, could add any value to the regional system of governance, 'since its proposed functions [could] be effectively discharged by a restructured secretariat, empowered by the Revised Treaty of Chaguaramas, and expanded to be more than 'the principal administrative Organ of the Community'.[35] He seemed particularly concerned about the need to rationalise institutions in order to achieve a level of systemic coherence – an objective which Gomes believed would be compromised by the fact that the proposed Commission's role in initiating proposals would likely duplicate the Community Council's role in strategic planning. Furthermore, like Brewster, he anticipated that the Commission would remain subject to the prevailing orthodoxy of informal inter-Prime-Ministerial and Presidential governance which had always characterised the whole CARICOM movement. Gomes summed up the state of the institutional framework and the agenda for reform, including Rose Hall, as follows: 'the principle of individual sovereignty gives rise to an operational dysfunctionality with which the secretariat (sic) is confined to a purely administrative role. Without the willingness on the part of Heads of Government to concede some of the sovereign rights as member states, in specific areas and spheres of action...decisions of the highest authority will continue to be subordinate and dependent on moral suasion of each individual member state'.[36] The strength of Gomes's argument appeared to cast doubt over the appropriateness of the PMEGG proposals, and ultimately, there was insufficient convergence of views to conclude the conference with a convincing plan of action to guide the continuing political debate on decentralisation of power and delegation of authority.

Edwin Jones's and Ivan Cruickshank's joint contribution to the colloquium intimated an understanding of the fact that the leaders were caught in a state of ambivalence, given the risky nature of proposals for supranationality, in light of their philosophical 'commitments to indivisible sovereignty and ultimately, ...the need to win elections and avoid second-guessing by the political opposition'.[37] In that context, the Conference concluded with an acknowledgment of the fact that advancement of the agenda required a new type of political leadership committed to improving national and regional governance, including enhancing the role of civil society in the decision-making process.[38] Indeed that point about leadership converged with George Lamming's view that a 'sovereignty of the imagination' was required to overcome the colonial and federal legacies.[39] The PMEGG and its three sub-groups were left to employ their creative imaginations in interpreting the political commitments of the Rose Hall Declaration, taking account of these latter intellectual contributions to understanding the imperatives of regional governance.

## THE PMEGG'S THREE IMPERATIVES FOR REFORM

The revised report of the PMEGG, incorporating the work of its technical sub-groups, was presented at a special meeting of Heads of Government convened in November 2003 in Castries, St Lucia. Entitled 'Regional Integration: Carrying the Process Forward', the document outlined three principal steps, in keeping with the Rose Hall agenda, towards the achievement of 'collective sovereignty'.[40] First, the creation of a body of 'Community Law', facilitated by the revision of the Treaty of Chaguaramas and the adoption of a Single CARICOM Act in all member states, was proposed as a means of securing governmental commitment to enact legislation for the implementation of treaty provisions and Community decisions. Secondly, the investment of a level of executive authority in a CARICOM Commission was intended to facilitate the translation of regional decisions into an appropriate legislative form – draft instruments of implementation – for adoption by national legislatures. The role of the Commission in this regard would be to interpret decisions and develop declarations of the 'rights and duties of Member States arising from the decision'. Finally, by endowing the CCJ, in its original jurisdiction, with authority to enforce this body of Community Law, CARICOM would, in theory, finally be able to attain the hitherto elusive goal of implementation. The PMEGG seemed convinced that these three levels of action – legislative, executive and judicial – would maintain a sense of collective sovereignty that simultaneously ensured that national sovereignty remained a pillar of the regional system and that the constitutions of each member state would be respected.[41]

In short, 'collective sovereignty' – akin to the 'shared sovereignty' concept proffered by Greene – had replaced supranationality in the lexicon of regional governance. The functions of the Commission outlined by the PMEGG confirmed the firm influence of national governments over regional executive authority. Although the Commission would have powers to initiate proposals to advance the integration process, that function could only be exercised within the parameters of the existing Community Council's strategic planning function, thereby granting political legitimacy to the Commission's authority and creating a level of coherence in the regional system. This theme of granting institutional legitimacy appears to have also precipitated the proposals for absorption of the CRNM – described by the PMEGG as a 'half-way house toward a central executive facility' – into the Commission or the Secretariat, given the Group's view that the Commission's remit should extend beyond the CSME to the coordination of external negotiations.[42]

With regard to the role of the Secretariat, the PMEGG seemed to have formed an erroneous impression that the 2002 Archer-Gomes report concurred with its own position that, the Secretariat should remain the administrative and technocratic arm of CARICOM. Although the Archer-Gomes team had restyled the Secretariat as the Implementation Support Arm, the report had, in fact, suggested that it should function as an Executive alternative to the Commission proposed by the WIC in 1992. Nonetheless, both reports agreed that the Secretariat should be reformed in terms of expansion and efficiency. It can be reasonably assumed that the PMEGG, having set the Archer-Gomes 'Secretariat-cum-Executive' model aside, was keen to avoid alienating the Secretary-General – perhaps both the office and the incumbent – from the process and therefore proposed that he be charged with developing the proposals for reform of the Secretariat. In addition, possibly in a bid to secure his support for its proposals, the PMEGG proposed that the position of Secretary-General be transformed into one of six posts of Commissioner – that is, a Commissioner for Administrative Affairs – and that a Director-General should be appointed to manage the Secretariat's daily administrative responsibilities. The new Commissioner for Administrative Affairs would operate at a political level, providing leadership in the implementation process along with four other Commissioners who would assume responsibility for one or more areas of the CSME. They would all report to a sixth Commissioner – the President (see figure 7.3). These proposed hierarchical reporting arrangements – from Director-General to Commissioner to President – correspond with the model utilized within the European Commission.

*Figure 7.3: The PMEGG's Pillars and Proposed Structure*

| Community Law | CARICOM Commission | Financing | ACCP |
|---|---|---|---|
| • Revised Treaty<br>• Decisions of Organs Enforcement by CCJ | • Initiate Proposals<br>• Facilitate National Implementation<br>• 6 Commissioners | • Automatic Transfers from Customs Duties to Regional Institutions | • Legitimately Represent People<br>• Deliberate on Decisions |

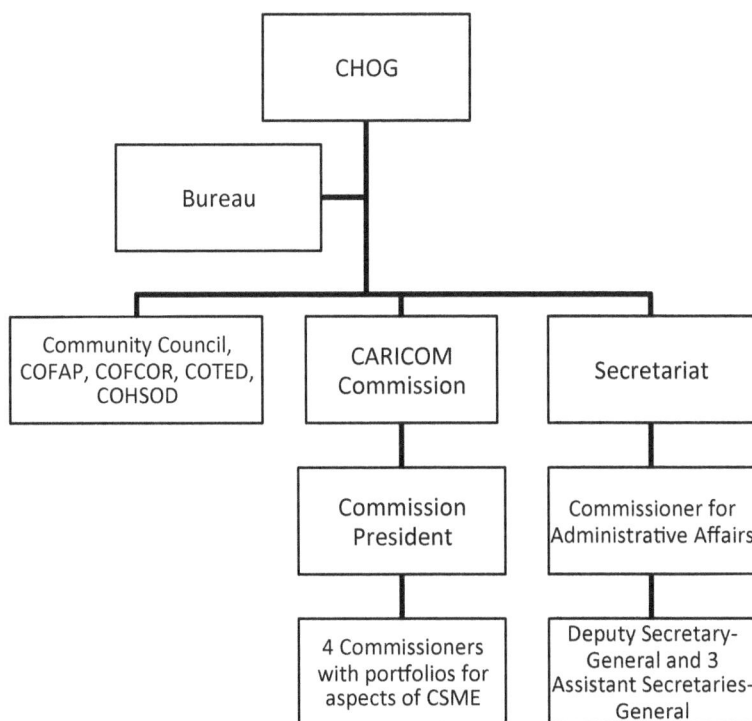

Apparently, the PMEGG was also keen to maintain the unique features of the regional movement – the Prime-Ministerial executive bodies. As such, the President of the Commission would join the new Commissioner of Administrative Affairs at the meetings of the Bureau and the other four Commissioners would liaise with Lead Heads in the Quasi-Cabinet in relation to their designated portfolios. That was perhaps another way of preserving a level of state control over the process, by allowing political leaders to maintain direct involvement in implementation. It was not clear, however, how these relationships would actually function – whether Heads would respond positively and proactively to proposals from Commissioners or ignore the regional Executive. In other words, as creative as the proposals were in seeking to craft a pragmatic compromise among various interests, the report did not clarify how the Commissioners would reverse, in a practical way, the embedded tradition of national actors ignoring regional decisions, best exemplified by the blatant and defiant disregard, since 2001, of the executive authority of the Secretary-General which was incorporated in the Revised Treaty.

Notwithstanding those weaknesses, the proposals on three imperatives for executive action were also buttressed by proposals for ensuring the adequacy and stability of financing for key regional institutions – a factor which had been significant in the success of several areas of functional cooperation. The technical subgroup chaired by Bourne had discussed the feasibility of mechanisms for direct popular ownership of regional institutions, as Brewster had suggested, but settled on an initial recommendation that a percentage of import duties be employed to meet the bulk of the US$30 million it estimated the Community would require annually.[43] Finally, in relation to the strengthening of the ACCP, the third technical subgroup proposed that the Assembly increase its level of non-governmental participation, mandate the participation of at least one opposition representative in each country delegation and admit other regional and international non-governmental groups as observers. The sub-group also argued for the provision of a sustainable source of financing for annual meetings of the Assembly and suggested that the ACCP be mandated to consider nominations for Commissioner posts.[44]

The PMEGG was apparently of the view that the Heads had sufficient information to warrant immediate implementation of its recommendations by 1 January, 2005. However, whether uncertain of the implications of accepting the advice of the PMEGG or whether reluctant and ill-prepared to make the changes it demanded, the Special Meeting of Heads requested that the report be released for public consultations.[45] For the next two years there was further review of the proposals without significant revision or progress on their implementation. Firstly, a 'Think Tank' on Governance was convened in February 2004 to discuss the public comments and then the Community Council further discussed them in October 2004. In the interim, even discussion of the proposals submitted by Secretary-General Carrington for further modernisation of the Secretariat was deferred by the 2004 regular meeting of the CHOG until the review of the PMEGG proposals had been finalised.[46] There does not appear to be any public information available about the outcome of those discussions. It is not surprising that, in the interval, views were expressed that the CSME would have to be foregone since there had been no decision on the delegation of sovereignty.[47]

However, the Port of Spain Statement issued at the conclusion of a Special Meeting of Heads in November 2004 demonstrated, at least diplomatically, a continued political commitment to 'the logic of the CSME [as an] embodiment of the essence of a mature economic integration enterprise'.[48] It was not expected then that, only a few months after that Statement, Owen Arthur would feel compelled to acknowledge a lingering contradiction inherent in the attempts to support the CSME logic without political institutional change. He suggested that, because of the Federal legacy, 'a false pragmatism' had asserted itself within the CARICOM movement, suggesting that 'economic and political affairs can be compartmentalised....and the very highest form of economic union known to mankind [could be achieved]...without major political readjustments'.[49] Having recognised this challenge, it remains moot why Arthur was not able to convince his colleagues to rise above the legacy.

Gonsalves at least, as Chair of the PMEGG, pleaded with his colleagues to move beyond it when he presented his final report in the July 2005 to the Bureau, which then comprised incumbent Chairman Kenny Anthony, incoming Chairman Patrick Manning and outgoing Chairman Runaldo Venetiaan, President of Suriname. The final PMEGG report had changed minimally from the 2003 version and acknowledged the need for further technical work in respect of proposals on financing and strengthening the ACCP. However, the Group called on the Conference to set a firm date for the establishment of the Commission.[50] There is little record of the Bureau's comments on the report, given the informal nature of the arrangement, save that it recommended that the proposed six Commissioner posts be reduced to four. However, the report had been deferred to the Bureau because the agenda of the annual Conference had been deemed to be too full, prompting Heads to mandate the Secretary-General to assess the effectiveness of their own forum.[51] It is unclear whether this assessment was ever completed. Thus, the delegation of responsibility to the Bureau, albeit by default, was perhaps appropriate since the Bureau had been established essentially as a mechanism to further implementation. However, the lack of authority of the Bureau to decide and implement on behalf of other members of the Conference, as well as the longstanding issue of the time constraints experienced by government ministers, meant that the governance agenda received limited attention particularly as Heads became more preoccupied with other matters, including the political challenges resulting from the coup in Haiti in the previous year and the subsequent suspension of that Member State from the Community.[52] Although the afore-mentioned developments seemed to imply the absence of collective political will to advance the reform agenda, the 2005 Conference did agree to establish a Technical Working Group on Governance (TWG) to be chaired by Vaughan Lewis, in order to translate the PMEGG recommendations into a workable strategy.

## THE TECHNICAL WORKING GROUP (TWG) ON GOVERNANCE

The Technical Working Group (TWG) received its official mandate at the Intersessional Meeting in Trinidad in February 2006, at which Haiti resumed membership. It was mandated to suggest the most feasible options for implementation of the PMEGG recommendations. The five-member TWG was chaired by Professor of International Relations, Vaughan Lewis, and comprised UWI Professor of Public Policy, Denis Benn, Professor of Law, Ralph Carnegie, former CARICOM Secretariat Director for Functional Cooperation, Angela Cropper, and regional private sector representative, James Moss-Solomon of the Caribbean Association of industry and Commerce (CAIC). The TWG in turn enlisted a team of advisors, including George Belle, Cuthbert Joseph, Roderick Rainford and Barton Scotland, to assist in its study which was concluded in October 2006.[53] Lewis was an interesting choice of Chairman, for while he was an academic and technocrat like most of the 'experts' appointed over the years, and a former Director-General of the OECS, he was also a former Prime Minister of St Lucia. It is conceivable that Heads had hoped that the Chairman's political leadership experience would have fostered an understanding, if not sympathy, for their sovereignty-based traditions. The TWG's Terms of Reference called for resolving the areas of contention within the PMEGG proposals. Specifically, the Group was asked to propose how to reconcile the idea of a Commission with that of a Community of Sovereign States; to rationalise the functions of Commissioners with the executive functions of Cabinets; to develop the legislative interventions required to invest the Commission with powers; to rationalise the Commission in relation to other Organs and Institutions; and to make concrete recommendations on the implementation of financing and strengthening of the ACCP. The TWG report entitled 'Managing Mature Regionalism: Regional Governance in the Caribbean Community' was, accordingly, completed on the basis of consultations with Heads of Government, Secretariat officials and EU representatives in Brussels and presented at the Intersessional meeting in February 2007.[54] It contained four principal recommendations which are discussed in turn below and summarised in figure 7.4 which also outlines the proposed organisational structure.

*Figure 7.4: The TWG's Proposed Regional Governance Framework*

| Community Law | Commission with Secretariat | ACCP | Financing |
|---|---|---|---|
| • Revised Treaty<br>• Decisions of Organs | • Initiate Proposals<br>• Facilitate National Implementation<br>• 4 Commissioners | • Legitimately Represent People<br>• Deliberate on Decisions<br>• Opposition, Government and Non-Governmental | • Automatic Transfers from Customs Duties to Commission, CRNM, ACCP |

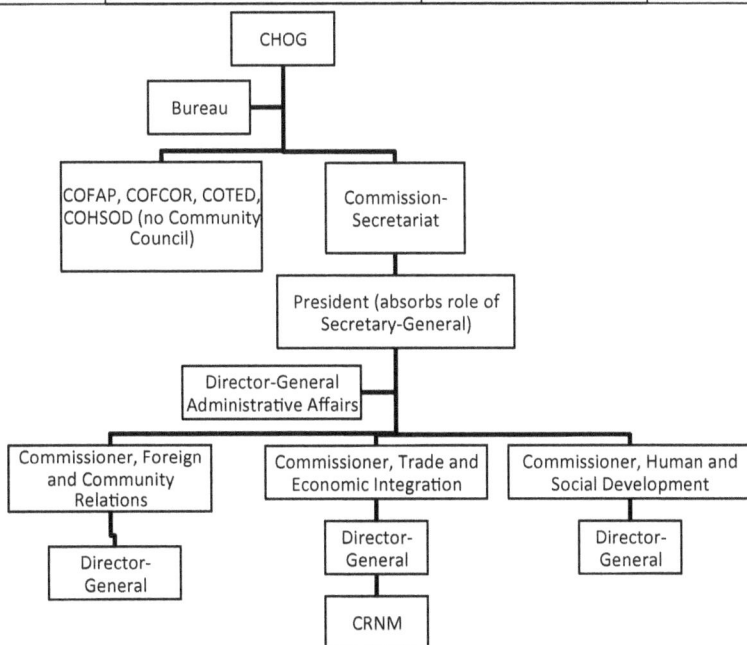

First, the TWG addressed the recommendation for the creation of a CARICOM Commission. In relation to the apparent disconnect between the concept of a Commission and the concept of a Community of Sovereign States, the TWG recommended that CARICOM adopt the principle of 'shared sovereignty' which, had initially been proposed by Eddie Greene in 2003 and dubbed 'collective sovereignty' in the PMEGG report. This effectively meant the collective exercise of sovereignty in agreed areas. The operationalisation of this shared sovereignty would be based on the principles of proportionality and subsidiarity, as employed in the EU context. In other words, the Commission would be accorded limited authority, delegated from member state cabinets, to act on behalf of member states only in areas necessary for the achievement of treaty objectives (authority proportional to treaty) and only if national action was not sufficient for the achievement of those objectives (authority subsidiary to areas of exclusive national competence).

The TWG also rationalised the relationships between the Commission and other Community Organs and Institutions by proposing that the Commission absorb the Secretariat completely, with the latter's technical and administrative staff serving the Commission. The role played by the Secretary-General would be undertaken by the Commission President. Three other Commissioners of equally high political profile and competence would be assigned to the three pillars of the Community (Foreign and Community Relations, Regional and International Trade and Economic Integration, Human and Social Development) and hence head the respective directorates of the Secretariat. Assistant Secretaries-General would be reappointed as Directors-General in the three areas and report to the respective Commissioners; while the Deputy Secretary-General would be designated as Director-General for Administration and would report to the President of the Commission. The Legal Counsel would also report directly to the President. The Commission would also absorb the CRNM within the office of the Commissioner for Regional and International Trade and Economic Integration.

In order for this new executive Commission-Secretariat mechanism to be effective, the TWG argued that it would have to maintain formalised and frequent relationships with the other Community Organs and organs in member states, specifically the Cabinets. The bridging of the gap between regional and national level was recognised to be important, since the TWG envisioned the Commission having the authority to intervene at both national and regional levels, enforcing Community decisions and participating in extra-regional negotiations. Equally, Organs would be expected to exercise the full authority accorded to them under the treaty to make decisions rather than ushering issues upward for the attention of the Heads of Government. The Commission would then be appropriately responsive to their decisions.

Interestingly, unlike the PMEGG, the TWG identified a certain redundancy in the existence of the Community Council. It argued, convincingly, that the Council had not functioned as had been intended, partly because of the lack of competence of Ministers of Foreign Affairs to address issues raised by technical Ministerial Councils and partly because its function in relation to implementation had been assumed by the Heads themselves in the Bureau and Quasi-Cabinet structures. In essence, the Council only functioned in relation to its responsibilities for approving the agenda for the CHOG and the budget of the Community. The former functions, it argued, could be handled by the Secretariat of the new Commission. The latter function, it concluded, would be better transferred to the specialist attention of the Ministers of COFAP. At the same time and surprisingly, in spite of the indictment of the alternative Prime-Ministerial executive structures (i.e. the Bureau and Quasi-Cabinet) in the expert reviews outlined in chapters 5 and 6, the TWG concurred with the PMEGG that they should be maintained, since 'their further institutional integration with the Commission's activities [could] only enhance the making and implementation of decisions'.[55] On the one hand, this recommendation sought to maintain a level of uniqueness in the CARICOM structure, by paying due deference to the political culture of Prime-Ministerial involvement. On the other hand, however, it ignored seemingly sound expert advice and arguably sought to perpetuate ineffectiveness.

Notwithstanding, the TWG also made proposals for rendering decision making among Heads more effective via the adoption of different types of agreement – whether binding regulations and decisions; discretionary directives which would permit flexibility in the pace and extent of national implementation; or advisory recommendations and opinions.

Secondly, the TWG recommended a stronger framework of Community Law. That was a significant recommendation because it held potential for preventing Heads from resorting to the permanent use of flexible directives or intangible recommendations. Indeed, implicit in its discussions, the TWG had perhaps recognised that even the 'high political experience' of Commissioners would not be sufficient to persuade Heads to adopt binding decisions and regulations in areas deemed to be critical to treaty objectives. The legitimacy of the Commission – beyond the political competence of its individual members – would have to rest on a legal foundation. It is in this respect that the TWG built on the PMEGG's advice for the creation of a body of Community Law. The TWG was of the view that enactment in each member state of a Single CARICOM Act would facilitate the entrenchment of all decisions of the Community Organs and Institutions in national law, eliminating the discretionary element in adoption of individual decisions. Once entrenched in national law, the authority of the Commission could be exercised at both national and regional levels. Only with the force of law behind its authority would the Commission be able to evade the predictably chilly reception of any proposals to intervene in a member state in order to secure implementation.

The third recommendation related to the creation of a sustainable system for financing regional institutions. TWG agreed with the PMEGG on the use of import duties for the financing of new institutions. As such, it proposed a two-phased approach, beginning in 2008, in which the Customs departments of all member states would make direct transfers to the Commission for financing the Commission-Secretariat, the ACCP and the CRNM. Once this was in place and working satisfactorily, member states could consider broadening the system to include other Institutions. Interestingly, the TWG noted in its report that there was no unanimous support for its recommendations among the Heads.

Finally, having agreed with the PMEGG proposals on strengthening the ACCP, the only adaptation suggested by the TWG was that the budget for the ACCP meetings be included in the budget of the Commission cum Secretariat.

Overall, the TWG report presented a pragmatic strategy for implementing governance reform. The Group suggested that, by creating an intergovernmentalist-neofunctionalist hybrid approach to regional integration, involving strict and relatively fixed demarcations of responsibilities between the national and regional levels of action, based on the principle of shared sovereignty, the governance framework would facilitate implementation. The report emphasised its point thus:

> ...the objectives of regional integration are unlikely to be achieved
> unless supported by a rational system of regional governance.
> However, the advocacy of enhanced regional decision-making, based
> on the collective exercise of sovereignty, as an indispensable element

of regional integration, should not be construed as a statement in favour of federation or other form of political union, which implies a permanent cessation of sovereignty. Instead, it should be seen as a pragmatic attempt to identify a creative and flexible form of governance in keeping with the logic of regional integration.[56]

The Intersessional Meeting approved the report and mandated the reconstitution of the Inter-Governmental Task Force to consider making further amendments to the treaty to accommodate the proposals.[57] Notwithstanding, alternatives to the executive Commission were still being proposed, even at that late stage, particularly by President Jagdeo of Guyana, who argued that the proposed Commission would be too powerful and expensive to maintain. Jagdeo outlined his disagreement by way of a letter to the TWG and requested that it consider, as an alternative, the establishment of a Council for Economic Cooperation which would function like a Committee of Ambassadors directly appointed by Heads to meet with national counterparts to facilitate action on behalf of Heads. The Conference agreed that those alternatives deserved proper discussion by social partners and opposition groups. A further three-member sub-committee of the TWG, comprising Denis Benn, Vaughan Lewis, and Cuthbert Joseph, was mandated to refine the proposals from the Intersessional and consider the alternative proposed by Jagdeo. However, the sub-group was unable to reconcile Jagdeo's proposals with the TWG recommendations by the time the Twenty-Eighth Regular Meeting of the Conference was convened in July 2007 in Barbados.

At the 2007 meeting, the Conference agreed that 'a system of commissioners, including a President and three Commissioners was the most appropriate option available for strengthening the governance of the Community, complemented by a council on policy implementation comprising representatives at the ministerial level of all Member States'.[58] The Heads further agreed to strengthen the executive management process by making links between the Bureau and Quasi-Cabinet and the directorates within the Secretariat and put in place mechanisms for automaticity of financing. Those decisions were taken in the context of a Nassau Declaration on Functional Cooperation, entitled 'A Community for All', which established a Task Force mandated to propose how best to make this functional aspect of the integration process a priority for the movement since it touched the everyday lives of CARICOM citizens.[59] It was certainly wise to shine the spotlight on the successes of functional cooperation rather than on the continued indecision with regard to reform of the central governance framework. However, the intention was to develop closer links between the institutions of functional cooperation and those central institutions concerned with the implementation of the CSME. Another 'small committee' – composed of the same members of the TWG subcommittee and headed by the Conference Chairman, Owen Arthur – was established to further refine the TWG recommendations.[60]

It is curious, therefore, that only a few months later, during an informal session at a special meeting convened in Port of Spain in April 2008, Heads decided to defer the establishment of the Commission as a longer-term governance instrument, arguing that focus should be placed instead on the streamlining and rationalisation of existing mechanisms. Heads commissioned a review of decision-making; a review of the Treaty provisions on non-compliance and non-implementation; a strategy to strengthen the Quasi-Cabinet; and a new strategy for restructuring the Secretariat to enhance its operations. Heads apparently also decided to establish a Council for Coordination and Implementation which would replace the Community Council. The subcommittee of the TWG eventually met with the Secretary-General in June 2008 to discuss the revised mandate of assessing existing structures. Focus was placed on enhancing the functioning of the Bureau, Quasi-Cabinet and the Secretariat and the revision of the Treaty to accommodate a new ministerial council – the Council for National Security and Law Enforcement (CONSLE). However, those involved in the process have indicated that much attention was placed on deciding whether to engage in or avoid an open discussion of sovereignty and supranationalism. Ultimately, it was decided not to reopen the philosophical debate on sovereignty, perhaps because it had not, hitherto, proved conducive to action. Certainly, there had been no evidence of any progress made on the strengthening of institutions since this subgroup was convened.

It is probable that the previous political commitments to the PMEGG-TWG reform agenda had in fact been eclipsed by changes in the global political economy which shifted the attention of Heads away from the region and towards their respective countries. In December 2007, a rise in oil prices and ballooning food costs were the priority of Heads of Government, particularly in Jamaica and Guyana.[61] Soon after, a global recession and financial crisis began to take its toll on the small Caribbean states and to impact on the prospects for establishment of new regional institutional mechanisms. The regional governance approach was not viewed, in these moments of crisis, as a viable solution to national problems. In the succeeding two years, commentators would suggest that continuing with CARICOM was an experiment in futility. For one, Former Jamaican Prime Minister Edward Seaga, during the course of an investment conference in Jamaica, suggested that the achievement of economic union was unlikely and therefore there was a need for the political leadership to develop innovative ways of promoting cooperation, rather than economic integration, which he argued had hitherto produced a structure which was 'top-heavy in bureaucracy and bottom-light in benefits'.[62] Seaga was of the view that changes in leadership had ushered into power younger leaders who had different objectives to their predecessors, but who now also had an opportunity to reverse the attachment to the CARICOM integration process as it had evolved and to pursue better options.

In contrast, Trinidad and Tobago Prime Minister Patrick Manning seemed to view integration as precisely the right strategy for the region, but agreed that the CARICOM economic union model, the CSME, was not the appropriate modality. During the 2008 Intersessional Meeting, Manning announced his intention to lead Trinidad and Tobago into the formation of a political union with three other OECS states. This proposal, discussed more substantively in chapter 9, suggested a level of frustration with the slow pace of CARICOM. For his part, Jamaican Prime Minister Bruce Golding was not convinced of the usefulness of either economic union to Jamaica's development prospects or sub-regional political union to stability within the CARICOM group.[63] These discussions raised the question of whether CARICOM was actually at risk of disintegration and whether the imperatives of dealing with economic and financial crises, including the negotiation of national agreements with international financial institutions, would take precedence over the continuation of a seemingly endless debate on modalities for political commitments to regionalism.[64]

Furthermore, it raised the question of whether, in the new context, regional integration was still an imperative for economic adjustment.[65] Against the background of advancement towards economic union in the OECS, Ralph Gonsalves expressed his obvious dissatisfaction with the CHOG reneging on its agreement to establish a Commission. During an OECS consultation on economic union, broadcast over radio, on 18 June 2008 Gonsalves stated:

> You have a ramshackle political apparatus in CARICOM. It
> doesn't even suit properly, the functional arrangements in health,

education and the like, and in foreign policy, much less to use the same arrangements – institutional, administrative, political arrangements: governance arrangements – for a single market and a single economy.[66]

Then, he frankly outlined why he thought CARICOM could not move forward:

The politics of a limited regional engagement in Jamaica, shackled as it is by the ghosts from the referendum; the politics of ethnicity in Trinidad and Tobago and Guyana; a mistaken sense of the uniqueness, specialness and separation among large sections of the Barbadian populace; the peculiar distinctiveness of Haiti and Suriname; and the cultivated aloofness from the regional enterprise by The Bahamas; are destined, in the foreseeable future, to keep CARICOM as a Community of Sovereign States in which several of its member states jealously guard a vaunted and pristine sovereignty.[67]

It seemed, then, that CARICOM had not moved much beyond its early history of insularity, nor had the conception of sovereignty changed from those early years of its first assertion. In that context, the members of CARICOM, compared to the members of the OECS, were, in Gonsalves' view, just too disparate to be able to reach a suitable sovereignty bargain to advance the integration process. Yet, at the same time, Gonsalves seemed to maintain a residual hope that the political will could be mustered to conquer diversity. His sensational remarks, carried around the region via the media, were perhaps intended to embarrass CARICOM into action and also warn the OECS about travelling the same path.

## WHITHER THE POLICY ON REGIONAL GOVERNANCE?

It had taken CARICOM some 15 years to develop a clear policy on regional governance reform, only to abandon it when the exigencies of global economic adjustment put pressure on its level of commitment and political will (see path of evolution in figure 7.5). The agenda outlined by the PMEGG and followed by the TWG strategy had refined the ideas of the 1992 West Indian Commission in order to present contemporary guidelines for governance of a mature system of regionalism. However, the protracted periods of indecision among Heads of Government, in relation to their willingness to undertake the requisite sovereignty bargains, in effect stifled the new stimulus for reform.

**Figure 7.5: Evolution of the Regional Governance Reform Agenda**

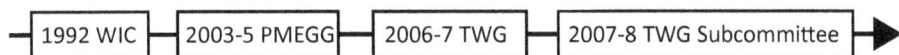

```
─┤ 1992 WIC ├─┤ 2003-5 PMEGG ├─┤ 2006-7 TWG ├─┤ 2007-8 TWG Subcommittee ├─►
```

In spite of the emerging consensus not to continue with the sovereignty debate, pursuant to the new mandate to focus on existing institutions, one member of the TWG, in particular, continued to analyse the implications of sovereignty on the reform agenda. Denis Benn lauded the evolution of the collective/shared sovereignty concept in Caribbean regionalism.[68]

Later, in a paper on the relationships between sovereignty, supranationalism and intergovernmentalism, Benn attempted to outline how the concept could be employed practically in different cases. Having identified different types of intergovernmentalism and models of supranationalism, in the context of the UN General Assembly and Security Council as well as the European Union, he concluded that, 'while an organisation may not be supranational in an absolute sense, parts of it may act supranationally'.[69] He challenged the relevance of the Rose Hall commitment to the overarching institution of intergovernmentalism and the concept of 'Community of Sovereign States', given the fact that the exercise of sovereignty in that context had failed to facilitate the achievements of the Community's economic goals, including the establishment of the CSME. Similarly, Vaughan Lewis noted that the concept was irrelevant because the collectivising of sovereignty was viewed purely from the perspective of a zero-sum game.[70] However, in spite of his commitment to the shared sovereignty concept, Benn was forced to acknowledge that the meaning of the three concepts at the centre of the debate – sovereignty, intergovernmentalism and supranationalism – remained imprecise.

He concluded that, 'without becoming caught up in a debate about the exact nature of sovereignty, intergovernmentalism and supranationalism which, as is seen from the foregoing discussion, are somewhat imprecise and mean different things to different people, it would be more productive to conceive of governance within the Community in terms of establishing a balance between national decision-making and regional or Community decision-making' and based on a 'redefinition of the Caribbean Community as a Community of States and Territory exercising sovereignty individually and collectively in support of the objectives of regional integration, based on the flexible exercise of sovereignty and a variable geometry of integration'.[71]

This was an insightful proposal, which not only took the agenda back to its inspiring origins in the Chairman's Rose Hall Perspective and the PMEGG proposals, but also acknowledged an emerging variable geometry resulting from the strengthening of the OECS and Trinidad's decision to form closer associations with that grouping. Benn's statement, in effect, described an appropriate context for modern Caribbean governance.

At the 30th Conference of Heads in Guyana in July 2009, Heads began to re-engage with the reform agenda. Two new proposals emerged. Firstly, Patterson, who had by then retired from politics and was being honoured with the Order of the Caribbean Community (OCC), called for a re-examination of executive authority in the Community. He proposed a new model – the appointment of a High-Level Independent Facilitator to help remove barriers to implementation at the national level. The appointee would be at the rank of a Cabinet Minister, although not necessarily exercising executive authority, but would have access to Heads and the Secretariat in order to fulfil a facilitative role. Secondly, during an informal discussion of governance in the Caucus of Heads, Bruce Golding expressed to his colleagues the desire for development of a Permanent High Level Body, comprising representatives of all members of CARICOM, mandated to resolve conflicts among members.[72] That such a proposal should emanate from Golding was reflective of a kind of pragmatism which gripped states in light of the economic crisis. It may have been that Golding had come to the realisation that should other states proceed to deeper levels of integration, Jamaica could be marginalised if it did not find a way to ensure the sustainability of CARICOM. His proposal was also, no doubt, precipitated by the tensions which had erupted among some states in relation to immigration and trade.

Immediately preceding the Conference, a dispute had erupted between Barbados and other member states over immigration under the regional policy on the free movement of persons. Barbados had threatened to remove CARICOM nationals living in the country without 'regularised status'. During the Summit, Gonsalves and Jagdeo charged that citizens from Jamaica, St Vincent and the Grenadines, and Guyana were being treated particularly badly by Barbadian authorities. It was perhaps the issue of mistreatment rather than the issue of deportation which was most hurtful. However, underpinning these events was a difference of perspective on the existence of a regional identity. The assumption of Gonsalves and Jagdeo, as reflected in their comments at the Summit, suggested a perception of Caribbean citizens as a single people. However, the comments made by some Barbadian citizens on the Nation newspaper discussion board dedicated to the immigration issue suggested otherwise.[73] Indeed, some of the national commentaries suggested that the new immigration policy reflected a welcome change in leadership in Barbados. Prime Minister David Thompson, only a few months in the position, was responding to his Caribbean neighbours in a manner decidedly distinct from Owen Arthur's prior administration. In response, a Barbados editorial suggested the promotion of a values-based regional identity which could embrace multiple identities rather than pushing a single identity.[74] Another similar row evolved between Jamaica and Trinidad and Tobago, and Barbados over the non-admission of Jamaican products and nationals to those countries.

Addressing some students ahead of the 2009 Summit, Ramphal made the profound observation that:

> ...at this moment, [the] smaller, narrower, insular impulse is dominant. We are turning inward just at the moment when the external environment of crisis demands responses driven by the spirit of community. Not only are we not going forward in fulfilment of professed goals – like the CARICOM Single Market – we are actually retreating from both the spirit and letter of community agreements – like those that bear on the movement of Caribbean people. If we allow these negative instincts to prevail; we will lose altogether the reality of 'community' which is within our grasp; and endanger the Caribbean personality which should be its underpinning. They must not prevail.[75]

It is in that context that Golding's proposal for a high level body was accepted in Caucus and the Conference reactivated the Arthur-led sub-committee of the TWG to discuss the feasibility of developing a Permanent Commission of CARICOM Representatives which would not initially have independent authority.[76] However, the political context in 2009 was a far cry from that which had obtained at the time of Gonsalves' call for advancement of a Caribbean civilisation six years previously in 2003. It seemed that the system would need to be built from scratch but with a focus on a new ideology for Caribbean development. From where such an ideology might emerge is still uncertain. Academics had, for some years, been setting an agenda for inspirational leadership aimed at reclaiming independence and sovereignty.[77] Central to that task would be a firm decision on the role that sovereignty should play in the evolution of the institutions of regionalism. Notwithstanding the lack of ideology, in the preceding four years, the institutional landscape of the Caribbean Community had nonetheless been altered. The first phase of the CSME, the Single Market, had been inaugurated; the CCJ had been inaugurated and some elements of the institutional framework had been rationalised with the Secretariat. Interestingly, however, these institutional changes evolved relatively separately from the ongoing debate on the Rose Hall agenda. The subsequent chapter will review these second generation changes and discuss their relationship with the overall reform agenda.

# SECOND GENERATION INSTITUTIONAL CHANGE

Notwithstanding the disappointing reversal of commitments to the principal elements of the agenda for governance reform, between 2005 and 2009 the institutional framework did in fact undergo a further period of change. This second wave of post-Rose Hall institutional change, which led to the realisation of some of the commitments discussed in chapter 6, emerged independently of the three-pronged reform proposals related to executive authority, automaticity of financing and effectiveness of parliamentary representation. This chapter briefly explores the relationship between the Rose Hall-inspired agenda for governance reform discussed in chapter 7 and three specific instances of institutional change. These cases have been highlighted in this brief discussion to separate the formative elements of the emerging agenda from the outcomes which have been driven by other contextual factors. Firstly, it discusses the controversial path to the full realisation of the supranational mode of governance, introduced in chapter 6, with the inauguration of the Caribbean Court of Justice (CCJ) in 2005. Secondly, it discusses the implications for governance of the launch of the Single Market in 2006 and the adoption of a Single Development Vision in 2007. Thirdly, it analyses the implications of the rationalisation of the Caribbean Regional Negotiating Machinery (CRNM) within the CARICOM Secretariat in 2009. The chapter concludes with a brief analysis of context and prospects for future governance reform.

## THE CCJ AND STATE SOVEREIGNTY

Undoubtedly, the CCJ was an important element of the Prime Ministerial Expert Group on Governance-Technical Working Group on Governance (PMEGG-TWG) proposals for governance reform. It was expected to play an important role in enforcing implementation of the treaty, via interpretation of the proposed body of Community Law and by resolving disputes among members. Indeed, some legal experts argued that its role was so crucial that it should be promoted to the status of a Community Organ, appropriately acknowledged under the revised treaty.[1] However, the Court remained separate from the central institutions recognised under the Treaty of Chaguaramas and its role in dispute settlement was defined by the Agreement by which it was established. The path leading to the Court's inauguration on 16 April 2005 was an arduous one, particularly for the Jamaican and Trinidadian governments. The inauguration date was postponed on two occasions as a result of challenges to the constitutional legitimacy of the Court's appellate jurisdiction in Jamaica. Its central role in the regional governance architecture, therefore, warrants a brief discussion of the process towards its establishment – one which further highlights the pronounced nature of the sovereignty paradox in the Caribbean.

Jamaica ratified the CCJ Agreement in June 2003 and moved in July 2004 to repeal judicial appeals to the Judicial Committee of the Privy Council of the United Kingdom (JCPC) in order to install the appellate jurisdiction of the CCJ in its place. Although three bills were passed by a simple majority of Parliament (33 People's National Party [PNP] government members of the total 60 representatives of the House), the process by which they were adopted was challenged by various state and non-state actors, including the Opposition Jamaica Labour Party (JLP). Ironically, the JLP had proposed the creation of a Caribbean court in 1970 when in government, but had maintained while in political Opposition, a critical view of the impending establishment of the CCJ and the deepening of Caribbean integration more generally. The challengers argued that a simple majority was not sufficient to satisfy the requirements of the Jamaican Constitution and that a full referendum of the Jamaican people was necessary. Unsurprisingly, the PNP government was reluctant to pursue this avenue, given the legacy of partisan politicisation of the referendum held during the Federal negotiations, and argued that a referendum was unnecessary.

Public resistance to the Court's appellate jurisdiction had emerged among human rights organisations, in particular, based on a perception that the Court had been conceived by political leaders as a tool to expedite the resumption of capital punishment. Capital punishment has been suspended in most Commonwealth Caribbean countries as a result of a landmark ruling by the JCPC in the Jamaican case of Pratt and Morgan v. AG.[2] The judgment which stipulated that, in cases where convicted persons had been sentenced to death and execution had not been carried out within five years, the sentences of the convicted person should be commuted to life imprisonment, since a delay constituted 'cruel and inhumane treatment'. Indeed, it was not unusual in the Jamaican justice system for inmates to be held on death row for longer than the stipulated five-year period to facilitate the extensive multiple appeals process. As a consequence, several death sentences were commuted to life imprisonment and executions suspended, although recourse to capital punishment remained enshrined in the Jamaican Constitution. The creation of the Caribbean Court staffed by Caribbean judges held potential for overturning the JCPC ruling and the resumption of capital punishment. However, as early as 2003, Prime Minister P.J. Patterson had decried all Opposition statements against the appellate jurisdiction, arguing that its raison d'être should not depend on the matter of capital punishment since at the time the court was first conceived in 1970, the United Kingdom also practised executions.[3] The fundamental role of the appellate jurisdiction was to allow Caribbean states to assert their independence from Britain and sovereignty over their judicial affairs.

Unfortunately, the resistance to the appellate jurisdiction extended to wider criticism of the Court's original jurisdiction in respect of the CARICOM Singel Market and Economy (CSME). Views were often expressed in the Jamaican national media that the judges would be subject to political interference, given the tribalism associated with partisan politics in the country, and that the Court would not be financially viable, relying heavily on government subventions.[4] On signing the agreement however, Heads had already decided to establish a Judicial Services Commission to ensure the independent appointment of judges and had also agreed to establish a US$100 million Trust Fund to ensure the Court's financial sustainability. In fact, it had been Jamaica's Leader of the Opposition, Edward Seaga, who had proposed the principle of financial independence. So, it was essentially the potential implications of the appellate jurisdiction for capital punishment which became the focus of attention of dissenting interest groups. While the controversy over the death penalty was of major focus the argument contained in the remarks made by Seaga on the implications of the CCJ for state sovereignty resonate. In his contribution to the debates on the three bills in 2004, for obvious reasons of partisan advantage, Seaga employed a definition of sovereignty which presented the adoption of the CCJ's appellate jurisdiction as a political dilemma. Seaga claimed in 2004 that:

> To wilfully expose the weak Jamaican economy to further battering and the weak justice system to further erosion, all in the name of strengthening Caribbean regionalism at Jamaica's expense, cannot be accepted as the patriotic goal of a national Government....These diversions from the true national goal of Jamaican development can only be denounced as an unpatriotic surrender of national sovereignty for dreams of a dubious Caribbean destiny.[5]

In essence, in Seaga's view, the extension of CARICOM's remit to judicial affairs, given its reputation for inefficiency and dysfunctionality, posed a threat to Jamaica's judicial sovereignty. Consequently, Seaga's JLP party, along with other civic action groups, took the matter of the passage of the Bills to the Jamaican Court of Appeal, which, ultimately, dismissed the claims of the group regarding unconstitutional process, but permitted them to launch a further appeal to the JCPC in the United Kingdom. The JCPC ruled in February 2005, just days ahead of the planned CCJ inauguration date, that the Jamaican process of adoption of the Court was unconstitutional. The ruling stated that, while the government had followed due process in removing appeals to the JCPC, the entrenchment of a new final court of appeal required a qualified majority vote. The implication of the ruling was that the government would require the support of Opposition Members of Parliament in order to install the CCJ. However, since the Opposition and Government could not agree on the holding of a referendum, Jamaica's adoption of the appellate jurisdiction was aborted. The Jamaican ruling reverberated across the region as other territories with similar constitutional provisions would have been required to follow the same process to avoid similar controversy. In Trinidad and Tobago, some political Opposition groups, which had previously supported the Court, decided to withdraw their support and Trinidad – ironically, the impending Headquarters of the CCJ – also rejected the appellate jurisdiction. As a result of these obstacles, CARICOM reviewed the Treaty of Chaguaramas and amended it by protocol to highlight the original jurisdiction of the Court – the most critical for CARICOM's functioning – and to ensure that its provisions did not suggest an intention to contravene national constitutions and judicial sovereignty.

It is worth noting that, Barbados had amended its constitution in September 2002 to facilitate the adoption of the appellate jurisdiction without needing to have separate processes for repeal of the JCPC and institution of the CCJ. It is interesting that, in that country, the political leadership was able to develop a sense of awareness of the symbolism of the Court as a rejection of West Indian colonialism and an embrace of Caribbean independence. The dynamics of the process leading to the passing of that national constitutional amendment is perhaps worthy of study elsewhere. Guyana, also adopted the appellate jurisdiction, having abolished appeals to the Privy Council in 1970 when it assumed the status of a Republic. So, when the CCJ was finally inaugurated on April 16, 2005, only Barbados and Guyana adopted the appellate jurisdiction. Nonetheless, all the member states adopted the CCJ in its original jurisdiction, creating at last the first pillar of supranational regional governance. However, the CSME had not yet been implemented. The lack of direct effect of regional decisions meant that the role of the CCJ in regional governance has been much more limited than many advocates of regionalism had initially hoped and the PMEGG and TWG agenda had intended.

In retrospect, the attempt to establish both the original regional and national appellate jurisdictions of the CCJ simultaneously, detracted somewhat from the imperative of creating an effective mechanism for enforcement and dispute settlement within the remit of the Revised Treaty of Chaguaramas.[6] However, a more nuanced understanding of the political context is necessary to grasp fully the significance of these events. The review of regional governance has thus far revealed that, in the Commonwealth Caribbean, national and regional institutions have always been closely intertwined because of the concurrent evolution of regionalism and nationalism. Placed within that context, the Jamaican PNP administration's attempt to adopt both jurisdictions was largely a matter of functional expediency. Indeed, while conceptually the issues of national judicial independence and judicial sovereignty are separate from issues of regionalism (the perspective offered by Seaga), the extent to which the building of governance capacity of small Caribbean states is highly dependent on regional functional cooperation is striking. Indeed, Tracy Robinson of the University of the West Indies (UWI) Cave Hill offered just such a perspective on the existence of a Caribbean Common Law, highlighting the fact that, although jurists treated the law as a purely national issue, the very study and practice of law in the Caribbean had long been framed by regional institutions – namely, the University of the West Indies and the UK Privy Council which made its rulings on the basis of a single Commonwealth legal framework. She affirmed that: 'Notwithstanding the independence and sovereignty of each territory, their highest laws (the constitutions) coalesced around a common set of principles of interpretation developed by judges; a common law of the constitution'.[7] In that regard, the attempt to extend the regional judicial framework – an indigenous rather than colonial one – was entirely appropriate.

However, the lesson learnt from the Jamaican controversy is that the symbiotic relationship between the national and regional frameworks relies heavily on the nature of the national context of partisan politics. In that regard, Patsy Lewis made a noteworthy observation about the significance of consensus-building at the national level between governments and opposition parties to the process of resolving the regional implementation deficit. She noted that:

> ...governments in power operate as a [unified] regional political party because they take decisions at the Heads of Government [where the] national is subordinated to region...[however,] the contradiction is that governing parties rely on Opposition support at national level to implement regional decisions.[8]

The process of national decision-making therefore lies at the heart of the implementation deficit. The reform agenda had not addressed this adequately. The weaknesses in Jamaica had posed, though briefly, a serious threat to the evolution of the entire system of regional governance. The lesson is relevant in light of the fact that the abolition of the JCPC in the UK in October 2009 in favour of a UK Supreme Court keen to shed the burden of Caribbean appeals, may very well prompt a resurgence of interest in installing the appellate jurisdiction of the CCJ. In that eventuality, there will certainly be need to develop a more cooperative regional approach to installing that jurisdiction.

Interestingly, in July 2005 the Heads of Government introduced an innovative consultative mechanism – an exchange of views between Heads of Government and Leaders of the Parliamentary Opposition – which reflected a significant progression towards the kind of consensus building that Lewis had identified. The extension of this olive branch appears, in retrospect, to have been influenced not only by the CCJ experience, but also by the proposals of the PMEGG and the TWG for increased involvement of Opposition representatives in the decision-making process through the Assembly of Caribbean Community Parliamentarians (ACCP). The exchange of views held significant potential for overcoming the legacy of partisan politicisation which was a particularly challenging aspect of the Federal legacy. It could have potentially enhanced the discussion at the national level towards the development of national instead of partisan positions on the regional agenda. However, regional civil servants who witnessed the process suggest that the encounter was so adversarial as to cause a permanent suspension of the dialogue at that level. Instead, a Committee, chaired by Kenny Anthony, as Lead CARICOM Head on Justice and Governance, was established to discuss other modalities for maintaining the dialogue between government and opposition at the regional level. The Heads of Government of Barbados and Guyana and the Leaders of the Opposition of Dominica, Guyana, Jamaica and the Turks and Caicos Islands joined the committee, which met in January 2006 and concluded that the Opposition should be updated on the progress of the integration movement via the sharing of important documentation.[9] The Committee further proposed that the Secretariat develop guidelines for sustaining that sharing process – an initiative which was subsequently endorsed by the Conference in 2007.[10] There is some uncertainty as to whether mechanisms were also proposed for ensuring the proper review and interpretation of the shared documents by Opposition groups or for the reception of feedback from these groups. Indeed, outside the context of the actual discussions in Community fora, the Opposition was likely to have several questions on the agenda. However, despite these potential challenges, the initiative to develop new methods of consensus-building with Opposition parties was a significant element of progress in Caribbean governance.

## The CARICOM Single Market and the Single Development Vision

Some 16 years after it had first been conceived, the first phase of the CSME was launched on January 30, 2006, when six CARICOM member states – Barbados, Belize, Jamaica, Guyana, Suriname and Trinidad and Tobago – signed the Declaration marking the inauguration of the CARICOM Single Market (CSM) in Kingston, Jamaica. Six OECS member states, which were celebrating the twenty-fifth anniversary of their sub-regional movement, deferred their signatures until the Regular meeting of CHOG in July 2006.[11] Their delayed participation is reminiscent of their approach to accession to CARIFTA and the transition to Common Market, and was based on a desire to ensure the maximum benefits from the arrangement. At the same time, the OECS states were in the process of revising their own treaty, signalling a move towards the implementation of an economic union by 2007.[12] Three states were not expected to join: The Bahamas, because of its preference not to participate in economic integration; Montserrat, because it was required to await permission from Britain; and Haiti, because of its suspension after the 2004 coup and general ill-preparedness to give effect to the treaty's economic obligations.

Although the desired model of mature regionalism had been partly realised, the governance framework lacked the appropriate legal, executive and operational mechanisms, including a body of Community Law, a regional executive and better administrative procedures to facilitate, *inter alia*, the free movement of people within the single market. It was the recognition of these gaps which prompted Prime Minister P.J. Patterson to raise the issue of the lagging governance agenda at the inauguration ceremony.[13] The implication of the CSM launch was that the time for deliberation on governance had come to an end and implementation had become an imperative. It was Patterson's observations that prompted the establishment of the TWG and the initial adoption of the strategy for governance reform which was reviewed in chapter 7. However, his remarks also precipitated the completion of a study on regional Institutions which had been commissioned under the Rose Hall Declaration, with regard to an agenda for rationalisation of Community structures.

Ralph Carnegie, who had also been a member of the TWG on Governance, completed the review of the Institutions of CARICOM in 2006. The UWI Professor of Law was concerned about a level of incoherence evident in the institutional system arising from ill-defined relationships among the CARICOM Organs, Institutions and Associate Institutions identified in the Treaty. Among the many issues raised by Carnegie was an observation of the need for greater coordination of the activities of those structures designated as Institutions which benefitted from greater levels of autonomy by virtue of their specialised technical functions. Specifically, Carnegie recommended the convening of annual meetings between the Secretary-General and the Heads of regional Institutions in order to share information and discuss priorities to reduce duplication of activities. The first such meeting of the Heads of 22 regional Institutions with the Secretary-General was convened in Georgetown in October 2007, providing an opportunity for discussion of the proposed governance reform agenda, including restructuring of the Secretariat, automaticity of financing and coordination of the activities among the Institutions.[14] In order to maintain the momentum of the discussions on governance, a second meeting was convened in July 2008 and a third followed in July 2009, which discussed similar issues.

Carnegie also identified two anomalies in relation to the designation of Institutions in the treaty. Firstly, he observed that, although the ACCP was designated as a Community Institution, unlike other organisations in this category, it did not play a functional cooperation or technical implementation role. As an alternative, he proposed that the Institution be promoted to the status of an Organ or Body of the Community.[15] Secondly, Carnegie observed that the status of the CRNM within the regional system was precarious, particularly because it lacked an explicitly defined legal status or legally-defined patron relationship with the CARICOM superstructure. The matter of the CRNM's legal status was simultaneously the subject of an unrelated set of studies commissioned internally by the CRNM which suggested that the mechanism should be granted independent legal personality as a Community Institution. However, Carnegie was concerned that the nature of the CRNM's remit – trade negotiations being one of the three principal objectives of CARICOM and a fundamentally political pursuit – would not warrant it being promoted to the status of an autonomous Institution in the same way that other technical entities had been so designated. However, he also acknowledged that the specialist nature of its work would qualify it for a greater level of independence than Community Organs. Therefore, Carnegie argued for it to be accorded formal status as an Institution, but not as a separate juridical entity from CARICOM.[16] He felt that the development of a separate juridical identity for the CRNM should only be considered as a matter of last resort.

Carnegie's observations on creating greater coherence and more appropriate institutional linkages between the Community structures highlighted the need for the development of an overall policy framework to guide the activities of all the Institutions. That framework was achieved by the development of a concept paper on the establishment of a regional development policy framework by a Special Task Force on the CSME, led by Norman Girvan. The paper, which was presented at the 'Caribbean Connect' symposium on the CSME convened in June 2006 in Barbados, on the initiative of Owen Arthur, was later transformed into a Single Development Vision (SDV) document that outlined a framework for transforming the policy context for integration from one based on open regionalism to developmental regionalism.

The SDV presented a road map for socio-economic development based on the Task Force's mission statement:

> We envision a Caribbean Community in which every citizen has the opportunity to realise his or her human potential and is guaranteed the full enjoyment of their human rights in every sphere; in which social and economic justice is enshrined in law and embedded in practice; a Community from which poverty, unemployment and

social exclusion have been banished; in which all citizens willingly accept a responsibility to contribute to the welfare of their fellow citizens and to the common good; and one which serves as a vehicle for the exercise of the collective strength of the Caribbean region, and the affirmation of the collective identity of the Caribbean people, in the world community.[17]

The statement certainly introduced the human element of the rationale for integration in a way in which the Treaty could not, as a legal document. The SDV went on to outline an industrial policy to support the Single Economy, scheduled for completion by 2015. It also proposed official recognition of social partners in relation to decision-making on the CSME, arguing that a social partnership, involving a Community Social Compact and full activation of the Charter of Civil Society, was imperative for CARICOM development. Against that background, Girvan's Task Force was convinced that the implementation of the Rose Hall Declaration and the anticipated recommendations of the TWG were instrumental to the entire development process. The Conference approved the final version of the vision entitled: 'Towards a Single Development Vision and the Role of the Single Economy' during its meeting in Barbados in July 2007 and mandated that a Strategic Development Plan, based on the SDV, be prepared by June 2008.[18]

The introduction of the Vision was a significant event for CARICOM since it provided an interim framework for decision-making and implementation. Indeed, the 22 regional Institutions which met with the Secretary-General for the first time in 2007 converged around the Vision in their discussions of governance. It presented a common agenda for each of the entities, working in different areas of functional cooperation, to coordinate their activities.[19] However, there is little evidence of its discussion and integration into the work of the Secretariat Directorates and the Councils. In addition, although the CRNM was represented at the 2007 meeting of Institutions, it seems that the SDV document was largely ignored as the CRNM pursued its mandate to negotiate an Economic Partnership Agreement with the EU. The lack of synergy between the negotiation strategy and the Vision perhaps occurred as a result of the lack of a clear statement from the political directorate that the Vision be treated as the guiding strategy for all regional Institutions – regardless of their formal or informal status vis-à-vis the Treaty.

## The Rationalisation of the CRNM

The lack of attention to the development framework outlined in the Vision eventually influenced the emergence of a perception of the need to alter the position of the CRNM within the regional governance framework. However, the move towards transformation of that entity began as early as 2005 when the Council on Trade and Economic Development (COTED) approved the recommendations of two reports commissioned by the CRNM – one by a consultancy firm International Development Management Advisory Group (IDMAG) and the other a legal opinion by UWI law professor Albert Fiadjoe, in January and February 2005, respectively – which suggested that legal status be granted to the entity. A quadripartite committee, comprising the CARICOM Secretary-General, OECS Director-General, the Prime Ministerial Subcommittee on External Negotiations (PMSCEN) Chairman and the CRNM Director-General, was established to conclude the arrangements in the following year. However, discussions with regional officials suggest that a meeting of that committee was never convened since there was no consensus on the matter of granting the CRNM independent status. However, in 2006, against the background of the Carnegie study, the CRNM took the initiative to contract a consultant to draft pre-emptory legal instruments for legal status. The Terms of Reference for this exercise outlined the justification for legal status as follows:

> The special mandate of the CRNM and the increasing complexity of its tasks...now require a further degree of formalization of CRNM's structures and procedures and a conferment of de jure legal status as an agency of CARICOM, which together will enhance its operational efficiency and effectiveness and reduce the substantial 'transaction costs' involved in present arrangements for the government of Barbados, CRNM and its limited human resources, and external funding agencies as well as contributing governments.[20]

The consultant was expected to present a strategy for a process of phased legalisation, involving first, the regularisation of the CRNM's status in Barbados in a similar fashion to that which obtained in Jamaica where the headquarters agreement was in place; and then, the finalisation of its procedures and functions, including the reporting status to CARICOM structures in order to ensure greater transparency in its operations.

However, without the approval of the quadripartite committee the matter could not be taken any further.

Another review of the CRNM's institutional and human resource capacity was conducted in 2007 by Roderick Rainford. It proposed the rationalisation of the CRNM's operations in a single location and the remedying of the relationships with the Secretariat and any other structures which had been expected to emerge at that time from the PMEGG-TWG recommendations.[21] However, Rainford also made a very instructive comment in relation to the need, at this stage of its existence, to think carefully about the rationalisation of the institution. He said:

> It is to be noted that the kind of entity that has tended to be established with [independent] legal capacity is an agency with a specific technical function that the CARICOM Secretariat could not itself feasibly undertake operationally, whether physically located within or without the Secretariat. Were it not for the entirely sui generis way in which the leadership of the CRNM was installed at its genesis, [interpreted here to mean a confusion of political and technical roles], the issue could have been moot whether the agency be settled as an operation of the Secretariat or be endowed with its own legal capacity.[22]

Essentially, he argued that the situation had arisen from what the PMEGG had previously interpreted as a 'half-way house' process of institutionalisation (see chapter 7), which had now created ambivalence about the actual role and position of the CRNM within the CARICOM framework. It was unclear whether it was a technical Institution or a part of the central machinery under the supervision of the Secretariat. Against that background, Rainford argued that, given the fact that the CRNM had evolved since 1997 to also represent the interests of non-CARICOM states – Cuba and the Dominican Republic in the context of European Union (EU) and Free Trade Area of the Americas (FTAA) negotiations – it should be warranted some level of independence from the central CARICOM structure. He also warned member states against the temptation to use the rationalisation process to 'straight-jacket' the operations of the CRNM by restricting its involvement in the negotiation process to the exact letter of its mandate, rather than the spirit of its negotiation instructions.[23]

Indeed, the reality was that the CRNM had been given significant leeway in coordinating the negotiation of the EU-CARIFORUM Economic

Partnership Agreement (EPA) since 2003. However, when Director-General Richard Bernal initialled the EPA on behalf of member states in December 2007, Heads of Government became embroiled in a debate about whether or not the CRNM had pursued its mandate (to the letter rather than the spirit) to negotiate an agreement which reflected the best interests of their countries. A 'Group of Concerned Citizens', including Girvan, launched a strong media-driven campaign against the EPA, based on a view that the governance arrangements contained in that inter-regional reciprocal trade arrangement would overshadow CARICOM's own governance arrangements and eclipse the role of the CSME as the primary regional development strategy. In a series of newspaper articles on the implications of the EPA, Girvan noted that it was

> ...ironic that, with virtually no consultation or discussion on the substantive issues involved, CARICOM governments have been prepared to endow a Joint Council set up with the Dominican Republic and with Europe, with legal powers that it has been unable to agree on giving its own organs of governance after several years of inconclusive discussion.[24]

The criticism pointed to a significant influence of external factors and actors on the environment for creating political will for reform.

Another principal criticism of the agreement was that it did not contain a sufficiently clear development plan, including guidelines for EU development assistance to facilitate the economic adjustment to trade reciprocity, particularly for the less-developed states. The critique raised two important issues about the way in which the CARICOM governance framework had functioned with respect to the CRNM. Firstly, it called into question the structures for accountability of the CRNM in its coordination role. It was not clear whether the blame for the weaknesses in the EPA agreement should be attributed to the CRNM coordinators or the political leaders who should have been providing oversight. Secondly, it raised the longstanding issue of weak national capacity – in this case, in relation to participation in and monitoring of international negotiations. Indeed, national representatives were participants in the College of Negotiators which had actually concluded the agreement and yet, several member states seemed to be unaware of the provisions being negotiated with the EU. A related issue which was likely to have precipitated the assault on the agreement – and by extension the CRNM and Heads of Government – by Girvan and the concerned citizens, was that the negotiation process seemed not to have been influenced at all by the SDV approved in 2007, even though Girvan and other experts familiar with the SDV served as advisors to the CRNM.

The debate created an atmosphere of tension among Heads of Government, similar to the type of conflict which had occurred so often in the mid-1970s. In particular, differences between Prime Minister Golding and President Jagdeo elicited a public war of words based on their evidently diverging visions of regional development and external cooperation. Jamaica focused essentially on an outward-looking neoliberal competitiveness strategy and, therefore, viewed the EPA as a model for that type of international engagement. In contrast, Guyana held fast to the maintenance of longer-term preferential treatment and, hence, challenged the agreement for its lack of attention to the special needs of small developing countries. Jagdeo's criticisms of the agreement extended to an attack on the legitimacy of the CRNM structure itself. He argued that it had been operating as if it 'was an independent entity vested with different [interpreted here as independent extra-national] powers'.[25] However, although it was true that the CRNM was somewhat autonomous of the Secretariat, the CRNM had, in fact, never been fully independent of the leaders' influence. Jagdeo and his colleagues would have been appropriately represented by the Lead Head on External Negotiations within the Quasi-Cabinet – first, P.J. Patterson, then, Portia Simpson-Miller and latterly, Bruce Golding.[26] In that regard, Golding's assumption of responsibility for those matters in 2008 had perhaps placed some obligation on him to defend the agreement.

In April 2008, as the conflict heated up over whether CARICOM Heads should or should not sign the agreement, Bernal announced his resignation from the post of Director-General. When the time came to appoint a successor to Bernal, Jagdeo initially insisted that the appointment be conditional on the immediate absorption of the CRNM into the Secretariat in Guyana. However, Golding and Trinidad's Manning worked together to secure the swift appointment of Bernal's deputy, a Trinidadian, Henry Gill, even before a decision on rationalisation could be made. That eventuality raises a suspicion as to whether Jamaica and Trinidad were concerned that Jagdeo's call for rationalisation with the Secretariat was based on a desire to have closer personal oversight of the CRNM. Nonetheless, over the next few months, Heads continued to discuss the matter of rationalisation informally, often in Caucus – a tool frequently employed by Heads to ease tensions and resolve conflicts amongst leaders. Jagdeo's unrelenting pressure on his colleagues – most likely with the support of the CARICOM Secretary-General – eventually resulted in a decision taken by the Bureau in March 2009 to rationalise the CRNM within the CARICOM framework by creating a new Specialised Department mandated to report directly to the CARICOM Secretariat. Interestingly, Guyana was the incoming member of the Bureau at the time of this decision. It is quite likely that Jagdeo was particularly pleased that he would have ultimate responsibility for implementation of the decision in the latter part of the year when he assumed the Chairmanship of the Conference. Prior to the decision, the Bureau had discussed the option of transforming the CRNM into a Community Institution, as Carnegie had proposed, but felt that, given the central role of negotiations to the political agenda, it should fall within Secretariat for closer surveillance.

The July 2009 Conference agreed to the Bureau's proposal and decided that the new Department should be called the Office of Trade Negotiations (OTN). Gail Mathurin, a Jamaican Ambassador, who had previously critiqued the functions of the CRNM, was appointed as the new Head of the Office. The OTN's mandate was extended beyond the CRNM's original remit over three negotiating arenas (EU, FTAA and World Trade Organization [WTO]) to include all external trade negotiations. It reported to the COTED and, by extension, the Heads of Government, through the Secretary-General. The OTN maintained its offices in Jamaica and Barbados as well as its representation to the WTO in Geneva but agreed to discontinue its representation in Brussels and Toronto once agreements with the EU and Canada were concluded.[27] In a significant related development, the CHOG appointed a Task Force to consider the Dominican Republic's most recent application for membership to CARICOM, in the context of that country's membership of the CRNM within the framework of the Caribbean Forum of ACP States (CARIFORUM).

The agreed approach to rationalisation, particularly the erosion of the CRNM brand, which had become an internationally recognised and respected name, was warily received in some quarters – both regional and international. Shantal Munro-Knight, a UWI lecturer and member of the regional civil society group Caribbean Policy Development Centre (CPDC), lamented that the dismantling process would place the new entity under the supervision of another organisation she viewed as in need of reform.[28] Similarly, the Dominican Republic's Ambassador to the EU, Federico Cuello-Camilo, who had served as a member of the College of Negotiators for the EPA, was deeply concerned about the CARICOM

Secretariat's management capacity, given what he described as 'severe financial irregularities' identified by the EC in relation to a Caribbean Regional Indicative Programme (CRIP) managed by the Secretariat in the past.[29] He also expressed concern that the change would lead several of the region's best negotiators to resign from their posts in the new OTN. EU representatives are also known to have informally expressed regret at the dismantling of the CRNM – which the EC acknowledges played a significantly positive role in the outcome of the negotiation of the CARIFORUM-EU Economic Partnership Agreement. The full implications of the decision are yet to be fully understood. However, at this early stage of the rationalisation process, it is clear that steps must be taken to ensure effectiveness of all the structures in the regional framework. Improvement of the legal position of the CRNM will be futile unless the structures with which it must now closely liaise are also able to function effectively.

## THE CONTEXT AND PROSPECTS FOR FURTHER REFORM

In conclusion, it is clear that the landscape of Caribbean regionalism had changed over the preceding four years. CARICOM had made significant progress in the realisation of judicial regulatory capacity with the inauguration of the CCJ's original jurisdiction to regulate the single market which was launched in 2006. However, the functioning of the market has since been limited and hence the CCJ has been underutilised. CARICOM also achieved greater policy coherence with the development of a Single Development Vision; however, the translation of that Vision into an implementable strategic document has been slow. Furthermore, the rationalisation of the CRNM – which presented a prominent anomaly in the tradition of direct Head of Government control – suggested a theoretically progressive step, though one which is risky without complementary reform of the framework in which the new OTN is expected to function. Indeed, what is interesting and revealing about this period is that the three cases of institutional change discussed briefly in this chapter seemed to have materialised independently of the emerging agenda for governance reform in relation to sharing sovereignty.

The protracted process of decision-making on the specifics of the governance reform agenda, between 2003 and 2008, when it was eventually decided to postpone further discussion of the establishment of an executive Commission, has underscored the futility and irrelevance of the CARICOM decision-making process. Indeed, the instances of institutional change reviewed here and in chapter 6 represented changes which had very little do with a conscious effort to bargain with aspects of formal sovereignty to create an effective regional executive. Although two further proposals for alternative structures – Patterson's High-Level Independent Facilitator and Golding's Permanent High Level Body which were highlighted in chapter 7 – may have temporarily reinvigorated the agenda, it is likely that a similar protracted period of indecision is likely to ensue in relation to the new proposals.

During the 2009 Conference, Heads mandated a further review of the effectiveness of the Quasi-Cabinet as a mechanism of shared sovereignty.[29] Significantly, that matter, as well as other governance issues, were notably absent from the agenda of the March 2010 Intersessional Meeting of the CHOG in Dominica. Instead, Heads focused largely on the reconstruction efforts in Haiti following the devastating earthquake in January 2010; and on the conclusions of the CARICOM-Canada Free Trade Area.[31] Nothing more has been said of the elements of the agenda related to strengthening the ACCP and creating a system of automatic financing for regional institutions.

Since 2010 no action on reform has taken place and the movement has been dogged by accusations of being in crisis. A recent review of the Secretariat, which was the principal subject of the 2012 Intersessional meeting convened in Suriname, called for increased managerial efficiency in the Secretariat but neglected to address any of the political aspects of governance. Within the context of pressing global economic challenges, attention to the governance agenda may continue to wane until a firm decision can be reached on the relevance of regionalism to the development agenda and on the most appropriate configuration of regional governance for Commonwealth Caribbean countries.

An interesting question is whether or not the current regional governance context would have been more effective had the integration process followed a different path. In light of this question, this analysis of the modern history of regional governance in CARICOM, takes a brief but significant departure from the CARICOM story to discuss alternatives which were proposed in the past and pursued by OECS states, parallel to CARICOM's evolution. This review provides insight into different contexts and prospects for regional governance and thus enhances the analysis of CARICOM's history and the subsequent concluding discussion of the dynamics of sovereignty, regionalism and governance.

# THE EASTERN CARIBBEAN SUBCULTURE OF GOVERNANCE

The conception of sovereignty, which became entrenched in the post-1962 independence era, has constrained the evolution of an appropriate regional governance framework. Notwithstanding, the evolution of relatively more progressive regional institutions in the Eastern Commonwealth Caribbean suggests that the prevailing tradition of sovereignty need not have precluded the development of supranational modes of governance in the wider region. It is in that context that the features of a subculture of regional governance which evolved between 1962 and 2009, both parallel to and within the broader CARICOM framework of national sovereignty are now explored. The emergence of the institutional foundations of the subculture – vis-à-vis the West Indian Associated States (WISA) framework and the Eastern Caribbean Common Market (ECCM) is reviewed. The consolidation of those institutions in 1981 into a centralised Organisation of Eastern Caribbean States (OECS) designed to strengthen the position of the sub-region within CARICOM is then examined. Thirdly, this chapter reflects on the potential inherent in the proposals for development of legislative executive capacity in an OECS Economic Union and in a Trinidad and Tobago-East Caribbean Integration Initiative. Finally, the chapter concludes with a brief discussion of the relevance of the Eastern Caribbean experience to the process of rethinking and perhaps restructuring CARICOM governance.

## THE SUBREGIONAL FOUNDATIONS OF CARICOM GOVERNANCE

The Eastern Caribbean political experience has significantly influenced the emergence of regional governance in the wider region. Indeed, the Caribbean politico-economic profile is conceptualised in the context of a Demasian paradox of sovereignty, has been most evident in the seven less developed countries (LDCs) of CARICOM:

Antigua and Barbuda, Dominica, Grenada, St Lucia, St Kitts and Nevis, St Vincent and the Grenadines and Montserrat.[1] Consequent on the limitations of human and natural development resources inherent in small size, these countries shared a long history of federal administration among the Windward Islands (1833–42) and among the Leeward Islands (1674–1798 and 1871–1958) that preceded the establishment of the West Indies Federation (WIF).[2] That common profile and federal legacy was the context of Eastern Caribbean political advocacy towards the creation of the WIF and the attempts to reinstate federal governance in the subregion, immediately following the collapse of the WIF in 1962. Arthur Lewis's account of the negotiations for a 'Federation of Eight', including Barbados, suggested that regional governance was viewed as a prerequisite to effective government administration.[3] Lewis argued that the risk of corruption and abuse of power in such small territories in which citizens held close personal or familial ties to government officials was too great to render island independence a realistic goal. The fact that four of the governments were, at that time, under investigation by the British Colonial Office for irregularities in financial management, seemed to lend some credence to that observation.[4] The interdependent federal framework was, therefore, expected to promote political accountability as well as economies of scale for development.

Barbados' involvement in the negotiations was rather curious given its eligibility for independent statehood based on a relatively better economic position and reputation for good financial regulation. Although Lewis argued that Barbados' participation had been secured primarily through the strength of the friendship between newly-elected Premier Errol Barrow and Antiguan Premier Vere Bird – a friendship which had also facilitated the emergence of the Dickenson Bay Agreement in 1965 – it is perhaps equally feasible that Barrow, who had not been directly involved in the WIF negotiations, retained an ideological commitment to West Indian Nationalism and an idealistic view of leading Barbados into an alternative federal union. Irrespective of the rationale, because the profile of these states included a level of dependence on more developed countries, Barbados' involvement was expected to accord the Federation greater economic viability and political legitimacy.

Ultimately, however, despite the enthusiasm of all the parties and the Eastern Caribbean predisposition to regional governance, the negotiations for a 'Federation of Eight' stalled under circumstances similar to the WIF experience, given a certain commonality of political culture across the

Commonwealth Caribbean. An impasse over the perceived inadequacy of the British Government's proposed contribution to the federal budget gave rise to opportunistic partisan politicisation of the agenda in several territories. Firstly, the new government elected in Grenada in September 1962 withdrew from the negotiations to pursue potentially greater benefits of unitary statehood with Trinidad and Tobago.[5] Then, following the St Lucian elections in 1964, the new Premier, John Compton reneged on the commitments made by his predecessor to the federal process and also disengaged from the process. Subsequently, a desire to preserve high levels of national autonomy from other Caribbean territories, exemplified by Antigua's decision not to federate its postal services, led to that country's withdrawal, along with Montserrat, which wished to display solidarity with Antigua, its closest neighbour and ally. Eventually, in 1965, with only five states remaining in the negotiation process, the government of Barbados, frustrated by these eventualities, took a unilateral decision to move towards its own independence, which it attained in 1966.

In the light of these events, Lewis concluded that deadlock, fatigue and silence from the British Treasury contributed to the demise of the initiative in 1965.[6] The abortion of the 'Federation of Eight' demonstrates that the subregional movement displayed similar characteristics of the wider CARICOM political culture, including an emphasis on maximising island autonomy and government control, despite the prominent sovereignty paradox. In fact, several subsequent proposals for deeper political integration in the subregion were abandoned over similar concerns, including the 1971 proposal for the creation of a West Indian State launched by the Grenada Declaration between six of the territories and Guyana;[7] a call for a new Federation of Eastern Caribbean States launched by the Tobago Declaration of 1972; a further political union proposed in 1987; and a Barbados-OECS confederation proposed in 1995. Notwithstanding those failures, the seven Eastern Caribbean territories continued to pursue a path to national independence which retained a strong regional dimension sustained by innovative institutional frameworks kept distinct from the wider CARICOM architecture.

In 1966 the seven territories of the Eastern Caribbean opted to pursue Associated Statehood with the United Kingdom – an unconventional form of quasi-independent governance which offered three primary benefits. Firstly, the Associated States became eligible for recognition as subjects of international law, pursuant to their gradual progression to full political independence. Secondly, they gained full control of their national constitutions, but continued to receive financial and administrative support from Britain which retained responsibility for foreign affairs and defence. Thirdly, they preserved a level of island autonomy through self-government while also benefitting from common functional services. In that regard, the states formed an intergovernmental Council of Ministers of the West Indian Associated States (WISA) to regulate the operations of the shared (colonial) institutions which were adopted under the associated framework, formally achieved in 1967. These institutions included a common currency supervised by an Eastern Caribbean Currency Authority (ECCA), which had evolved from the British Currency Board previously dissolved in 1965, following Jamaica's and Trinidad's establishment of independent central banks. The states were served by an administrative WISA Secretariat established in St Lucia. They also shared a common judicial system supported by an Eastern Caribbean Supreme Court (ECSC) and Judicial Services Commission; a tourist association; a civil aviation authority; and joint diplomatic missions in the UK and Canada. These regional institutions were empowered to exercise supranational powers of implementation in their very specifically defined areas of responsibility. The supranational competencies entrusted to the regional institutions enabled WISA to sustain elements of regional economic (monetary), political (judicial; diplomatic) and functional (aviation; tourism) union within an intergovernmental policy framework. The fact that the supranational executive competencies were viewed as specific, rather than overarching, facilitated the acceptance of and support for the institutions among political leaders, which further encouraged them to deepen the level of economic integration.

In 1968, parallel to the establishment of the Caribbean Free Trade Association (CARIFTA), the Associated States built on these functional foundations by establishing an Eastern Caribbean Common Market (ECCM) governed by a separate intergovernmental Council of Ministers and a Secretariat based in Antigua.[8] Predictably, in spite of the existing supranational infrastructure, the intergovernmental policy framework for the WISA Council and the ECCM Council adopted the same tradition of unanimous voting as had become characteristic of the wider integration movement (see Article 18(5)). There are two important initial observations which must be made about the creation of these two intergovernmental councils. Firstly, the WISA and ECCM were separate institutions which served to maintain an institutional distinction between political cooperation and economic integration. Secondly, both Councils were viewed as rather informal fora for policy coordination since none of the states had yet assumed full independent statehood. Given the pronounced nature of the sovereignty paradox, none of the Associated States were sufficiently equipped to assume the responsibilities of implementing monetary and judicial policies without the support of joint institutions. In that regard, the intergovernmental fora served as temporary testing grounds for building the capacity for policymaking – until the states had resolved the issue of whether they would assume full formal sovereignty within the framework of statehood or political union. The level of informality and the distinction between the political and economic aspects of integration are likely to have contributed significantly to the acceptance of supranationality as a necessary aspect of political life in the subregion.

Consequently, the dual institutional modes – an intergovernmental policy framework coupled with a supranational functional architecture – facilitated the emergence of a subculture of regional governance in two ways. Firstly, the supranational institutions such as the common currency and judicial system became embedded within the popular consciousness, strengthening the human bonds of regional unity and facilitating greater interaction among citizens in the common market – notwithstanding the pre-existence of strong inter-island familial ties.[9] Secondly, the WISA/ ECCM policy framework, while making a modest contribution to levels of intra-regional trade, served to strengthen the position of the subregion vis-à-vis its more developed CARIFTA partners. As such, the subregion created an overarching political institution, reflecting a unique subregional identity, which was employed as a bargaining mechanism for preferential treatment in the wider region and internationally. The establishment of the Caribbean Development Bank (CDB) in 1969, with a special mandate to support the economic development interests of the LDCs, was closely related to the success of their joint bargaining. Subsequently, when CARIFTA was transformed into the CARICOM Common Market in 1973, WISA negotiated continued recognition of the group within the Treaty of Chaguaramas as LDCs eligible for special preferential support for industrial development.

There is a further observation to be made about the complementarity of supranationalism and intergovernmentalism in this context. Unlike in the rest of the region, individual territorial nationalisms were not yet strong enough, in the late 1960s, to co-opt sovereignty within a nationalist conception of independence. In the subregion, sovereignty was still closely associated with West Indian Nationalism which was the patron of the independence movement. In that regard, even though independent statehood appeared to be an inescapable future for these states – given the institutionalisation of statehood as a convention of international relations – the Eastern Caribbean states worked towards strengthening the subregional movement even as each eventually abandoned Associated Statehood for independent statehood. Grenada was the first to achieve that status in 1974; followed by Dominica in 1978; St Lucia and St Vincent and the Grenadines in 1979; Antigua and Barbuda in 1981 and finally St Kitts and Nevis in 1983 without Anguilla. Notwithstanding those events, it is likely that the challenges of independence, exemplified by Jamaica and Guyana's experiences of economic decline in the early 1970s, stood as prominent reminders of the significance of regional integration to economic development. Even Montserrat, which remained a dependent territory of the UK, continued to participate in the ECCM and in CARICOM, advocating for continued strengthening of both frameworks.

The ECCM had provided a framework in which the Associated States could pursue economic growth through free market access to factors of production and cooperation in industrial development. For example, an Industry Allocation Scheme was launched to support the development of over 30 manufacturing industries and distribute them equitably among the seven members so as to avoid duplication of activities. However, the functioning of this scheme was not without its problems, including a perception that allocation was based on political rather than economic grounds.[10] Perhaps because of those weaknesses and an emerging sense that looming deadlines for independence threatened to weaken the commitment to sustaining the common institutions managed under WISA, new proposals were developed for deepening the subregional movement.

The earliest proposal for further strengthening regional integration was a 1972 governmental proposal for renewed political integration as an alternative to statehood. Some of the academic community endorsed the proposal and suggested various ways of upgrading the existing supranational governance architecture to support political union. In particular, Swinburne Lestrade and Ralph Gonsalves, who were undertaking postgraduate research at the University of the West Indies (UWI) Mona at the time, proposed the adoption of supranational executive structures including a multi-level parliament composed of a directly-elected senate in each of the seven territory and one regional senate which would be responsible for oversight of a fully-fledged regional civil service.[11] It is likely that the proposal for union was not adopted because the suggested supranational political executive was seen in a very different light to the existing functional executive institutions. In light of the fact that the states were now actively pursuing state sovereignty, the proposal may have been viewed as a threat to emerging national executive competences.

A few years later when the process of national independence was well under way, Antigua assumed a leadership role in providing an alternative to the existing framework. We recall that Antigua had also played a leading role in catalysing the emergence of the CARIFTA. It was during the 23rd Meeting of the WISA Council of Ministers in October 1978 in St John's that the Deputy Premier of Antigua and Barbuda, Lester Bird, son of Premier Vere Bird, proposed a new way of strengthening the subregional movement. He said: 'I will suggest that in order to preserve the benefits of interdependence after independence, we need to work out a formal relationship between what we know as WISA and the ECCM...To abandon WISA would be the start of a chain of fragmentation among us...a step which we cannot afford. The concept of WISA is rooted in the recognition of our interdependence and it is that concept which we must concretise'.[12] The fact was that, in the preceding years, the move towards separate independence was emerging as a threat to the common institutions upon which the states relied. Bird was clear, however, that he was not advocating a return to federation. He was proposing the development of a stronger framework which would be complementary to national independence. In addition, the gains which had been expected to have accrued to the LDCs from the CARICOM framework had not materialised, particularly as tensions among CARICOM Heads of Government and the economic and financial crises in the MDCs from the mid-1970s onwards had contributed to increasing fragility in the wider movement.[13] Bird argued further that the strengthening of the subregional movement held potential for resolving the tensions in the wider movement. He declared: 'If we prove that we have the capacity to work together, ending competition and creating instead the atmosphere and basis for economic integration, we will be better placed to persuade the MDCs to pursue this course with us'.[14] So, on Bird's prompting, the WISA Council of Ministers adopted a resolution at its next meeting in May 1979 in St Lucia on the consolidation of the disparate elements of the subregional institutional identity within a single regional economic organisation. The new organisation was intended, firstly, to enhance the capacity of the emerging independent states to engage in external affairs, once they assumed responsibility for those matters, and, secondly, to catalyse a renewal of the wider integration process upon which the subregion remained dependent.

## THE ORGANISATION OF EASTERN CARIBBEAN STATES (OECS)

The seven WISA states signed the Treaty of Basseterre Establishing the Organisation of Eastern Caribbean States (OECS) on 18 June, 1981.[15] The new Organisation had six principal objectives: to promote regional and international cooperation; to promote unity and solidarity in defence of sovereignty, territorial integrity and independence; to facilitate member states' fulfilment of their international obligations; to harmonise foreign policy; to promote economic integration within the ECCM; and to further joint action in 18 areas of functional cooperation (Article 3). The objectives were akin to those of the CARICOM Common Market and implied the existence of a similar discourse on the defence of sovereignty. In particular, the general undertaking to implement, as outlined in Article 4, reflected a similar preoccupation with regard to the retention by national governments of exclusive responsibility for legislation of regional decisions. It is in that context that the five primary governance mechanisms outlined in Article 5 of the Treaty of Basseterre were also predictably reminiscent of the CARICOM framework (see figure 9.1).

The mechanisms included the Authority of Heads of Government of member states of the Organisation as the principal policymaking institution; together with three ministerial committees – the Foreign Affairs Committee, the Defence and Security Committee and the Economic Affairs Committee – which made recommendations to the Authority and other

*Figure 9.1: The OECS Governance Framework*

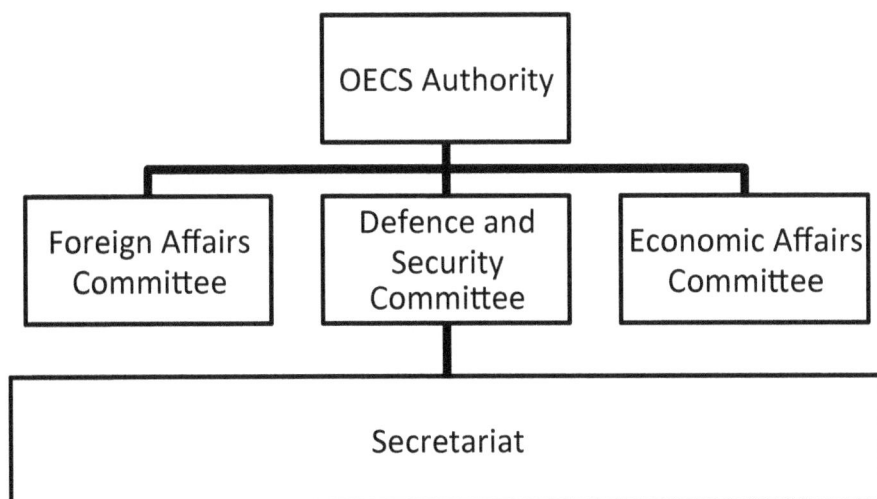

Institutions. The WISA Secretariat was replaced by an OECS Secretariat established in St Lucia to manage the administrative affairs of the Organisation. The ECCM Secretariat continued to function remotely from Antigua as a part of the OECS until 1997 when its operations were formally merged with the OECS Secretariat in St Lucia. The full integration of the political and economic governance structures was thus achieved. The supranational functional institutions, including the ECCA which was upgraded to a Central Bank the Eastern Caribbean Central Bank (ECCB) in 1983, were made subordinate to these intergovernmental arrangements.

The tradition of unanimous decision-making was preserved in these intergovernmental institutions and decisions did not take effect until ratified by national legislatures, according to the 'sovereign competence of member states to implement' (Article 6(5)). This clause may have been included to acknowledge the lack of competence of non-independent members like Montserrat to act in respect of some matters without permission from the colonial state. However, it may well have been inserted within the arrangement in order to provide an opportunity for member states to benefit from a loophole for avoiding implementation. The three ministerial councils were empowered to make unanimous recommendations to the Authority and take decisions binding on subordinate institutions (unless overruled by the Authority) but not on member states (Articles 7, 8, 9).

The Secretariat was supervised by a Director-General who, although dubbed the Chief Executive Officer of the Organisation, was essentially responsible for the general efficiency of administrative service. However, in many ways, it is arguable that the mandate of the Director-General held greater political significance than that of the CARICOM Secretary-General, given the extensive jurisdiction of the OECS institutions in each member state. Interestingly, despite the existence of a supranational judicial framework for criminal cases, the states did not make reference within the Treaty to a role for a specialised judicial framework to enforce the rules of the ECCM and adjudicate disputes between members. Instead, the Treaty specified a role for informal and amicable dispute settlement as was also customary in CARICOM in this period (Article 14).

During the first ten years of its operation, the OECS sought to strengthen subregional governance by establishing new functional institutions, including an investment promotion service, an export development agency, a pharmaceutical procurement framework and the Regional Security System (RSS) formed with Barbados in 1983. In addition, it also continued to advocate the advancement of CARICOM and the special interests of the LDCs within that wider framework. At the same time, many political leaders continued to pursue a vision of subregional political integration. For example, at the 11th meeting of the OECS Authority in May 1987, the Prime Minister of St Vincent and the Grenadines, James Mitchell, initiated another proposal for the creation of an OECS political union. The deliberations on the proposal and provisions of the resulting Tortola Declaration have been carefully outlined by Patsy Lewis and therefore, do not require detailed elaboration here.[16] However, the initiative revealed two interesting aspects of an intensifying subculture of governance which served to distinguish the OECS from CARICOM.

The first notable feature of the subculture was the entrenchment of principles of participatory regional governance, based on a commitment to public consultation and the legitimisation of regional decision-making by political referenda. The Tortola Declaration mandated such action as a matter of respect for the rights of citizens and a political responsibility to ensure responsiveness of the regional framework to the concerns of the people.[17] This approach is interesting in light of the negative connotation associated with public consultation and referenda in the wider region, as a result of the Jamaican experience in the early 1960s. The opening up of national debate on the subregional agenda encouraged non-governmental groups to develop regional responses. For example, some democratic opposition groups formed a regional alliance in the Standing Committee of Opposition Parties of Eastern Caribbean States (SCOPE)[18] in 1987 as an expression of their support for the concept of union. Other Opposition groups, which espoused more socialist agendas, converged around concerns about the perceived elitist nature of the proposals.[19] In spite of the inevitable debate among political parties on the merits and faults of the proposal, the creation of space for all ideas to contend was quite innovative in the region, given that a comparable participatory approach in CARICOM was not fully achieved until after the appointment of the West Indian Commission in 1989. It is only reasonable to concede that the participatory culture had perhaps been fostered by the even smaller size of these territories and the closer relationships between some government officials and the citizens.

The second interesting aspect of the subculture arising from the discussions on political union was the identification of a dual role for the subregional framework. The union was proposed as a way to enhance OECS capacity to act not only as a distinct entity for subregional governance but also as a catalyst for deeper CARICOM integration. Committed West

Indians like Demas had encouraged the adoption of political union in the OECS as a precursor to promoting unification in the wider region.[20] As such, the CARICOM Heads of Government meeting in St Lucia in 1987 expressed the view that the subregional initiative was of importance 'not only to the aspirations of the people of those States concerned, but also the strengthening of the wider integration movement in CARICOM'. The MDCs, in particular, expressed their 'strong support of any action towards unity among those states'.[21] The duality present in the subculture of governance sustained a contrived competitiveness between the OECS and CARICOM. Although the organisations were designed to be legally complementary and the advancement of OECS institutions was intended to inspire greater supranationality in CARICOM, the institutional distinction sustained a measure of rivalry between the LDCs and MDCs in relation to the distribution of the gains of integration.[22] That rivalry has since pervaded the ongoing pursuit of deeper integration.

Eventually, the 1987 political union initiative also floundered as various OECS members lost interest, particularly in the Leeward Islands, which had maintained relatively more prosperous economies and, above all, in Antigua whose new Prime Minister, Vere Bird, viewed the union proposal as a representation of neocolonialism. Notwithstanding the failure of the initiative, the OECS states continued to support the supranational institutions which sustained aspects of economic and political integration. The ECCB and common currency, in particular, were viewed as examples of good governance mechanisms, given the contribution of both the bank and the currency to greater economic and financial stability in OECS states at a time when the MDCs were struggling with the regulation of floating monetary policy and the administration of individual central banks.[23] By 1990 Grenadian Prime Minister Nicholas Brathwaite was able to boast to his CARICOM MDC colleagues about the relatively superior record of economic growth and stability which had been achieved through OECS monetary policy.[24] The apparent success and dynamism of the OECS process perhaps also contributed to Prime Minister Owen Arthur's expression of interest in leading Barbados into closer union with the OECS, based on the existing Regional Security System. Arthur signed an Agreement for Economic Coordination in 1995 in rejection of what he perceived to be a 'ruling paradigm [in CARICOM] that integration in the Caribbean should be constrained to strictly economic and functional matters; that considerations of political unity and integration should entirely be eschewed as being altogether dangerous, unachievable and in the realm of fantasy'.[25] He argued that 'economic integration without political unity in the Caribbean [would] be shown increasingly to be nonsense'.[26] Much to Arthur's regret, his proposal for a Barbados-OECS confederation did not materialise for a lack of popular support among Barbadian citizens who, although apparently supportive of integration generally, were concerned about the implications of closer union on the labour market in Barbados.[27]

Against the background of those aborted initiatives, the OECS 20th anniversary celebrations in June 2001 inspired member states to pursue a new attempt at further strengthening the political arrangements for economic integration. Gonsalves, the postgraduate student who had proposed an innovative architecture for union in 1972, had been elected as the Prime Minister of St Vincent and the Grenadines in March 2001, based on a manifesto which included a commitment to lead the country along a 'Path to Caribbean Nationhood'. Perhaps by then better acquainted with the dynamics of partisan politics, Gonsalves seized the opportunity of his Anniversary address to the Authority to outline a new proposal for a confederal arrangement, instead of a full political union, in order to support his vision of Caribbean civilisation. He described it as 'a more minimalist approach to political integration but...with resolution and with commitment to achieving something deeper and larger when the circumstances [became] more propitious...a strategy and bundle of tactics which emphasise[d] both prudence and enterprise'.[28] He proposed that the states seek to develop a framework which balanced power between the centre and the constituent members via rotational political leadership. Gonsalves' address inspired two new initiatives for the further institutionalisation of regional governance which called for the investment of even greater political responsibility at the regional level. First, the OECS decided in 2002 to establish an Economic Union with centralised legislative executive structures. Subsequently, in 2008 some Members of the OECS agreed to pursue an economic and political union with Trinidad and Tobago. The modes of supranationalism proposed in these initiatives are discussed, hereafter, in relation to their potential contribution to enhancing the effectiveness of the subregional framework.

## New Configurations of Eastern Caribbean Governance

The path of Eastern Caribbean governance has diverged on more than one occasion towards new institutional forms (see figure 9.2).

*Figure 9.2: Eastern Caribbean Path of Governance and Integration*

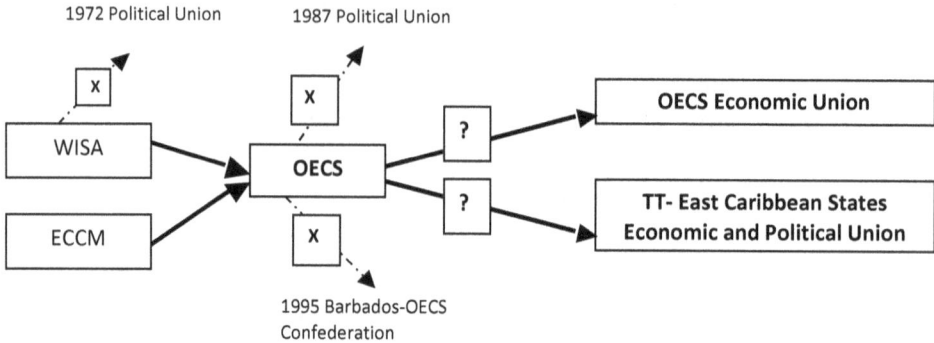

However, like CARICOM, several proposals have floundered in the face of a general reluctance to delegate political authority to regional institutions. At the same time, the subregion has been confronted with a greater level of powerlessness and desperation evident in the sovereignty paradox. This has perhaps forced more instances of governmental agreement to institutional reform in the Eastern Caribbean. Those factors have also created the impression of a greater level of political maturity in the subregion in respect of translating principles of sovereign power into workable institutional modes for regional integration. The two most recent propositions for supranationalism are the most innovative to date.

The first contemporary branch of new OECS integration emerged in 2001 with the decision to pursue an OECS Economic Union. The 34th meeting of the OECS Authority in June 2001 agreed that a Prime Ministerial Task Force, led by Gonsalves with participation from St Lucia's Kenny Anthony and Dominica's Pierre Charles, should develop proposals for institutionalisation of an 'East Caribbean Union of Independent States' by January 2002.[29] The fact that both Anthony and Gonsalves were also involved in the emerging proposals for governance reform in CARICOM meant that the subregional process was likely to reflect a similar discourse on the relationship between sovereignty and supranationalism. Indeed, that debate featured prominently in the discussions. Over a six year period the Task Force guided a three-stage process to operationalisation of the decision, discussed below, having regard to the formulation of a Development Charter; completion of research on appropriate modes of governance; and the drafting of a new legislative framework.

The first step towards the realisation of an economic union was the signing of an OECS Development Charter by the Heads of Government at a Special Summit convened in Basseterre, St Kitts and Nevis, in

October 2002.[30] The Charter outlined a people-centred development vision which identified the economic union as the principal instrument for development.[31] It highlighted specific human, economic and institutional development goals for the union, including the achievement of annual real growth rates of 6 per cent and the reduction of unemployment and poverty levels below 6 per cent by 2007. The goals were not overambitious since the states were already achieving average economic growth rates of 5.4 per cent of GDP in 2005, rising to some 7.2 per cent by 2006. However, the states were also highly indebted, carrying a collective debt in 2006 as high as 95 per cent of regional GDP.[32] Interestingly, unlike the process which had ensued from the development of the 2007 CARICOM Single Development Vision (see chapter 8), the OECS Development Charter was submitted to national parliamentary debate which suggested a seriousness of purpose in relation to the regional agenda. The Charter further outlined an intention to 'fashion and enhance institutions and modalities of governance, relevant to a [distinct] OECS approach to governance that recognises and is consistent with the Treaty of Basseterre and the objectives of the integration movement'.[33] Unfortunately, the statement provided no details of the type of governance architecture which would be required to support the union. Acknowledging the need for a deeper understanding of the requisite governance arrangements, the Heads commissioned two studies – one on the necessary executive arrangements including the possible adoption of an EU-style Commission and the other on the legal requirements for revision of the Treaty of Basseterre.[34]

## THE 2004 ECONOMIC UNION STUDIES

The completed studies were discussed at the 38th Meeting of the Authority in Castries in January 2004 against the background of an address by Prime Minister Kenny Anthony which contextualised the political foundations of the union as an act of 'balancing sovereignty and efficiency'. Like Gonsalves, Anthony acknowledged the importance of ensuring that 'new or upgraded political arrangements [took] into consideration the tenor of [each country's] constitutions and political culture'. However, he acknowledged that the OECS' existing governance framework had already been functioning on the basis of a 'joint sovereignty' which had served the subregion effectively and he therefore argued that the adoptions of new options for collective action as proposed by the studies would not be difficult.

Notably, the findings of the first study conducted by the OECS Secretariat on modalities of executive governance mirrored many of the conclusions of the CARICOM Rose Hall Agenda. It argued that there was a need for legislative effect in regional decision-making. It highlighted the OECS' predisposition to supranationalism and suggested therefore that the Organisation could learn from two principal features of the EU decision-making process. First, the new union would benefit from the adoption of majority voting in some intergovernmental fora. Second, the union would benefit from the institution of different types of deliberative outputs – whether regulations, directives, decisions and recommendations – which would enable states to reserve the right to make some agreements non-binding while assuring that others achieved immediate legislative effect at the national level.[35]

In that regard, the second study prepared by Earl Huntley argued that 'the most critical implication of an economic union [was the requirement for] a single legal/political authority to govern the new single economic space... those countries joining the union must establish a supranational entity to legislate and administer the laws that will govern the union'.[36] Clearly recognising that the amendment of the Treaty of Basseterre would not adequately accommodate the new legal authority, he recommended that member states negotiate an entirely new treaty.

Pleased with the indications from these studies of a variety of available options for improved governance, the Heads of Government reactivated the Task Force which established a technical group chaired by the Governor of the ECCB, Sir Dwight Venner, to assist in the preparation of a new draft Treaty of Union.[37] Venner's technical team engaged Ralph Carnegie, who had prepared the 2006 study on CARICOM institutions and was a member of the CARICOM Technical Working Group on Governance (TWG), to formulate the first draft of the Treaty which was finally unveiled during the OECS' 25th Anniversary celebrations in June 2006, at which time the Authority also signed a Declaration of Intent to Implement by 1st July 2007, after a year of public consultations.[38] Consequent on the comments of the Heads, the draft was further revised to include a role for parliamentary representatives. The final revised draft, which was made available to the public after the official launch, outlined the following governance framework.

The Treaty proposed enhanced legislative and executive procedures to support the pre-existing 'supranational architecture' in order to ensure timely implementation of a single financial and economic space.[39] The objectives of the Union as outlined in Article 4 were the same as those of the OECS, including the reference to the protection of sovereignty, territorial integrity and independence. However, the tradition of 'general undertaking for implementation' was completely eclipsed by the innovation contained in Article 5 with regard to the delegation of legislative authority from national parliaments to the union in specific areas. The union was granted exclusive competence to formulate binding legislation which would have direct effect in national law. Article 14 outlined exclusive competence of the union in five areas – the common market; monetary policy; trade policy; maritime jurisdiction; and civil aviation. In these areas, national legislatures would be expected to cease making legislation. The framework, as proposed, was not expected to require any amendment to national constitutions nor remove national government responsibility for public participation and consultation. In addition to the areas of exclusive legislative competence, the union was also empowered with overriding authority to legislate in respect of three other areas – common commercial policy; the environment; and immigration. In these areas, national legislatures would continue making laws if the union had declined to exercise its authority based on an assessment that national action was sufficient for the achievement of the intended objectives. This concept was derived from the principles of proportionality and subsidiarity which, had also been adapted from the EU context and inserted into the Prime Ministerial Expert Group on Governanace (PMEGG) and TWG proposals for CARICOM reform.

The Draft Treaty presented, in Article 6, three Institutions of the Union– the Supreme Court (ECSC), the ECCB and the Eastern Caribbean Civil Aviation Authority (ECCAA); and in Article 7, five principal Organs – the Authority; the Council of Ministers; the OECS Assembly; the Economic Affairs Council and the OECS Commission, as reflected in figure 9.3.

The strength of the proposed framework was found in its legislative and not its political executive competence. In fact, the Organs of the Union retained the political tradition of unanimous affirmative voting (see Articles 8 and 9), save for procedural matters where a simple majority vote was employed. However, it was empowered to make 'Acts of the Organisation' with direct effect. The Council of Ministers, which would comprise the appropriate Ministers of Government according to the matters to be discussed at each sitting, was empowered to pass binding 'Regulations and Orders' which would serve as subsidiary legislative instruments of implementation. The Council would consult with the OECS Assembly when instructed to do so by the Authority in the development of regulations

*Figure 9.3 Proposals for Governance Structure of OECS Union (2006)*

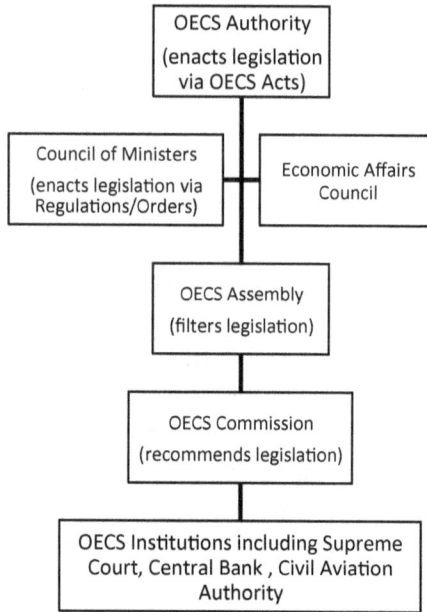

```
                    ┌─────────────────────┐
                    │    OECS Authority    │
                    │  (enacts legislation │
                    │    via OECS Acts)    │
                    └─────────────────────┘

┌─────────────────────┐      ┌─────────────────────┐
│  Council of Ministers│      │   Economic Affairs  │
│ (enacts legislation  │      │       Council       │
│   via Regulations/   │      │                     │
│      Orders)         │      │                     │
└─────────────────────┘      └─────────────────────┘

                    ┌─────────────────────┐
                    │    OECS Assembly     │
                    │ (filters legislation)│
                    └─────────────────────┘

                ┌─────────────────────────┐
                │     OECS Commission      │
                │ (recommends legislation) │
                └─────────────────────────┘

        ┌─────────────────────────────────────┐
        │ OECS Institutions including Supreme  │
        │ Court, Central Bank , Civil Aviation │
        │             Authority                │
        └─────────────────────────────────────┘
```

and orders. The Assembly was, therefore, positioned to act as a 'legislative filter' between the recommendations made by a technical Commission and the legislative competence of the Organs. It would be composed of elected Members of Parliaments and Legislatures – five from each full member state and three from each associate member state, according to the proportions of representation abiding in each member state once at least one Opposition Member and at least two government representatives agreed to participate in each delegation (see Article 10). Provisions were also made for the election of a Speaker and Deputy Speaker from among citizens eligible for election to national Parliament and a Clerk to be appointed by the Commission.

Interestingly, the OECS Commission was designed to act as the administrative and research arm of the union and not as a political executive, as proposed by the PMEGG and TWG in the CARICOM context (Article 12). It would comprise a Director-General and one Ambassador appointed by each member state, who would also represent the OECS Union in the member state which appointed him or her. The Commission was empowered in the draft treaty to recommend legislation to be pursued by the Council and the Authority; monitor implementation; and conduct relevant research. Its non-binding decisions would be made by majority vote. The Director-General, still described as the CEO, would have responsibility for the administration of a Secretariat within the Commission and for convening the dispute resolution mechanisms (see Article 13).

The foregoing suggests that the proposed arrangements were not intended to remove the union from the prevailing tradition of Head of Government control. However, the draft treaty did provide a framework for more effective decision-making by developing legislative rather than political supranational institutions which were intended to facilitate the national implementation process. Notwithstanding this legislative competence, it is interesting that the clause present in the previous treaty which subjected the implementation process to the 'sovereign competence of member states' was retained in the new draft. The meaning of the clause in this revised context is uncertain, given the legislative power of the new Authority and the Council. However, it is not likely that it would have had the wide interpretation and loophole effect which the previous treaty may have permitted. The phrase can only be considered as a legitimate provision of regional governance if it is meant to remove any threat of sanction should states default on implementation as a result of events outside government control. The Treaty was further revised in January 2007 at the 44th meeting of the Authority in St Johns, Antigua in order to permit the Speaker of the Assembly to invite technical experts and civil society representatives to participate in its deliberations.

As the OECS states prepared to accede to the CARICOM Single Market (CSM) in 2006, the Authority established a special unit within the Secretariat to spearhead the OECS Union process, including a public education initiative.[40] Subsequently, at a retreat in St Kitts in October 2007, Heads proposed that special units be established in the Offices of Prime Ministers/Chief Minister to facilitate the implementation process by creating better administrative synergies between the national and regional levels of governance.[41] This proposal reflected the traditional preoccupation with Head of Government control which also held the potential to enhance the likelihood of national implementation by giving the regional agenda high priority within the national cabinet. These units were fully in place by January 2008.[42] The following year, the Prime-Ministerial Task Force proposed that Cabinet and Parliamentary committees be convened to assist in the consultation and implementation process. In addition, the Task Force proposed that a subcommittee of Heads, including the incoming and outgoing chair of the Authority (reminiscent of the CARICOM Bureau structure), meet to ensure clarity of roles of different actors in the process.[43] The public consultation process eventually began in Dominica in April 2008 and proceeded slowly in the other territories over the next year.[44]

However, consequent on the slow pace of the consultation process, the deadlines for implementation of the union were postponed on several occasions. The states faced two principal challenges which affected the implementation process. First, a level of political instability had emerged in relation to the desire of Nevis to secede from St Kitts.[45] At the 38th meeting of the Authority in Castries, St Lucia, Heads expressed 'deep concern [in relation to] the proclaimed intention to have a referendum for Nevis to secede from St Kitts' and urged that 'the matter be re-examined with a view to preserving the integrity of the state of St Kitts and Nevis'.[46] Second, the states, which were carrying high levels of debt, faced a challenge of financial unsustainability. For several years some member states had been in arrears in their contributions to the OECS budget. The problem was compounded by the fact that Hurricane Ivan in 2004 destroyed most of the island of Grenada. However, the other members responded by agreeing to shoulder Grenada's financial responsibilities for a 12-month period while it pursued reconstruction.[47] It is not evident whether the members were successful in meeting that commitment, but there has certainly been no record of a comparable collective responsibility for regional arrangements and spirit of solidarity in the CARICOM context.

In summary, notwithstanding the long process of consultation, the OECS had on this occasion made a relatively smooth transition between the 1981 OECS and the upgraded Economic Union, compared with the protracted analysis still underway in CARICOM. In May 2009, at their 49th meeting in Tortola, in the British Virgin Islands, Heads agreed to finalise and sign the Treaty.[48] By December of the same year, six member states signed a charter of commitment to implement the Economic Union, at the headquarters of the ECCB in St Kitts-Nevis. Chairman of the Authority and host of the ceremony, Prime Minister Denzil Douglas indicated that in his view, the signing of the charter represented a 'fundamental philosophical transformation and political commitment to deepening the level of integration among member states'.[49] Unfortunately, Montserrat did not receive the requisite entrustments from the British Government to join the Union. The final Revised Treaty of Basseterre, establishing the OECS Economic Union was signed by the six states, at a formal ceremony, during the 51st meeting of the Authority in June 2010, in order to mark the 29th anniversary of the signing of the original treaty.

The second branch of new configurations for the OECS was proposed as an Economic and Political Union between the OECS states and Trinidad and Tobago. Parallel to the OECS Economic Union process, St Vincent and the Grenadines and Grenada announced in March 2008 their intention to pursue the formation of a southern Caribbean political union with Trinidad and Tobago. During a meeting among the prospective parties, convened the following August in Port of Spain, newly-elected Prime Minister of Grenada Tillman Thomas explained that he and his Prime-Ministerial colleagues, Patrick Manning and Ralph Gonsalves, were willing to relinquish a certain amount of sovereignty in the interest of developing appropriate structures to advance the integration process.[50] As such, the participating states were prepared to create a new space for the 'convergence' (not 'sharing') of sovereignties in order to link decision-making to decision-implementation in a more effective way. The underlying rationale for this bold step was that a political union was more likely to develop the kind of space for economic development which neither the OECS Union nor the CARICOM Single Economy, if eventually realised, was likely to achieve.[51]

This particular South-Eastern Caribbean geopolitical alliance did not come as a surprise to many commentators. In fact, Rosina Wiltshire-Brodber had anticipated the strengthening of relationships between the three territories which she had regarded as the core of the 1980s integration movement.[52] In recent times, it had become apparent that Trinidad had an interest in building a 400-mile gas pipeline through the Eastern Caribbean in order to enhance its capacity to supply the region.[53] It is not surprising therefore that Trinidad and Tobago, and Prime Minister Patrick Manning in particular, assumed a leadership role in the process. Manning undertook an impromptu official tour of the CARICOM region in August 2008 to encourage participation of other states. In a matter of weeks, St Lucia had signed up to participate in the Trinidad and Tobago-Eastern Caribbean States Integration Initiative (referred to as the Manning Initiative) and the four states signed a 'Joint Declaration on Collaboration towards the achievement of the Single Economy and Political Integration among Grenada, St Lucia, St Vincent and the Grenadines and the Republic of Trinidad and Tobago'.[54]

However, critics of the initiative were sceptical of the potential for success, given the differences in economic status and political subcultures in the OECS and in Trinidad and Tobago respectively. Some suggested that there was greater potential in achieving an OECS political union.[55] When Manning visited Jamaica, Prime Minister Bruce Golding assured him that Jamaica had no interest in participating in any configuration of political union but expressed no objection to the initiative among other states, while recommending that the matter be discussed in CARICOM.

However, the following year when Manning raised the issue at a People's National Movement (PNM) meeting in Trinidad in June 2009 and the oil-driven economic interests of Trinidad became more apparent, Golding reversed his prior opinion to suggest that the initiative was in fact an imperialist move by Manning into the rest of the region and represented a threat to the stability of CARICOM.[56] The effect of Golding's statement may have been to dissuade other states, particularly other MDCs, from joining the initiative. The Joint Declaration signed by the four states had argued that the initiative was based on a

> ...spirit of solidarity, cooperation and friendship borne out of shared membership in CARICOM...the imperatives of responding in a more immediate manner to increasing changes in the international economic and political environment...[and a resolution to] continue the process of creating an ever closer union among the peoples of the Caribbean on the basis of principles of equality and mutual benefit.[57]

It sought to allay fears of a threat to the existing CARICOM framework by declaring an intention to develop a single economy by 2011 and to develop an appropriate form of political integration which would not undermine the framework established by the Revised Treaty of Chaguaramas. Notwithstanding these remarks, the Declaration made clear that a primary rationale of the initiative was to move the participating states beyond the Rose Hall conception of 'Community of Sovereign States'. In that regard, the Declaration was intended to challenge other CARICOM Heads of Government to take steps to advance the CARICOM Single Market and Economy (CSME) agenda. On behalf of the signatory states, Trinidad and Tobago commissioned St Lucian Vaughan Lewis, who had been the first Director-General of the OECS, and Trinidadian Cuthbert Joseph – both having participated in the PMEGG and TWG processes – to lead a Task Force in undertaking the feasibility study.

The Lewis-Joseph Task Force presented its report to a meeting of Signatory States of CARICOM Heads of Government in May 2009.[58] In his address to Heads, Vaughan Lewis reinforced the argument that the initiative was being pursued as a mechanism for strengthening the CARICOM integration process and therefore suggested that the Task Force's recommendations did not undermine the ongoing thrust towards the CSME.[59] In fact, Lewis acknowledged that the report had been influenced by the long series of studies that had sought to advance

CARICOM governance including the WIC, PMEGG and TWG reports. His address included reference to two primary proposals to secure achievement of the union which were perhaps directed at the CARICOM directorate. First, he suggested that the traditional ambivalence about the sovereignty-supranationalism debate – a continuation of which was likely to be much more harmful to the smaller economies than the larger – could be resolved by approaching the union from the perspective of creating several designated spaces for economies of scale, as opposed to the creation of a single highly centralised unitary economic space. The delegation of sovereignty would, therefore, be limited to specific areas. Secondly, he recommended that States adopt a gradual evolutionary approach to the achievement of union, involving a two-phased process of first economic integration and then political integration upon review of the initial process.

The report of over 500 pages was presented in two volumes – the latter containing detailed thematic reports on proposed spaces of integration and governance which had informed the preparation of the former volume containing the official recommendations on the modalities of economic and political union which were presented to Heads.[60] The recommendations were contained in six chapters. In the tradition of all CARICOM expert reports, chapter 1 provided a detailed overview of the historical precedents and contemporary context of CARICOM integration, followed by identification in chapter 2 of six primary spaces of integration. The Task Force recommended that decision-making competencies be merged in order to create selective supranationalism in respect of economic spaces for facilitation of production (that is, land, maritime and air spaces); human resource spaces; monetary spaces; security spaces; external relations spaces; and legal and judicial spaces.[61] The proposed role for each of these spaces was elaborated in chapters 3 and 4, along with the profile of the states which represented a combined population of only 1.7 million people, including a labour force of 738,000; a collective land size of only 2501 square miles and a combined GDP in 2007 of US$22.8 billion (over 85 per cent of which was accounted for by Trinidad's GDP).[62] In chapter 5, the concept of political integration was presented not as an end in itself (West Indian Nationalism) but as a means to supporting the economic union as an imperative for economies of scale.

Finally, chapter 6 tackled the important issue of governance arrangements for the union. The Task Force outlined two institutional models for governance as illustrated in figures 9.4 and 9.5. The evolutionary approach which Lewis had recommended in his address to

Heads proposed the pursuit of an initial Model 1 for a Trinidad and Tobago Eastern Caribbean States Economic Union and then, upon review of Model 1, the formulation of a Modified Model for Political Union. In the first stage of equipping the region with appropriate governance architecture, the states would create six principal tiers of governance. The Union Council of States, comprising each Head of Government of the member states, would act as the supreme decision-making authority of the union, exercising policy formulation and executive responsibility for each of the economic integration spaces within the union. Each Head would be assigned portfolio responsibility for one dimension of the union and elect from among themselves a Chairman of the Council of States to act as President of the Union. At the second tier of regional governance, a Union Council of Ministers would be convened to assist the Council of States

*Figure 9.4: Model 1 for Trinidad-OECS Economic Union*

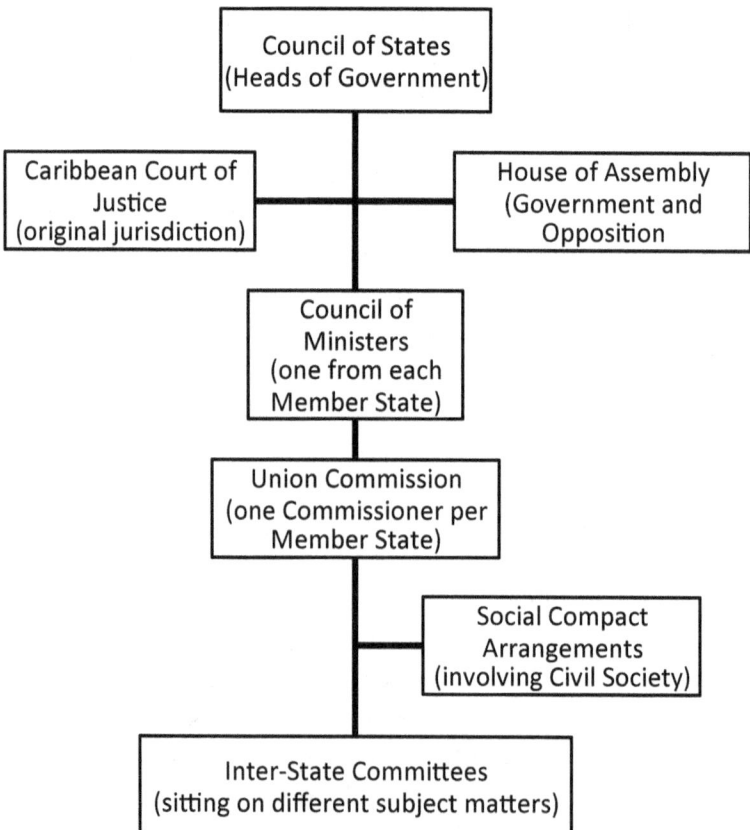

in its decision-making. The Council of Ministers would be composed of one representative from each member state having responsibility in the national cabinet for decision-making according to the subject matter of the sitting. The third tier would be managed by the Union Commission, acting as the technical arm supporting the decision-making processes of the Council of Ministers and the Council of States. The Commission would facilitate the intergovernmental negotiation process at the level of the Council of Ministers; prepare proposals in consultation with Inter-State Committees and national ministries; and implement, as directed by the Councils of States and Ministers. It would be led by a Commissioner-General appointed by the Council of States from among the other Commissioners representing each State and nominated by their Heads of Government for a period of five years. The administrative aspects of the Commission's role would be led by an Executive Secretary. These three principal tiers would function as the regional executive of the union.

At the fourth level of the governance arrangement, a Union House of Assembly comprising both governmental and non-governmental representatives from each member state, would take responsibility for approving the budget of the union; approving public policy; assessing programmes; and making recommendations on issues referred to it by the executive structures. The Assembly would also play a key role in monitoring the actions of the executive structures. Union legislation would be passed by the Council of States in cooperation with the Assembly and would have direct effect in each member state once the Treaty of Union was ratified by Single Acts of Union passed in each member state. Pursuant to that process, the Caribbean Court of Justice (CCJ) would be entrusted as a fifth tier of judicial enforcement of legislation. Rather than create a new mechanism, the group perhaps decided to make use of the CCJ, which had, after all, already been established so as to accommodate the differences in judicial administration in the OECS and the CARICOM MDCs. Furthermore, the entrustment of the protection of the Treaty of Chaguaramas to the CCJ would also ensure that interpretations of the Treaty of Union would not contravene the provisions of CARICOM. These five regional tiers would be supported by a sixth tier of governance comprising Inter-State Committees and other mechanisms for civil society participation convened at regional and national levels to support the work of the Commission and the Council of Ministers. The inclusion of these consultative mechanisms certainly reinforced the subcultural predisposition to participatory governance, relative to what obtained in CARICOM.

Overall, the arrangement proposed in Model 1 could be viewed as a hybrid of CARICOM and OECS governance traditions. In many ways, it reflected the tradition of intergovernmental control common to both CARICOM and the OECS. It adopted the CARICOM's preference for portfolio allocation to Heads as an executive mechanism. However, it also embraced the more progressive aspects of the OECS economic union model in respect of legislative supranationalism, via Single Acts of Union. Analytically, it appears that the proposal, having been spearheaded by two key figures of the TWG, was a reworked version of the CARICOM reform agenda which had benefitted from the progress made by the OECS Economic Union initiative.

In the event that Model 1 functioned effectively, the Task Force expected the group of states to be in a position to establish a political union by 2013. The team proposed that an Inter-State Conference be convened to review the initial model and recommend a new structure, but it also specified its own scenario in which the Council of Ministers and the Commission were replaced by a Cabinet of the Union and Ministerial Departments. In the second model, shown in figure 9.5, the Council of States would retain its position as the principal decision-making body but its members would not participate in the Assembly. The most prominent changes have been highlighted in black. Most notably, in this model, a Cabinet would be established comprising appointed representatives from each member state not holding ministerial office or positions as members of national Parliaments. It would be presided over by an appointed First Minister. Each regional Cabinet Minister would be assigned responsibility for a regional portfolio and participate in the Assembly to which he or she would be accountable.

The second principal change was that the Cabinet Members would lead Union Ministerial Departments staffed by public officers recruited on an equitable basis from all the states of the union by a Union Public Service Commission. The House of Assembly would operate in the same manner as it had under the economic union but would have increased powers to legislate. The CCJ, Inter-State Committees and civil society consultative mechanisms would operate as under Model 1. The implications of the changes in Model 2 include the opening up of the regional agenda to the kind of partisan debate typical of the legislative process at national level. The empowerment of the Assembly to make legislation would require more stringent debate rather than general discussion. The overall policy framework of the Union, guided by the Council of States, would remain

## Figure 9.5: Model 2 for Trinidad-OECS Political Union

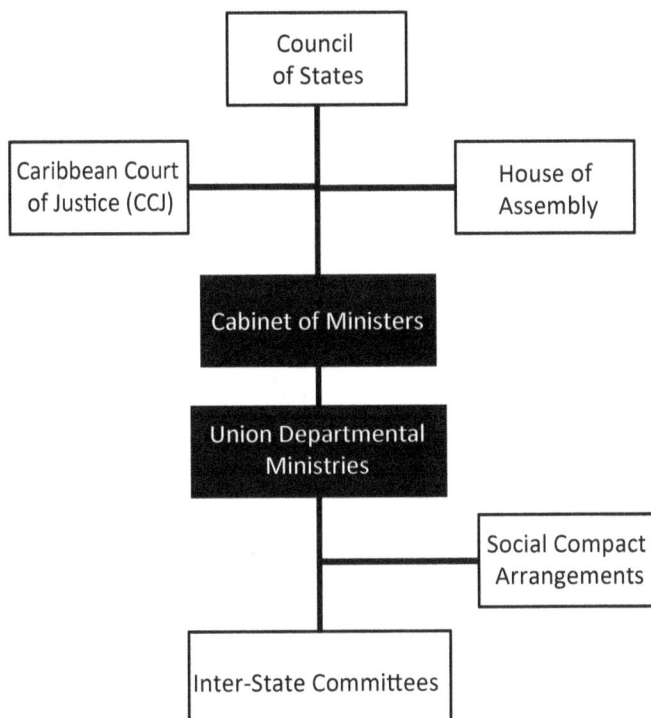

intergovernmental. However, once legislation was agreed by the Council of States and the Assembly, the supranational legal framework – empowered by Single Acts in each state – would ensure that regional decisions had direct effect at the national level. Furthermore, regional Ministerial Departments, if properly staffed with the competent policy and technical personnel, would be able to facilitate national implementation.

This second more sophisticated model of integration perhaps reflected a utopian view of the prospects for political union. While the establishment of a regional Cabinet and regional Government bureaucracy was quite likely in the context of the OECS, given the interdependence we have explored in this chapter, the difference in political culture between Trinidad and the OECS certainly made the proposal seem less feasible. However, if we reflect on the fact that the whole initiative had been conceived as a means to influence CARICOM's decision making on governance reform, then we can more easily understand that Trinidad perhaps hoped to cause controversy over the possible adoption of Model 2 as a means of securing CARICOM's agreement to pursue a version of Model 1 – akin to the PMEGG-TWG proposals. In that regard, Lewis and Joseph were very strategic appointees to the Task Force. To date, however, there has been no further progress on the Manning Initiative and its realisation remains doubtful in light of changes in government leadership in Trinidad and Tobago and observations of that country having to bear the brunt of financial support in the region.

## INSIGHTS FROM EASTERN CARIBBEAN GOVERNANCE

The proposals for supranational legislative competence ascribed to regional structures in the OECS Economic Union and in the Trinidad and Tobago-Eastern Caribbean Union provide alternative frameworks for effectively translating regional decisions into implementable policies at the national level. Drawing on the overview of the OECS experience in general, it is possible to isolate some important features of an Eastern Caribbean subculture of governance which has thus far sustained distinct institutional modes of governance founded on greater levels of and types of supranationality in an attempt to make regional integration more effective.

The discussion has shown that the features peculiar to Caribbean political culture and the sovereignty tradition observed in CARICOM also persist in the subregional movement. The OECS member states are perhaps equally preoccupied with Head of Government control and unanimous voting procedures and obsessed with the maintenance of the highest levels of island autonomy. As a consequence, regional deliberative structures retain a fixed intergovernmental character. However, the prominence of the sovereignty paradox within the Eastern Caribbean political economic profile has fostered the development of different institutional approaches to balancing the safeguarding of the aforementioned dimensions of sovereignty with the need to create common spaces for economic development. The OECS states have sustained common institutions which have adopted supranational competencies which are not deemed to be in conflict with the sovereignty of each state or the power of national governments. For instance, the ECCB and the ECSC have effectively and successfully governed those aspects of economic and political union present in the OECS. The persistence of these supranational institutions is not only related to the prominence of the paradox, given the relatively smaller size of the OECS territories. It is also the outcome of the distinct historical path of the subregional framework. Even after the collapse of the Federation, the Eastern Caribbean territories continued to pursue other forms of regionalism in parallel to the pursuit of nationalism. The absence of an interruption in the regional movement between 1961 and 1968 when

CARIFTA was established is enough to suggest that the subculture reflects, in some ways, a continued commitment to the concept of West Indian Nationalism. The conceptual rupture between territorial nationalisms and a 'regional nationalism' never occurred in the way that it did, for example, in Jamaica and Trinidad and Tobago. Rather, a culture of interdependence has been fostered.

Consequent on that commitment to a regional nationalism, and despite the failure to date of various initiatives towards closer political union, the dynamism in conceptions of regional governance in the OECS has facilitated the continued evolution of new proposals for strengthening the political arrangements for economic integration. In particular, the most recent decision to employ legislative supranationalism in specific areas of an OECS Economic Union, as an alternative to political executive supranationalism, has presented an innovative option for facilitating implementation of regional decisions while respecting traditions of intergovernmental decision making. Although the areas for exclusive regional legislative competence are areas in which the OECS has already developed advanced common administrative procedures, the proposed framework is likely to embed the regional agenda within the national policy implementation process. Consequently, the correction of weaknesses in national public administration remains an imperative for its effective functioning.

The second proposal for a Trinidad and Tobago-Eastern Caribbean economic and political union has employed a similar approach to giving legislative effect to regional decisions. However, the differences between the OECS and Trinidad and Tobago – particularly in relation to their distinct histories of common administration and unique nationalist traditions – may complicate the adoption of this kind of legislative competence. This MDC-LDC context is quite similar to the context of diverse political views in the wider CARICOM group. In that regard, the Manning Initiative may have been proposed as a way of presenting the recommendations of the PMEGG and TWG on Governance within a subregional context which is more predisposed to regional governance, in order to make the proposals appear more feasible at the wider regional level. The OECS structures have always been intended to catalyse similar approaches in the wider CARICOM integration process, so that Eastern Caribbean states can reap the benefits of even greater economies of scale. The flaws in this rationale, however, are two-fold. First, because the OECS states remain dependent on the wider Caribbean political economy, including the success of the CSME, the subculture loses some viability. In other words, even with relatively more progressive and effective governance institutions, the prospects for OECS development are limited without the support of the larger states in the region. Secondly, the subculture is a result of the unique history of the Eastern Caribbean and therefore cannot be imposed on the wider region. It remains comfortably nested within the wider CARICOM tradition of sovereignty safeguards, but is, nevertheless, confined to its subregional space. The improbability of achievement of the Trinidad and Tobago-OECS initiative is testament to that fact. The wider CARICOM group must, therefore, reach its own separate compromise on new approaches to developing supranational competence for the CSME based on a more appropriate interpretation of sovereignty.

The principal theme of the OECS experience and the proposals for new branches of subregional governance is that alternative bargains between supranationalism and intergovernmentalism are possible in the Caribbean. CARICOM has long been apprised through its expert studies of a continuum of possibilities which neither require the full surrender of sovereignty nor its full retention. However, in light of the diversity of positions on sovereignty in the region, the geographical context in which sovereignty bargains are persued may change. Indeed, while CARICOM is currently an important forum for regional solidarity and cooperation, it may not be considered the most appropriate configuration for the furtherance of regional economic integration. In that regard, the region may become more polarised as each state seeks to find the best geographical configuration to suit its conception of sovereignty. Some polarisation is already evident in the increased interest shown by some CARICOM states in alternative frameworks, including the Bolivarian Alternative for Latin America (ALBA), which involves Dominica, St Vincent and the Grenadines and St Lucia with Latin America; CARIFORUM, which engages CARICOM states in an international cooperation framework with the Dominican Republic and Europe; the Central American Integration System (SICA), which engages Belize in Central America; and the Union of South American Nations (UNASUR), which engages Guyana and Suriname in the South American subcontinent.

There is, however, a caveat, which must be placed on this pursuit of alternatives. It is possible that, if the strengthening of these alternative mechanisms leads to a decline in commitment to CARICOM, some states which do not have comparably strong allegiances to alternative frameworks, may be marginalised from the regional (and perhaps international) political economy. CARICOM, therefore, is likely to continue to have an important role in the region. In that regard, the concluding chapter consolidates the review of the mode of CARICOM governance that has operated hitherto, in relation to the tradition of sovereignty and the sovereignty paradox. This understanding of CARICOM governance is then complemented by an examination of the implications for moving beyond the current CARICOM impasse towards a more effective approach to regional governance, regardless of the model or geometry of integration which may evolve henceforth.

# ► 10

# CARIBBEAN SOVEREIGNTY: LEGACY AND PROSPECTS

The process towards establishing a framework for regional governance in the West Indies began at the 1947 Montego Bay Conference on Closer Association, and yet, more than six and a half decades later, that goal of regional governance remains the single most pressing issue on the Caribbean political and development agendas. Interestingly, the July 2010 meeting of Heads of Government brought leaders back to Montego Bay to discuss, *inter alia*, new proposals for reform of the governance structures of the 37-year-old Caribbean Community (CARICOM). That meeting was being heralded, by politicians and civic commentators alike, as another potential watershed in the evolution of CARICOM.[1] The issue of leadership was raised as a potential starting point for renewing governance. However, the meeting did not bring about the anticipated change and since then, the discourse has deteriorated to one of 'CARICOM in crisis'. Although, the Community appointed a new Secretary-General in 2011, the perpetuation of 'crisis' led St Vincent and the Grenadines Prime Minister Ralph Gonsalves to pen on open letter to the new Secretary-General in early 2012 describing his frustrations with the stagnation in the movement. Furthermore, shortly thereafter, a team of consultants commissioned to review the functioning of the Secretariat, concluded that without urgent attention to pressing governance issues, CARICOM would potentially 'expire slowly' by 2017.[2]

This concluding chapter, therefore, consolidates the principal themes that have emerged from the review of the experience of regional governance in the CARICOM region between 1947 and 2010. Specifically, the three sections examine the relationship between the dynamics of the CARICOM case and the theoretical assumptions regarding regional governance in the context of a conceptual problematic and an institutional imperative. The first section explains the special paradoxical relationship between sovereignty and regionalism, which distinguishes

CARICOM's mode of governance from other models discussed in the broader literature. In the second section, the chapter revisits the three-tiered framework for regional governance analysis elaborated in chapter 2, by way of highlighting the distinctive characteristics of Caribbean political culture, CARICOM institutions and elite conceptions of sovereignty, which have influenced the evolution and effective functioning of regional governance systems. Finally, the chapter concludes with a discussion of the strategic implications of CARICOM's governance history for future reform.

## CARICOM's Unorthodox Paradox

From a perspective of traditional regionalist scholarship, there are three principal themes relating to the emergence of Caribbean regionalism which highlight certain unique aspects of the case. The first theme relates to the traditional expectations of a chronological progression from the attainment of sovereignty to the pursuit of regionalism. The conceptual introduction to regional governance assumed, *a priori*, the achievement and consolidation of sovereignty in individual state territories prior to any agreement to embark on a strategy of regional integration. Indeed, that was the experience of Europe and Latin America. Conversely, West Indian regionalism was not a post-sovereignty phenomenon. The political campaigns for sovereign independence in each territory were conceptualised within the regionalist framework of West Indian Nationalism. In that regard, the first opportunity for the colonies to claim sovereignty arose within the context of the 1958 West Indies Federation. Sovereignty and regionalism emerged concurrently, further suggesting that, paradoxically, regionalism was endorsed as an integral component of the movement for sovereign independence. Consequent on that special relationship between sovereignty and regionalism, neither the collapse of the Federation in 1962, nor Jamaica and Trinidad and Tobago's early assumption of separate independent statehood, precluded the emergence of a new regionalism in the post-independence period. In fact, the Demasian paradox of sovereignty, manifested in the features of small size, vulnerability to external pressures and quasi-state incapacity, as observed in the empirical discussion, ensured that the strengthening of regionalism continued to be viewed as an indispensable strategy for the consolidation of an effective national sovereignty.

The continued pursuit of regionalism after the disintegration of the Federation, despite the geographical and psychological predispositions to fragmentation, highlighted a second interesting theme in the CARICOM case, in relation to traditional assumptions about the logical progression of regional integration. Consequent on the legacy of the neo-functionalist hypothesis of spillover, even 'new regionalist' literature has assumed that regional integration usually involves the deepening of institutional relationships from functional to economic and then to political integration. A distinct reversal of those assumptions is evident in the CARICOM case, since the West Indian territories followed an unorthodox path, involving the transition from a state of near complete political integration in Federation to one of complete disintegration. This was followed by the construction and then reconstruction of apolitical economic integration models in the form of the 1968 CARIFTA followed by the 1973 Caribbean Community and Common Market and currently the 2006 CARICOM Single Market. Notwithstanding the early reversal of the neofunctionalist assumption of spillover however, CARICOM's current ambitions to establish a single economy by 2015 have now raised the imperative of proceeding towards greater integration of political institutions at the regional level.

That reversed path of integration was complemented by a third interesting theme in Caribbean regionalism – the parallel evolution of a distinct subregional governance framework which is nested within the CARICOM framework. Although limited attention has been given to subregional movements in the broader literature, the coexistence of two highly-institutionalised formal systems of regional governance within such a small geographical area provided an interesting opportunity to examine the relationships between the two frameworks. The history of the OECS has been treated in this case as a significant part of the CARICOM analysis for two principal reasons. Firstly, the experience of relatively higher levels of institutional integration among the smallest territories in the Eastern Caribbean has reinforced the significance of the small size factor to understanding the Caribbean sovereignty paradox, which compels deeper integration. Secondly, the OECS experience preserves a link to CARICOM's past through its retention of shared supranational judicial and monetary systems which reflect the spirit of West Indian Nationalism; while also pointing to a possible future for CARICOM via the innovative governance proposals for legislative supranationalism within a fully-fledged OECS Economic Union.

Against the background of those dynamics – the convergence of sovereignty and regionalism and the unorthodox progression, as well as the variable geometry of regionalism – regionalism in Caribbean development appears to have been inevitable. In the broader regionalism literature, the phenomenon is treated as an optional but complementary strategy to sovereign governance, which emerged as a part of the post-1945 trend towards the internationalisation of governance. However, the Caribbean case has presented regionalism as an integral part of ongoing strategies to improve the capacity of new states to participate effectively in national and international governance regimes. Regionalism represents an important part of CARICOM's trade policy (with regional trade agreements becoming a norm of international relations), economic and financial policy (as the current global economic crisis calls for a common response), and socio-economic development policy (taking account of natural disasters such as the January 2010 earthquake in Haiti, as well as the social and economic challenges of crime and violence and youth development which also demand joint action). Because regionalism is inextricably linked to the struggle to achieve effective sovereignty, the viability of regional governance remains a salient point. In spite of recent discussions which have suggested that the commitment of political elites to regionalism is waning because of the weaknesses of the governance framework, the region continues to struggle with this deep-seated paradox and the associated contradictory forces of 'oneness' and 'otherness' which have been a fundamental part of the history of the process of Caribbean state-building.[3] In this sense, the case bears out the ongoing debate in the new regionalism literature in respect of the tensions between the endogenous search for regional identity and the utilitarian search for a solution to small size, captured by CARICOM's 'means-end' debate.

The definition of regional governance, encapsulates some of these tensions. It refers to a process of transforming the political context for national development into shared development outcomes that reflect the identity and aspirations of the people. It involves the regulation of power by the state, within a multi-level institutional system, via a process of bargaining with attributes of sovereignty in order to achieve an optimum balance between national authority and legitimacy, on the one hand, and effective autonomy and control, on the other hand, in the pursuit of defined national and regional development goals. Against the background of that understanding and the acknowledgement of the persistence of a special paradox in the conceptualisation of CARICOM governance, there are specific elements of the case which help to engage the findings on CARICOM's experimentation with addressing the institutional imperative.

In order to explain how CARICOM's governance framework has evolved over time, the three-tiered analytical framework which has guided the empirical discussion is revisited. CARICOM's political culture and context, the institutional framework and the tradition of sovereignty which determined the overall mode of governance are all reviewed.

## THE POLITICAL CONTEXT OF INTEGRATION

The historical review of the political context of CARICOM's evolution has highlighted three significant aspects of political culture which have influenced the institutionalisation of regionalism. The first is related to a Federal legacy which has significantly impinged on the institutional choices made by the architects of the CARICOM governance framework. The second aspect relates to a political tradition of personalised politics which has influenced the way in which the implications for sovereignty of pursuing regionalism have been understood by political elites. The third aspect is the emergence of a regional ideological vacuum in relation to the adoption of a purpose for Caribbean regionalism.

The first issue relates to the emergence of a strong aversion, among political elites, to delegating authority to supranational institutions, which is a legacy of the collapse of the Federation in 1962. Consequent on the fact that the joint Federal institutions had remained under the control of the British colonial government, and therefore, prevented local leaders from exerting full authority, supranational institutions became strongly associated with colonialism as an illegitimate form of governance. In contrast, with the emergence of national sovereignty after 1962, state institutions were viewed as the more appropriate and legitimate vehicles for governance, and subsequent models of regionalist governance sought to emphasise the role of state institutions and thus avoided the establishment of supranational authority.

It cannot be denied that the pre-independence West Indian and subsequent Caribbean political culture emphasises the role of individual political leaders, over other actors, in the development process. The second aspect of political culture is evident in the direct exertion of authority by Heads of Government over the CARICOM project. From the inauguration of the first Conference of Heads of Government of the Commonwealth Caribbean in 1963, Heads have assumed direct responsibility for the protection and safeguarding of national sovereignty against the intrusion of external or supranational authority. Having been denied the right to rule over centuries of colonisation, post-independence rulers have perhaps, understandably, adopted regimes which emphasise their authority. In fact, the influence of the Heads has been so prominent as to suggest that the political culture has equated national sovereignty with personal sovereignty.

A related issue which must be taken into account here, is the special role played by individual nationals and 'nations' in catalysing or frustrating the integration process. In this regard, there has been a popular perception that a post-independence polarisation has emerged in the region emanating from the distinctiveness of Jamaica's political tradition. The unfolding of the events in Jamaica, which of course, precipitated the collapse of the Federation and also inaugurated the prominence of national sovereignty, initiated a perception that the sovereignty tradition in Jamaica is an absolutist model, opposed to that prevailing in other parts of the region, where there has instead been demonstration of a greater willingness to bargain with some attributes of sovereignty. However, despite the view that, in the wake of the Federal legacy, Jamaica has been the principal bug-bear of modern integration, as recently as July 2010 CARICOM leaders and the Secretary-General alike acknowledged the special significance of Montego Bay and the facilitative role of Jamaicans in the history of Caribbean integration. Since the 1947 Conference on Closer Association, Jamaica has played a significant role in inaugurating CARICOM in 1973, in reviving the integration movement in 1982 following a seven-year hiatus of the Conference, and in developing a new conception of regional governance at the 2003 Rose Hall Conference. Certainly, Jamaican nationals such as Norman Manley, Michael Manley and P.J. Patterson are among those counted as stalwarts of the integration movement. In spite of its geographical separateness and often perceived political aloofness, Edwin Carrington has referred to Jamaica as 'the cradle of modern Caribbean integration'.[4] Certainly, Carrington's remarks may have been made merely out of conviction or made as a part of a deliberate strategy to instil greater confidence in Jamaica's leadership (particularly under Bruce Golding's Chairmanship), in relation to CARICOM's imperative of moving forward at a critical juncture in the regional integration and governance processes. He may have been, no doubt, mindful that successive administrations of the Jamaica Labour Party (JLP), to which Golding was a member, had traditionally been viewed as lacking empathy for the deepening of integration.

Notwithstanding the special role Jamaica has played, there is no evidence that any single nation or individual is wholly responsible for

CARICOM's successes or failures. For example, Jamaica's leadership at Rose Hall in 2003, under Patterson's Chairmanship, would undoubtedly have been less momentous had it not been for the inspiration provided by the anniversary lecture of St Vincent and the Grenadines' Prime Minister Gonsalves and the governance papers produced by Barbados' Prime Minister Owen Arthur and Trinidad and Tobago's Prime Minister Patrick Manning. Similarly, the post-independence movement would not have materialised without the initiative of Prime Minister Eric Williams of Trinidad and Tobago. Furthermore, the foresight of Antigua's Premier Vere Bird (along with Barbados' Barrow and Guyana's Burnham) in catalysing the move to CARIFTA and later, Lester Bird in relation to the deepening of the OECS, cannot be overlooked. Indubitably, there have been some outstanding contributions made by the leaders of that era. At the same time, while there is no evidence to suggest that the current leaders, which still include a few from the earlier years, are incapable of the same level of distinguished contribution to advancing regional integration, the lack of progress on governance, over a protracted period, could well serve to give credence to Gonsalves' argument that they are perhaps not serious about the process.[5]

The third aspect of political culture has been a predisposition to the development of ideas without political action. The demise of the Federation led to the abandonment in the wider CARICOM group of the West Indian Nationalist (WIN) ideology, which had clearly defined the elements of an ideology of governance, and its replacement with a more vague philosophy of economic cooperation. Since then, the region has operated within an ideological vacuum. However, ideology has not been highlighted in the broader literature as a necessary condition for the proper institutionalisation of regionalism. Yet, the potential value-added of a role for ideology has featured prominently in the CARICOM discourse. Following the resurgence of regionalism in the 1968 CARIFTA, academic and technocratic elites, in particular, have been in pursuit of the development of a new indigenous ideology of regional integration. Although several elites, including politicians, have, at different points in history, sought to fill the gap left by WIN by inventing new ideational foundations for the movement, none of these efforts have ever been successfully transformed into a coherent plan of action on governance.

The first and most prominent attempt at reinstating an ideological grounding was William Demas's intrepid effort between 1965 and 1972 to develop an indigenous ideology of regional integration, which took into account the desire for West Indian unity, the quest for economic independence, the commitment to 'Third World' solidarity and the ideal of legitimate participatory governance. Demas had hoped that his ideas, which inspired the move from CARIFTA to CARICOM, would lead to a strategy towards effective sovereignty. In the final analysis, CARICOM's emergent governance structure, as proposed by Demas, did more to address the need for institutional coherence among existing regional structures than to address the ideological gap in the regional strategic outlook. Subsequently, a second, and perhaps less conscious, attempt at ideological development occurred at the end of the 1980s when Guyana's Desmond Hoyte and Jamaica's P.J. Patterson, speaking at Grande Anse in 1989 and in Kingston in 1990 respectively, sought to encourage the region's ideational commitment to popular participation as driving forces of the integration process. However, again, the outcome of those discussions reflected a preoccupation with the specific objectives of creating a single market and economy, rather than with developing the broad-based values which underpinned the integration movement as a whole.[6] Nonetheless, the Grande Anse and Kingston Conferences inspired the emergence of a new set of proposals for 'indigenous moorings' which were published in the West Indian Commission's 1992 report. The Chairman Shridath Ramphal's critique centred on what he perceived to be the great loss of the commitment to West Indian unity. He proposed, therefore, the adoption of a holistic governance ideology focused not only on the economic aspects of integration, but also the indigenous values, institutional structures and administrative processes. Indeed, those proposals precipitated the development of new models of institutionalising the Caribbean brand of regionalism, including a revised Treaty of Chaguaramas, the Bureau, the Quasi-Cabinet, the CRNM and the CCJ. However, the unimplemented proposals on enhancing the institutional structure under a framework of West Indian values – aptly entitled 'Time for Action' – remain relevant today.

The quest to grant the regional movement some ideological purpose continued into the new millennium with Prime Minister Gonsalves proposing, in 2001 and again in 2003, the adoption of a commitment to Caribbean civilisation as the fundamental basis of a new ideological focus for the regionalist agenda. Like his predecessors, Gonsalves attempted to move the region towards a values-based ideology of integration which reasserted the importance of citizen involvement in regional governance. Notwithstanding critiques of Gonsalves' theory of Caribbean civilisation, the concept held potential for making the regionalist strategy more relevant, pointing to the need for the development of stronger regional political arrangements. Indeed, if the critics were right to suggest that, in 2003, the region represented merely a culture zone because it lacked a distinct centre among the diverse societies, nations and peoples, then the Gonsalves' proposal for the establishment of a central governance authority could have easily assumed the role of the required 'centre' for 'Civilization'.[7] Subsequently, Gonsalves' ideas were complemented by the collective sovereignty concept – emerging from P.J. Patterson's initiative at the 2003 Rose Hall Conference – which represents the most recent ideational principle with potential for precipitating an ideological reinterpretation of the place and role of sovereignty in Caribbean development. The members of the Prime Ministerial and Technical Groups on governance, particularly Denis Benn, have continued to support the embedding of this concept in the CARICOM framework.[8] However, to date, these ideas have not converged into a single ideology which could support action, as evidenced by the fact that much of the institutional change which occurred after 2003 was independent of the ideational principles discussed at the beginning of the new millennium.

These attempts at ideological development have shown the strength of the personalised sovereignty and Federal legacy factors in relation to the development of new frameworks for governance. None of the ideas explored convinced Heads of Government of the potential effectiveness of engaging in sovereignty bargains in order to make the regional integration project a success. Certainly, there were notable differences among the approaches to the presentation of the ideas to Heads. For example, Demas's idea for a new regionalism may have been presented in too moderate a tone, thereby compromising his vision for a centralised political governance system, because he anticipated rather than pre-empted the reluctance of Heads to compromise sovereignty. Then, Ramphal's Commission may have been too radical in calling for a full overhaul of the precedent foundations of the movement. Finally, the Rose Hall experts seemed, at least, to have attempted to adopt a 'middle-ground' approach between the two extremes – but still, even those proposals have not found collective favour. This is particularly interesting since Heads were always either among the group of 'aspiring ideologues' or worked closely with the technocrats and experts to develop several of these proposals. Yet, there has remained a division between radical thought in the technostructure and the cautious response from the political superstructure because of the unwillingness to be seen to be relinquishing their personal authority in the context of a political culture which recalls the legacy of colonial governance and which has appointed them as the de facto guardians of national sovereignty. The concept of personal sovereignty has prevented the transformation of regionalist ideas into concrete action plans. Perhaps, in some way, therefore, the missing ideological foundation has been replaced by the ideational paradigm of personal sovereignty. The lack of progress towards effective regional integration begs the question as to whether the pre-eminence of national sovereign authority as an ideational paradigm for development has served to deliberately frustrate implementation of the longstanding acceptance of regional governance as the most effective path towards the attainment of the development goals of small states.

Against that background, it is understandable as to why the failure to adopt a collective ideology has been pinpointed as a significant factor in the evolution of CARICOM regionalism. The analysis has demonstrated that, due to an absence of ideology, having regard to an appropriate role for national sovereign authority in a regional context, the Caribbean problem has primarily been with the implementation of decisions. While there has been continuous attention to the formulation of new ideas, these have not been followed up with the necessary associated implementation strategies. There is no single understanding of what CARICOM should be doing and how – an understanding that gives the region a governance identity consistent with the definition of regional governance, as a reflection of who the people are, what they want and how they intend to portray themselves to the rest of the world. In that context, the absence of a regional ideology – that is, ideas supported by measurable collective action – has been one of CARICOM's major shortcomings and has likely contributed considerably to its acknowledged implementation deficit.[9] In that regard, ideology – the 'why' of governance – is potentially the missing link between the theoretical promise of regionalism and the disappointing record of CARICOM to date.

Building on the understanding of the political culture of personalised sovereignty, the legacy of supranational aversion and the ideological vacuum, we now discuss the specific institutional choices made by CARICOM and their effect on the effectiveness of the system in transforming the national context for development into shared development outcomes is discussed below.

## THE CHARACTERISTICS OF CARICOM'S INSTITUTIONS

The review of institutions has shown convincingly that CARICOM's institutional choices have been viewed within and outside the region as inappropriate for the goals which the Community has set for itself. Our definition of regional governance and discussion of the institutional options available to states suggested a need for a level of synergy between national and regional levels of governance in order to encourage effectiveness. However, political culture has had a lasting impact on the CARICOM institutional structure, minimising the efficiency of regional decision-making and slowing national and regional implementation because of a lack of coherence in the framework. Those weaknesses can be summarised by reference to four main features of CARICOM's institutional mode of governance.

Firstly, CARICOM has created a dominant system of 'Head of Government Control'. Regional political authority has remained firmly invested in the Conference of Heads of Government (CHOG) since its inception in 1963. The reliance on unanimous voting procedures in the CHOG has reinforced this culture of individual and personal control. In some cases, subordinate regional institutions, such as the various sectoral Councils, have not been given the authority to make binding decisions without the approval of the CHOG. Yet, despite the desire to control all aspects of the regional system, the decisions reached by the CHOG have often lacked the requisite strategic direction or specificity to guide effective implementation.

The primary implication of this personalised system of control is that the institutional framework relies heavily on the strength of the interpersonal relationships among the Heads. These relationships have shown potential to either catalyse or constrain the integration process. For example, several Heads became personally embroiled in conflicts over political philosophy in the 1970s which prevented the convening of the CHOG between 1975 and 1982. Once those meetings ceased, the integration movement fell into a leadership crisis of sorts, during which time, limited progress was made towards the achievement of the goals of the Common Market. Indeed, the prevailing climate of conflict among Heads certainly contributed to and perhaps even fuelled the involvement of CARICOM Members in the threat to the sovereignty posed by the United States' invasion of Grenada in 1983. At the same time, it is only fair to note, that the outstanding leadership exercised by individual Heads of Government over the years has often served to catalyse the processes of positive change in the institutional framework. In the same vein, the use of the informal caucus among Heads has been helpful, on more than one occasion, in resolving conflict. However, even if relationships among the Heads of Government were always free of tension, the CARICOM framework would still have faltered. Since the end of the Cold War, relationships among Heads have generally been less tense and yet, CARICOM's record of implementation has not improved. The system of control which relies on inter-personal relationships is not, however, the sole contributing factor to ineffectiveness. The lack of authority of regional structures and the inefficiency of procedures have also affected implementation.

The second feature of the CARICOM's institutional mode of governance is its weak legislative framework. In the first instance, national sovereignty has been embedded within all the treaties and agreements reached among states, whether in the 1968 CARIFTA Agreement, the 1973 original Treaty of Chaguaramas or the 2001 Revised Treaty of Chaguaramas, in such a way that the implementation process has been extremely tardy. In that legislative context summed up by Article 240(1) of the Revised Treaty, implementation is left to the discretion of each Member State under the principle of respect for its sovereign competence and constitutional procedures. Since the majority of CARICOM states prescribe to dualist legal systems which require the adoption of each provision and decision of the Organs by national legislatures, the process of enacting regional decisions has been extremely slow. Until the national process is complete, agreements lack legislative effect and are therefore not legally-binding. In addition, despite the fact that Article 240 (2) of the Revised Treaty of Chaguaramas requests that states act expeditiously to give regional decisions effect at the national level, there are no complementary enforcement mechanisms to compel the expeditious action. The contrasting approach to the adoption of legislative supranationalism in the OECS Economic Union is, therefore, instructive for CARICOM.

The implementation deficit is also closely related to a third issue of the inefficiency of the regional decision-making process which relies, in some cases, on unanimous voting procedures and consensus-building among fifteen different postures of sovereignty. Even when unanimous decision-making was abandoned in CARICOM Councils upon revision of the Treaty of Chaguaramas in 2001, it was retained in the CHOG where all decisions are ultimately concluded. The removal of the unanimous procedures in subsidiary organs was initially helpful in giving impetus to the pace of decision-making at lower levels of the CARICOM system. However, this effect was nullified by the overpowering role played by Heads of Government. The informal practice of referring even procedural matters to the attention of Heads, coupled with the lack of legislative effect, indicate worrying levels of inefficiency in regional decision-making, particularly before the revision of the Treaty.

In a related issue, the lack of non-state participation in the decision-making process has also been a CARICOM weakness. In spite of the acknowledgement of roles for non-state actors in wider new regionalisms, CARICOM has maintained a very government-centric view of regional governance. The abandonment of early traditions of engaging the political opposition, business, labour and civil society in the highest levels of the CARICOM system has led to legitimate concerns about the relevance of CARICOM decision-making. Furthermore, the Assembly of Caribbean Community Parliamentarians (ACCP) established in 1994 as a forum for reintegration of popular sovereignty into the governance framework has now been obscured within the system. No sittings have occurred since 2000 and the Caribbean people remain detached from the representatives and their deliberations. Interestingly, the irrelevance of the ACCP is also symbolised by its ambivalent position in the institutional architecture. It has been denied a place alongside the other deliberative Organs of the Community, but has been considered in the ranks of the semi-autonomous Institutions, even though it does not exercise a technical function. There may be reason to wonder whether the ACCP has been deliberately abandoned since it has never been convened again, despite calls in the most recent proposals for governance reform to have it strengthened.

The fourth, and perhaps most prominent, feature of the CARICOM institutional framework of governance is its weak capacity for executive action. Since the establishment of the Federation, all institutional forms have been criticised by the experts for the lack of an appropriate regional mechanism responsible for coordinating the implementation process. However, particularly since the mid-1980s there has been disagreement among political leaders, technocrats and academics on whether the requisite form of executive capacity should be established as an administrative Secretariat or a quasi-political Commission.

The first option of strengthening the role of the Secretariat in the regional governance process is not without validity. The first Secretariat had been proposed by Burnham in 1963 as a facility to give the decisions of the Conference 'teeth'. It had always been intended to play a central role in the implementation process. And, true to form, in the early years, the staff of the Commonwealth Caribbean Regional Secretariat and then the CARICOM Secretariat, appeared to play a pivotal role in the growth and progression of the movement. However, by the 1980s, the management capacity and poor resourcing of the Secretariat, including its location in Guyana (viewed by some as being remote and underdeveloped), became a frequent point of criticism. The role played by the Secretariat had been confined, by this time, largely, to the servicing of the meetings of CARICOM Organs and Institutions and responding to individual government agencies, rather than the implementation of region-wide technical and programmatic strategies. Those weaknesses gave credence to the view that the Secretariat should not, and indeed, could not play the role of regional executive.

In 1992, the West Indian Commission proposed the establishment of a high level political Commission, with supranational competencies, as an alternative. That proposal and all subsequent proposals modelled on it have been rejected by the Heads of Government as part of their traditional sovereignty defence. That defence, exemplified by the pursuit of innovative models of executive governance, including the 1993 Bureau of Heads and the Quasi-Cabinet which was fully constituted in 2001, was eventually acknowledged, by leaders themselves and critics alike, to be no more appropriate to filling the gap of executive competence than the Secretariat had been. Indeed, few individual Heads had time to dedicate to the implementation process.

However, Heads continued to view the strengthening of the Secretariat's administrative capacity as a priority. Since the 1980s, beginning with Roderick Rainford's reforms and then, from 1992 onwards, under the longstanding leadership of Edwin Carrington, the Secretariat has undergone various phases of reorganisation, including an upgrade of its physical and telecommunications infrastructure, the creation of a new senior management system of Assistant Secretaries-General at ambassadorial rank, and the development of linkages among the various directorates. Furthermore, in the Revised Treaty of Chaguaramas, the Secretary-General was nominated as CARICOM's Chief Executive Officer (CEO). However, the staff of the Secretariat has still operated within directorates and divisions which were organised and only authorised to support and respond to Member States with respect to the administrative agenda. Neither the Secretary-General nor his staff held supranational authority to act independently of the Heads in the interest of the Community as a whole. In that regard, one prominent expert review proposed that the Secretariat's machinery be upgraded to support the post of CEO by granting the Secretariat greater responsibility for the implementation of decisions.[10] Others were not convinced of the feasibility of the proposal. One wonders whether the Secretariat's record of poor administration suggested the need for a completely new structure to be developed and whether, as a part of that perspective, proponents of the Commission model were of the view that a new Commission structure would shed the ghosts of inefficiency, even perhaps, finding a new location. However, it must be acknowledged that, even if the Commission had been established in a more 'developed' location, it could have, potentially, succumbed to the other problems which have plagued the Secretariat – and specifically, those associated with the limited and inconsistent funding provided for regional institutions. The challenge of arrears in Member States' assessed contributions continues to be raised at the regional meetings.[11]

It is fair to say, perhaps, that, there is still no consensus among the experts as to the preferable option for executive capacity-building. However, the most recent proposal of the TWG on governance in relation to the establishment of a Commission including Secretariat, which defines the relationship between the executive and administrative competences, is an encouraging compromise. The indecision among Heads on this matter over the 17 years since the 'Time for Action' report has been one of the most disappointing aspects of CARICOM leadership. At some points, the impression has been given that Heads had agreed to implement a Commission only for the decision to be reversed shortly thereafter. Since the tabling of the last report of the TWG, it appears that the further restructuring of the Secretariat is likely to be a prominent aspect of the post-2010 reform agenda. The establishment of a supranational Commission has been replaced by a proposal for a Permanent Committee of Ambassadors which is likely to ensure that executive capacity is firmly entrenched in the intergovernmentalist tradition.

The weaknesses of the regional mechanisms for implementation have also been complemented by weaknesses in national bureaucracy where executive authority has been legally enshrined. National ministerial departments lack the capacity and the incentive to support the implementation of regional decisions. Given the lack of legislative effect, national agencies have reason to disregard regional decisions, in light of the burden of their national portfolios and their capacity constraints. Therefore, CARICOM does not function within an institutional framework which creates a seamless and coherent relationship between regional decisions and national action; nor between regional coordination and regulation and national action. Even in the few cases where regional executive structures were equipped with the resources and the authority to implement decisions of the Conference – the most notable cases being the Institutions and Associate Institutions of CARICOM which operate autonomously of CARICOM – the lack of legislative effect at national level discourages state departments from following up or complementing the action initiated by the regional mechanisms.

The overall effect of the four features of the institutional mode of governance, highlighted in this section, has been to generate a system of slow decision-making and implementation deficit. It strongly supports the argument that supranational institutions are likely to improve the efficiency of regional governance. To date, the Single Economy of the CSME announced in 1989 is far from complete and its realisation remains threatened by an apparent lack of commitment to the process. Already, some Member States have begun to show interest in alternative regional arrangements, and the states in the Eastern Caribbean have begun to pay closer attention to strengthening their subculture of governance which acknowledges the institutional imperative of creating supranational institutions to address the paradox.

When the findings on political context are linked to those on the CARICOM institutions, contrary to the customary aversion to supranational authority, two prominent anomalies are revealed. Firstly, CARICOM inaugurated a fully supranational Caribbean Court of Justice in 2005 with jurisdiction to interpret and adjudicate in disputes with respect to the Revised Treaty of Chaguaramas. The Court is the only fully supranational entity, having an independently appointed judiciary and an independent source of financing. In theory, its decisions are legally binding and enforceable. However the lack of progress on implementation of the CSME has meant it rarely exercises its original jurisdiction in respect of the Treaty. In one respect the existence of supranationalism in CARICOM goes counter to the political culture; however, at the same time, there is a second anomalous aspect of this example. The rejection of the court's appellate jurisdiction in all but three Member States, in favour of the retention of civil appeals to the Judicial Committee of the Privy Council (JCPC) in the United Kingdom, reflects a curious willingness of Member States to surrender their judicial authority to an external (colonial) influence but not to enhance their judicial sovereignty by delegating authority to an indigenous system, which already sustains a collective legal education framework. That decision becomes more curious by the fact that OECS countries also retain appeals to the JCPC in the UK even though they already have a shared regional supreme court. Encouragingly, Guyana which has strong popular association with regional institutions as the home of the Secretariat, adopted the appellate jurisdiction, given the fact that it had established its own appellate court on becoming a Republic in 1970. Furthermore, Barbados, under the leadership of Owen Arthur, amended its constitution specifically in order to adopt the CCJ's appellate jurisdiction and later Belize also adopted the jurisdiction.

The second anomaly in the pattern of intergovernmental institution-building presents itself in the establishment of the Caribbean Regional Negotiating Machinery in 1997 as a quasi-supranational institution which, though not fully independent of national governments, exercised increasing autonomy from the rest of the regional framework throughout its evolution. The CRNM for most of its history bypassed the intergovernmental Ministerial Councils and the Secretariat, commanding its own administrative machinery and reporting directly to a single Lead Head of Government on external affairs – the Prime Minister of Jamaica. While this model of executive governance emerged from an agreement to the formulation of a temporary project unit, the evolution of the CRNM under the leadership of the Chairman of the WIC led to the entity's ironic assumption of the proposed characteristics and competencies of the executive Commission which had been proposed and rejected by Heads in 1992. The existence of this anomaly within the CARICOM anti-supranationalist culture for an initial four years until its minimal revamping by Patterson in 2001 and for a further eight years until its complete submergence within the Secretariat (as the Office of Trade Negotiations (OTN)) in 2009, illustrates, at least, the feasibility of the coexistence of quasi-supranational modes of governance with intergovernmental traditions. The challenges of effectively positioning the newly-created OTN in the framework were perhaps related to the informal way in which the CRNM had emerged without legal status, which ultimately contributed to an overshadowing of its technical competences and the emergence of a perception among political leaders that it was an illegitimate institution.

These two anomalies imply that contrary to an aversion to supranationalism, the concept of delegating limited supranational authority is not in any way in complete contradiction to even the most absolutist interpretation of sovereignty in the region. Those two cases, coupled with the historical experience of the OECS, including its adoption of legislative supranationalism in its recently signed Economic Union Treaty, are ample testament to that fact.

## SOVEREIGNTY BARGAINING AND THE CARICOM TRADITION OF SOVEREIGNTY

Against the background of that description of a mode of governance which lacks the appropriate institutions, it is reasonable to conclude that CARICOM has not achieved the balance between national authority and national legitimacy on one hand, and shared autonomy and control on the other. The reason for this failing is interrogated here by reference to the third tier of the analytical framework – the sovereignty bargains analysis. In spite of the comments in the wider literature that, theoretically, the significance of sovereignty as an ontological bedrock of international relations is waning, in the Caribbean, sovereignty has played a dominant role in the regional governance process.[12]

Interestingly, our introduction to sovereignty bargains made two assumptions about analysing the bargaining process which have not evolved as expected. Firstly, the discussion here had assumed that the bargaining process was part of a conscious and informed calculus by state representatives. However, it is difficult to pinpoint from the CARICOM case the conscious and deliberate bargaining by political leaders in the creation of the institutional framework. In fact, the overarching political culture of 'pure sovereignty' has persisted and intensified over CARCIOM's history, creating a general resistance to sovereignty bargaining. The problem is that there have been no bargains at all – indeed concessions have had to be made, at least on paper, in the move from CARIFTA to CARICOM to CSME. However, the challenge has been that those bargains, which have not been enforced, have also been ad hoc and not reflective of a conscious acceptance of sovereignty, as a 'bargainable' concept.

Secondly, the introduction to sovereignty bargaining also assumed that the each participating state had acquired full command of each of the four attributes of sovereignty in order to bargain with them. In the CARICOM context, the evolution of sovereignty is still a part of an ongoing independence movement. The constraints of the internal political economy, coupled with the challenging dynamics of globalisation, mean that few Caribbean states have ever been able to fully command all dimensions of sovereignty. Nonetheless, the analysis of CARICOM has revealed a putative understanding of the hierarchy among the attributes of authority, control, Autonomy and Legitimacy in the CARICOM tradition of sovereignty, which makes a useful contribution to explaining the reluctance of political leaders to engage deliberately in sovereignty bargains. The proposed hierarchy is outlined and explained in figure 10.1.

Overall, it can be argued that CARCIOM has placed an inordinately high value on governmental Authority and Control, thereby resulting in slow decision-making and an implementation deficit. In turn, actual control has not been achieved with regard to facilitation of the development process. Conversely, an inordinately low value has been placed on the attribute of Legitimacy. The people's objectives and development aspirations have been ignored in favour of making the system a personal project of Heads of Government who, once elected, are not held accountable for implementation of regional decisions.

### Figure 10.1: Hierarchy of Attributes in CARICOM Sovereignty

| 1 | Authority (High Position) | Authority is understood as an integral aspect of the achievement of national independence. |
|---|---|---|
| | | However, within the Caribbean political culture, authority is invested within individual Heads of Government who are personally responsible for political and socio-economic affairs, including the safeguarding of sovereignty. |
| 2 | Control (Highest Position) | Control is perhaps the most important attribute to CARICOM governments because it is conceptualised as a symbol of the authority of Heads of Government. |
| | | At the regional level it is translated into various mechanisms which reinforce the authority of Heads above other institutions so as to avoid the delegation of authority. |
| | | However, actual control outside the deliberative fora, as defined in our study in relation to the ability to produce a developmental effect, is not achieved. The capacity for effective control over state affairs remains weak or non-existent. |
| 3 | Autonomy (Ambivalent Position) | There is some ambivalence about the position of Autonomy in the CARICOM tradition. |
| | | While it has been a part of the diplomatic rhetoric in treaties and agreements and has been fiercely preserved among the Members of the regional group, it has also been surrendered completely to external authorities, for example with regard to external judicial appeals to the UK Privy Council. |
| 4 | Legitimacy (Low Position) | Legitimacy is interpreted in a very narrow sense in CARICOM. It is viewed solely in respect of the role of the electoral process in establishing the authority of national governments. |
| | | Beyond the ballot, Legitimacy of regional decision-making and citizen participation at both regional and national level is not given high priority. In fact, regional issues are not generally a part of national political manifestos. |

The sovereignty bargains analysis has assisted in highlighting two interesting analytical issues in relation to the CARICOM conception of sovereignty. First, it has shown that in the CARICOM tradition of sovereignty formal authority has been confused with effective control. In theory, control is conceptualised as an ability to produce a developmental effect. In CARICOM, control has been conceptualised as an authoritarian system of supervision by leaders which does not extend beyond control of deliberations and decision-making to embrace effective executive action. Secondly, the analysis reveals that sovereignty bargains have been viewed in the region as a zero-sum game, rather than a beneficial trade-off. Leaders seem not to have come to a full grasp of the implications of holding unswervingly to attributes of national sovereignty vis-à-vis the potential gain in effective control from bargaining some aspects of authority. The overall implication of the tradition and its associated ineffective institutions is that the region has not been able to pursue the construction of a modern re-aggregated concept of shared sovereignty, which could guide the process of regional governance and catalyse the integration process.

Against that background, this investigation concludes that the way in which the paradox of sovereignty has been construed and constructed by political elites has impinged negatively on regional governance in CARICOM. While the theoretical paradox compels the voluntary pursuit of transnational modes of cooperative governance, based on a reconfiguration of sovereignty, Caribbean leaders have interpreted the state of paradox as a clarion call to safeguard the purity of sovereignty – that is, absolute governmental authority and control – from any intrusive elements of the external environment which might seek to erode it. In that context, concessions of sovereignty have been perceived as threats to the sanctity of the concept and a betrayal of the struggle for emancipation and national independence. Having placed such an inordinately high value on the concept of national sovereignty as a guiding principle for the exercise of political authority and control, the strong urge to safeguard the purity of sovereignty has stymied the evolution of efficient and effective regional institutions. The four negative features of the CARICOM institutional framework highlighted above are directly related to the tradition of safeguarding sovereignty. The emergence of this prominent sense of duty to safeguard national sovereignty is directly linked to the Federal experience. While West Indian Nationalism was initially able to accommodate a sense of duty to a national sovereignty couched within a broader regional sovereignty, the weaknesses of the Federation's colonial institutional framework had, in fact, betrayed the West Indian Nationalist ideals. The vision of sovereignty, a national-regional fusion, was never realised under the Federation. Consequently, when individual states were finally able to attain full sovereignty in 1962, a dominant concept of national sovereignty emerged in defiance of its regional heritage. The exception to the rule, of course, has been found in the OECS experience of sovereignty which continues to embrace an association with a regional nationalism. The question remains as to whether the wider CARICOM group will be able to formulate strategies to overcome the historical legacy.

## IMPLICATIONS OF THE SOVEREIGNTY TRADITION AND PROSPECTS FOR THE FUTURE

At the end of the analysis, it is difficult to say that CARICOM has in fact achieved regional governance in the way it has been theorised. CARICOM's mode of governance has fallen short of the definition which has been adopted. There have been few instances of conscious bargaining; the appropriate balance between national and regional levels of governance has not been created; the institutions established have, largely, been inefficient and ineffective; and, as a result, many of CARICOM's development goals remain unrealised. The longitudinal perspective has shown that CARICOM has struggled with a single issue throughout its history. The paradox of sovereignty has posed a significant challenge in the context of an overvalued national sovereignty, which has been divorced from the more modern concept of a flexible and 'bargainable' people's sovereignty. In that regard, this conclusion argues that the transformation of the meaning and role of sovereignty in Caribbean politics is imperative to the consolidation and sustainability of Caribbean regionalism. The evolution and entrenchment of a more popular concept of sovereignty, as an alternative to personal sovereignty vis-à-vis elite authority and control, is essential to moving the integration process forward.

The analytical imperative at this stage relates not only to reinterpreting sovereignty as an academic exercise but also a more practical imperative of rethinking the relationship between governance, sovereignty and power. When sovereignty is interpreted as the individual power of government leaders, it is transformed into an unnatural attempt to maintain personal control over thoughts and action. Sovereignty becomes disconnected from, and consequently, irrelevant to the people's concerns about good governance and development. The achievement of effective control will require the relinquishment of the individual power of Heads in order to allow participation of other actors at national, regional and supranational levels of governance. In light of our findings, the rethinking exercise will require a reconfiguration of Caribbean political culture – a task which can only be undertaken with the support and participation of the people, including non-state actors, who drive the processes of regionalisation. The process will require more informed popular debate at national levels. Therefore, the public will have to demand the commencement of the debate and to insist that the emerging consensus on resolving the sovereignty paradox comes to bear on the electoral process.

Theoretically, there are three major scenarios in which the reconfiguration exercise might be initiated. The first is the emergence of a major crisis which impacts on CARICOM, thereby obliging states to delegate authority and pool resources in order to gain the development benefit they need to mitigate the negative effects of small size and the context of paradox. Further natural or man-made disasters, like the January 2010 earthquake in Haiti and the May 2010 security crisis in Jamaica, may be among the types of crises, which if on a large scale, might highlight the imperative of interdependence. The second scenario is the pursuit of a more extensive and improved public education programme by CARICOM on the significance of regionalism to development. In addition to greater understanding of regionalism as a useful phenomenon in the context of globalisation as well as improved knowledge of CARICOM's goals, the education experience should, more fundamentally, involve the reconceptualisation of regionalism as an imperative of nationalism. CARICOM's inability to appropriately address the institutional imperative of regional governance is directly related to the ambivalence created by the conceptual disintegration of the symbiotic relationship between regionalism and nationalism after 1962. In the contemporary era, Caribbean regionalism is still, fundamentally, an issue of nationalist independence. The third scenario is to allow regional civil society groups, like the Caribbean Congress of Labour (CCL), the Caribbean Policy Development Centre (CPDC), the Caribbean Association of Industry and Commerce (CAIC) as well as the regional universities to introduce the institutional imperative into the national political dialogue. The eventual incorporation of a debate on the future of regionalism on the agenda of the national election campaigns and manifestos would be an important part of the reinterpretation exercise. This latter scenario may be the least effective, in light of the substantial amount of work which has already been done by experts from these groups – to no avail.

In reality, it is perhaps most likely that a combination of these three options will precipitate the change. Indeed, the most recent focus on the crisis of regional governance since 2010 emerged from a combined context of the struggle of member states to survive the current global recession and the increased media and academic commentary and critique of Heads of Government leadership of CARICOM. In 2010, Chairman of the Conference, Jamaican Prime Minister, Bruce Golding sensed that it was time for change in the wake of popular demand for meaningful action. In his words, it was 'time to do or die'.[13]

It is now essential that the action is clearly identified and the modalities for implementation are concrete. In that regard, the renewed attempt of Heads to address the ineffectiveness of the CARICOM integration process is encouraging. Against the background of provocative innuendos then, and more recently in 2012 by Gonsalves, that the region lacks serious leadership, the new agenda for regional governance reform includes a new review process which is to be undertaken by a subcommittee of Heads of Government, with the support of a technical working group. The subcommittee has been mandated to look at the proposals on the table specifically for: the restructuring of the Secretariat; the establishment of a Permanent Committee of Ambassadors; a system of sanctions for non-implementation; the use of dispute settlement mechanisms; and the greater involvement of Ministries of Finance in the decision-making process.[14] The movement has benefitted from a new Secretary-General appointed in 2011 and from the recent report on restructuring the Secretary-General's machinery which was the focus of the 2012 Intersessional meeting.

So, in conclusion, a return to the three-pronged question of the 'who?', 'why?' and 'how?' of regional governance in small states, in a context where the answers to those questions are likely to bring influence to bear on the current attempt to develop a new CARICOM strategy.

## WHO?

A new cadre of decisive and accountable leadership could play a significant inspirational role in crafting a new governance response to the challenges of states that are likely to remain, because of limitations related to their small size, permanently within the realm of a sovereignty paradox. The nature of the 2012 mandate clearly anticipates that the calibre of that leadership will have a more open and transparent approach. It is encouraging therefore that the a CARICOM Civil Society Project was launched to engage civil society in debate on the future of regional development.[15] It remains to be seen whether Heads will take full advantage of a vehicle such as this, in pursuit of new governance objectives and that they will be able to think 'outside of the narrow box' of national sovereignty and personal authority.

## WHY?

The adoption of a new Caribbean regional ideology – if not in name, in meaning – could serve to capture what one commentator has referred to as the 'public imagination'.[16] Against the background of an apparent waning of support for integration, there is a need to provide a signal to the Caribbean people that there is a rationale for the integration process. The finding of an ideological rationale may pale in significance given the pressing context of economic crisis but it is imperative for developing a level of political legitimacy. In that regard, in support of a new cadre of leadership, the public will need to be engaged in some form of collective social partnership which will enable the formulation of new ideas and associated strategies for regional governance.

## HOW?

Finally, but most significantly, in the pursuit of the development of more effective governance institutions, the new leadership and renewed ideological principles must acknowledge the institutional imperative of bargaining with attributes of national sovereignty in order to achieve a more effective collective sovereignty. Unfortunately, the recent 2012 consultancy report on the Secretariat focused on the managerial aspects of administrative efficiency rather than addressing the fundamental issues of political governance which constrain the effective functioning of the Secretariat. Without addressing the limited conception of sovereignty held by political leaders, the Secretariat and the Secretary-General are likely to fail to re-energise the movement.

Admittedly, CARICOM Member States are still 'youthful', and therefore, the novelty of sovereignty, makes the prospect of bargaining a significant political challenge. However, in light of contemporary development imperatives, a system of bargains could enable these new states to equip regional and national institutions with the requisite authority to pursue the implementation of pressing development goals. It is clear that the role of stronger legislative institutions will be pivotal in this process and that special attention will have to be devoted to the provision of adequate financial and human resources.

From the analysis, it becomes clear that notwithstanding the failures in leadership and the dominance of the personal sovereignty concept in Caribbean politics, the predicted collapse of CARICOM is not inevitable. There is potential for the movement to be better equipped with effective governance institutions. In sum, under a serious and radical reform process, individual sovereign leadership may be transformed into a more strategic collective leadership; the ideological vacuum may be filled; and more efficient, flexible and adaptable institutions may emerge to support the regional development process. The fundamental dynamics of power within regionalism, including the implications for sovereign authority, control, autonomy and legitimacy, is critical to the question of whether the development of such reform within CARICOM will actually, at last, be initiated.

# NOTES

## INTRODUCTION

1. For examples of studies in these regions see H.E.S. Nesadurai, 'ASEAN and Regional Governance after the Cold War: From Regional Order to Regional Community', *The Pacific Review* 22, no. 1 (2009); Shaun Naraine, 'The English School and ASEAN', *The Pacific Review* 19, no. 2 (2006); Shaun Naraine, 'State Sovereignty, Political Legitimacy and Regional Institutionalism in the Asia-Pacific', *The Pacific Review* 17, no. 3 (2004); Jean Grugel, 'New Regionalism and Modes of Governance – Comparing US and EU Strategies in Latin America', *European Journal of International Relations* 10 (2004); Fredrik Söderbaum, 'Regionalisation and Civil Society: The Case of Southern Africa', *New Political Economy* 12, no. 3 (2007); Kennedy Graham, ed. *Models of Regional Governance for the Pacific: Sovereignty and the Future Architecture of Regionalism* (Christchurch: Canterbury University Press, 2008).
2. The member states of the Caribbean Community (CARICOM) are Antigua and Barbuda, The Bahamas, Barbados, Belize, Dominica, Grenada, Guyana, Haiti, Jamaica, Montserrat, Saint Kitts and Nevis, Saint Lucia, Saint Vincent and the Grenadines, Suriname and Trinidad and Tobago. Montserrat is the only full member which is not an independent state.
3. Haiti attained independence in 1804; Jamaica and Trinidad and Tobago gained independence in 1962.

## CHAPTER ONE

1. F.H. Hinsley, *Sovereignty,* 2nd ed (Cambridge: Cambridge University Press, 1986), 1.
2. For more on this early history see S.E. Finer, *The History of Government from the Earliest Times. Volume 3. Empires, Monarchies and the Modern State,* 3 vols., vol. Volume III. *Empires, Monarchies and the Modern State* (Oxford: Oxford University Press, 1999); Robert Jackson, ed. *Sovereignty at the Millennium* (Oxford: Blackwell Publishers, 1999).
3. Bodin's ideas are discussed in John Boli, 'Sovereignty from a World Polity Perspective,' in *Problematic Sovereignty: Contested Rules and Political Possibilities,* ed. Stephen D. Krasner (New York: Columbia University Press, 2001), 56.
4. Robert Jackson, *Quasi-States: Sovereignty, International Relations and the Third World, Cambridge Studies in International Relations* 12 (Cambridge: Cambridge University Press, 1990); Stephen D. Krasner, *Sovereignty: Organised Hypocrisy* (New Jersey: Princeton University Press, 1999).

5.  Georg Sorenson, 'Sovereignty: Change and Continuity in a Fundamental Institution,' in *Sovereignty at the Millennium*, ed. Robert Jackson (Oxford: Blackwell Publishers, 1999), 169.
6.  See James A. Camilleri and Jim Falk, *The End of Sovereignty? The Politics of a Shrinking and Fragmenting World* (Hants: Edward Elgar, 1992); Jon Pierre, ed. *Debating Governance: Authority Steering and Democracy* (Oxford: Oxford University Press, 2000).
7.  Finer, *The History of Government* John Gaffar La Guerre, 'Organic and Mechanistic Theories of the State and the Individual,' in *Issues in the Government and Politics of the West Indies. A Reader*, ed. John Gaffar La Guerre (St Augustine: School of Continuing Studies, University of the West Indies, 1997).
8.  James A. Camilleri, 'Rethinking Sovereignty in a Shrinking, Fragmented World,' in *Contending Sovereignties: Redefining Political Community*, ed. R.B.J. Walker and Saul H. Mendlovitz (Boulder: Lynne Rienner Publishers, 1990).
9.  Jackson, *Quasi-States* Andrew Linklater, 'Citizenship and Sovereignty in the Post-Westphalian European State,' in *Re-Imagining Political Community. Studies in Cosmopolitan Democracy*, ed. Daniele Archibugi, David Held, and Martin Kohler (Cambridge: Polity Press, 1998); Christopher Rudolph, 'Sovereignty and Territorial Borders in a Global Age', *International Studies Review* 7 (2005).
10. Jackson, ed. *Sovereignty at the Millennium*.
11. See definition in James Crawford, *The Creation of States in International Law, Second* ed. (Oxford: Clarendon Press, 2006).
12. Jackson, ed. *Sovereignty at the Millennium*; Alexander B. Murphy, 'The Sovereign State System as Political-Territorial Ideal: Historical and Contemporary Considerations,' in *State Sovereignty as Social Construct*, ed. Thomas J. Biersteker and Cynthia Weber, *Cambridge Studies in International Relations* 46 (Cambridge: Cambridge University Press, 1996).
13. Jackson, ed. *Sovereignty at the Millennium*; Jackson, *Quasi-States:*.
14. Jackson, *Quasi-States.*
15. Daniel Philpott, 'Westphalia, Authority and International Society,' in *Sovereignty at the Millennium*, ed. Robert Jackson (Oxford: Blackwell Publishers, 1999).
16. James N. Rosenau, 'Governance and Democracy in a Globalizing World,' in *Re-Imagining Political Community. Studies in Cosmopolitan Democracy*, ed. Daniele Archibugi, David Held, and Martin Kohler (Cambridge: Polity Press, 1998); Camilleri and Falk, *The End of Sovereignty?*
17. James N. Rosenau, 'Governance in the Twenty-First Century', *Global Governance* 1 (1995); James N. Rosenau, 'Governance in the New Global Order,' in *Governing Globalization*, ed. David Held and Anthony McGrew (Cambridge: Polity Press, 2002); Gerry Stoker, 'Governance as Theory: Five Propositions', *International Social Science Journal*, no. 155 (1998).
18. Hendrik Spruyt, 'The Origins, Development and Possible Decline of the Modern State', *Annual Review of Political Science* 5 (2002): 140.
19. See Dag Anckar, 'Islandness or Smallness? A Comparative Look at Political Institutions in Small Island States', *Island Studies Journal* 1, no. 1 (2006).
20. Jackson, *Quasi-States*, 21; Robert Jackson, ed. *Sovereignty, Key Concepts* (Cambridge: Polity Press, 2007), 14.

21. Christopher Clapham, 'Sovereignty and the Third World State,' in *Sovereignty at the Millennium*, ed. Robert Jackson (Oxford: Blackwell Publishers, 1999); Fredrik Söderbaum, 'Modes of Regional Governance in Africa: Neo-Liberalism; Sovereignty Boosting, and Shadow Networks', *Global Governance* 10 (2004).

22. European Commission, 'Cotonou Agreement,' European Commission, http://europa.eu.int/comm/development/body/cotonou/agreement/agr06_en.htm; Selwyn Ryan and Ann Marie Bissessar, 'Overview: Governance,' in *Governance in the Caribbean*, ed. Selwyn Ryan and Ann Marie Bissessar (St Augustine: Sir Arthur Lewis Institute for Social and Economic Studies (SALISES), The University of the West Indies, 2002).

23. Graham Harrison, 'Governance States in Africa: Conceptualising the Encounter between the World Bank and the Sovereign Frontier,' in *The World Bank and Africa: The Construction of Governance States*, ed. Graham Harrison, Routledge Advances in International Political Economy (London: Routledge, 2004), 24.

24. Commission on Global Governance, 'Our Global Neighbourhood. The Report of the Commission on Global Governance', (New York: Oxford University Press, 1995); Ramesh Thakur and Luk Van Langenhove, 'Enhancing Global Governance through Regional Integration', *Global Governance* 12 (2006).

25. Marie-Claude Smouts, 'The Proper Use of Governance in International Relations', *International Social Science Journal L*, no. 155 (1998).

26. Mark Beeson, 'Sovereignty under Siege: Globalisation and the State in Southeast Asia', *Third World Quarterly* 24, no. 2 (2003): 361.

27. Stephen D. Krasner, ed. *Problematic Sovereignty: Contested Rules and Political Possibilities* (New York: Columbia University Press, 2001); Krasner, *Sovereignty: Organised Hypocrisy*.

28. Krasner, *Sovereignty: Organised Hypocrisy*, 3–4.

29. William Wallace, 'The Sharing of Sovereignty: The European Paradox,' in *Sovereignty at the Millennium*, ed. Robert Jackson (Oxford: Blackwell Publishers, 1999).

30. In contrast, regionalisation is described as an informal process, manifest in the ongoing international transnational economic processes. For explanations of regionalisation see Judith Wedderburn, 'Organisations and Social Actors in the Regionalization Process,' in *Elements of Regional Integration: The Way Forward*, ed. Peter Wickham, et al. (Kingston: Ian Randle Publishers, 1998); Fredrik Söderbaum, 'Regionalisation and Civil Society: The Case of Southern Africa', *New Political Economy* 12, no. 3 (2007). For explanations of regionalism see Andrew Gamble and Anthony Payne, eds., *Regionalism and World Order* (London: Macmillan Press, 1996), 2; Jean Grugel, 'New Regionalism and Modes of Governance – Comparing US and EU Strategies in Latin America', *European Journal of International Relations* 10 (2004): 204.

31. James D. Sidaway, *Imagined Regional Communities. Integration and Sovereignty in the Global South* (London: Routledge, 2002), 16; UNU-CRIS, 'Regional Integration Knowledge System,' UNU-CRIS, http://www.cris.unu.edu/riks/web/arrangement.

32. Ernst B. Haas, 'The Challenge of Regionalism', *International Organization* 12, no. 4 (1958): 441.

33. Louise Fawcett, 'Regionalism in World Politics: Past and Present' in *Elements*

*of Regional Integration: A Multidimensional Approach,* ed. Ariane Kösler and Martin Zimmek (Baden-Baden: Nomos, 2008).

34. See also Haas, 'The Challenge of Regionalism', 441.

35. William G. Demas, *The Economics of Development in Small Countries with Special Reference to the Caribbean* (Montreal: McGill University Press, 1965); William G. Demas, *Essays on Caribbean Integration and Development* (Kingston: Institute of Social and Economic Research (ISER), University of the West Indies, 1976).

36. Ramesh Thakur and Luk Van Langenhove, 'Enhancing Global Governance through Regional Integration,' in *Regionalisation and Global Governance. The Taming of Globalisation?,* ed. Andrew F. Cooper, Christopher W. Hughes, and Philippe De Lombaerde (London: Routledge, 2008).

37. Luk Van Langenhove and Daniele Marchesi, 'The Lisbon Treaty and the Emergence of Third Generation Regional Integration', in *The Jean Monnet/ Robert Schumann Paper Series* (Miami: Miami European Union Centre, 2008).

38. See summaries of these frameworks in Kenneth Hall and Denis Benn, eds., *Caribbean Imperatives. Regional Governance and Integrated Development* (Kingston: Ian Randle Publishers, 2005), xvi.

39. Björn Hettne, 'Beyond the 'New' Regionalism', *New Political Economy* 10, no. 4 (2005): 546.

40. See Ernst Haas's notion as quoted in ibid., 545.

41. Sidaway, *Imagined Regional Communities,* 8.

42. Shaun Breslin and Richard Higgott, 'Studying Regions: Learning from the Old, Constructing the New', *New Political Economy* 5, no. 3 (2000): 335.

43. Haas in Hettne, 'Beyond the 'New' Regionalism', 545; Breslin and Higgott, 'Studying Regions: Learning from the Old, Constructing the New', 335.

44. For references to the former see Björn Hettne, András Inotai, and Osvaldo Sunkel, eds., *Globalism and the New Regionalism* (Basingstoke: Macmillan Press, 1999); Björn Hettne and Fredrik Söderbaum, 'Theorising the Rise of Regionness', *New Political Economy* 5, no. 3 (2000); Fredrik Söderbaum, 'The International Political Economy of Regionalism,' in *Globalising International Political Economy,* ed. Nicola Phillips (Basingstoke: Palgrave Macmillan, 2005). For references to the latter see Jean Grugel and Wil Hout, eds., *Regionalism across the North-South Divide: State Strategies and Globalisation* (London: Routledge, 1999).

45. See also Anthony Payne, ed. *The New Regional Politics of Development* (Basingstoke: Palgrave Macmillan, 2004), 20.

46. Breslin and Higgott, 'Studying Regions: Learning from the Old, Constructing the New'; Peter J. Katzenstein, 'Regionalism and Asia', *New Political Economy* 5, no. 3 (2000).

47. Grugel and Hout, eds., *Regionalism across the North-South Divide*; Hettne, 'Beyond the 'New' Regionalism'; Kanishka Jayasuriya, 'Embedded Mercantilism and Open Regionalism: The Crisis of a Regional Political Project', *Third World Quarterly* 24, no. 2 (2003).

48. Fawcett, 'Regionalism in World Politics: Past and Present'.

49. Nikki Slocum-Bradley, 'Regional Integration, Identity and Culture,' in *Elements of Regional Integration: A Multidimensional Approach* ed. Ariane Kösler and Martin Zimmek (Baden-Baden: Nomos, 2008).

50. Liesbet Hooghe and Gary Marks, *Multi-Level Governance and European Integration* (Oxford: Rowman and Littleford Publishers, 2001); Liesbet Hooghe and Gary Marks, 'The Making of a Polity: The Struggle over European Integration,' *European Integration Online Papers (EIOP)* 1, no. 004 (1997), http://eiop.or.at/eiop/texte/1997-004a.htm.

51. Mattias Albert and Tanja Kopp-Malek, 'The Pragmatism of Global and European Governance: Emerging Forms of the Political 'Beyond Westphalia', Millennium: Journal of International Studies 31, no. 3 (2002); Nicola Phillips, 'Globalisation and the "Paradox of State Power": Perspectives from Latin America', in CSGR Working Paper No. 16/98 (Coventry: Centre for the Study of Globalisation and Regionalisation, University of Warwick, 1998).

52. Glenn Hook and Ian Kearns, eds., *Subregionalism and World Order* (Basingstoke: Macmillan Press, 1999). Examples of European Studies include Ariane Kösler and Martin Zimmek, eds., *Elements of Regional Integration: A Multidimensional Approach*, Schriften Des Zentrum Für Europäische Integrationsforschung/Centre for European Integration Studies (Baden-Baden: Nomos, 2008); Jeffrey T. Checkel, 'It's the Process Stupid! Process Tracing in the Study of European and International Politics', (Oslo: Centre for European Studies, 2005); Thomas Risse, 'Neofunctionalism, European Identity, and the Puzzles of European Integration', *Journal of European Public Policy* 12, no. 2 (2005); Michael Keating, 'European Integration and the Nationalities Question', *Politics and Society* 32 (2004); Jeffrey Stacey and Berthold Rittberger, 'Dynamics of Formal and Informal Institutional Change in the EU', *Journal of European Public Policy* 10, no. 6 (2003); Albert and Kopp-Malek, 'The Pragmatism of Global and European Governance: Emerging Forms of the Political "Beyond Westphalia"'; Liesbet Hooghe and Gary Marks, 'Unravelling the Central State, but How? Types of Multi-Level Governance', *American Political Science Review* 97, no. 2 (2003); Hooghe and Marks, *Multi-Level Governance and European Integration*; Helen Wallace, 'Europeanisation and Globalisation: Complementary or Contradictory Trends?', *New Political Economy* 5, no. 3 (2000); Wallace, 'The Sharing of Sovereignty.'

53. See for example Thakur and Van Langenhove, 'Enhancing Global Governance'; Hall and Benn, eds., *Caribbean Imperatives*; Anthony Payne, 'The Study of Governance in a Global Political Economy,' in *Globalising International Political Economy*, ed. Nicola Phillips (Basingstoke: Palgrave Macmillan, 2005); Grugel, 'New Regionalism and Modes of Governance'; Söderbaum, 'Modes of Regional Governance in Africa; Dwight K. Venner, 'Sub-Regional Governance: The OECS Experience,' in *Governance in the Age of Globalisation: Caribbean Perspectives*, ed. Kenneth O. Hall and Denis Benn (Kingston: Ian Randle Publishers, 2003); Anthony Payne, 'Globalisation and Modes of Regionalist Governance,' in *Debating Governance: Authority, Steering and Democracy*, ed. Jon Pierre (Oxford: Oxford University Press, 2000).

54. Söderbaum, 'Modes of Regional Governance in Africa', 422.

55. Jayasuriya, 'Embedded Mercantilism and Open Regionalism', 339.

56. See Albert and Kopp-Malek, 'The Pragmatism of Global and European Governance', 458.

57. Wallace, 'The Sharing of Sovereignty: The European Paradox.'

58. Hooghe and Marks, *Multi-Level Governance and European Integration*.
59. Simon J. Bulmer, 'New Institutionalism and the Governance of the Single European Market', *Journal of European Public Policy* 5, no. 3 (1998).

CHAPTER TWO

1. Bruce Byers, 'Ecoregions, State Sovereignty and Conflict', *Bulletin of Peace Proposals* 22, no. 1 (1991); Karen T. Litfin, 'Sovereignty in World Ecopolitics', *Mershon International Studies Review* 41, no. 2 (1997); Karen T. Litfin, *The Greening of Sovereignty in World Politics* (Cambridge, Massachussets: MIT Press, 1998); Walter Mattli, 'Sovereignty Bargains in Regional Integration', *International Studies Review* 2, no. 2 (2000); Kathryn Hochstetler, Ann Marie Clark, and Elisabeth J. Friedman, 'Sovereignty in the Balance: Claims and Bargains at the UN Conferences on the Environment, Human Rights, and Women', *International Studies Quarterly* 44, no. 4 (2000).
2. Byers, 'Ecoregions, State Sovereignty and Conflict'.
3. Nincic in ibid., 72.
4. Ibid., 73.
5. Litfin, 'Sovereignty in World Ecopolitics'; Litfin, *The Greening of Sovereignty*.
6. Litfin, 'Sovereignty in World Ecopolitics', 170.
7. Mattli, 'Sovereignty Bargains in Regional Integration'.
8. Ibid., 152.
9. Christopher Rudolph, 'Sovereignty and Territorial Borders in a Global Age', *International Studies Review* 7 (2005).
10. James A. Caporaso, 'Changes in the Westphalian Order: Territory, Public Authority, and Sovereignty', *International Studies Review* 2, no. 2 (2000): 9; Hochstetler, Clark, and Friedman, 'Sovereignty in the Balance'.
11. Mattli, 'Sovereignty Bargains in Regional Integration', 151.
12. Ibid., 152.
13. Shaun Naraine, 'State Sovereignty, Political Legitimacy and Regional Institutionalism in the Asia-Pacific', *The Pacific Review* 17, no. 3 (2004): 437.
14. A more sophisticated matrix of the trade-offs between Litfin's three attributes in the context of international bargains in UN fora can be found in Hochstetler, Clark, and Friedman, 'Sovereignty in the Balance', 595.
15. Autonomy, Authority, Control and Legitimacy are concepts to which this book returns as the Caribbean experience in the pursuit of sovereignty is examined at greater length.
16. Hochstetler, Clark, and Friedman, 'Sovereignty in the Balance', 610.
17. A. Moravcsik and K. Nicolaidis, 'Explaining the Treaty of Amsterdam: Interests, Influence, Institutions', *Journal of Common Market Studies* 37, no. 1 (1999); Jonas Tallberg, 'Delegation to Supranational Institutions: Why, How and with What Consequences?', *West European Politics* 25, no. 1 (2002).
18. See H.E.S. Nesadurai, 'Asean and Regional Governance after the Cold War: From Regional Order to Regional Community', *The Pacific Review* 22, no. 1 (2009); Mark Beeson, 'Geopolitics and the Making of Regions: The Fall and Rise of East Asia', *Political Studies* 57 (2009).
19. See for example Ariane Kösler and Martin Zimmek, eds., *Elements of Regional*

*Integration: A Multidimensional Approach*, Schriften Des Zentrum Für Europäische Integrationsforschung/Centre for European Integration Studies (Baden-Baden: Nomos, 2008); Andrew F. Cooper, Christopher W. Hughes, and Philippe De Lombaerde, 'Regionalisation and the Taming of Globalisation,' in *Regionalisation and Global Governance. The Taming of Globalisation?*, ed. Andrew F. Cooper, Christopher W. Hughes, and Philippe De Lombaerde (London: Routledge, 2008); Fredrik Söderbaum, 'The International Political Economy of Regionalism,' in *Globalising International Political Economy*, ed. Nicola Phillips (Basingstoke: Palgrave Macmillan, 2005); Anthony Payne, ed. *The New Regional Politics of Development* (Basingstoke: Palgrave Macmillan, 2004); Jean Grugel, 'New Regionalism and Modes of Governance – Comparing Us and EU Strategies in Latin America', *European Journal of International Relations* 10 (2004); Nicola Phillips, 'The Rise and Fall of Open Regionalism? Comparative Reflections on Regional Governance in the Southern Cone of Latin America', *Third World Quarterly* 24, no. 2 (2003); Shaun Breslin et al., *New Regionalism in the Global Political Economy. Theories and Cases* (London: Routledge, 2002); Timothy M. Shaw, 'New Regionalisms in Africa in the New Millennium: Comparative Perspectives on Renaissance, Realisms and/or Regressions', *New Political Economy* 5, no. 3 (2000); Morten Boas, Marianne H. Marchand, and Timothy M. Shaw, 'The Weave-World: Regionalisms in the South in the New Millennium', *Third World Quarterly* 20, no. 5 (1999); Marianne H. Marchand, Morten Boas, and Timothy M. Shaw, 'The Political Economy of New Regionalisms', *Third World Quarterly* 20, no. 5 (1999).
20. Alex Warleigh-Lack, 'Towards a Conceptual Framework for Regionalisation: Bridging "New Regionalism" and "Integration Theory"', *Review of International Political Economy* 13, no. 5 (2006): 760; Alex Warleigh-Lack, 'Studying Regionalisation Comparatively. A Conceptual Framework,' in *Regionalisation and Global Governance. The Taming of Globalisation?*, ed. Andrew F. Cooper, Christopher W. Hughes, and Philippe De Lombaerde (London: Routledge, 2008), 52.
21. Tallberg, 'Delegation to Supranational Institutions', 25.
22. Paul Pierson, 'The Path to European Integration. A Historical Institutionalist Analysis', *Comparative Political Studies* 29 (1996); Jeffrey Stacey and Berthold Rittberger, 'Dynamics of Formal and Informal Institutional Change in the EU', *Journal of European Public Policy* 10, no. 6 (2003).
23. Johan P. Olsen, 'Organising European Institutions of Governance. A Prelude to an Institutional Account of Political Integration,' ARENA Working Papers WP00, no. 2 (2000), http://www.erena.uio.no/publications/wp00_2.htm.
24. Patricia Luíza Kegel and Mohamed Amal, 'The Problem of Legal Implementation and Sovereignty' in *Elements of Regional Integration: A Multidimensional Approach*, ed. Ariane Kösler and Martin Zimmek (Baden-Baden: Nomos, 2008), 216.
25. Cuthbert Joseph, 'Institutional and Structural Patterns of Integration in Latin America and the Caribbean: A Legal Critique Presentado a Comitè Juridico Interamericano: Un Siglo De Aportes Al Derecho Internacional', (Washington, D.C.: Organizacion de los Estados Americanos Secretaria General, 2006); Kegel and Amal, 'The Problem of Legal Implementation and Sovereignty'.

26. See Duke E. Pollard, 'Juridical and Constitutional Implication of CARICOM Treaty Practice', *Commonwealth Law Bulletin* 35, no. 1 (2009).
27. See Tallberg, 'Delegation to Supranational Institutions'.
28. Thomas Risse, 'Neofunctionalism, European Identity, and the Puzzles of European Integration', *Journal of European Public Policy* 12, no. 2 (2005).
29. See Pollard, 'Juridical and Constitutional Implication of CARICOM Treaty Practice'.
30. Duke E. Pollard, 'Unincorporated Treaties and Small States', *Commonwealth Law Bulletin* 33, no. 3 (2007); Anthony Payne, 'The Study of Governance in a Global Political Economy,' in *Globalising International Political Economy*, ed. Nicola Phillips (Basingstoke: Palgrave Macmillan, 2005); Etel Solingen, 'The Genesis, Design and Effects of Regional Institutions: Lessons from East Asia and the Middle East', *International Studies Quarterly* 52, no. 2 (2008).
31. Jan-Erik Lane, 'International Organisation Analysed with the Power Index Method', in CSGR Working Paper No.181/05 (Coventry: Centre for the Study of Globalisation and Regionalisation, University of Warwick, 2005), 3.
32. J. Lodge, 'Federalism and the European Parliament', *Publius – The Journal of Federalism* 26, no. 4 (1996).
33. Nicola Phillips, 'Governance after Financial Crisis: South American Perspectives on the Reformulation of Regionalism', *New Political Economy* 5, no. 3 (2000); Joseph, 'Institutional and Structural Patterns of Integration in Latin America and the Caribbean'.
34. Joseph, 'Institutional and Structural Patterns of Integration'.
35. Naraine, 'State Sovereignty'; Solingen, 'The Genesis, Design and Effects of Regional Institutions'.
36. Solingen, 'The Genesis, Design and Effects of Regional Institutions', 270; also Naraine, 'State Sovereignty'.
37. See Kennedy Graham, 'Models of Regional Governance: Is There a Choice for the Pacific?,' in *Models of Regional Governance for the Pacific: Sovereignty and the Future Architecture of Regionalism*, ed. Kennedy Graham (Christchurch: Canterbury University Press, 2008); Kennedy Graham and Graham Hassall, 'Sovereignty and the Future Architecture of Pacific Regionalism,' in *Models of Regional Governance for the Pacific: Sovereignty and the Future Architecture of Regionalism*, ed. Kennedy Graham (Christchurch: Canterbury University Press, 2008); Ian Frazer and Jenny Bryant-Tokalau, 'Introduction: The Uncertain Future of Pacific Regionalism,' in *Redefining the Pacific?*, ed. Jenny Bryant-Tokalau and Ian Frazer (Aldershot: Ashgate, 2006).
38. The League was founded by Egypt, Iraq, Jordan, Lebanon, Saudi Arabia and Syria and has since expanded to a total of 22 members.
39. Solingen, 'The Genesis, Design and Effects of Regional Institutions', 281.
40. Naraine, 'State Sovereignty': 437; Shaun Naraine, 'The English School and ASEAN', *The Pacific Review* 19, no. 2 (2006): 215.
41. Shaun Breslin and Richard Higgott, 'Studying Regions: Learning from the Old, Constructing the New', *New Political Economy* 5, no. 3 (2000): 337–38; Helen E.S. Nesadurai, 'Asia-Pacific Approaches to Regional Governance: The Globalisation-Domestic Politics Nexus,' in *Asian Regional Governance: Crisis and Change*, ed. Kanishka Jayasuriya (London: Routledge, 2004); Nesadurai, 'ASEAN and Regional Governance after the Cold War'.

42. H.E.S. Nesadurai, 'Attempting Developmental Regionalism through Afta: The Domestic Sources of Regional Governance', *Third World Quarterly* 24, no. 2 (2003): 239.

43. Amitav Acharya, 'Democratization and the Prospects for Participatory Regionalism in Southeast Asia,' in *Asian Regional Governance: Crisis and Change*, ed. Kanishka Jayasuriya (London: Routledge, 2004).

44. Fredrik Söderbaum, 'Modes of Regional Governance in Africa: Neo-Liberalism; Sovereignty Boosting, and Shadow Networks', *Global Governance* 10 (2004).

45. Nesadurai, 'ASEAN and Regional Governance after the Cold War'; Benny Teh Cheng Guan, 'ASEAN's Regional Integration Challenge: The ASEAN Process', *The Copenhagen Journal of Asian Studies* 20 (2004); Acharya, 'Democratization'.

46. Dorothee Heisenberger and Amy Richmond, 'Supranational Institution-Building in the European Union: A Comparison of the European Court of Justice and the European Central Bank', *Journal of European Public Policy* 9, no. 2 (2002).

47. Roberto Ridolfi, 'The EU as Integration Model: How Relevant Is the European Experience?,' in *Models of Regional Governance for the Pacific: Sovereignty and the Future Architecture of Regionalism*, ed. Kennedy Graham (Christchurch: Canterbury University Press, 2008), 51.

48. Nicolas Jabko, 'In the Name of the Market: How the European Commission Paved the Way for Monetary Union', *Journal of European Public Policy* 6, no. 3 (1999); Moravcsik and Nicolaidis, 'Explaining the Treaty of Amsterdam'.

49. Teh Cheng Guan, 'ASEAN's Regional Integration Challenge', 90.

50. Söderbaum, 'Modes of Regional Governance in Africa'.

51. Naraine, 'State Sovereignty'; Solingen, 'The Genesis, Design and Effects of Regional Institutions'.

52. Phillips, 'Governance after Financial Crisis', 387; James D. Sidaway, *Imagined Regional Communities. Integration and Sovereignty in the Global South* (London: Routledge, 2002), 94.

53. Margaret Weir, 'Ideas and the Politics of Bounded Innovation,' in *Structuring Politics. Historical Institutionalism in Comparative Analysis*, ed. Sven Steinmo, Kathleen Thelen, and Frank Longstreth (Cambridge: Cambridge University Press, 1992); Peter A. Hall and Rosemary C. R. Taylor, 'Political Science and the Three Institutionalisms', *Political Studies* XLIV (1996); Simon J Bulmer, 'New Institutionalism and the Governance of the Single European Market', *Journal of European Public Policy* 5, no. 3 (1998).

54. See Anthony Payne, *The Politics of the Caribbean Community 1961–79* (Manchester: Manchester University Press, 1980); Anthony Payne, *The Political History of CARICOM* (Kingston: Ian Randle Publishers, 2008); Norman Girvan, 'Societies at Risk? The Caribbean and Global Change. Discussion Paper Series', in Caribbean Regional Consultation on the Management of Social Transformations (MOST) Programme of UNESCO, Discussion Paper No. 17 (Kingston: UNESCO, 1997); Norman Girvan, 'Creating and Recreating the Caribbean,' in *Contending with Destiny: The Caribbean in the 21st Century*, ed. Kenneth Hall and Denis Benn (Kingston: Ian Randle Publishers, 2000); Vaughan Lewis, 'The Eastern Caribbean States: Fledgling Sovereignties in the Global Environment,' in *Democracy in the Caribbean*, ed. Jorge I.

Dominguez, Robert A. Pastor, and R. Delisle Worrell (Baltimore: Johns Hopkins University Press, 1993); Vaughan Lewis, 'Regional Integration Institutional Arrangements: Underlying Assumptions and Contemporary Appropriateness,' in *Governance in the Age of Globalisation: Caribbean Perspectives*, ed. Kenneth O. Hall and Denis Benn (Kingston: Ian Randle Publishers, 2003); Vaughan Lewis, 'The Changing Environment of Oecs International Economic Relations and Some External Policy Implications', in *The Integrationist – Survival and Sovereignty in the Caribbean Community*, ed. Kenneth Hall and Myrtle Chuck-A-Sang (Kingston: Ian Randle Publishers, 2005); Kari Levitt, *Reclaiming Development: Independent Thought and Caribbean Community* (Kingston: Ian Randle Publishers, 2005); Vaughan Lewis, 'What Purposes for CARICOM Integration Today?' (paper presented at the Third Distinguished Lecture in a series in honour of Sir Arthur Lewis, the English-speaking Caribbean's first Nobel Laureate, 15 April 2007); Vaughan Lewis, 'Concept Paper: Parameters of Changing European Union-Caribbean Relations' (paper presented at the Seminar on "The Future of Caribbean-European Union Relations: Defining a Research Agenda", Maastricht, Holland, 8–9 October 2009); Clive Y. Thomas, 'The Development Glass: Half Empty or Half Full. Perspectives on Caribbean Development' (paper presented at the Sixth William G. Demas Memorial Lecture, Georgetown, Guyana, 17 May 2005).

## CHAPTER THREE

1.  Antigua and Barbuda, Barbados, Dominica, Grenada, Jamaica, St Kitts-Nevis-Anguilla, St Lucia, Montserrat, Trinidad and Tobago, and St Vincent and the Grenadines.

2.  For more on this early history, see for example, Byron Blake, 'The Caribbean – Geography, Culture, History and Identity: Assets for Economic Integration and Development,' in *Contending with Destiny: The Caribbean in the 21st Century*, ed. Kenneth Hall and Denis Benn (Kingston: Ian Randle Publishers, 2000); Gordon K. Lewis, *The Growth of the Modern West Indies* (London: McGibbon and Kee, 1968; reissued Kingston: Ian Randle Publishers, 2004).

3.  J.J. Thomas in Denis Benn, 'West Indian Nationalism: The Intellectual Dimensions,' in *The Caribbean: An Intellectual History 1774–2003*, ed. Denis Benn (Kingston: Ian Randle Publishers, 2004), 69.

4.  See ibid., 75.

5.  Christoph Müllerleile, *CARICOM Integration: Progress and Hurdles. A European View* (Kingston: Kingston Publishers, 1996), 12; Hugh W. Springer, 'Federation in the Caribbean: An Attempt That Failed', *International Organization* 16, no. 4 (1962): 758.

6.  Springer, 'Federation in the Caribbean', 759.

7.  See Benn, 'West Indian Nationalism'.

8.  In ibid., 77.

9.  Jesse Harris Proctor, 'The Functional Approach to Political Union: Lessons from the Effort to Federate the British Caribbean Territories', *International Organization* 10, no. 1 (1956).

10. Ibid.

11. See Springer, 'Federation in the Caribbean', 758.

12. See Gordon K. Lewis, 'The Federal Venture: The Formative Years,' in *The Growth of the Modern West Indies* (London: MacGibbon and Kee, 1968; reissued Kingston: Ian Randle Publishers, 2004), 352.

13. In Hugh Wooding, 'Lecture on the Failure of the West Indies Federation by Sir Hugh Wooding, C.B.E. Chief Justice of Trinidad and Tobago', (Port of Spain, Trinidad, 1964), 10; Springer, 'Federation in the Caribbean', 762.

14. In Wooding, 'Lecture on the Failure of the West Indies Federation', 3.

15. In ibid., 3.

16. In Springer, 'Federation in the Caribbean', 763.

17. Proctor, 'The Functional Approach to Political Union', 39.

18. Ibid.

19. Ibid.

20. John Mordecai, *The West Indies. The Federal Negotiations* (London: George Allen and Unwin, 1968), 88.

21. Ibid., 85–86.

22. Hugh W. Springer, *Reflections on the Failure of the First West Indian Federation*, vol. 4, Occasional Papers in International Affairs (Cambridge: Centre for International Affairs, Harvard University, 1962), 17.

23. Eric Williams, *Inward Hunger: The Education of a Prime Minister* (Princeton: Markus Wiener Publishers, 2006), 176.

24. In ibid., 177.

25. See Shelton Michael Anthony Nicholls, 'Economic Integration in the Caribbean Community (CARICOM): From Federation to Single Market' (The University of London, 1995), 42.

26. See Lewis, 'The Federal Venture: The Road to Failure.'

27. In Darrel E. Levi, *Michael Manley: The Making of a Leader* (London: Andre Deutsch, 1989), 77.

28. David Lowenthal and Lambros Comitas, eds., *The Aftermath of Sovereignty: West Indian Perspectives* (New York: Anchor Books, 1973), 164.

29. A.N.R. Robinson, 'Federation and Tobago. A Speech Delivered in Federal House of Representatives', (Chaguaramas, Trinidad and Tobago, 1960), 1.

30. See literature including Mordecai, *The West Indies. The Federal Negotiations*; Lewis, 'The Federal Venture: The Formative Years'; Lewis, 'The Federal Venture: The Road to Failure'; Arthur W. Lewis, *The Agony of the Eight* (Bridgetown: Advocate Commercial Printery, 1965); Wooding, 'Lecture on the Failure of the West Indies Federation by Sir Hugh Wooding, C.B.E. Chief Justice of Trinidad and Tobago'; Springer, *Reflections*.

31. That experience is discussed in greater detail in chapter 9.

32. In P.J. Patterson, 'The Present State of Caribbean Sovereignty' (paper presented at the Regional Seminar on Caribbean Sovereignty: Mobilization for Development and Self-Reliance. The Tasks of Political Education, Kingston, Jamaica, December 1984), 10.

33. See Anthony Payne, *The Political History of CARICOM* (Kingston: Ian Randle Publishers, 2008), 16.

34. In Kenneth O. Hall, ed. *Integrate or Perish: Perspectives of the Heads of Government of the Caribbean Community and the Commonwealth Caribbean Countries 1963–2002*, 2nd ed. (Kingston: Ian Randle Publishers, 2003), 514.

35. In Payne, *The Political History of CARICOM*.

36. In Hall, ed. *Integrate or Perish*, 146–47.
37. In Payne, *The Political History of CARICOM*, 17.
38. Heads of Governments of Commonwealth Caribbean Countries, 'Declaration on Foreign Policy Issued at the Second Conference of Heads of Governments of Commonwealth Caribbean Countries', (Kingston, Jamaica: CARICOM Secretariat, 1964).
39. Hall, ed. *Integrate or Perish*, 5.
40. In ibid., 545.
41. For the positive report see Heads of Governments of Commonwealth Caribbean Countries, 'Communiqué Issued at the Conclusion of the Third Conference of Heads of Government of Commonwealth Caribbean Countries' (Georgetown, Guyana, 8–10 March 1965).
42. Hall, ed. *Integrate or Perish*, 581.
43. Anthony Payne, 'The Rise and Fall of Caribbean Regionalisation', *Journal of Common Market Studies* XIX, no. 3 (1981): 256.
44. Alister McIntyre, 'Aspects of Trade and Development in the Commonwealth Caribbean', Economic Bulletin for Latin America 10, no. 2 (1965).
45. William G. Demas, Essays on Caribbean Integration and Development (Kingston: Institute of Social and Economic Research (ISER), University of the West Indies, 1976), 68.
46. Shridath Ramphal, 'Remembering to Score,' CARICOM Perspective, June 1995.
47. In Hall, ed. *Integrate or Perish*, 123.
48. Havelock Brewster and Clive Y. Thomas, *The Dynamics of West Indian Integration, vol. 1, Studies in Regional Economic Integration* (Kingston: Institute for Social and Economic Research, University of the West Indies, 1967), 29, 334.
49. Ibid., 19.
50. Heads of Governments of Commonwealth Caribbean Countries, 'Summary of Conclusions of the Fourth Conference of the Heads of Governments of Commonwealth Caribbean Countries' (Bridgetown, Barbados, 23–27 October 1967).
51. Trinidad joined Antigua and Barbuda, Barbados and Guyana in May 1968; Dominica, Grenada, St Kitts-Nevis-Anguilla, St Lucia, St Vincent and the Grenadines joined in July 1968 and Montserrat and Jamaica in August 1968. British Honduras finally joined CARIFTA in 1971 becoming the twelfth member.
52. See the preamble of Preamble, Governments of Antigua, Barbados, and British Guiana, 'The Dickenson Bay Agreement. Agreement Establishing the Caribbean Free Trade Association', (Georgetown: Commonwealth Caribbean Regional Secretariat, 1965).
53. Caribbean Development Bank (CDB), 'Agreement Establishing the Caribbean Development Bank', (1969).
54. See CARICOM Secretariat, *CARICOM: Our Caribbean Community. An Introduction* (Kingston: Ian Randle Publishers, 2005), 42–43.
55. Anthony Payne, *The Politics of the Caribbean Community 1961–1979* (Manchester: Manchester University Press, 1980).
56. In Hall, ed. *Integrate or Perish*, 137.

57. Lightbourne, Burnham, Bird and Gairy in ibid., 548–49, 122, 79, 441; Burnham and Bird in ibid., 122, 79.
58. The initiator's future policy position on that judicial entity will be discussed in chapter 8.
59. Proposals of the 1971 Grenada Declaration will be discussed in chapter 9.
60. See Godfrey Baldacchino, 'The Coming of Age of Island Studies', *Tijdschrift voor Economische en Sociale Geografie* 95, no. 3 (2004); Percy Selwyn, 'Smallness and Islandness', *World Development* 8 (1980).

## CHAPTER FOUR

1. Dominica, Grenada, Guyana, St Kitts-Nevis-Anguilla, St Lucia and St Vincent and the Grenadines.
2. Shridath Ramphal, 'Dialogue of Unity. A Search for West Indian Identity' (paper presented at the Address delivered at the Caribbean Ecumenical Consultation for Development, Chaguaramas, Trinidad, 16 November 1971).
3. Ibid., 9.
4. See Norman Girvan and Owen Jefferson, eds., *Readings in the Political Economy of the Caribbean* (Kingston: New World Group Ltd.,1974); Havelock Brewster and Clive Y. Thomas, *The Dynamics of West Indian Integration, vol. 1, Studies in Regional Economic Integration* (Kingston: Institute for Social and Economic Research, University of the West Indies, 1967).
5. See discussion of these various strands in Kari Levitt and Michael Witter, eds., *The Critical Tradition of Caribbean Political Economy. The Legacy of George Beckford* (Kingston: Ian Randle Publishers, 1996).
6. United Nations General Assembly, 'Declaration on the Establishment of a New International Economic Order – Unga Resolution 3201 (S-Vi)', in Official Records: Sixth Special Session Supplement No. 1 (A9559) (New York: United Nations, 1974); United Nations General Assembly, 'Programme of Action on the Establishment of a New International Economic Order – Unga Resolution 3202 (S-Vi)', in Official Records: Sixth Special Session Supplement No.1 (A/9559) (New York: United Nations, 1974); see also Duke E. Pollard, *Law and Policy of Producers' Associations* (Oxford: Clarendon, 1984).
7. These essays were eventually compiled in William G. Demas, *West Indian Nationhood and Caribbean Integration*, ed. David I. Mitchell, *Challenges in the New Caribbean* No. 1 (Bridgetown: CCC Publishing House, 1974).
8. William G. Demas, 'Building the New West Indies,' in *Change and Renewal in the Caribbean*, ed. William G Demas (Bridgetown: CCC Publishing House, 1971), 8.
9. Demas, *West Indian Nationhood and Caribbean Integration*, 16–18.
10. Commonwealth Caribbean Regional Secretariat, 'From CARIFTA to Caribbean Community', (Georgetown: Commonwealth Caribbean Regional Secretariat, 1972).
11. Ibid; see also Shridath Ramphal, 'The Prospect for Community in the Caribbean' (paper presented at the Address to the Royal Commonwealth Society, London, 22 January 1973).
12. In William G. Demas, 'Some Thoughts on the Caribbean Community', (Georgetown: CARICOM Secretariat, 1974), 127.

13. See Michael Manley, 'The Caribbean Community Envisioned by Its Forefathers and a Reality 25 Years After,' *CARICOM Perspective*, June 1995.

14. In Kenneth O. Hall and Denis Benn, eds., *Governance in the Age of Globalisation: Caribbean Perspectives* (Kingston: Ian Randle Publishers, 2003), 92.

15. Commonwealth Caribbean Regional Secretariat, 'From CARIFTA to Caribbean Community', 115.

16. Heads of Government of Commonwealth Caribbean Countries, 'Communiqué Issued at the Conclusion of the Seventh Conference of Heads of Government of Commonwealth Caribbean Countries' (Chaguaramas, Trinidad, 9–14 October 1972).

17. Heads of Government of Commonwealth Caribbean Countries, 'The Georgetown Accord', (Georgetown, Guyana, 1973).

18. Heads of Government of Commonwealth Caribbean Countries, 'Communiqué Issued at the Conclusion of the Eighth Meeting of Heads of Government of the Commonwealth Caribbean Countries' (Georgetown, Guyana, 9–12 April 1973).

19. In Kenneth O. Hall, ed. *Integrate or Perish: Perspectives of the Heads of Government of the Caribbean Community and the Commonwealth Caribbean Countries 1963–2002*, 2nd ed. (Kingston: Ian Randle Publishers, 2003), 88.

20. In Pollard, *Law and Policy of Producers' Associations*, 157.

21. See Article 4 in *CARICOM Conference of Heads of Government*, 'Treaty of Chaguaramas Establishing the Caribbean Community', (Georgetown: CARICOM Secretariat, 1973).

22. See Roderick Rainford, 'El Proceso De Adopción De Decisiones Y La Estructura Institucional De La Comunidad Del Caribe', Integraciòn Latinoamericana 91 (1984).

23. Anthony Payne, *The Political History of CARICOM* (Kingston: Ian Randle Publishers, 2008), 203.

24. See Vaughan Lewis, 'The Caribbean in Emerging World Political/Economic Trends', *Caribbean Quarterly* 25, no. 3 (1979).

25. This alternative is discussed in greater detail in chapter 9.

26. See Deirdre Jessamy, 'The Role of Personality in Commonwealth Caribbean Politics. The CARICOM Experiment 1973–1986' (MSc dissertation, University of the West Indies, 1986).

27. See ibid; Eric Williams, *Inward Hunger: The Education of a Prime Minister* (Princeton: Markus Wiener Publishers, 2006).

28. Editor, 'Third Time around – Perspective Interviews Prime Minister Manley,' *CARICOM Perspective*, January/June 1989, 37.

29. Republic of Trinidad and Tobago, White Paper on CARICOM, 1973–1978 (Port of Spain: Government Printery, 1979).

30. See Port of Spain Jamaican High Commission, 'Developments since July 1983 CARICOM Heads of Government Conference', (Port of Spain: Jamaican High Commission, 1984), 9.

31. See Rosina Wiltshire-Brodber, 'The Caribbean Integration Movement: An Alternative Prospective,' *CARICOM Perspective* 1983; Rainford, 'El Proceso De Adopción De Decisiones'.

32. See Ramesh Ramsaran, 'CARICOM: The Integration Process in Crisis', *Journal of World Trade Law* 12, no. 3 (1978); Mahindra Naraine, 'The Caribbean Community's Tenth Anniversary', *The Round Table: The Commonwealth*

*Journal of International Affairs* 288 (1983); Anthony Payne, *The Politics of the Caribbean Community 1961–1979* (Manchester: Manchester University Press, 1980); Anthony Payne, 'The Rise and Fall of Caribbean Regionalisation', *Journal of Common Market Studies* XIX, no. 3 (1981); Anthony Payne, 'Whither CARICOM? The Performance and Prospects of Caribbean Integration in the 1980s', *International Journal* XL, no. 2 (1985); Trevor Farrell, 'Five Major Problems for CARICOM', in *The Caribbean Community: Beyond Survival*, ed. Kenneth O. Hall (Kingston: Ian Randle Publishers, 2001); Norman Girvan, 'Three Areas of Regional Crisis', in *The Caribbean Community: Beyond Survival*, ed. Kenneth O. Hall (Kingston: Ian Randle Publishers, 2001); Ramesh Ramsaran, 'CARICOM's Soft Belly', in *The Caribbean Community: Beyond Survival*, ed. Kenneth O. Hall (Kingston: Ian Randle Publishers, 2001).

33. Shridath Ramphal, 'To Care for CARICOM. The Need for an Ethos of Community' (paper presented at the Speech delivered by Secretary-General of the Commonwealth at the Dinner held in his Honour by the CARICOM Council of Ministers, Montego Bay, Jamaica, 5 July 1975), 8.

34. Clive Y. Thomas, 'The Community is a Big Paper Tiger', in *The Caribbean Community: Beyond Survival*, ed. Kenneth O. Hall (Kingston: Ian Randle Publishers, 2001), 29.

35. Andrew W. Axline, 'Integration and Development in the Commonwealth Caribbean: The Politics of Regional Negotiations', *International Organisation* 32, no. 4 (1978): 973.

36. See Payne, *The Political History of CARICOM*, 200.

37. See Naraine, 'The Caribbean Community's Tenth Anniversary', 441.

38. Alister McIntyre and William G. Demas, 'Towards the More Effective Functioning of the Caribbean Common Market. Presented to the Tenth Meeting of the Common Market Council', (Georgetown: CARICOM Secretariat, 1977), 24–26.

39. See also Demas, 'Some Thoughts on the Caribbean Community'; William G. Demas, *Essays on Caribbean Integration and Development* (Kingston: Institute of Social and Economic Research (ISER), University of the West Indies, 1976); William G. Demas, 'The Three Aspects of the Caribbean Community. Keynote Address Delivered by President of the Caribbean Development Bank' (paper presented at the National Youth Leaders Conference of the Barbados Youth Council, Barbados, 18 February 1979).

40. Demas, 'Some Thoughts on the Caribbean Community', 125.

41. See first four chapters of Carmen Diana Deere et al., *In the Shadows of the Sun: Caribbean Development Alternatives and U.S. Policy* (Boulder: Westview Press, 1990).

42. Group of Caribbean Experts, 'The Caribbean Community in the 1980s. Report by a Group of Caribbean Experts', (Georgetown: CARICOM Secretariat, 1981), 7.

43. CARICOM Conference of Heads of Government, 'The Ocho Rios Declaration', (Ocho Rios, Jamaica 1982).

44. See also *IDB, Ten Years of CARICOM* (Washington: IDB-INTAL, 1984).

45. Naraine, 'The Caribbean Community's Tenth Anniversary'.

46. Wiltshire-Brodber, 'The Caribbean Integration Movement'; Ralph Premdas, 'Secession in Nevis: Symbolic and Instrumental Explanations,' in *Beyond*

*Walls: Multidisciplinary Perspectives*, ed. Simone Augier and Olivia Edgecombe-Howell (Basseterre: School of Continuing Studies, University of the West Indies, 2002).

47. In Hall, ed. *Integrate or Perish*, 594.
48. CARICOM Conference of Heads of Government, 'Communiqué Issued at the Conclusion of the Fifth Meeting of the Conference of Heads of Government of the Caribbean Community' (Nassau, Bahamas, 4–7 July 1984).
49. CARICOM Secretariat, 'CARICOM Analysis: The Unanimity Rule: Constraint or Blessing,' *CARICOM Perspective 1983*.
50. Rainford, 'El Proceso De Adopción De Decisiones'.
51. In Hall, ed. *Integrate or Perish*, 289.
52. CARICOM Conference of Heads of Government, 'The Nassau Understanding: Structural Adjustment and Closer Integration for Accelerated Development in the Caribbean Community', (Nassau, Bahamas: CARICOM Secretariat, 1984).
53. In Christoph Müllerleile, *CARICOM Integration: Progress and Hurdles. A European View* (Kingston: Kingston Publishers, 1996), 78.
54. Compton Bourne, 'Caribbean Development to the Year 2000. Challenges, Prospects and Policies', (Georgetown: CARICOM Secretariat, 1988).
55. In Hall, ed. *Integrate or Perish*, 721; ibid., 398.
56. Ibid.
57. CARICOM Conference of Heads of Government, 'Communiqué Issued at the Conclusion of the Ninth Meeting of the Conference of Heads of Government of the Caribbean Community' (Deep Bay, Antigua, 4–8 July 1988). That report, which was published in 1990 by Don Mills, is discussed in chapter 5 along with other expert perspectives.
58. William G. Demas, 'Consolidating Our Independence: The Major Challenges for the West Indies' (paper presented at the Distinguished Lecture Series, Institute of International Relations, St Augustine, Trinidad, 1986), 10.
59. Jessamy, 'The Role of Personality', 146.
60. Cuthbert Joseph, 'Caribbean Economic Integration: Reflections on Some Legal and Institutional Issues,' in *Towards a Caribbean Economy in the Twenty-First Century. Essays in Honour of William G. Demas*, ed. Laurence Clarke and M.G. Zephirin (Port of Spain: Caribbean Centre for Monetary Studies, University of the West Indies, 1997), 410.
61. Ibid., 143.
62. Roderick Rainford, 'Awaiting the Dawn of a Greater Unity,' *CARICOM Perspective*, June 1995, 67.

## CHAPTER FIVE

1. See Anthony P. Gonzales, 'Recent Trends in International Economic Relations of the CARICOM States', *Journal of Interamerican Studies and World Affairs* 31, no. 3 (1989).
2. See Shridath Ramphal, 'To Be a Canoe. Presentation to the 12th Conference of Heads of Government of the Caribbean Community, Basseterre, St Kitts,' in *No Island is an Island. Selected Speeches of Sir Shridath Ramphal*, ed. David Dabydeen and John Gilmore (London: Macmillan Press, 1991).

3.  In Kenneth O. Hall, ed. *Integrate or Perish: Perspectives of the Heads of Government of the Caribbean Community and the Commonwealth Caribbean Countries 1963–2002*, 2nd ed. (Kingston: Ian Randle Publishers, 2003), 423–24.
4.  Ibid., 481.
5.  Ibid., 866.
6.  CARICOM Conference of Heads of Government, 'Communiqué Issued at the Conclusion of the Tenth Meeting of the Conference of Heads of Government of the Caribbean Community' (Grande Anse, Grenada, 3–7 July 1989).
7.  See Manley in Hall, ed. *Integrate or Perish*, 85.
8.  CARICOM Conference of Heads of Government, 'Grande Anse Declaration and Work Programme for the Advancement of the Integration Movement', (Georgetown: CARICOM Secretariat, 1989); CARICOM Conference of Heads of Government, 'Communiqué Issued at the Conclusion of the Tenth Meeting of the Conference of Heads of Government of the Caribbean Community'.
9.  CARICOM Conference of Heads of Government, 'Annex Ii – Grande Anse Resolution on Preparing the Peoples of the West Indies for the 21st Century' (paper presented at the Tenth Meeting of the Conference of Heads of Government of the Caribbean Community, Grande Anse, Grenada, 1989).
10. Duke E. Pollard, 'Decision-Making in the Caribbean Community', (Georgetown: CARICOM Secretariat 1985).
11. Ibid., 34.
12. Ibid., 11.
13. Gladstone E. Mills et al., 'Report on a Comprehensive Review of the Programmes, Institutions and Organisations of the Caribbean Community', (Georgetown: CARICOM Secretariat, 1990).
14. See preliminary report submitted to CARICOM Conference of Heads of Government, 'Communiqué Issued at the Conclusion of the Eleventh Meeting of the Conference of Heads of Government of the Caribbean Community' (Kingston, Jamaica, 31 July–2 August 1990).
15. Mills et al., 'Report on a Comprehensive Review', v.
16. Ibid., 23.
17. Patterson in Hall, ed. *Integrate or Perish*, 576.
18. CARICOM Conference of Heads of Government, 'The Kingston Declaration', (Kingston, Jamaica: CARICOM Secretariat, 1990).
19. William G Demas, 'The New Caribbean Man', in *Change and Renewal in the Caribbean*, ed. William G Demas (Bridgetown: CCC Publishing House, 1970).
20. Bradshaw in Hall, ed. *Integrate or Perish*, 631.
21. Shridath Ramphal, 'Progress Report of the Independent West Indian Commission', in *The Caribbean Community: Beyond Survival*, ed. Kenneth O. Hall (Kingston: Ian Randle Publishers, 2001), 229; see also Ramphal, 'To Be a Canoe'.
22. Roderick Rainford, 'Review of the Achievements and Shortcomings of CARICOM', in Paper Prepared for the West Indian Commission (Black Rock: West Indian Commission, 1991).
23. Tripartite Regional Economic Conference, 'The Port of Spain Consensus' (paper presented at the CARICOM Tripartite Regional Economic Conference, Port of Spain, Trinidad and Tobago, 27 February–1 March 1991).

24. Vaughan Lewis, 'Compulsions of Integration [West Indian Commission's Occasional Paper No. 6]', in *The Caribbean Community: Beyond Survival*, ed. Kenneth O. Hall (Kingston: Ian Randle Publishers, 2001), 180.
25. Ramphal, 'To Be a Canoe'.
26. CARICOM Conference of Heads of Government, 'Communiqué Issued at the Conclusion of the Twelfth Meeting of the Conference of Heads of Government of the Caribbean Community' (Basseterre, St Kitts and Nevis, 2–4 July 1991).
27. This particular institutional model of governance was extended in subsequent years and is discussed further in chapter 6.
28. CARICOM Conference of Heads of Government, 'Communiqué Issued at the Conclusion of the Third Intersessional Meeting of the Conference of Heads of Government of the Caribbean Community' (Kingston, Jamaica, 19 February 1992).
29. In Hall, ed. *Integrate or Perish*, 570–71.
30. West Indian Commission, 'Time for Action. The Report of the West Indian Commission', (Blackrock: The West Indian Commission, 1992).
31. Ibid., 35.
32. Ibid., 489.
33. Ibid., 475.
34. See for example Joycelin Massiah, 'The Report of the West Indian Commission: An Appreciation', *Caribbean Quarterly* 39, no. 1 (1993).
35. Havelock Brewster, 'The Report of the West Indian Commission, Time for Action – A Critical Appreciation', *Caribbean Quarterly* 39, no. 1 (1993); Peter Wickham, 'More Shadow Than Substance', in *The Caribbean Community: Beyond Survival*, ed. Kenneth O. Hall (Kingston: Ian Randle Publishers, 2001).
36. Fauzya A. Moore, 'The Report of the West Indian Commission: New Directions for CARICOM?', *Social and Economic Studies* 43, no. 2 (1994): 165.
37. Norman Girvan, 'Labour and Caribbean Integration', *Caribbean Labour Journal* 1, no. 1 (1991): 5.
38. Shridath Ramphal, 'Time to Act', *Caribbean Quarterly* 39, no. 1 (1993): 2.
39. CARICOM Conference of Heads of Government, 'Communiqué of the Special Meeting of the Conference of Heads of Government of the Caribbean Community' (Port of Spain, Trinidad, 28–31 October 1992).
40. See Anthony Payne, *The Political History of CARICOM* (Kingston: Ian Randle Publishers, 2008), 267.
41. Kenneth O. Hall and Byron Blake, 'CARICOM Administration,' in *The Caribbean Community: Beyond Survival*, ed. Kenneth O. Hall (Kingston: Ian Randle Publishers, 2001), 208.
42. Brewster, 'The Report of the West Indian Commission'.
43. CARICOM Standing Committee of Ministers of Foreign Affairs, 'Report of Second Meeting of Standing Committee of Ministers Responsible for Foreign Affairs', (Georgetown: CARICOM Secretariat, 1976).
44. See CARICOM Secretariat, 'Report' (paper presented at the 'Think Tank' on Joint Representation, Barbados, 27–28 August 1990).
45. CARICOM Conference of Heads of Government, 'Protocol of Port of Spain', (Georgetown: CARICOM Secretariat, 1992).
46. CARICOM Conference of Heads of Government, 'Communiqué Issued at the

Conclusion of the Fourth Intersessional Meeting of the Conference of Heads of Government of the Caribbean Community' (Roseau, Dominica, 22–23 March 1993); CARICOM Conference of Heads of Government, 'Communiqué Issued at the Conclusion of the Fourteenth Meeting of the Conference of Heads of Government of the Caribbean Community' (Nassau, Bahamas, 5–8 July 1993).

47. CARICOM Conference of Heads of Government, 'Communiqué Issued at the Conclusion of the Fifteenth Meeting of the Conference of Heads of Government of the Caribbean Community' (Bridgetown, Barbados, 4–7 July 1994).

48. CARICOM Conference of Heads of Government, 'Agreement for the Establishment of an Assembly of Caribbean Community Parliamentarians', (Kingston, Jamaica: CARICOM Secretariat, 1992).

49. See Duke Pollard, 'Revisiting Chaguaramas: Institutional Development in CARICOM since 1973', in *The Caribbean Community: Beyond Survival*, ed. Kenneth O. Hall (Kingston: Ian Randle Publishers, 2001), 224.

50. Ibid., 225.

51. Assembly of Caribbean Community Parliamentarians (ACCP), 'Motion to Consider Proposal for the Caribbean Non-Governmental Organisations (NGOs) to Be Granted Observer Status in the Assembly of Caribbean Community Parliamentarians' (paper presented at the Inaugural Meeting of the Assembly of Caribbean Community Parliamentarians, St Michael, Barbados, 27–29 May 1996).

52. Girvan, 'Labour and Caribbean Integration', 7.

53. Duke E. Pollard, ed. *The CARICOM System. Basic Instruments* (Kingston: The Caribbean Law Publishing Company, 2003), 227.

54. CARICOM Conference of Heads of Government, 'Communiqué Issued at the Conclusion of the Sixteenth Meeting of the Conference of Heads of Government of the Caribbean Community' (Georgetown, Guyana, 4–7 July 1995).

55. Assembly of Caribbean Community Parliamentarians, 'Resolution on the Caribbean Court of Justice' (paper presented at the Second Sitting of the Assembly of Caribbean Community Parliamentarians, St Georges, Grenada, 15 October 1999).

56. Wendy Grenade, 'An Overview of Regional Governance Arrangements within the Caribbean Community,' in *The European Union and Regional Integration. A Comparative Perspective and Lessons for the Americas*, ed. Joaquìn Roy and Roberto Dominguez (Miami: Office of the Jean Monnet Chair, University of Miami, 2005); David Hinds, 'Internal Political Tribalism and Regional Integration in the Caribbean,' in *The European Union and Regional Integration. A Comparative Perspective and Lessons for the Americas*, ed. Joaquìn Roy and Roberto Dominguez (Miami: Office of the Jean Monnet Chair, University of Miami, 2005).

57. Caribbean Engineering and Management Consultants Limited (CEMCO), 'Study to Determine Technical Assistance Needs for Implementation of Caribbean Community Decisions in Member States. Final Report', (Georgetown: CEMCO, 1994), vii.

58. Joseph Farier, 'Aligned for Global Change: Restructuring in the Caribbean Community', in *The Caribbean Community: Beyond Survival*, ed. Kenneth O. Hall (Kingston: Ian Randle Publishers, 2001), 272.

59. Duke Pollard, 'The Caribbean Single Market and Economy: The Legal Implications', in *The Caribbean Community: Beyond Survival*, ed. Kenneth O. Hall (Kingston: Ian Randle Publishers, 2001).
60. CARICOM Conference of Heads of Government, 'Communiqué Issued at the Conclusion of the Seventeenth Meeting of the Conference of Heads of Government of the Caribbean Community' (Bridgetown, Barbados, 3–6 July 1996).
61. See William G. Demas, *West Indian Development and the Deepening and Widening of the Caribbean Community, vol. 1, Critical Issues in Caribbean Development* (Kingston: Ian Randle Publishers, 1997), 34.

## CHAPTER SIX

1. The incremental revision process, by Protocol, was intended to facilitate the incremental mobilisation of grant funding by the Secretariat to support the requisite national consultations as well as to permit the demonstration of quick progress, for the benefit of critics of CARICOM's record of slow implementation.
2. Other protocols outlined provisions for the right of establishment, provisions of services and the movement of capital and nationals (Protocol II); industrial policy (Protocol III); trade policy (Protocol IV); agricultural policy (Protocol V); transport policy (Protocol VI); treatment of disadvantaged countries, regions and sectors (Protocol VII); competition policy and consumer protection (VIII); and disputes settlement (Protocol IX). All nine protocols were completed in March 2000 and then integrated into the 2001 Revised Treaty of Chaguaramas.
3. CARICOM Conference of Heads of Government, 'Communiqué Issued at the Conclusion of the Eighth Intersessional Meeting of the Conference of Heads of Government of the Caribbean Community' (St John's, Antigua and Barbuda, 20–21 February 1997).
4. CARICOM Conference of Heads of Government, 'Protocol Amending the Treaty Establishing the Caribbean Community Signed at Chaguaramas on 4 July 1973', (Georgetown: CARICOM Secretariat, 1997).
5. All subsequent references to legislative 'articles' in this section of the discussion refer to the articles of Protocol I as adopted in February 1997 and not to their subsequent numeration or wording after integration into the 2001 Revised Treaty of Chaguaramas. In that regard, the CSME is referred to here as the Caribbean Single Market and Economy but after 2001 as the CARICOM Single Market and Economy – an appellation adopted in the Revised Treaty.
6. See Duke E. Pollard, 'Personal Interview', (Port of Spain, Trinidad and Tobago, 2008).
7. See Bishnodat Persaud and Michael Davenport, 'The Implications for the Bahamas of Participation in the CARICOM Single Market and Economy', (Nassau: Ministry of Foreign Affairs, 2000).
8. See CARICOM, 'Agreement between the Caribbean Community and the Government of the Bahamas Including Declaration of the Commonwealth of the Bahamas on Signing the Agreement between the Caribbean Community and the Government of the Bahamas', (Port of Spain, Trinidad and Tobago, 2006).

9. CARICOM Conference of Heads of Government, 'Charter of Civil Society for the Caribbean Community', (Georgetown: CARICOM Secretariat, 1997).
10. Ibid.
11. CARICOM Conference of Heads of Government, 'The Liliendaal Statement of Principles on 'Forward Together', (Georgetown: CARICOM Secretariat, 2002).
12. See William G. Demas, *West Indian Development and the Deepening and Widening of the Caribbean Community., vol. 1, Critical Issues in Caribbean Development* (Kingston: Ian Randle Publishers, 1997), 30, 44; Cuthbert Joseph, 'Caribbean Economic Integration: Reflections on Some Legal and Institutional Issues,' in *Towards a Caribbean Economy in the Twenty-First Century. Essays in Honour of William G. Demas*, ed. Laurence Clarke and M.G. Zephirin (Port of Spain: Caribbean Centre for Monetary Studies, University of the West Indies, 1997).
13. Bird in Kenneth O. Hall, ed. *Integrate or Perish: Perspectives of the Heads of Government of the Caribbean Community and the Commonwealth Caribbean Countries 1963–2002*, 2nd ed. (Kingston: Ian Randle Publishers, 2003), 201.
14. CARICOM Conference of Heads of Government, 'Communiqué Issued at the Conclusion of the Tenth Intersessional Meeting of the Conference of Heads of Government of the Caribbean Community' (Paramaribo, Suriname, 4–5 March 1999); Owen Arthur, 'Towards a New Governance', in *Governance in the Caribbean*, ed. Selwyn Ryan and Ann Marie Bissessar (St Augustine: Sir Arthur Lewis Institute of Social and Economic Studies (SALISES), 1999), 35.
15. CARICOM Conference of Heads of Government, 'Communiqué Issued at the Conclusion of the Twentieth Meeting of the Conference of Heads of Government of the Caribbean Community' (Port-of-Spain, Trinidad and Tobago, 4–7 July 1999).
16. CARICOM Conference of Heads of Government, 'Consensus of Chaguaramas', (Georgetown: CARICOM Secretariat, 1999).
17. Kenny Anthony, 'The Caribbean in the New Century: Challenges to the Emergence of a New Political Culture' (paper presented at the Address by the Prime Minister of St Lucia to the Caribbean Studies Association, Castries, St Lucia, 30 May 2000).
18. CARICOM Conference of Heads of Government, 'Communiqué Issued at the Conclusion of the Eleventh Intersessional Meeting of the Conference of Heads of Government of the Caribbean Community' (Basseterre, St Kitts and Nevis, 13–14 March 2000).
19. See CARICOM Conference of Heads of Government, 'Communiqué Issued at the Conclusion of the Seventeenth Meeting of the Conference of Heads of Government of the Caribbean Community' (Bridgetown, Barbados, 3–6 July 1996).
20. See Alister McIntyre, 'The Importance of Negotiation Preparedness', in *The Caribbean Community: Beyond Survival*, ed. Kenneth O. Hall (Kingston: Ian Randle Publishers, 2001).
21. Cedric Grant, 'An Experiment in Supra-National Governance: The Caribbean Regional Negotiating Machinery,' in *Contending with Destiny: The Caribbean in the 21st Century*, ed. Kenneth Hall and Denis Benn (Kingston: Ian Randle Publishers, 2000), 459.

22. Ibid., 463–64.

23. Ibid., 494.

24. Ibid.

25. CARICOM Conference of Heads of Government, 'Communiqué Issued at the Conclusion of the Eighteenth Meeting of the Conference of Heads of Government of the Caribbean Community' (Montego Bay, Jamaica, 30 June–4 July 1997).

26. In Rickey Singh, 'Changing Leadership in CRNM, *Trinidad and Tobago Express*, 30 April 2008.

27. CARICOM Conference of Heads of Government, 'Communiqué Issued at the Conclusion of the Nineteenth Meeting of the Conference of Heads of Government of the Caribbean Community' (Castries, St Lucia, 30 June–4 July 1998).

28. P.J. Patterson, 'Report of the Chairman of the Prime-Ministerial Sub-Committee (PMSC) on External Negotiations on the Reviews of the Structure and Budget of the RNM, (2001), 14.

29. Ibid., 17.

30. In Hall, ed. *Integrate or Perish*, 707–708.

31. CARICOM Conference of Heads of Government, 'Communiqué Issued at the Conclusion of the Nineteenth Meeting of the Conference of Heads of Government of the Caribbean Community'; Anthony in Hall, ed. *Integrate or Perish*, 698–705.

32. CARICOM Conference of Heads of Government, 'Agreement Establishing the Caribbean Court of Justice', (Georgetown: CARICOM Secretariat, 2001).

33. Chapter Nine of CARICOM Conference of Heads of Government, 'Revised Treaty of Chaguaramas Establishing the Caribbean Community and the CARICOM Single Market and Economy', (Georgetown: CARICOM Secretariat, 2001).

34. Gonsalves in Hall, ed. *Integrate or Perish*, 750.

35. Havelock Brewster, 'CARICOM: From Community to Single Market and Economy,' in *Governance in the Age of Globalisation: Caribbean Perspectives*, ed. Kenneth O. Hall and Denis Benn (Kingston: Ian Randle Publishers, 2003), 504.

36. The consultant team was chaired by Ambassador Leonard Archer of the Ministry of Foreign Affairs of Bahamas and a former Member of the West Indian Commission; and also included, Dr. P.I. Gomes of the CARICAD, Dr Didacus Jules, Permanent Secretary in the Ministry of Education and Human Resource Development of St Lucia, Dr. Henley Morgan of the Caribbean Applied Technology Centre in Jamaica and Ms. Maria Smart, an Information Systems specialist from Trinidad and Tobago.

37. Leonard Archer et al., 'A Review of the Structure of the Functioning of the Caribbean Community Secretariat. Final Report', (Georgetown: CARICOM Secretariat, 2002), x.

38. Ibid., 37.

39. Ibid., iii.

40. Ibid., 36.

41. Duke E. Pollard, ed. *The CARICOM System: Basic Instruments* (Kingston: The Caribbean Law Publishing Company, 2003), 463; Duke E. Pollard, 'The Revised Treaty of Chaguaramas,' in *CARICOM Single Market and Economy: Genesis and Prognosis*, ed. Kenneth Hall and Myrtle Chuck-A-Sang (Kingston: Ian Randle Publishers, 2007), 9.

42. See Clive Y. Thomas, 'The Interrelationship between Economic and Social Development,' in *Poverty, Empowerment and Social Development in the Caribbean*, ed. Norman Girvan (Kingston: Canoe Press, University of the West Indies, 1997).

43. Edwin Jones, 'Governance in CARICOM – A 2000 Perspective,' *CARICOM Perspective. A Century of Achievement* (June 2000).

44. Kim Ho-Fatt, 'Region Versus Nation: An Examination of Identity Formation in the Caribbean' (MSc diss., University of the West Indies, 2000), 26–29.

45. See Havelock RH Ross-Brewster, 'Identity, Space and the West Indian Union,' in *Contending with Destiny: The Caribbean in the 21st Century*, ed. Kenneth Hall and Denis Benn (Kingston: Ian Randle Publishers, 2000).

46. CARICOM Secretariat, 'Implementation of Caribbean Community Foreign Policy Strategy', in *Part I – Revised Strategy for the Coordination of the Foreign Policies of CARICOM States* (Baracara Island, Guyana, 2002); CARICOM Conference of Heads of Government, 'Framework for Stabilising and Transforming Caribbean Economies' (paper presented at the Special Meeting of Conference of Heads of Government, Castries, St Lucia, 17 August 2002).

47. Manning in Hall, ed. *Integrate or Perish: Perspectives of the Heads of Government of the Caribbean Community and the Commonwealth Caribbean Countries 1963–2002*, 814.

48. Jagdeo in ibid., 524.

49. Norman Girvan, 'Creating and Recreating the Caribbean,' in *Contending with Destiny: The Caribbean in the 21st Century*, ed. Kenneth Hall and Denis Benn (Kingston: Ian Randle Publishers, 2000), 35.

## CHAPTER SEVEN

1. Ralph Gonsalves, 'Our Caribbean Civilisation and Its Political Prospects' (paper presented at the Inaugural Lecture in the Distinguished Lecture Series Supported by CARICOM to Commemorate the Thirtieth Anniversary, Port of Spain, Trinidad, 12 February 2003), 26.

2. Ibid., 22.

3. Compton Bourne, 'A Caribbean Community for All' (paper presented at the Fifth Lecture in the Distinguished Lecture Series Celebrating the Thirtieth Anniversary of the Caribbean Community, Grenada, 25 June 2003); Rex Nettleford, 'The Caribbean's Creative Diversity: The Defining Point of the Region's History. Lecture Delivered by the Vice Chancellor of the University of the West Indies' (paper presented at the Second Lecture in the Distinguished Lecture Series Commemorating the Thirtieth Anniversary of the Caribbean Community, University Of Guyana, Guyana, 21 March 2003); Maxine Henry-Wilson, 'Culture in the Future of the Caribbean Community. Third Lecture in the Distinguished Lecture Series Sponsored by CARICOM to Commemorate its Thirtieth Anniversary' (paper presented at the Eighth Meeting of the Council for Human and Social Development, Paramaribo, Suriname, 24–26 April 2003); Bhoendradatt Tewarie, 'Redesigning a Strategy for Caribbean Success in the Age of Globalization' (paper presented at the Sixth Lecture of the Distinguished Lecture Series Celebrating the 30th Anniversary of the Caribbean Community, Belize, 17 September 2003).

4. William G. Demas, 'The New Caribbean Man', in *Change and Renewal in the Caribbean*, ed. William G. Demas (Bridgetown: CCC Publishing House, 1970); Lloyd Best, 'Independence and Responsibility: Self-Knowledge as an Imperative,' in *The Critical Tradition of Caribbean Political Economy. The Legacy of George Beckford*, ed. Kari Levitt and Michael Witter (Kingston: Ian Randle Publishers, 1996); see discussion of Best in Kirk Meighoo, 'Organic Theorising in Inorganic Societies, or the Need for Epistemic Sovereignty,' in *The Caribbean Integration Process: A People Centred Approach*, ed. Kenneth Hall and Myrtle Chuck-A-Sang (Kingston: Ian Randle Publishers, 2005).

5. See Cedric Grant, 'Democracy and Governance in the Caribbean Community' (paper presented at the Fourth Lecture in the Distinguished Lecture Series Sponsored by CARICOM to Commemorate its Thirtieth Anniversary, Kingstown, St Vincent and the Grenadines, 7 May 2003).

6. P.J. Patterson, 'CARICOM Beyond Thirty: Connecting with the Diaspora' (paper presented at the Seventh Lecture in the Distinguished Lecture Series Commemorating the 30th Anniversary of the Caribbean Community, Brooklyn, New York, 2 October 2003).

7. See Cynthia Barrow-Giles and Don Marshall, eds., *Living at the Borderlines: Issues in Caribbean Sovereignty and Development* (Kingston: Ian Randle Publishers, 2003).

8. Cynthia Barrow-Giles, 'Dangerous Waters: Sovereignty, Self-Determinism and Resistance,' in *Living at the Borderlines: Issues in Caribbean Sovereignty and Development*, ed. Cynthia Barrow-Giles and Don Marshall (Kingston: Ian Randle Publishers, 2003), 51.

9. Compton Bourne, 'Small States in the Context of Global Change', in Fourth Annual SALISES Conference – Development Strategy and Policy for Small States in the Context of Global Change (Cave Hill, Barbados, 2003).

10. Havelock Brewster, 'The CARICOM Single Market and Economy: Is it Realistic without Commitment to Political Unity?', *Journal of Eastern Caribbean Studies* 28, no. 3 (2003).

11. Barrow-Giles, 'Dangerous Waters,' 54.

12. Ibid.

13. CARICOM Conference of Heads of Government, 'Communiqué Issued at the Conclusion of the Fourteenth Intersessional Meeting of the Conference of Heads of Government of the Caribbean Community' (Port of Spain, Trinidad and Tobago, 14–15 February 2003).

14. P.J. Patterson, 'CARICOM Beyond Thirty: Charting New Directions. Chairman's Perspective', in 24th Meeting of the Conference of Heads of CARICOM (Montego Bay, Jamaica, 2003), 7.

15. Ibid.

16. CARICOM Prime Ministerial Expert Group on Governance, 'Regional Integration: Carrying the Process Forward. Report on the Establishment of a CARICOM Commission or Other Executive Mechanism', (Georgetown: CARICOM Secretariat, 2003).

17. P.J. Patterson, 'Opening Address by the Prime Minister of Jamaica at the 24th Regular Meeting of the Conference of CARICOM Heads of Government' (Montego Bay, Jamaica, 2 July 2003 2003).

18. CARICOM Conference of Heads of Government, 'Communiqué Issued at the Conclusion of the Twenty-Fourth Meeting of the Conference of Heads of Government of the Caribbean Community' (Montego, Bay, Jamaica 2–5 July 2003); CARICOM Conference of Heads of Government, 'The Rose Hall Declaration on 'Regional Governance and Integrated Development' Adopted on the Occasion of the Thirtieth Anniversary of the Caribbean Community (CARICOM)', in Twenty-Fourth Meeting of the Conference of Heads of Government of CARICOM (Montego Bay: CARICOM Secretariat, 2003).

19. Havelock Brewster, 'Review of the Rose Hall Declaration: Provisions on Regional Governance', in *CARICOM Single Market and Economy: Genesis and Prognosis*, ed. Kenneth Hall and Myrtle Chuck-A-Sang (Kingston: Ian Randle Publishers, 2003), 49.

20. Ibid., 56.

21. See Kenneth Hall and Denis Benn, eds., *Caribbean Imperatives. Regional Governance and Integrated Development* (Kingston: Ian Randle Publishers, 2005).

22. Cedric Grant, 'Civil Society, Governance and Conflict Resolution in the Caribbean,' in *Governance in the Age of Globalisation: Caribbean Perspectives*, ed. Kenneth O. Hall and Denis Benn (Kingston: Ian Randle Publishers, 2003), 293.

23. Edward Greene, 'Striving toward a Reconfiguration of a Rational Community through Shared Sovereignty,' in *Caribbean Imperatives: Regional Governance and Integrated Development*, ed. Kenneth Hall and Denis Benn (Kingston: Ian Randle Publishers, 2005), 7–8.

24. Adapted from ibid., 6.

25. Trevor Munroe, 'On Strengthening Foundations for Regional Governance,' in *Caribbean Imperatives: Regional Governance and Integrated Development*, ed. Kenneth Hall and Denis Benn (Kingston: Ian Randle Publishers, 2005), 66.

26. Ibid.

27. Ian Boxill, 'Sovereignty and the Search for Recognition,' in *Caribbean Imperatives: Regional Governance and Integrated Development*, ed. Kenneth Hall and Denis Benn (Kingston: Ian Randle Publishers, 2005).

28. See Neville Duncan et al., 'Jamaican Perspectives of Regional Integration', in SALISES Internal Paper (Mona, Jamaica: University of the West Indies, 2004), unpublished; and also Jimmy Kazaara Tindigarukayo, 'Perceptions and Opinions of Jamaicans on CARICOM Single Market Economy', in SALISES 5th Annual Conference on the CARICOM Single Market Economy (St Augustine, Trinidad and Tobago, 2004).

29. Shridath Ramphal, 'The CARICOM Commission: Towards a Mature Regionalism,' in *Caribbean Imperatives: Regional Governance and Integrated Development*, ed. Kenneth Hall and Denis Benn (Kingston: Ian Randle Publishers, 2005); Roderick Rainford, 'Towards a Commission or Executive Authority for the Community,' in *Caribbean Imperatives: Regional Governance and Integrated Development*, ed. Kenneth Hall and Denis Benn (Kingston: Ian Randle Publishers, 2005).

30. Cuthbert Joseph, 'Reconceptualising the Caribbean Community: Reconciling Individual and Collective Exercise of Sovereignty – A Legal Perspective,' in

*Caribbean Imperatives: Regional Governance and Integrated Development*, ed. Kenneth Hall and Denis Benn (Kingston: Ian Randle Publishers, 2005), 14.

31. Ramphal, 'The CARICOM Commission: Towards a Mature Regionalism.'

32. Ibid., 77.

33. Havelock Brewster, 'Mature Regionalism and the Rose Hall Declaration on Regional Governance,' in *Caribbean Imperatives: Regional Governance and Integrated Development*, ed. Kenneth Hall and Denis Benn (Kingston: Ian Randle Publishers, 2005).

34. see Gail Mathurin, 'Governance Structures for the Formulation and Negotiation of Trade Policy,' in *Caribbean Imperatives: Regional Governance and Integrated Development*, ed. Kenneth Hall and Denis Benn (Kingston: Ian Randle Publishers, 2005), 234; Jessica Byron, 'CARICOM at Thirty: New and Old Foreign Policy Challenges', *Social and Economic Studies* 53, no. 4 (2004).

35. P.I. Gomes, 'Rationalizing the Functions of the Organs of the Community,' in *Caribbean Imperatives: Regional Governance and Integrated Development*, ed. Kenneth Hall and Denis Benn, (Kingston: Ian Randle Publishers, 2005), 23.

36. Ibid., 101.

37. Edwin Jones and Ivan Cruickshank, 'Making the CARICOM Administrative Machinery Work: The Decentralisation and Leadership Factor,' in *Caribbean Imperatives: Regional Governance and Integrated Development*, ed. Kenneth Hall and Denis Benn (Kingston: Ian Randle Publishers, 2005), 105, 19.

38. See Robert Buddan, 'My Generation Comes to Power: A Time for Caribbean Leadership and Political Transformation,' in *Caribbean Imperatives: Regional Governance and Integrated Development*, ed. Kenneth Hall and Denis Benn (Kingston: Ian Randle Publishers, 2005).

39. In George Lamming, *The Sovereignty of the Imagination* (Kingston: Arawak Publications, 2004), 31.

40. CARICOM Prime Ministerial Expert Group on Governance, 'Regional Integration: Carrying the Process Forward. Report on the Establishment of a CARICOM Commission or Other Executive Mechanism'.

41. Ibid., 3.

42. Ibid., 6.

43. Prime Ministerial Expert Group on Governance, 'Draft Report of the Technical Group on Automaticity of Financing', ed. Compton Bourne (2003).

44. Prime Ministerial Expert Group on Governance, 'Report of the Technical Sub-Group on the Assembly of Caribbean Community Parliamentarians (Accp)', ed. Denis Benn (2003).

45. CARICOM Conference of Heads of Government, 'Press Statement Issued at the Conclusion of the Ninth Special Meeting of the Conference of Heads of Government of the Caribbean Community' (Castries, St Lucia, 13–14 November 2003).

46. CARICOM Conference of Heads of Government, 'Communique Issued at the Conclusion of the Twenty-Fifth Meeting of the Conference of Heads of Government of the Caribbean Community' (St George's, Grenada, 8 July 2004).

47. See Norman Girvan, 'Reflections on the CARICOM Single Market and Economy. Keynote Address' (paper presented at the SALISES Fifth Annual Conference, St Augustine, 31 March 2004).

48. CARICOM Conference of Heads of Government, 'Communiqué Issued at the Conclusion of the Tenth Special Meeting of the Conference of Heads of Government of the Caribbean Community' (Port of Spain, Trinidad and Tobago, 10 November 2004); CARICOM Conference of Heads of Government, 'Delivering the CSME by 2005: The Port of Spain Statement on the CARICOM Single Market and Economy' (paper presented at the Issued at the Conclusion of the Tenth Special Meeting of the Conference of Heads of Government of the Caribbean Community, Port of Spain, Trinidad and Tobago, 9 November 2004).

49. Owen Arthur, 'The Caribbean Single Market and Economy: The Way Forward', in *Integration: CARICOM's Key to Prosperity*, ed. Kenneth Hall and Myrtle Chuck-A-Sang (Kingston: Ian Randle Publishers, 2004), 131.

50. Prime Ministerial Expert Group on Governance, 'Final Report of the Expert Group of Heads of Government on the Establishment of a CARICOM Commission or Other Executive Mechanism, Automatic Resource Transfers and the Assembly of Caribbean Community Parliamentarians', ed. Ralph Gonsalves (Kingston, Jamaica, 2005).

51. CARICOM Conference of Heads of Government, 'Communiqué Issued at the Conclusion of the Twenty-Sixth Meeting of the Conference of Heads of Government of the Caribbean Community' (Castries, St Lucia, 6 July 2005).

52. see CARICOM Conference of Heads of Government, 'Communiqué Issued at the Conclusion of the Fifteenth Inter-Sessional Meeting of the Conference of Heads of Government of the Caribbean Community' (Basseterre, St Kitts and Nevis, 25–26 March 2004).

53. CARICOM Conference of Heads of Government, 'Communiqué Issued at the Conclusion of the Seventeenth Intersessional Meeting of the Conference of Heads of Government of the Caribbean Community' (Port of Spain, Trinidad and Tobago, 10 February 2006).

54. Vaughan Lewis, 'Managing Mature Regionalism: Regional Governance in the Caribbean Community. Report of the Technical Working Group on Governance Appointed by CARICOM Heads of Government', (Georgetown: CARICOM Secretariat, 2006).

55. Ibid., 17.

56. Ibid., 29.

57. CARICOM Conference of Heads of Government, 'Communiqué Issued at the Conclusion of the Eighteenth Inter-Sessional Meeting of the Conference of Heads of Government of the Caribbean Community' (Kingstown, St Vincent and the Grenadines, 12–14 February 2007); CARICOM Secretariat, 'Summary of Recommendations and Conclusions of the 28th Meeting of Heads of Government of CARICOM' (St Michael, Barbados, 1–4 July 2007).

58. CARICOM Secretariat, 'Summary of Recommendations and Conclusions of the 28th Meeting of Heads of Government of CARICOM', 44.

59. Ibid.

60. CARICOM Conference of Heads of Government, 'Communiqué Issued at the Conclusion of the Twenty-Eighth Meeting of the Conference of Heads of Government of the Caribbean Community' (Needham's Point, Barbados, 1–4 July 2007).

61. CARICOM Conference of Heads of Government, 'Statement by CARICOM Heads of Government on Poverty and Rising Cost of Living in Member States' (paper presented at the Twelfth Special Meeting of the Conference of Heads of Government of the Caribbean Community, Georgetown, Guyana, 7 December 2007).

62. Seaga in John Myers, 'After 35 Years, CARICOM Needs Fresh Thinkers – Seaga – Bats for Regional Cooperation over Integration', The Jamaica Gleaner, Wednesday, 13 February 2008; see also similar discussion in Edward Seaga, 'Integration vs. Cooperation: Rethinking CARICOM,' in *Production Integration in CARICOM: From Theory to Action*, ed. Denis Benn and Kenneth Hall (Kingston: Ian Randle Publishers, 2006).

63. See CARICOM Conference of Heads of Government, 'Communiqué Issued at the Conclusion of the Twentieth Inter-Sessional Meeting of the Conference of Heads of Government of the Caribbean Community' (Belize City, Belize, 12–13 March 2009).

64. See David Jessop, 'The View from Europe – the World Will Be a Different Place', *Sunday Gleaner*, 23 October 2009; Norman Girvan, 'Is CARICOM at Risk?,' www.normangirvan.info.

65. See Vaughan Lewis, 'Concept Paper: Parameters of Changing European Union-Caribbean Relations' (paper presented at the Seminar on "The Future of Caribbean-European Union Relations: Defining a Research Agenda", Maastricht, Holland, 8–9 October 2009), 14.

66. Ralph Gonsalves, 'Remarks on the CARICOM Single Market and Economy Delivered During Oecs Consultation on Economic Union on June 18 [Audio Recording],' BBC, http://www.bbc.co.uk/caribbean/news/story/2008/06/printable/080627_havesaycaricom.shtml, http://www.bbc.co.uk/mediaselector/check/caribbean/meta/dps/2008/07/080702_gonsalves_caricom?size=au&bgc=003399&lang=en-cb&nbram=1&nbwm=1.

67. Ibid.

68. See Denis Benn, 'The Caribbean Community: Reflections on a Variable Geometry of Integration', (Kingston: Office of the Michael Manley Professor of Public Affairs/Public Policy, University of the West Indies Mona, 2007).

69. Denis Benn, 'Tip-Toeing through the Raindrops: The Exercise of Sovereignty in the Caribbean Community', (Kingston: Office of the Michael Manley Professor of Public Affairs/Public Policy, University of the West Indies, 2008), 3–4.

70. Vaughan Lewis, 'Governing Our Caribbean Region: To What End and in What Ways?', (St Augustine, Trinidad and Tobago: Institute of International Relations, 2008).

71. Benn, 'Tip-Toeing through the Raindrops', 6–7.

72. In Rickey Singh, 'New Ideas to Push Region Forward', *Observer*, Saturday, 4 July 2009.

73. See Tracy Moore, '"Not All the Facts"', *Nation News*, 3 July 2009; Iana Seales, 'Immigration Row Heats up at Summit Launch', *Stabroek News*, 3 July 2009.

74. Editor, 'One Caribbean People?', *Barbados Advocate*, 23 January 2009.

75. In David Jessop, 'The View from Europe – Caribbean Regionalism', (London: Caribbean Council, 2009).

76. CARICOM Conference of Heads of Government, 'Communiqué Issued at the

Conclusion of the Thirtieth Regular Meeting of the Conference of Heads of Government of the Caribbean Community' (Georgetown, Guyana, 2–5 July 2009).

77. David Austin, 'Development, Change and Society: An Interview with Kari Levitt', *Race & Class* 49, no. 2 (2007); Anthony Payne and Paul Sutton, 'Repositioning the Caribbean within Globalisation', in *The Caribbean Paper*, No. 1 (Waterloo: The Centre for International Governance Innovation (CIGI), 2007); Kari Levitt, *Reclaiming Development: Independent Thought and Caribbean Community* (Kingston: Ian Randle Publishers, 2005).

## CHAPTER EIGHT

1. See Duke E. Pollard, 'The CSME, CCJ and Private Sector,' in *The CARICOM Single Market and Economy: Genesis and Prognosis*, ed. Kenneth Hall and Myrtle Chuck-A-Sang (Kingston: Ian Randle Publishers, 2007); Cuthbert Joseph, 'The Caribbean Court of Justice: Some Aspects of Its Original Jurisdiction', in *SALISES Fifth Annual Conference on the CARICOM Single Market Economy* (St Augustine, Trinidad and Tobago, 2004).
2. *Pratt and Morgan v. The Attorney-General of Jamaica* (1993) 30 JLR 473.
3. P.J. Patterson, 'Seize the Moment. Address by the Prime Minister of Jamaica' (paper presented at the Opening Session of the Fourteenth Inter-Sessional Meeting of CARICOM Heads of Government, Port of Spain, Trinidad and Tobago, 14 February 2003), 12.
4. See for example Rose Blenman, 'Caribbean Court of Justice – Bringing People on Board', Caribbean Court of Justice – Issues and Perspectives 1(2001); Robert Hart, 'House Passes Bill on CCJ', *Jamaica Gleaner*, Wednesday, 28 July 2004; Robert Buddan, 'A New Debate on Federation: The Hard Facts', *Sunday Gleaner*, Sunday, 6 February 2005.
5. In Hart, 'House Passes Bill on CCJ'.
6. See advice against the approach in Victor Jordan, 'The Caribbean Court of Justice as a Part of a Wider Integration Movement' (paper presented at the Fourth Annual SALISES Conference on Development Strategy and Policy for Small States in the Context of Global Change, Cave Hill, Barbados, 15–17 January 2003 2003); Victor Jordan, 'A Critique of the Caribbean Court of Justice. With Special Reference to the European Court of Justice', in Fifth Annual SALISES Conference on the CARICOM Single Market and Economy (St Augustine, Trinidad and Tobago, 2004).
7. T. Robinson, 'A Caribbean Common Law', *Race & Class* 49, no. 2 (2007): 122.
8. Patsy Lewis, 'The Agony of the Fifteen: The Crisis of Implementation', *Social and Economic Studies* 54, no. 3 (2005): 163.
9. CARICOM Committee of Heads of Government and Leaders of Parliamentary Opposition, 'Communiqué Issued at the Conclusion of the First Meeting of the Committee Established by Heads of Government and Leaders of the Parliamentary Opposition of the Caribbean Community' (Kingston, Jamaica, 30 January 2006).
10. CARICOM Secretariat, 'Summary of Recommendations and Conclusions of the 28th Meeting of Heads of Government of CARICOM' (St Michael, Barbados, 1–4 July 2007).

11. CARICOM Conference of Heads of Government, 'Communiqué Issued at the Conclusion of the Twenty-Seventh Meeting of the Conference of Heads of Government of the Caribbean Community' (Bird Rock, St Kitts and Nevis, 6 July 2006).

12. Ralph Gonsalves, 'Address by the Prime Minister of St. Vincent and the Grenadines at the Inauguration of the CARICOM Single Market,' in *CARICOM Single Market and Economy: Genesis and Prognosis*, ed. Kenneth Hall and Myrtle Chuck-A-Sang (Kingston: Ian Randle Publishers, 2006).

13. See P.J Patterson, 'Statement by Prime Minister of Jamaica on the Occasion of the Formal Launch of the CARICOM Single Market' (Kingston, Jamaica, 30 January 2006).

14. CARICOM Secretariat, 'Report of the Meeting of the Secretary-General of the Caribbean Community and Heads of Regional Institutions, 25–26 October', (Georgetown, Guyana, 2007).

15. A.R. Carnegie, 'Preliminary Report on the Relationship of CARICOM with the Institutions of the Revised Treaty of Chaguaramas', (Georgetown: CARICOM Secretariat, 2006), 10.

16. Ibid., 13.

17. Norman Girvan, 'Towards a Single Development Vision and the Role of the Single Economy', in Report Approved by the Twenty-Eighth Meeting of the Conference of Heads of Government of the Caribbean Community (CARICOM), 1–4 July, 2007, Needham's Point, Barbados (Georgetown: Special Task Force on the Single Economy, CARICOM Secretariat, 2007), 7.

18. CARICOM Secretariat, 'Summary of Recommendations and Conclusions of the 28th Meeting of Heads of Government of CARICOM'; CARICOM Conference of Heads of Government, 'Communiqué Issued at the Conclusion of the Eighteenth Inter-Sessional Meeting of the Conference of Heads of Government of the Caribbean Community' (Kingstown, St Vincent and the Grenadines, 12–14 February 2007).

19. CARICOM Secretariat, 'Report of the Meeting of the Secretary-General of the Caribbean Community and Heads of Regional Institutions, 25–26 October'.

20. Caribbean Regional Negotiating Machinery (CRNM), 'Caribbean Regional Negotiating Machinery: Regularization of Legal Status', in Summary of Terms of Reference for Consultant Legal Status of the Caribbean Regional Negotiating Machinery (CRNM) (Bridgetown: CRNM, 2006), 3.

21. Roderick Rainford, 'Caribbean Regional Negotiating Machinery. Institutional and Human Resources Review', (Georgetown: CARICOM Secretariat, 2007).

22. Ibid., 48.

23. Ibid., 29.

24. Norman Girvan, 'Implications of the EPA: Supranational Cariforum-EC Joint Council Consensus Decisions Supreme', *Jamaica Gleaner*, Friday, 15 February 2008.

25. In Barbados Business Authority, 'Why Change Now?', *Nation Newspaper*, Monday, 27 April 2009.

26. See similar argument in Tony Best, 'If It Aint Broke....', *Nation Newspaper*, Monday, 27 April 2009.

27. CARICOM Conference of Heads of Government, 'Communiqué Issued at the

Conclusion of the Twentieth Inter-Sessional Meeting of the Conference of Heads of Government of the Caribbean Community' (Belize City, Belize, 12–13 March 2009); see also Caribbean Regional Negotiating Machinery (CRNM), 'From CRNM to OTN', in CRNM Press Release No.25/2009 (Bridgetown: CRNM, 2009).

28. In Jewel Brathwaite, 'CARICOM Warned: Be Careful in Dismantling CRNM', *Nation Newspaper*, 27 February 2009.
29. Federico Cuello-Camilo, 'Answers Needed First', *Nation Newspaper*, Monday, 27 April 2009.
30. CARICOM Conference of Heads of Government, 'Communiqué Issued at the Conclusion of the Thirtieth Regular Meeting of the Conference of Heads of Government of the Caribbean Community' (Georgetown, Guyana, 2–5 July 2009), 47.
31. CARICOM Conference of Heads of Government, 'Communiqué Issued at the Conclusion of the Twenty-First Intersessional Meeting of the Conference of Heads of Government of the Caribbean Community' (Roseau, Dominica, 11–12 March 2010).

## CHAPTER NINE

1. See again *William G. Demas, The Economics of Development in Small Countries with Special Reference to the Caribbean* (Montreal: McGill University Press, 1965).
2. The Windward Islands are located in the south-east of the region and include Grenada, St Lucia and St Vincent and the Grenadines. The Leeward Islands are located in the north-east of the region and include Antigua and Barbuda, Dominica, St Kitts and Nevis and Montserrat.
3. Arthur W. Lewis, *The Agony of the Eight* (Bridgetown: Advocate Commercial Printery, 1965).
4. Ibid., 16.
5. The Trinidad-Tobago-Grenada unitary statehood initiative dissipated by 1965.
6. Lewis, *The Agony of the Eight*, 38–39.
7. Heads of Government of the Commonwealth Caribbean Countries, 'The Grenada Declaration' (paper presented at the Meeting of Signatory Heads of Government, Georgetown, Guyana, 8 November 1971).
8. Governments of the Signatory States, 'Agreement Establishing the East Caribbean Common Market (ECCM)', (Castries: WISA Secretariat, 1968).
9. See cases cited in Patsy Lewis, *Surviving Small Size. Regional Integration in Caribbean Ministates* (Kingston: University of the West Indies Press, 2002), 32.
10. Ibid., 53.
11. Swinburne Lestrade and Ralph Gonsalves, 'Political Aspects of Integration of the Windward and Leeward Islands', *Caribbean Quarterly* 18, no. 2 (1972): 33.
12. Editor, 'Bird Calls for More Unity after Independence', *Virgin Islands Daily News*, 31 October 1978.
13. See Earl Huntley, 'The LDCs and CARICOM', in *The Caribbean Community. Beyond Survival*, ed. Kenneth O. Hall (Kingston: Ian Randle Publishers, 2001).
14. Editor, 'Bird Calls for More Unity after Independence'.

15. Heads of Government of Antigua and Barbuda; Dominica; Grenada; Montserrat; St Kitts/Nevis; St Lucia and St Vincent and the Grenadines, 'Treaty Establishing the Organisation of Eastern Caribbean States', (Basseterre: OECS Secretariat, 1981).
16. Lewis, Surviving Small Size. Regional Integration in Caribbean Ministates.
17. See Vaughan Lewis, 'The OECS and Closer Political Union', in *The Caribbean Community. Beyond Survival*, ed. Kenneth O. Hall (Kingston: Ian Randle Publishers, 2001), 309; Vaughan Lewis, 'Political Integration Revived,' *CARICOM Perspective* 1989.
18. The name was later changed to the Standing Conference of Popular Democratic Parties of the Eastern Caribbean (SCOPE) in March 1988.
19. Anti-Imperialist Organisations of the Caribbean and Central America, 'A People's Agenda for Caribbean Unity' (paper presented at the Conference on Caribbean Unity, Kingstown, St Vincent and the Grenadines, 22 November 1987), 48–49.
20. William G. Demas, 'Consolidating Our Independence: The Major Challenges for the West Indies' (paper presented at the Distinguished Lecture Series, Institute of International Relations, St Augustine, Trinidad, 1986).
21. CARICOM Conference of Heads of Government, 'Communiqué Issued at the Conclusion of the Eighth Meeting of the Conference of Heads of Government of the Caribbean Community' (Castries, St Lucia, 29 June–3 July 1987).
22. See David S. Berry, 'Nested Communities. The Implications of a Changing CARICOM for St Kitts and Nevis,' in *Beyond Walls: Multidisciplinary Perspectives*, ed. Simone Augier and Olivia Edgecombe-Howell (Basseterre: School of Continuing Studies, University of the West Indies, 2002); Patsy Lewis, 'Is the Goal of Regional Integration Still Relevant among Small States? The Case of the OECS and CARICOM,' in *Living at the Borderlines: Issues in Caribbean Sovereignty and Development*, ed. Cynthia Barrow-Giles and Don Marshall (Kingston: Ian Randle Publishers, 2003); Lewis, *Surviving Small Size. Regional Integration in Caribbean Ministates.*
23. Vaughan Lewis, 'The Eastern Caribbean States: Fledgling Sovereignties in the Global Environment,' in *Democracy in the Caribbean*, ed. Jorge I. Dominguez, Robert A. Pastor, and R. Delisle Worrell (Baltimore: Johns Hopkins University Press, 1993), 118.
24. In Kenneth O. Hall, ed. *Integrate or Perish: Perspectives of the Heads of Government of the Caribbean Community and the Commonwealth Caribbean Countries 1963–2002*, 2nd ed. (Kingston: Ian Randle Publishers, 2003), 433.
25. Owen Arthur, 'Prospects for Caribbean Political Unity', *Journal of Eastern Caribbean Studies* 23 (1998): 27–28; ibid., 27–28.
26. Ibid., 31.
27. See Cynthia Barrow-Giles, 'From National Independence to a Single Caribbean State. Views on the Barbados-OECS Initiative,' in *Living at the Borderlines: Issues in Caribbean Sovereignty and Development*, ed. Cynthia Barrow-Giles and Don Marshall (Kingston: Ian Randle Publishers, 2003), 374.
28. Ralph Gonsalves, 'The OECS in Our Caribbean Civilisation' (paper presented at the Address by Prime Minister of St Vincent and the Grenadines on the

Occasion of the 20th Anniversary of the Organisation of Eastern Caribbean States (OECS), Castries, St Lucia, 18 June 2001).

29. OECS Authority, 'Communiqué – 34th Meeting of the OECS Authority' (Roseau, Dominica, 26 July 2001).

30. OECS Authority, 'Communiqué – Special Meeting of the OECS Authority on the Economy' (Basseterre, St Kitts and Nevis, 10 October 2002).

31. OECS Authority, 'OECS Development Charter' (Castries, 10 October 2002).

32. See OECS Authority, 'Communiqué – 45th Meeting of the OECS Authority' (Grande Anse, Grenada, 23–25 May 2007).

33. OECS Authority, 'OECS Development Charter', 16.

34. OECS Authority, 'Communiqué – Special Meeting of the OECS Authority on the Economy'.

35. OECS Secretariat Economic Union Project Unit, 'Towards Developing a Model of Governance for Economic Union in the OECS: A Case Study of the European Union', in Presented at Thirty Eighth Meeting of the OECS Authority (Castries, St Lucia: OECS Secretariat, 2004).

36. Earl Huntley, 'The Treaty of Basseterre and Economic Union' (paper presented at the Paper Presented at Thirty-Eighth Meeting of the OECS Authority, Castries, St Lucia, January 2004), 4.

37. OECS Authority, 'Communiqué – 40th Meeting of the OECS Authority' (Tortola, British Virgin Islands, 10–12 November 2004).

38. OECS Authority, 'Declaration of Intent by Heads of Government of the Oecs on the Participation of Their Countries in the Oecs Economic Union' (paper presented at the 43rd Meeting of the OECS Authority, Basseterre, St Kitts and Nevis, 21–23 June 2006); OECS Authority, 'Communiqué – 43rd Meeting of the Oecs Authority' (Basseterre, St Kitts and Nevis, 21–23 June 2006).

39. Organisation of Eastern Caribbean States (OECS), 'Draft of the New Treaty', (Castries: OECS Secretariat, 2006).

40. OECS Authority, 'Communiqué – 45th Meeting of the OECS Authority'.

41. OECS Secretariat, 'Communiqué – OECS Economic Union Retreat' (Basseterre, St Kitts, 13 October 2007).

42. OECS Authority, 'Communiqué – 46th Meeting of the OECS Authority' (Roseau, Dominica, 23–25 January 2008).

43. OECS Authority, 'Communiqué – 47th Meeting of the OECS Authority' (Rodney Bay Gros Islet, St Lucia, 23-24 May 2008).

44. OECS Authority, 'Communiqué – 48th Meeting of the OECS Authority' (Little Bay, Montserrat, 19–21 November 2008).

45. For more information on that campaign see Neville Duncan, 'Caribbean Governance: Solving the St Kitts-Nevis Dilemma and the Caribbean-Atlantic Wide Participation Conundrum,' in *Caribbean Imperatives: Regional Governance and Integrated Development*, ed. Kenneth Hall and Denis Benn (Kingston: Ian Randle Publishers, 2005); Berry, 'Nested Communities. The Implications of a Changing CARICOM for St Kitts and Nevis'; Ralph Premdas, 'Secession in Nevis: Symbolic and Instrumental Explanations,' in *Beyond Walls: Multidisciplinary Perspectives*, ed. Simone Augier and Olivia Edgecombe-Howell, St Kitts and Nevis (Basseterre: School of Continuing Studies, University of the West Indies, 2002).

46. OECS Authority, 'Communiqué – 38th Meeting of the OECS Authority' (Castries, St Lucia, 22–23 January 2004).

47. OECS Authority, 'Communiqué – 40th Meeting of the OECS Authority'.

48. OECS Authority, 'Communiqué – 49th Meeting of the OECS Authority' (Tortola, British Virgin Islands, 20–22 May 2009).

49. Editor, 'OECS in Economic Union', *Stabroek News*, 30 December 2009.

50. In Peter Ischyrion, 'Caribbean Political Union Endorsed', *Terra Viva: South-South Executive Brief* 1 (8), no. 4 (2008).

51. See Ralph Gonsalves, 'Prospects for Economic Union in the Caribbean' (paper presented at the Department of Economics Distinguished Lecture Series, University of the West Indies, Mona, 3 November 2008).

52. Rosina Wiltshire-Brodber, 'The Caribbean Integration Movement: An Alternative Prospective,' *CARICOM Perspective* 1983.

53. See Robert Buddan, 'A New Debate on Federation: The Hard Facts', The Sunday Gleaner, Sunday, 6 February 2005.

54. Governments of Grenada et al., 'Joint Declaration on Collaboration Towards the Achievement of the Single Economy and Political Integration among Grenada, St Lucia, St Vincent and the Grenadines and the Republic of Trinidad and Tobago' (Port of Spain, Trinidad and Tobago, 14 August 2008).

55. See Sanders in Ischyrion, 'Caribbean Political Union Endorsed'.

56. See Editor, 'The Unravelling of Logic', *Jamaica Gleaner*, 23 June 2009; Editor, 'Manning Reiterates Support for Political Union with OECS', *Jamaica Gleaner*, 23 June 2009.

57. Governments of Grenada et al., 'Joint Declaration on Collaboration Towards the Achievement of the Single Economy and Political Integration among Grenada, St Lucia, St Vincent and the Grenadines and the Republic of Trinidad and Tobago'.

58. The Task Force also comprised other eminent Eastern Caribbean nationals including Velma Newton, an independent senator of Barbados; Wayne Sandiford, a Professor of Economics at St George's University Grenada; Ambassador Earl Huntley, CARICOM Representative to Haiti and formerly Ambassador of St Lucia to the United Nations; and Dr Carlyle Mitchell, a Grenadian economist and former Director of Economic Affairs in the OECS Secretariat.

59. Vaughan Lewis, 'Presentation to the CARICOM Heads of State and Government on the Report of the Task Force on the Trinidad and Tobago-Eastern Caribbean States Integration Initiative' (Port of Spain, Trinidad, 24 May 2009).

60. Office of the Prime Minister Trinidad and Tobago, 'Trinidad and Tobago – Eastern Caribbean States Integration Initiative', in *Task Force Report* ed. Vaughan Lewis (Port of Spain: Office of the Prime Minister, 2009); Office of the Prime Minister Trinidad and Tobago, 'Trinidad and Tobago – Eastern Caribbean States Integration Initiative', in *Task Force Report* Volume 2, ed. Vaughn Lewis (Port of Spain: Office of the Prime Minister, 2009).

61. The detailed studies in Volume 2 suggested that Barbados would participate in some of these spaces.

62. Trinidad and Tobago, 'Trinidad and Tobago – Eastern Caribbean States Integration Initiative', 29–31.

CHAPTER TEN

1. CARICOM Conference of Heads of Government, 'Communiqué Issued at the Conclusion of the Thirty-First Regular Meeting of the Conference of Heads of Government of the Caribbean Community, 4–7 July' (Montego Bay, Jamaica, 7 July 2010); CARICOM Secretariat, 'Jamaica's Contribution to Integration has always Been Pivotal – CARICOM Secretary General', in CARICOM Press Release No. 272/2010 (Georgetown: CARICOM Secretariat, Public Information Unit, 2010); Bruce Golding, 'Address by Jamaica's Prime Minister' (paper presented at the Opening Ceremony of the 31st Meeting of Heads of Government of CARICOM, Montego Bay, Jamaica, 3 July 2010); Jamaica Office of the Prime Minister, 'Changes Coming for CARICOM Administration – PM Golding', in News Release (2010); Rickey Singh, 'CARICOM – Decisions Minus Theatrics', *Jamaica Observer*, 7 July 2010.
2. Richard Stoneman, Justice Duke Pollard, and Hugo Inniss. 'Turning around CARICOM: Proposals to Restructure the Secretariat,' (Guyana: CARICOM Secretariat, 2012).
3. David Jessop, 'Caribbean Integration Losing Appeal', *Sunday Gleaner*, Sunday, 27 June 2010. See also Shridath Ramphal, 'Careless with CARICOM – Part 1', *Guyana Chronicle*, Wednesday, 5 May 2010.
4. CARICOM Secretariat, 'Jamaica's Contribution to Integration Has Always Been Pivotal – CARICOM Secretary General'.
5. Caribbean Media Corporation, 'Lack of Leadership Stifling Caribbean Integration - Gonsalves', *Jamaica Gleaner*, 2 July 2010; Caribbean Media Corporation, 'Lack of Leadership Stifling CARICOM Integration, Says Gonslaves', *Jamaica Observer*, 30 June 2010.
6. Havelock Brewster, 'CARICOM: From Community to Single Market and Economy,' in *Governance in the Age of Globalisation: Caribbean Perspectives*, ed. Kenneth O. Hall and Denis Benn (Kingston: Ian Randle Publishers, 2003).
7. See Kirk Meighoo, 'Organic Theorising in Inorganic Societies, or the Need for Epistemic Sovereignty,' in *The Caribbean Integration Process: A People Centred Approach*, ed. Kenneth Hall and Myrtle Chuck-A-Sang (Kingston: Ian Randle Publishers, 2005).
8. See Denis Benn, 'The Caribbean Community: Reflections on a Variable Geometry of Integration', (Kingston: Office of the Michael Manley Professor of Public Affairs/Public Policy, University of the West Indies Mona, 2007); Denis Benn, 'Tip-Toeing through the Raindrops: The Exercise of Sovereignty in the Caribbean Community', (Kingston: Office of the Michael Manley Professor of Public Affairs/Public Policy, University of the West Indies, 2008).
9. Rickey Singh, 'CARICOM Needs the 'Obama Spirit' – Action , Not Ole' Talk', *Sunday Chronicle*, 13 September 2009; Rickey Singh, 'New Ideas to Push Region Forward', *Observer*, Saturday, 4 July 2009; Ian Boxill, *Ideology and Caribbean Integration* (Kingston: Consortium Graduate School of the Social Sciences, University of the West Indies, Mona, 1996); David Jessop, 'The View from Europe – Caribbean "New Thinking"', *Sunday Gleaner*, 7 March 2008.
10. Leonard Archer et al., 'A Review of the Structure of the Functioning of the

Caribbean Community Secretariat. Final Report', (Georgetown: CARICOM Secretariat, 2002).

11. CARICOM Conference of Heads of Government, 'Communiqué Issued at the Conclusion of the Thirty-First Regular Meeting of the Conference of Heads of Government of the Caribbean Community, 4-7 July'.

12. Mark Beeson, 'Sovereignty under Siege: Globalisation and the State in Southeast Asia', *Third World Quarterly* 24, no. 2 (2003).

13. Golding, 'Address by Jamaica's Prime Minister'.

14. CARICOM Conference of Heads of Government, 'Communiqué Issued at the Conclusion of the Thirty-First Regular Meeting of the Conference of Heads of Government of the Caribbean Community, 4–7 July'.

15. CARICOM Secretariat, 'Government of Trinidad and Tobago Commits to Engaging Civil Society', in CARICOM Press Release No. PR 327/2010 (Georgetown: CARICOM Secretariat, Public Information Unit, 2010).

16. Jessop, 'Caribbean Integration Losing Appeal'.

# SELECT BIBLIOGRAPHY

Acharya, Amitav. 'Democratization and the Prospects for Participatory Regionalism in Southeast Asia.' In *Asian Regional Governance: Crisis and Change*, edited by Kanishka Jayasuriya, 127–44. London: Routledge, 2004.

Albert, Mattias, and Tanja Kopp-Malek. 'The Pragmatism of Global and European Governance: Emerging Forms of the Political "Beyond Westphalia"'. *Millennium: Journal of International Studies* 31, no. 3 (2002): 453–71.

Anckar, Dag. 'Islandness or Smallness? A Comparative Look at Political Institutions in Small Island States.' *Island Studies Journal* 1, no. 1 (2006): 43–54.

Anthony, Kenny. 'Transcending Critical Constraints.' Paper presented at the Address by Prime Minister of St Lucia to the Thirty Eighth Conference of the OECS Authority, Castries, St Lucia, 22 January 2004.

Anti-Imperialist Organisations of the Caribbean and Central America. 'A People's Agenda for Caribbean Unity.' Paper presented at the Conference on Caribbean Unity, Kingstown, St Vincent and the Grenadines, 22 November 1987.

Archer, Leonard, Patrick I. Gomes, Didacus Jules, Henley Morgan, and Maria Smart. 'A Review of the Structure of the Functioning of the Caribbean Community Secretariat. Final Report.' Georgetown: CARICOM Secretariat, 2002.

Arthur, Owen. 'The Caribbean Single Market and Economy: The Way Forward.' In *Integration: CARICOM's Key to Prosperity*, edited by Kenneth Hall and Myrtle Chuck-A-Sang, 130–49. Kingston: Ian Randle Publishers, 2004.

———. 'Prospects for Caribbean Political Unity.' *Journal of Eastern Caribbean Studies* 23 (1998): 27–34.

———. 'Towards a New Governance.' In *Governance in the Caribbean*, edited by Selwyn Ryan and Ann Marie Bissessar, 32–36. St Augustine: Sir Arthur Lewis Institute of Social and Economic Studies (SALISES), 1999.

Assembly of Caribbean Community Parliamentarians. 'Resolution on the Caribbean Court of Justice.' Paper presented at the Second Sitting of the Assembly of Caribbean Community Parliamentarians, St Georges, Grenada, 15 October 1999.

———. 'Motion to Consider Proposal for the Caribbean Non-Governmental Organisations (Ngos) to Be Granted Observer Status in the Assembly of Caribbean Community Parliamentarians.' Paper presented at the Inaugural Meeting of the Assembly of Caribbean Community Parliamentarians, St Michael, Barbados, 27–29 May 1996.

Austin, David. 'Development, Change and Society: An Interview with Kari Levitt.' *Race & Class* 49, no. 2 (2007): 1–19.

Axline, Andrew W. 'Integration and Development in the Commonwealth Caribbean: The Politics of Regional Negotiations.' *International Organisation* 32, no. 4 (1978): 953–73.

Baldacchino, Godfrey. 'The Coming of Age of Island Studies.' *Tijdschrift voor Economische en Sociale Geografie* 95, no. 3 (2004): 272–83.

Barbados Business Authority. 'Why Change Now?' *The Nation Newspaper*, Monday, 27 April 2009.

Barrow-Giles, Cynthia. 'Dangerous Waters: Sovereignty, Self-Determinism and Resistance.' In *Living at the Borderlines: Issues in Caribbean Sovereignty and Development*, edited by Cynthia Barrow-Giles and Don Marshall, 51–62. Kingston: Ian Randle Publishers, 2003.

———. 'From National Independence to a Single Caribbean State. Views on the Barbados-OECS Initiative.' In *Living at the Borderlines: Issues in Caribbean Sovereignty and Development*, edited by Cynthia Barrow-Giles and Don Marshall, 353–75. Kingston: Ian Randle Publishers, 2003.

Barrow-Giles, Cynthia, and Don Marshall, eds. *Living at the Borderlines: Issues in Caribbean Sovereignty and Development*. Kingston: Ian Randle Publishers, 2003.

Beeson, Mark. 'Geopolitics and the Making of Regions: The Fall and Rise of East Asia.' *Political Studies* 57 (2009): 498–516.

———. 'Sovereignty under Siege: Globalisation and the State in Southeast Asia.' *Third World Quarterly* 24, no. 2 (2003): 357–74.

Benn, Denis. 'The Caribbean Community: Reflections on a Variable Geometry of Integration.' Kingston: Office of the Michael Manley Professor of Public Affairs/ Public Policy, University of the West Indies Mona, 2007.

———. 'Tip-Toeing through the Raindrops: The Exercise of Sovereignty in the Caribbean Community.' Kingston: Office of the Michael Manley Professor of Public Affairs/Public Policy, University of the West Indies, 2008.

———. 'West Indian Nationalism: The Intellectual Dimensions.' In *The Caribbean: An Intellectual History 1774–2003*, edited by Denis Benn, 65–102. Kingston: Ian Randle Publishers, 2004.

Berry, David S. 'Nested Communities. The Implications of a Changing CARICOM for St Kitts and Nevis.' In *Beyond Walls: Multidisciplinary Perspectives*, edited by Simone Augier and Olivia Edgecombe-Howell, 107–38. Basseterre: School of Continuing Studies, University of the West Indies, 2002.

Best, Lloyd. 'Independence and Responsibility: Self-Knowledge as an Imperative.' In *The Critical Tradition of Caribbean Political Economy. The Legacy of George Beckford.*, edited by Kari Levitt and Michael Witter, 3–18. Kingston: Ian Randle Publishers, 1996.

Best, Tony. '"If It Aint Broke...."' *Nation Newspaper*, Monday, 27 April 2009.

Blake, Byron. 'The Caribbean – Geography, Culture, History and Identity: Assets for Economic Integration and Development.' In *Contending with Destiny: The Caribbean in the 21st Century*, edited by Kenneth Hall and Denis Benn, 45–32. Kingston: Ian Randle Publishers, 2000.

Blenman, Rose. 'Caribbean Court of Justice – Bringing People on Board.' *Caribbean Court of Justice – Issues and Perspectives* 1 (2001): 74–78.

Boli, John. 'Sovereignty from a World Polity Perspective.' In *Problematic Sovereignty: Contested Rules and Political Possibilities*, edited by Stephen D. Krasner, 53–82. New York: Columbia University Press, 2001.

Bourne, Compton. 'A Caribbean Community for All.' Paper presented at the

Fifth Lecture in the Distinguished Lecture Series Celebrating the Thirtieth Anniversary of the Caribbean Community, Grenada, 25 June 2003.

———. 'Caribbean Development to the Year 2000. Challenges, Prospects and Policies.' Georgetown: CARICOM Secretariat, 1988.

———. 'Small States in the Context of Global Change.' In *Fourth Annual SALISES Conference – Development Strategy and Policy for Small States in the Context of Global Change*. Cave Hill, Barbados, 2003.

Boxill, Ian. *Ideology and Caribbean Integration*. Kingston: Consortium Graduate School of the Social Sciences, University of the West Indies, Mona., 1996.

———. 'Sovereignty and the Search for Recognition.' In *Caribbean Imperatives: Regional Governance and Integrated Development*, edited by Kenneth Hall and Denis Benn, 22–30. Kingston: Ian Randle Publishers, 2005.

Brathwaite, Jewel. 'CARICOM Warned: Be Careful in Dismantling Crnm.' *Nation Newspaper*, 27 February 2009.

Breslin, Shaun, and Richard Higgott. 'Studying Regions: Learning from the Old, Constructing the New.' *New Political Economy* 5, no. 3 (2000): 333–52.

Brewster, Havelock. 'The CARICOM Single Market and Economy: Is It Realistic without Commitment to Political Unity?' *Journal of Eastern Caribbean Studies* 28, no. 3 (2003): 1–11.

———. 'CARICOM: From Community to Single Market and Economy.' In *Governance in the Age of Globalisation: Caribbean Perspectives*, edited by Kenneth O. Hall and Denis Benn, 499–508. Kingston: Ian Randle Publishers, 2003.

———. 'Mature Regionalism and the Rose Hall Declaration on Regional Governance.' In *Caribbean Imperatives: Regional Governance and Integrated Development*, edited by Kenneth Hall and Denis Benn, 88–93. Kingston: Ian Randle Publishers, 2005.

———. 'The Report of the West Indian Commission, Time for Action – a Critical Appreciation.' *Caribbean Quarterly* 39, no. 1 (1993): 29–42.

———. 'Review of the Rose Hall Declaration: Provisions on Regional Governance.' In *CARICOM Single Market and Economy: Genesis and Prognosis*, edited by Kenneth Hall and Myrtle Chuck-A-Sang, 46–59. Kingston: Ian Randle Publishers, 2003.

Brewster, Havelock, and Clive Y. Thomas. *The Dynamics of West Indian Integration*. Vol. 1, Studies in Regional Economic Integration. Kingston: Institute for Social and Economic Research, University of the West Indies, 1967.

Buddan, Robert. 'My Generation Comes to Power: A Time for Caribbean Leadership and Political Transformation.' In *Caribbean Imperatives: Regional Governance and Integrated Development*, edited by Kenneth Hall and Denis Benn, 55–65. Kingston: Ian Randle Publishers, 2005.

———. 'A New Debate on Federation: The Hard Facts.' *Sunday Gleaner*, Sunday, 6 February 2005.

Bulmer, Simon J. 'New Institutionalism and the Governance of the Single European Market.' *Journal of European Public Policy* 5, no. 3 (1998): 365–86.

Byers, Bruce. 'Ecoregions, State Sovereignty and Conflict.' *Bulletin of Peace Proposals* 22, no. 1 (1991): 65–76.

Byron, Jessica. 'CARICOM at Thirty: New and Old Foreign Policy Challenges.' *Social and Economic Studies* 53, no. 4 (2004): 1–36.

Camilleri, James A. 'Rethinking Sovereignty in a Shrinking, Fragmented World.' In *Contending Sovereignties: Redefining Political Community*, edited by R.B.J. Walker and Saul H. Mendlovitz, 13–44. Boulder: Lynne Rienner Publishers, 1990.

Camilleri, James A., and Jim Falk. *The End of Sovereignty? The Politics of a Shrinking and Fragmenting World*. Hants: Edward Elgar, 1992.

Caporaso, James A. 'Changes in the Westphalian Order: Territory, Public Authority, and Sovereignty.' *International Studies Review* 2, no. 2 (2000): 1–28.

Caribbean Development Bank (CDB). 'Agreement Establishing the Caribbean Development Bank.' 1969.

Caribbean Engineering and Management Consultants Limited (CEMCO). 'Study to Determine Technical Assistance Needs for Implementation of Caribbean Community Decisions in Member States. Final Report.' Georgetown: CEMCO, 1994.

Caribbean Media Corporation. 'Lack of Leadershiip Stifling Caribbean Integration – Gonsalves.' *Jamaica Gleaner*, 2 July 2010.

———. 'Lack of Leadership Stifling CARICOM Integration, Says Gonslaves.' *Jamaica Observer*, 30 June 2010.

Caribbean Regional Negotiating Machinery (CRNM). 'Caribbean Regional Negotiating Machinery: Regularization of Legal Status ' In *Summary of Terms of Reference for Consultant Legal Status of the Caribbean Regional Negotiating Machinery (CRNM)*. Bridgetown: CRNM, 2006.

———. 'From Crnm to Otn.' In *CRNM Press Release No.25/2009*. Bridgetown: CRNM, 2009.

CARICOM. 'Agreement between the Caribbean Community and the Government of the Bahamas Including Declaration of the Commonwealth of the Bahamas on Signing the Agreement between the Caribbean Community and the Government of the Bahamas.' Port of Spain, Trinidad and Tobago, 2006.

CARICOM Committee of Heads of Government and Leaders of Parliamentary Opposition. 'Communiqué Issued at the Conclusion of the First Meeting of the Committee Established by Heads of Government and Leaders of the Parliamentary Opposition of the Caribbean Community.' Kingston, Jamaica, 30 January 2006.

CARICOM Conference of Heads of Government. 'Agreement Establishing the Caribbean Court of Justice.' Georgetown: CARICOM Secretariat, 2001.

———. 'Agreement for the Establishment of an Assembly of Caribbean Community Parliamentarians.' Kingston, Jamaica: CARICOM Secretariat, 1992.

———. 'Annex Ii – Grande Anse Resolution on Preparing the Peoples of the West Indies for the 21st Century.' Paper presented at the Tenth Meeting of the Conference of Heads of Government of the Caribbean Community, Grande Anse, Grenada, 1989.

———. 'Charter of Civil Society for the Caribbean Community.' Georgetown: CARICOM Secretariat, 1997.

———. 'Communiqué Issued at the Conclusion of the Eighteenth Inter-Sessional Meeting of the Conference of Heads of Government of the Caribbean Community.' Kingstown, St Vincent and the Grenadines, 12–14 February 2007.

———. 'Communiqué Issued at the Conclusion of the Eighth Inter-Sessional Meeting of the Conference of Heads of Government of the Caribbean Community.' St John's, Antigua and Barbuda, 20–21 February 1997.

———. 'Communiqué Issued at the Conclusion of the Eighth Meeting of the Conference of Heads of Government of the Caribbean Community.' Castries, St Lucia, 29 June–3 July 1987.

———. 'Communiqué Issued at the Conclusion of the Eigteenth Meeting of the Conference of Heads of Government of the Caribbean Community.' Montego Bay, Jamaica, 30 June–4 July 1997.

———. 'Communiqué Issued at the Conclusion of the Eleventh Inter-Sessional Meeting of the Conference of Heads of Government of the Caribbean Community.' Basseterre, St Kitts and Nevis, 13–14 March 2000.

———. 'Communiqué Issued at the Conclusion of the Eleventh Meeting of the Conference of Heads of Government of the Caribbean Community.' Kingston, Jamaica, 31 July–2 August 1990.

———. 'Communiqué Issued at the Conclusion of the Fifteenth Inter-Sessional Meeting of the Conference of Heads of Government of the Caribbean Community.' Basseterre, St Kitts and Nevis, 25–26 March 2004.

———. 'Communiqué Issued at the Conclusion of the Fifteenth Meeting of the Conference of Heads of Government of the Caribbean Community.' Bridgetown, Barbados, 4–7 July 1994.

———. 'Communiqué Issued at the Conclusion of the Fifth Meeting of the Conference of Heads of Government of the Caribbean Community.' Nassau, Bahamas, 4–7 July 1984.

———. 'Communiqué Issued at the Conclusion of the Fourteenth Inter-Sessional Meeting of the Conference of Heads of Government of the Caribbean Community.' Port of Spain, Trinidad and Tobago, 14–15 February 2003.

———. 'Communiqué Issued at the Conclusion of the Fourteenth Meeting of the Conference of Heads of Government of the Caribbean Community.' Nassau, Bahamas, 5–8 July 1993.

———. 'Communiqué Issued at the Conclusion of the Fourth Intersessional Meeting of the Conference of Heads of Government of the Caribbean Community ', Roseau, Dominica, 22–23 March 1993.

———. 'Communiqué Issued at the Conclusion of the Nineteenth Meeting of the Conference of Heads of Government of the Caribbean Community.' Castries, St Lucia, 30 June–4 July 1998.

———. 'Communiqué Issued at the Conclusion of the Ninth Meeting of the Conference of Heads of Government of the Caribbean Community.' Deep Bay, Antigua, 4–8 July 1988.

———. 'Communiqué Issued at the Conclusion of the Seventeenth Inter-Sessional Meeting of the Conference of Heads of Government of the Caribbean Community.' Port of Spain, Trinidad and Tobago, 10 February 2006.

———. 'Communiqué Issued at the Conclusion of the Seventeenth Meeting of the Conference of Heads of Government of the Caribbean Community.' Bridgetown, Barbados, 3–6 July 1996.

———. 'Communiqué Issued at the Conclusion of the Sixteenth Meeting of the Conference of Heads of Government of the Caribbean Community.' Georgetown, Guyana, 4–7 July 1995.

———. 'Communiqué Issued at the Conclusion of the Tenth Inter-Sessional Meeting of the Conference of Heads of Government of the Caribbean Community.' Paramaribo, Suriname, 4–5 March 1999.

———. 'Communiqué Issued at the Conclusion of the Tenth Meeting of the Conference of Heads of Government of the Caribbean Community.' Grande Anse, Grenada, 3–7 July 1989.

———. 'Communiqué Issued at the Conclusion of the Tenth Special Meeting of the Conference of Heads of Government of the Caribbean Community.' Port of Spain, Trinidad and Tobago, 10 November 2004.

———. 'Communiqué Issued at the Conclusion of the Third Intersessional Meeting of the Conference of Heads of Government of the Caribbean Community.' Kingston, Jamaica, 19 February 1992.

———. 'Communiqué Issued at the Conclusion of the Thirtieth Regular Meeting of the Conference of Heads of Government of the Caribbean Community.' Georgetown, Guyana, 2–5 July 2009.

———. 'Communiqué Issued at the Conclusion of the Thirty-First Regular Meeting of the Conference of Heads of Government of the Caribbean Community, 4–7 July.' Montego Bay, Jamaica, 7 July 2010.

———. 'Communiqué Issued at the Conclusion of the Twelfth Meeting of the Conference of Heads of Government of the Caribbean Community.' Basseterre, St Kitts and Nevis, 2–4 July 1991.

———. 'Communiqué Issued at the Conclusion of the Twentieth Inter-Sessional Meeting of the Conference of Heads of Government of the Caribbean Community.' Belize City, Belize, 12–13 March 2009.

———. 'Communiqué Issued at the Conclusion of the Twentieth Meeting of the Conference of Heads of Government of the Caribbean Community.' Port-of-Spain, Trinidad and Tobago, 4–7 July 1999.

———. 'Communiqué Issued at the Conclusion of the Twenty-Eighth Meeting of the Conference of Heads of Government of the Caribbean Community.' Needham's Point, Barbados, 1–4 July 2007.

———. 'Communique Issued at the Conclusion of the Twenty-Fifth Meeting of the Conference of Heads of Government of the Caribbean Community.' St George's, Grenada, 8 July 2004.

———. 'Communiqué Issued at the Conclusion of the Twenty-First Intersessional Meeting of the Conference of Heads of Government of the Caribbean Community.' Roseau, Dominica, 11–12 March 2010.

———. 'Communiqué Issued at the Conclusion of the Twenty-Fourth Meeting of the Conference of Heads of Government of the Caribbean Community.' Montego, Bay, Jamaica 2–5 July 2003.

———. 'Communiqué Issued at the Conclusion of the Twenty-Seventh Meeting of the Conference of Heads of Government of the Caribbean Community.' Bird Rock, St Kitts and Nevis, 6 July 2006.

———. 'Communiqué Issued at the Conclusion of the Twenty-Sixth Meeting of the Conference of Heads of Government of the Caribbean Community.' Castries, St Lucia, 6 July 2005.

———. 'Communiqué of the Special Meeting of the Conference of Heads of Government of the Caribbean Community.' Port of Spain, Trinidad, 28–31 October 1992.

——. 'Consensus of Chaguaramas.' Georgetown: CARICOM Secretariat, 1999.

——. 'Delivering the Csme by 2005: The Port of Spain Statement on the CARICOM Single Market and Economy.' Paper presented at the Issued at the Conclusion of the Tenth Special Meeting of the Conference of Heads of Government of the Caribbean Community, Port of Spain, Trinidad and Tobago, 9 November 2004.

——. 'Framework for Stabilising and Transforming Caribbean Economies.' Paper presented at the Special Meeting of Conference of Heads of Government, Castries, St Lucia, 17 August 2002.

——. 'Grande Anse Declaration and Work Programme for the Advancement of the Integration Movement.' Georgetown: CARICOM Secretariat, 1989.

——. 'The Kingston Declaration.' Kingston, Jamaica: CARICOM Secretariat, 1990.

——. 'The Liliendaal Statement of Principles on 'Forward Together'.' Georgetown: CARICOM Secretariat, 2002.

——. 'The Nassau Understanding: Structural Adjustment and Closer Integration for Accelerated Development in the Caribbean Community.' Nassau, Bahamas: CARICOM Secretariat, 1984.

——. 'The Ocho Rios Declaration.' Ocho Rios, Jamaica, 1982.

——. 'Press Statement Issued at the Conclusion of the Ninth Special Meeting of the Conference of Heads of Government of the Caribbean Community.' Castries, St Lucia, 13–14 November 2003.

——. 'Protocol Amending the Treaty Establishing the Caribbean Community Signed at Chaguaramas on 4 July 1973.' Georgetown: CARICOM Secretariat, 1997.

——. 'Protocol of Port of Spain.' Georgetown: CARICOM Secretariat, 1992.

——. 'Revised Treaty of Chaguaramas Establishing the Caribbean Community and the CARICOM Single Market and Economy.' Georgetown: CARICOM Secretariat, 2001.

——. 'The Rose Hall Declaration on 'Regional Governance and Integrated Development' Adopted on the Occasion of the Thirtieth Anniversary of the Caribbean Community (CARICOM).' In *Twenty-Fourth Meeting of the Conference of Heads of Government of CARICOM*. Montego Bay: CARICOM Secretariat, 2003.

——. 'Statement by CARICOM Heads of Government on Poverty and Rising Cost of Living in Member States.' Paper presented at the Twelfth Special Meeting of the Conference of Heads of Government of the Caribbean Community, Georgetown, Guyana, 7 December 2007.

——. 'Treaty of Chaguaramas Establishing the Caribbean Community.' Georgetown: CARICOM Secretariat, 1973.

CARICOM Prime Ministerial Expert Group on Governance. 'Regional Integration: Carrying the Process Forward. Report on the Establishment of a CARICOM Commission or Other Executive Mechanism.' Georgetown: CARICOM Secretariat, 2003.

CARICOM Secretariat. 'CARICOM Analysis: The Unanimity Rule: Constraint or Blessing.' *CARICOM Perspective*, 1983, 1–5.

——. *CARICOM: Our Caribbean Community. An Introduction.* Kingston: Ian Randle Publishers, 2005.

————. 'Government of Trinidad and Tobago Commits to Engaging Civil Society.' In *CARICOM Press Release No. PR 327/2010*. Georgetown: CARICOM Secretariat, Public Information Unit, 2010.

————. 'Implementation of Caribbean Community Foreign Policy Strategy.' In *Part I – Revised Strategy for the Coordination of the Foreign Policies of CARICOM States*. Baracara Island, Guyana, 2002.

————. 'Jamaica's Contribution to Integration Has Always Been Pivotal – CARICOM Secretary General.' In *CARICOM Press Release No. 272/2010*. Georgetown: CARICOM Secretraiat, Public Information Unit, 2010.

————. 'Report.' Paper presented at the "Think Tank" on Joint Representation, Barbados, 27–28 August 1990.

————. 'Report of the Meeting of the Secretary-General of the Caribbean Community and Heads of Regional Institutions, 25–26 October.' Georgetown, Guyana, 2007.

————. 'Summary of Recommendations and Conclusions of the 28th Meeting of Heads of Government of CARICOM.' St Michael, Barbados, 1–4 July 2007.

CARICOM Standing Committee of Ministers of Foreign Affairs. 'Report of Second Meeting of Standing Committee of Ministers Responsible for Foreign Affairs.' Georgetown: CARICOM Secretariat, 1976.

Carnegie, A.R. 'Preliminary Report on the Relationship of CARICOM with the Institutions of the Revised Treaty of Chaguaramas.' Georgetown: CARICOM Secretariat, 2006.

Checkel, Jeffrey T. 'It's the Process Stupid! Process Tracing in the Study of European and International Politics.' 11–39. Oslo: Centre for European Studies, 2005.

Clapham, Christopher. 'Sovereignty and the Third World State.' In *Sovereignty at the Millennium*, edited by Robert Jackson, 100–15. Oxford: Blackwell Publishers, 1999.

Commission on Global Governance. 'Our Global Neighbourhood. The Report of the Commission on Global Governance.' New York: Oxford University Press, 1995.

Commonwealth Caribbean Regional Secretariat. 'From Carifta to Caribbean Community.' Georgetown: Commonwealth Caribbean Regional Secretariat, 1972.

Crawford, James. *The Creation of States in International Law*. Second ed. Oxford: Clarendon Press, 2006.

Cuello-Camilo, Federico. 'Answers Needed First.' *Nation Newspaper*, Monday, 27 April 2009.

Deere, Carmen Diana, Peggy Antrobus, Lynne Bolles, Edwin Melendez, Peter Phillips, Marcia Rivera, and Helen Safa. *In the Shadows of the Sun: Caribbean Development Alternatives and U.S. Policy*. Boulder: Westview Press, 1990.

Demas, William G. 'Building the New West Indies.' In *Change and Renewal in the Caribbean*, edited by William G. Demas. Bridgetown: CCC Publishing House, 1971.

————. 'Consolidating Our Independence: The Major Challenges for the West Indies.' Paper presented at the Distinguished Lecture Series, Institute of International Relations, St Augustine, Trinidad, 1986.

————. *The Economics of Development in Small Countries with Special Reference to the Caribbean*. Montreal: McGill University Press, 1965.

————. *Essays on Caribbean Integration and Development*. Kingston: Institute of Social and Economic Research (ISER), University of the West Indies, 1976.

————. The New Caribbean Man.' In *Change and Renewal in the Caribbean*, edited by William G Demas, 1–7. Bridgetown: CCC Publishing House, 1970.

————. 'Some Thoughts on the Caribbean Community.' Georgetown: CARICOM Secretariat, 1974.

————. 'The Three Aspects of the Caribbean Community. Keynote Address Delivered by President of the Caribbean Development Bank.' Paper presented at the National Youth Leaders Conference of the Barbados Youth Council, Barbados, 18 February 1979.

————. *West Indian Development and the Deepening and Widening of the Caribbean Community*. Vol. 1, Critical Issues in Caribbean Development. Kingston: Ian Randle Publishers, 1997.

————. *West Indian Nationhood and Caribbean Integration*. Edited by David I. Mitchell, Challenges in the New Caribbean No. 1. Bridgetown: CCC Publishing House, 1974.

Duncan, Neville. 'Caribbean Governance: Solving the St Kitts-Nevis Dilemma and the Caribbean-Atlantic Wide Participation Conundrum.' In *Caribbean Imperatives: Regional Governance and Integrated Development*, edited by Kenneth Hall and Denis Benn, 126–32. Kingston: Ian Randle Publishers, 2005.

Duncan, Neville, Kristin Fox, Aldrie Henry-Lee, Patsy Lewis, and Jimmy Tindigarukayo. 'Jamaican Perspectives of Regional Integration.' In *SALISES Internal Paper*. Mona, Jamaica: University of the West Indies, 2004.

Editor. 'Bird Calls for More Unity after Independence.' *Virgin Islands Daily News*, 31 October 1978, 4.

————. 'Manning Reiterates Support for Political Union with OECS.' *Jamaica Gleaner*, 23 June 2009.

————. 'OECS in Economic Union.' *Stabroek News*, 30 December 2009.

————. 'One Caribbean People?' *Barbados Advocate*, 23 January 2009.

————. 'Third Time around – Perspective Interviews Prime Minister Manley.' *CARICOM Perspective*, January/June 1989, 36–39.

————. 'The Unravelling of Logic.' *Jamaica Gleaner*, 23 June 2009.

European Commission. 'Cotonou Agreement.' European Commission, http://europa.eu.int/comm/development/body/cotonou/agreement/agr06_en.htm.

Farier, Joseph. 'Aligned for Global Change: Restructuring in the Caribbean Community.' In *The Caribbean Community: Beyond Survival*, edited by Kenneth O. Hall, 269–76. Kingston: Ian Randle Publishers, 2001.

Farrell, Trevor. 'Five Major Problems for CARICOM ' In *The Caribbean Community: Beyond Survival*, edited by Kenneth O. Hall, 8–16. Kingston: Ian Randle Publishers, 2001.

Fawcett, Louise. 'Regionalism in World Politics: Past and Present.' In *Elements of Regional Integration: A Multidimensional Approach*, edited by Ariane Kösler and Martin Zimmek, 15–28. Baden-Baden: Nomos, 2008.

Finer, S.E. *The History of Government from the Earliest Times. Volume 3. Empires, Monarchies and the Modern State*. 3 vols. Vol. Volume III. Empires, Monarchies and the Modern State. Oxford: Oxford University Press, 1999.

Frazer, Ian, and Jenny Bryant-Tokalau. 'Introduction: The Uncertain Future of Pacific Regionalism.' In *Redefining the Pacific?*, edited by Jenny Bryant-Tokalau and Ian Frazer, 1–23. Aldershot: Ashgate, 2006.

Gamble, Andrew, and Anthony Payne, eds. *Regionalism and World Order.* London: Macmillan Press, 1996.

Girvan, Norman. 'Creating and Recreating the Caribbean.' In *Contending with Destiny: The Caribbean in the 21st Century*, edited by Kenneth Hall and Denis Benn, 31–36. Kingston: Ian Randle Publishers, 2000.

———. 'Implications of the EPA: Supranational Cariforum-EC Joint Council Consensus Decisions Supreme.' *Jamaica Gleaner*, Friday, 15 February 2008.

———. 'Is CARICOM at Risk?' www.normangirvan.info.

———. 'Labour and Caribbean Integration.' *Caribbean Labour Journal* 1, no. 1 (1991): 4–9.

———. 'Reflections on the CARICOM Single Market and Economy. Keynote Address.' Paper presented at the SALISES Fifth Annual Conference, St Augustine, 31 March 2004.

———. 'Three Areas of Regional Crisis.' In *The Caribbean Community: Beyond Survival*, edited by Kenneth O. Hall, 17–21. Kingston: Ian Randle Publishers, 2001.

———. 'Towards a Single Development Vision and the Role of the Single Economy.' In *Report Approved by the Twenty-Eigth Meeting of the Conference of Heads of Government of the Caribbean Community (CARICOM), 1–4 July, 2007, Needham's Point, Barbados.* Georgetown: Special Task Force on the Single Economy, CARICOM Secretariat, 2007.

Girvan, Norman, and Owen Jefferson, eds. *Readings in the Political Economy of the Caribbean.* Kingston: New World Group Ltd., 1974.

Golding, Bruce. 'Address by Jamaica's Prime Minister.' Paper presented at the Opening Ceremony of the 31st Meeting of Heads of Government of CARICOM, Montego Bay, Jamaica, 3 July 2010.

Gomes, P.I. 'Rationalizing the Functions of the Organs of the Community.' In *Caribbean Imperatives: Regional Governance and Integrated Development*, edited by Kenneth Hall and Denis Benn, 94–103. Kingston: Ian Randle Publishers, 2005.

Gonsalves, Ralph. 'Address by the Prime Minister of St Vincent and the Grenadines at the Inauguration of the CARICOM Single Market.' In *CARICOM Single Market and Economy: Genesis and Prognosis*, edited by Kenneth Hall and Myrtle Chuck-A-Sang, 33–36. Kingston: Ian Randle Publishers, 2006.

———. 'The OECS in Our Caribbean Civilisation.' Paper presented at the Address by Prime Minister of St Vincent and the Grenadines on the Occasion of the 20th Anniversary of the Organisation of Eastern Caribbean States (OECS), Castries, St Lucia, 18 June 2001.

———. 'Our Caribbean Civilisation and Its Political Prospects.' Paper presented at the Inaugural Lecture in the Distinguished Lecture Series Supported by CARICOM to Commemorate the Thirtieth Anniversary, Port of Spain, Trinidad, 12 February 2003.

———. 'Prospects for Economic Union in the Caribbean.' Paper presented at the Department of Economics Distinguished Lecture Series, University of the West Indies, Mona, 3 November 2008.

———. 'Remarks on the CARICOM Single Market and Economy Delivered During OECS Consultation on Economic Union on June 18 [Audio Recording].' BBC, http://www.bbc.co.uk/caribbean/news/story/2008/06/printable/080627_havesaycaricom.shtml, http://www.bbc.co.uk/mediaselector/check/caribbean/meta/dps/2008/07/080702_gonsalves_caricom?size=au&bgc=003399&lang=en-cb&nbram=1&nbwm=1.

Gonzales, Anthony P. 'Recent Trends in International Economic Relations of the CARICOM States.' *Journal of Interamerican Studies and World Affairs* 31, no. 3 (1989): 63–95.

Governments of Antigua, Barbados, and British Guiana. 'The Dickenson Bay Agreement. Agreement Establishing the Caribbean Free Trade Association.' Georgetown: Commonwealth Caribbean Regional Secretariat, 1965.

Governments of Grenada, St Lucia, St Vincent and the Grenadines, and Trinidad and Tobago. 'Joint Declaration on Collaboration Towards the Achievement of the Single Economy and Political Integration among Grenada, St Lucia, St Vincent and the Grenadines and the Republic of Trinidad and Tobago.' Port of Spain, Trinidad and Tobago, 14 August 2008.

Governments of the Signatory States. 'Agreement Establishing the East Caribbean Common Market (ECCM).' Castries: WISA Secretariat, 1968.

Graham, Kennedy, ed. *Models of Regional Governance for the Pacific: Sovereignty and the Future Architecture of Regionalism.* Christchurch: Canterbury University Press, 2008.

Graham, Kennedy, and Graham Hassall. 'Sovereignty and the Future Architecture of Pacific Regionalism.' In *Models of Regional Governance for the Pacific: Sovereignty and the Future Architecture of Regionalism*, edited by Kennedy Graham, 211–16. Christchurch: Canterbury University Press, 2008.

Grant, Cedric. 'Civil Society, Governance and Conflict Resolution in the Caribbean.' In *Governance in the Age of Globalisation: Caribbean Perspectives*, edited by Kenneth O. Hall and Denis Benn, 291–316. Kingston: Ian Randle Publishers, 2003.

———. 'Democracy and Governance in the Caribbean Community.' Paper presented at the Fourth Lecture in the Distinguished Lecture Series Sponsored by CARICOM to Commemorate its Thirtieth Anniversary, Kingstown, St Vincent and the Grenadines, 7 May 2003.

———. 'An Experiment in Supra-National Governance: The Caribbean Regional Negotiating Machinery.' In *Contending with Destiny: The Caribbean in the 21st Century*, edited by Kenneth Hall and Denis Benn, 447–99. Kingston: Ian Randle Publishers, 2000.

Greene, Edward. 'Striving toward a Reconfiguration of a Rational Community through Shared Sovereignty.' In *Caribbean Imperatives: Regional Governance and Integrated Development*, edited by Kenneth Hall and Denis Benn, 3–9. Kingston: Ian Randle Publishers, 2005.

Grenade, Wendy. 'An Overview of Regional Governance Arrangements within the Caribbean Community.' In *The European Union and Regional Integration. A Comparative Perspective and Lessons for the Americas*, edited by Joaquín Roy and Roberto Dominguez, 167–83. Miami: Office of the Jean Monnet Chair, University of Miami, 2005.

Group of Caribbean Experts. 'The Caribbean Community in the 1980s. Report by a Group of Caribbean Experts.' Georgetown: CARICOM Secretariat, 1981.

Grugel, Jean. 'New Regionalism and Modes of Governance – Comparing Us and Eu Strategies in Latin America.' *European Journal of International Relations* 10 (2004): 603–26.

Grugel, Jean, and Wil Hout, eds. *Regionalism across the North-South Divide: State Strategies and Globalisation.* London: Routledge, 1999.

Haas, Ernst B. 'The Challenge of Regionalism.' *International Organization* 12, no. 4 (1958): 440–58.

Hall, Kenneth O., ed. *Integrate or Perish: Perspectives of the Heads of Government of the Caribbean Community and the Commonwealth Caribbean Countries 1963–2002.* 2nd ed. Kingston: Ian Randle Publishers, 2003.

Hall, Kenneth O., and Byron Blake. 'CARICOM Administration.' In *The Caribbean Community: Beyond Survival,* edited by Kenneth O. Hall, 203–21. Kingston Ian Randle Publishers, 2001.

Hall, Kenneth, and Denis Benn, eds. *Caribbean Imperatives. Regional Governance and Integrated Development.* Kingston: Ian Randle Publishers, 2005.

———, eds. *Governance in the Age of Globalisation: Caribbean Perspectives* Kingston: Ian Randle Publishers, 2003.

Hall, Peter A., and Rosemary C. R. Taylor. 'Political Science and the Three Institutionalisms.' *Political Studies* XLIV (1996): 936–57.

Harrison, Graham. 'Governance States in Africa: Conceptualising the Encounter between the World Bank and the Sovereign Frontier.' In *The World Bank and Africa: The Construction of Governance States,* edited by Graham Harrison. London: Routledge, 2004.

Hart, Robert. 'House Passes Bill on CCJ.' *Jamaica Gleaner,* Wednesday, 28 July 2004.

Heads of Government of Antigua and Barbuda; Dominica; Grenada; Montserrat; St Kitts/Nevis; St Lucia and St Vincent and the Grenadines. 'Treaty Establishing the Organisation of Eastern Caribbean States.' Basseterre: OECS Secretariat, 1981.

Heads of Government of Commonwealth Caribbean Countries. 'Communiqué Issued at the Conclusion of the Eighth Meeting of Heads of Government of the Commonwealth Caribbean Countries.' Georgetown, Guyana, 9–12 April 1973.

———. 'Communiqué Issued at the Conclusion of the Seventh Conference of Heads of Government of Commonwealth Caribbean Countries.' Chaguaramas, Trinidad, 9–14 October 1972.

———. 'The Georgetown Accord.' Georgetown, Guyana, 1973.

———. 'The Grenada Declaration.' Paper presented at the Meeting of Signatory Heads of Government, Georgetown, Guyana, 8 November 1971.

———. 'Communiqué Issued at the Conclusion of the Third Conference of Heads of Government of Commonwealth Caribbean Countries.' Georgetown, Guyana, 8–10 March 1965.

———. 'Declaration on Foreign Policy Issued at the Second Conference of Heads of Governments of Commonwealth Caribbean Countries.' Kingston, Jamaica: CARICOM Secretariat, 1964.

———. 'Summary of Conclusions of the Fourth Conference of the Heads of

Governments of Commonwealth Caribbean Countries.' Bridgetown, Barbados, 23–27 October 1967.

Heisenberger, Dorothee, and Amy Richmond. 'Supranational Institution-Building in the European Union: A Comparison of the European Court of Justice and the European Central Bank.' *Journal of European Public Policy* 9, no. 2 (2002): 201–18.

Henry-Wilson, Maxine. 'Culture in the Future of the Caribbean Community. Third Lecture in the Distinguished Lecture Series Sponsored by CARICOM to Commemorate Its Thirtieth Anniversary.' Paper presented at the Eighth Meeting of the Council for Human and Social Development, Paramaribo, Suriname, 24–26 April 2003.

Hettne, Björn. 'Beyond the 'New' Regionalism.' *New Political Economy* 10, no. 4 (2005): 543–71.

Hettne, Björn, András Inotai, and Osvaldo Sunkel, eds. *Globalism and the New Regionalism*. Basingstoke: Macmillan Press, 1999.

Hettne, Björn, and Fredrik Söderbaum. 'Theorising the Rise of Regionness.' *New Political Economy* 5, no. 3 (2000): 457–72.

Hinds, David. 'Internal Political Tribalism and Regional Integration in the Caribbean.' In *The European Union and Regional Integration. A Comparative Perspective and Lessons for the Americas*, edited by Joaquín Roy and Roberto Dominguez, 167–83. Miami: Office of the Jean Monnet Chair, University of Miami, 2005.

Hinsley, F.H. *Sovereignty*. London: C.A. Watts and Co. Ltd, 1966.

Hochstetler, Kathryn, Ann Marie Clark, and Elisabeth J. Friedman. 'Sovereignty in the Balance: Claims and Bargains at the Un Conferences on the Environment, Human Rights, and Women.' *International Studies Quarterly* 44, no. 4 (2000): 591–614.

Ho-Fatt, Kim. 'Region Versus Nation: An Examination of Identity Formation in the Caribbean.' MSc diss., University of the West Indies, 2000.

Hooghe, Liesbet, and Gary Marks. 'The Making of a Polity: The Struggle over European Integration.' *European Integration Online Papers (EIoP)*,no. 004 (1997), http://eiop.or.at/eiop/texte/1997-004a.htm.

———. *Multi-Level Governance and European Integration*. Oxford: Rowman and Littleford Publishers, 2001.

———. 'Unravelling the Central State, but How? Types of Multi-Level Governance.' *American Political Science Review* 97, no. 2 (2003): 233–43.

Hook, Glenn, and Ian Kearns, eds. *Subregionalism and World Order*. Basingstoke: Macmillan Press, 1999.

Huntley, Earl. 'The LDCs and CARICOM.' In *The Caribbean Community. Beyond Survival*, edited by Kenneth O. Hall, 35–38. Kingston: Ian Randle Publishers, 2001.

———. 'The Treaty of Basseterre and Economic Union.' Paper presented at the Paper Presented at Thirty-Eighth Meeting of the OECS Authority, Castries, St Lucia, January 2004.

IDB. *Ten Years of CARICOM*. Washington: IDB-INTAL, 1984.

Ischyrion, Peter. 'Caribbean Political Union Endorsed.' *Terra Viva: South-South Executive Brief* 1 (8), no. 4 (2008): 4–5.

Jabko, Nicolas. 'In the Name of the Market: How the European Commission Paved the Way for Monetary Union.' *Journal of European Public Policy* 6, no. 3 (1999): 475–95.

Jackson, Robert. *Quasi-States: Sovereignty, International Relations and the Third World*, Cambridge Studies in International Relations:12. Cambridge: Cambridge University Press, 1990.

———. *Sovereignty.* Edited by Key Concepts. Cambridge: Polity Press, 2007.

———. *Sovereignty at the Millennium.* Oxford: Blackwell Publishers, 1999.

———. 'Sovereignty in World Politics: A Glance at the Conceptual and Historical Landscape.' In *Sovereignty at the Millennium*, edited by Robert Jackson, 9–34. Oxford: Blackwell Publishers, 1999.

Jamaican High Commission, Port of Spain. 'Developments since July 1983 CARICOM Heads of Government Conference.' Port of Spain: Jamaican High Commission, 1984.

James, Alan. 'The Practice of Sovereign Statehood in Contemporary International Society.' In *Sovereignty at the Millennium*, edited by Robert Jackson, 35–51. Oxford: Blackwell Publishers, 1999.

Jayasuriya, Kanishka. 'Embedded Mercantilism and Open Regionalism: The Crisis of a Regional Political Project.' *Third World Quarterly* 24, no. 2 (2003): 339–55.

Jessamy, Deirdre. 'The Role of Personality in Commonwealth Caribbean Politics. The CARICOM Experiment 1973–1986.' MSc diss., University of the West Indies, 1986.

Jessop, David. 'Caribbean Integration Losing Appeal.' *Sunday Gleaner*, Sunday, 27 June 2010.

———. 'The View from Europe – Caribbean "New Thinking."' *Sunday Gleaner*, 7 March 2008.

———. 'The View from Europe – Caribbean Regionalism.' London: Caribbean Council, 2009.

———. 'The View from Europe – the World Will Be a Different Place.' *Sunday Gleaner*, 23 October 2009.

Jones, Edwin. 'Governance in CARICOM – a 2000 Perspective.' *CARICOM Perspective. A Century of Achievement*, June 2000, 61–64.

Jones, Edwin, and Edwin Cruickshank. 'Making the CARICOM Administrative Machinery Work: The Decentralisation and Leadership Factor.' In *Caribbean Imperatives: Regional Governance and Integrated Development*, edited by Kenneth Hall and Denis Benn, 104–25. Kingston: Ian Randle Publishers, 2005.

Jordan, Victor. 'The Caribbean Court of Justice as a Part of a Wider Integration Movement.' Paper presented at the Fourth Annual SALISES Conference on Development Strategy and Policy for Small States in the Context of Global Change, Cave Hill, Barbados, 15–17 January 2003.

———. 'A Critique of the Caribbean Court of Justice. With Special Reference to the European Court of Justice.' In *Fifth Annual SALISES Conference on the CARICOM Single Market and Economy.* St Augustine, Trinidad and Tobago, 2004.

Joseph, Cuthbert. 'The Caribbean Court of Justice: Some Aspects of Its Original Jurisdiction.' In *SALISES Fifth Annual Conference on the CARICOM Single Market Economy.* St Augustine, Trinidad and Tobago, 2004.

———. 'Caribbean Economic Integration: Reflections on Some Legal and Institutional Issues.' In *Towards a Caribbean Economy in the Twenty-First Century. Essays in Honour of William G. Demas*, edited by Laurence Clarke and M.G. Zephirin, 137–48. Port of Spain: Caribbean Centre for Monetary Studies, University of the West Indies, 1997.

———. 'Institutional and Structural Patterns of Integration in Latin America and the Caribbean: A Legal Critique Presentado a Comitè Juridico Interamericano: Un Siglo De Aportes Al Derecho Internacional.' Washington, D.C.: Organizacion de los Estados Americanos Secretaria General, 2006.

———. 'Reconceptualising the Caribbean Community: Reconciling Individual and Collective Exercise of Sovereignty – a Legal Perspective.' In *Caribbean Imperatives: Regional Governance and Integrated Development*, edited by Kenneth Hall and Denis Benn, 10–21. Kingston: Ian Randle Publishers, 2005.

Katzenstein, Peter J. 'Regionalism and Asia.' *New Political Economy* 5, no. 3 (2000): 353–68.

Keating, Michael. 'European Integration and the Nationalities Question.' *Politics and Society* 32 (2004): 367–87.

Kegel, Patricia Luiza, and Mohamed Amal. 'The Problem of Legal Implementation and Sovereignty.' In *Elements of Regional Integration: A Multidimensional Approach*, edited by Ariane Kösler and Martin Zimmek, 209–26. Baden-Baden: Nomos, 2008.

Kösler, Ariane, and Martin Zimmek, eds. *Elements of Regional Integration: A Multidimensional Approach*. Edited by Ludger Kühnhardt, Schriften Des Zentrum Für Europäische Integrationsforschung/ Centre for European Integration Studies. Baden-Baden: Nomos, 2008.

Krasner, Stephen D. 'Globalization and Sovereignty.' In *States and Sovereignty in the Global Economy*, edited by David A. Smith, Dorothy J. Solinger and Steven C. Topik, 34–52. London: Routledge, 1999.

———. *Problematic Sovereignty: Contested Rules and Political Possibilities*. New York: Columbia University Press, 2001.

———. 'Rethinking the Sovereign State Model.' In *Empires, Systems and States*, edited by Michael Cox, Tim Dunne and Ken Booth, 17–42. Cambridge: Cambridge University Press, 2001.

———. *Sovereignty: Organised Hypocrisy*. New Jersey: Princeton University Press, 1999.

Kühnhardt, Ludger. 'Prospects for Regional Integration.' In *Elements of Regional Integration: A Multidimensional Approach* edited by Ariane Kösler and Martin Zimmek, 261–76. Baden-Baden: Nomos, 2008.

La Guerre, John Gaffar. 'Organic and Mechanistic Theories of the State and the Individual.' In *Issues in the Government and Politocs of the West Indies. A Reader*, edited by John Gaffar La Guerre, 16–38. St Augustine: School of Continuing Studies, University of the West Indies, 1997.

Lamming, George. *The Sovereignty of the Imagination*. Kingston: Arawak Publications, 2004.

Lane, Jan-Erik. 'International Organisation Analysed with the Power Index Method.' In *CSGR Workign Paper No.181/05*. Coventry: Centre for the Study of Globalisation and Regionalisation, University of Warwick, 2005.

Lestrade, Swinburne, and Ralph Gonsalves. 'Political Aspects of Integration of the Windward and Leeward Islands.' *Caribbean Quarterly* 18, no. 2 (1972): 28–37.

Levi, Darrel E. *Michael Manley: The Making of a Leader*. London: Andre Deutsch, 1989.

Levitt, Kari. *Reclaiming Development: Independent Thought and Caribbean Community*. Kingston: Ian Randle Publishers, 2005.

Levitt, Kari, and Michael Witter, eds. *The Critical Tradition of Caribbean Political Economy. The Legacy of George Beckford*. Kingston: Ian Randle Publishers, 1996.

Lewis, Arthur W. *The Agony of the Eight*. Bridgetown: Advocate Commercial Printery, 1965.

Lewis, Gordon K. *The Growth of the Modern West Indies*. London: McGibbon and Kee, 1968; reissued Kingston: Ian Randle Publishers, 2004.

Lewis, Patsy. 'The Agony of the Fifteen: The Crisis of Implementation.' *Social and Economic Studies* 54, no. 3 (2005): 145–75.

———. 'Is the Goal of Regional Integration Still Relevant among Small States? The Case of the OECS and CARICOM.' In *Living at the Borderlines: Issues in Caribbean Sovereignty and Development*, edited by Cynthia Barrow-Giles and Don Marshall. Kingston: Ian Randle Publishers, 2003.

———. *Surviving Small Size. Regional Integration in Caribbean Ministates*. Kingston: University of the West Indies Press, 2002.

Lewis, Vaughan. 'The Caribbean in Emerging World Political/Economic Trends.' *Caribbean Quarterly* 25, no. 3 (1979): 44–62.

———. 'The Changing Environment of OECS International Economic Relations and Some External Policy Implications.' In *The Integrationist – Survival and Sovereignty in the Caribbean Community*, edited by Kenneth Hall and Myrtle Chuck-A-Sang, 36–49. Kingston: Ian Randle Publishers, 2005.

———. 'Compulsions of Integration [West Indian Commission's Occasional Paper No. 6].' In *The Caribbean Community: Beyond Survival*, edited by Kenneth O. Hall, 176–81. Kingston: Ian Randle Publishers, 2001.

———. 'Concept Paper: Parameters of Changing European Union-Caribbean Relations.' Paper presented at the Seminar on The Future of Caribbean-European Union Relations: Defining a Research Agenda, Maastricht, Holland, 8–9 October 2009.

———. 'The Eastern Caribbean States: Fledgling Sovereignties in the Global Environment.' In *Democracy in the Caribbean*, edited by Jorge I. Dominguez, Robert A. Pastor and R. Delisle Worrell, 99–121. Baltimore: Johns Hopkins University Press, 1993.

———. 'Governing Our Caribbean Region: To What End and in What Ways?' St Augustine, Trinidad and Tobago: Institute of International Relations, 2008.

———. 'Managing Mature Regionalism: Regional Governance in the Caribbean Community. Report of the Technical Working Group on Governance Appointed by CARICOM Heads of Government.' Georgetown: CARICOM Secretariat, 2006.

———. 'The OECS and Closer Political Union.' In *The Caribbean Community. Beyond Survival*, edited by Kenneth O. Hall, 301–14. Kingston: Ian Randle Publishers, 2001.

———. 'Political Integration Revived.' *CARICOM Perspective*, 1989, 3–4.

———. 'Presentation to the CARICOM Heads of State and Government on the Report of the Task Force on the Trinidad and Tobago-Eastern Caribbean States Integration Initiative.' Port of Spain, Trinidad, 24 May 2009.

———. 'Regional Integration Institutional Arrangements: Underlying Assumptions and Contemporary Appropriateness.' In *Governance in the Age of Globalisation: Caribbean Perspectives*, edited by Kenneth O. Hall and Denis Benn, 509–26. Kingston: Ian Randle Publishers, 2003.

———. 'What Purposes for CARICOM Integration Today?' Paper presented at the Third Distinguished Lecture in a series in honour of Sir Arthur Lewis, the English-speaking Caribbean's first Nobel Laureate, 15 April 2007.

Linklater, Andrew. 'Citizenship and Sovereignty in the Post-Westphalian European State.' In *Re-Imagining Political Community. Studies in Cosmopolitan Democracy*, edited by Daniele Archibugi, David Held and Martin Kohler, 113–37. Cambridge: Polity Press, 1998.

Litfin, Karen T. *The Greening of Sovereignty in World Politics*. Cambridge, Massachussets: MIT Press, 1998.

———. 'Sovereignty in World Ecopolitics.' *Mershon International Studies Review* 41, no. 2 (1997): 167–204.

Lodge, J. 'Federalism and the European Parliament.' *Publius – The Journal of Federalism* 26, no. 4 (1996): 63–79.

Lowenthal, David, and Lambros Comitas, eds. *The Aftermath of Sovereignty: West Indian Perspectives*. New York: Anchor Books, 1973.

Manley, Michael. 'The Caribbean Community Envisioned by Its Forefathers and a Reality 25 Years After.' *CARICOM Perspective*, June 1995, 12–14, 31.

Massiah, Joycelin. 'The Report of the West Indian Commission: An Appreciation.' *Caribbean Quarterly* 39, no. 1 (1993): 22–38.

Mathurin, Gail. 'Governance Structures for the Formulation and Negotiation of Trade Policy.' In *Caribbean Imperatives: Regional Governance and Integrated Development*, edited by Kenneth Hall and Denis Benn, 233–36. Kingston: Ian Randle Publishers, 2005.

Mattli, Walter. 'Sovereignty Bargains in Regional Integration.' *International Studies Review* 2, no. 2 (2000): 149–80.

McIntyre, Alister. 'Aspects of Trade and Development in the Commonwealth Caribbean.' *Economic Bulletin for Latin America* 10, no. 2 (1965): 125–59.

———. 'The Importance of Negotiation Preparedness.' In *The Caribbean Community: Beyond Survival*, edited by Kenneth O. Hall, 674–80. Kingston: Ian Randle Publishers.

McIntyre, Alister, and William G. Demas. 'Towards the More Effective Functioning of the Caribbean Common Market.' Presented to the Tenth Meeting of the Common Market Council.' Georgetown: CARICOM Secretariat, 1977.

Meighoo, Kirk. 'Organic Theorising in Inorganic Societies, or the Need for Epistemic Sovereignty.' In *The Caribbean Integration Process: A People Centred Approach*, edited by Kenneth Hall and Myrtle Chuck-A-Sang, 10–23. Kingston: Ian Randle Publishers, 2005.

Mills, Gladstone E., Carlisle Burton, J. Oneil Lewis, and Crispin Sorhaindo. 'Report on a Comprehensive Review of the Programmes, Institutions and Organisations of the Caribbean Community.' Georgetown: CARICOM Secretariat, 1990.

Moore, Fauzya A. 'The Report of the West Indian Commission: New Directions for CARICOM?' *Social and Economic Studies* 43, no. 2 (1994): 149–72.

Moore, Tracy. 'Not All the Facts.' *Nation News*, 3 July 2009.

Moravcsik, A., and K. Nicolaidis. 'Explaining the Treaty of Amsterdam: Interests, Influence, Institutions.' *Journal of Common Market Studies* 37, no. 1 (1999): 59–85.

Mordecai, John *The West Indies. The Federal Negotiations*. London: George Allen and Unwin, 1968.

Müllerleile, Christoph. *CARICOM Integration: Progress and Hurdles. A European View*. Kingston: Kingston Publishers, 1996.

Munroe, Trevor. 'On Strengthening Foundations for Regional Governance.' In *Caribbean Imperatives: Regional Governance and Integrated Development*, edited by Kenneth Hall and Denis Benn, 66–70. Kingston: Ian Randle Publishers, 2005.

Murphy, Alexander B. 'The Sovereign State System as Political-Territorial Ideal: Historical and Contemporary Considerations.' In *State Sovereignty as Social Construct*, edited by Thomas J. Biersteker and Cynthia Weber, 81–120. Cambridge: Cambridge University Press, 1996.

Myers, John. 'After 35 Years, CARICOM Needs Fresh Thinkers – Seaga – Bats for Regional Cooperation over Integration.' *Jamaica Gleaner*, Wednesday, 13 February 2008.

Naraine, Mahindra. 'The Caribbean Community's Tenth Anniversary.' *The Round Table: The Commonwealth Journal of International Affairs* 288 (1983): 433–42.

Narine, Shaun. 'The English School and ASEAN.' *The Pacific Review* 19, no. 2 (2006): 199–218.

———. 'State Sovereignty, Political Legitimacy and Regional Institutionalism in the Asia-Pacific.' *The Pacific Review* 17, no. 3 (2004): 423–50.

Nesadurai, H.E.S. 'ASEAN and Regional Governance after the Cold War: From Regional Order to Regional Community.' *The Pacific Review* 22, no. 1 (2009): 91–118.

———. 'Attempting Developmental Regionalism through Afta: The Domestic Sources of Regional Governance.' *Third World Quarterly* 24, no. 2 (2003): 235–53.

Nettleford, Rex. 'The Caribbean's Creative Diversity: The Defining Point of the Region's History – Lecture Delivered by the Vice Chancellor of the University of the West Indies.' Paper presented at the Second Lecture in the Distinguished Lecture Series Commemorating the Thirtieth Anniversary of The Caribbean Community, University Of Guyana, Guyana, 21 March 2003.

Nicholls, Shelton Michael Anthony. 'Economic Integration in the Caribbean Community (CARICOM): From Federation to Single Market.' The University of London, 1995.

OECS Authority. 'Commuique – 43rd Meeting of the OECS Authority.' Basseterre, St Kitts and Nevis, 21–23 June 2006.

———. 'Communiqué – 34th Meeting of the OECS Authority.' Roseau, Dominica, 26 July 2001.

———. 'Communiqué – 38th Meeting of the OECS Authority.' Castries, St Lucia, 22–23 January 2004.

———. 'Communiqué – 40th Meeting of the OECS Authority.' Tortola, British Virgin Islands, 10–12 November 2004.

———. 'Communiqué – 45th Meeting of the OECS Authority.' Grande Anse, Grenada, 23–25 May 2007.

———. 'Communiqué – 46th Meeting of the OECS Authority.' Roseau, Dominica, 23–25 January 2008.

———. 'Communiqué – 47th Meeting of the OECS Authority.' Rodney Bay Gros Islet, St Lucia, 23–24 May 2008.

———. 'Communiqué – 48th Meeting of the OECS Authority.' Little Bay, Montserrat, 19–21 November 2008.

———. 'Communiqué – 49th Meeting of the OECS Authority.' Tortola, British Virgin Islands, 20–22 May 2009.

———. 'Communiqué – Special Meeting of the OECS Authority on the Economy.' Basseterre, St Kitts and Nevis, 10 October 2002.

———. 'Declaration of Intent by Heads of Government of the OECS on the Participation of Their Countries in the OECS Economic Union.' Paper presented at the 43rd Meeting of the OECS Authority, Basseterre, St Kitts and Nevis, 21–23 June 2006.

———. 'OECS Development Charter.' Castries, 10 October 2002.

OECS Secretariat. 'Communiqué – OECS Economic Union Retreat.' Basseterre, St Kitts, 13 October 2007.

OECS Secretariat Economic Union Project Unit. 'Towards Developing a Model of Governance for Economic Union in the OECS: A Case Study of the European Union.' In *Presented at Thirty Eighth Meeting of the OECS Authority*. Castries, St Lucia: OECS Secretariat, 2004.

Office of the Prime Minister, Jamaica. 'Changes Coming for CARICOM Administration – PM Golding.' In *News Release*, 2010.

Olsen, Johan P. 'Organising European Institutions of Governance. A Prelude to an Institutional Account of Political Integration.' *ARENA Working Papers*, no. 2 (2000), http://www.erena.uio.no/publications/wp00_2.htm.

Organisation of Eastern Caribbean States (OECS). 'Draft of the New Treaty.' Castries: OECS Secretariat, 2006.

Patterson, P.J. 'CARICOM Beyond Thirty: Charting New Directions. Chairman's Perspective.' In *24th Meeting of the Conference of Heads of CARICOM*. Montego Bay, Jamaica, 2003.

———. 'CARICOM Beyond Thirty: Connecting with the Diaspora.' Paper presented at the Seventh Lecture in the Distinguished Lecture Series Commemorating the 30th Anniversary of the Caribbean Community, Brooklyn, New York, 2 October 2003.

———. 'Opening Address by the Prime Minister of Jamaica at the 24th Regular Meeting of the Conference of CARICOM Heads of Government.' Montego Bay, Jamaica, 2 July 2003 2003.

———. 'The Present State of Caribbean Sovereignty.' Paper presented at the Regional Seminar on Caribbean Sovereignty: Mobilization for Development and Self-Reliance. The Tasks of Political Education, Kingston, Jamaica, December 1984.

———. 'Report of the Chairman of the Prime-Ministerial Sub-Committee (Pmsc) on External Negotiations on the Reviews of the Structure and Budget of the Rnm.' 2001.

——. 'Seize the Moment. Address by the Prime Minister of Jamaica.' Paper presented at the Opening Session of the Fourteenth Inter-Sessional Meeting of CARICOM Heads of Government, Port of Spain, Trinidad and Tobago, 14 February 2003.

——. 'Statement by Prime Minister of Jamaica on the Occasion of the Formal Launch of the CARICOM Single Market.' Kingston, Jamaica, 30 January 2006.

Payne, Anthony. 'Globalisation and Modes of Regionalist Governance.' In *Debating Governance: Authority, Steering and Democracy*, edited by Jon Pierre, 201–18. Oxford: Oxford University Press, 2000.

——. *The New Regional Politics of Development*. Basingstoke: Palgrave Macmillan, 2004.

——. *The Political History of CARICOM*. Kingston: Ian Randle Publishers, 2008.

——. *The Politics of the Caribbean Community 1961–1979*. Manchester: Manchester University Press, 1980.

——. 'The Rise and Fall of Caribbean Regionalisation.' *Journal of Common Market Studies* XIX, no. 3 (1981): 255–80.

——. 'The Study of Governance in a Global Political Economy.' In *Globalising International Political Economy*, edited by Nicola Phillips, 55–81. Basingstoke: Palgrave Macmillan, 2005.

——. 'Whither CARICOM? The Performance and Prospects of Caribbean Integration in the 1980s.' *International Journal* XL, no. 2 (1985): 207–28.

Payne, Anthony, and Andrew Gamble. 'Introduction: The Political Economy of Regionalism and World Order.' In *Regionalism and World Order*, edited by Andrew Gamble and Anthony Payne, 1–20. London: Macmillan Press, 1996.

Payne, Anthony, and Paul Sutton. 'Repositioning the Caribbean within Globalisation.' In *The Caribbean Paper, No. 1*. Waterloo: The Centre for International Governance Innovation (CIGI), 2007.

Persaud, Bishnodat, and Michael Davenport. 'The Implications for the Bahamas of Participation in the CARICOM Single Market and Economy.' Nassau: Ministry of Foreign Affairs, 2000.

Phillips, Nicola. 'Globalisation and the "Paradox of State Power": Perspectives from Latin America.' In *CSGR Working Paper No. 16/98*. Coventry: Centre for the Study of Globalisation and Regionalisation, University of Warwick, 1998.

——. 'Governance after Financial Crisis: South American Perspectives on the Reformulation of Regionalism.' *New Political Economy* 5, no. 3 (2000): 383–98.

——. 'The Rise and Fall of Open Regionalism? Comparative Reflections on Regional Governance in the Southern Cone of Latin America.' *Third World Quarterly* 24, no. 2 (2003): 217–34.

Philpott, Daniel. 'Westphalia, Authority and International Society.' In *Sovereignty at the Millennium*, edited by Robert Jackson, 144–67. Oxford: Blackwell Publishers, 1999.

Pierre, Jon, ed. *Debating Governance: Authority Steering and Democracy*. Oxford: Oxford University Press, 2000.

Pierson, Paul. 'The Path to European Integration. A Historical Institutionalist Analysis' *Comparative Political Studies* 29 (1996): 123–63.

Pollard, Duke. 'The Caribbean Single Market and Economy: The Legal Implications.' In *The Caribbean Community: Beyond Survival*, edited by Kenneth O. Hall, 294–300. Kingston: Ian Randle Publishers, 2001.

———. 'Revisiting Chaguaramas: Institutional Development in CARICOM since 1973.' In *The Caribbean Community: Beyond Survival*, edited by Kenneth O. Hall, 222–28. Kingston: Ian Randle Publishers, 2001.

———. *The CARICOM System: Basic Instruments*. Kingston: The Caribbean Law Publishing Company, 2003.

———. 'The CSME, CCJ and Private Sector.' In *The CARICOM Single Market and Economy: Genesis and Prognosis*, edited by Kenneth Hall and Myrtle Chuck-A-Sang, 91–114. Kingston: Ian Randle Publishers, 2007.

———. 'Decision-Making in the Caribbean Community.' Georgetown: CARICOM Secretariat 1985.

———. *Law and Policy of Producers' Associations*. Oxford: Clarendon, 1984.

———. 'The Revised Treaty of Chaguaramas.' In *CARICOM Single Market and Economy: Genesis and Prognosis*, edited by Kenneth Hall and Myrtle Chuck-A-Sang, 3–19. Kingston: Ian Randle Publishers, 2007.

———. 'Unincorporated Treaties and Small States.' *Commonwealth Law Bulletin* 33, no. 3 (2007): 389–421.

———. 'Juridical and Constitutional Implication of CARICOM Treaty Practice.' *Commonwealth Law Bulletin* 35, no. 1 (2009): 7–29.

Premdas, Ralph. 'Secession in Nevis: Symbolic and Instrumental Explanations.' In *Beyond Walls: Multidisciplinary Perspectives*, edited by Simone Augier and Olivia Edgecombe-Howell, 49–76. Basseterre: School of Continuing Studies, University of the West Indies, 2002.

Prime Ministerial Expert Group on Governance. 'Draft Report of the Technical Group on Automaticity of Financing.' edited by Compton Bourne, 2003.

———. 'Final Report of the Expert Group of Heads of Government on the Establishment of a CARICOM Commission or Other Executive Mechanism, Automatic Resource Transfers and the Assembly of Caribbean Community Parliamentarians.' edited by Ralph Gonsalves. Kingston, Jamaica, 2005.

———. 'Report of the Technical Sub-Group on the Assembly of Caribbean Community Parliamentarians (Accp).' edited by Denis Benn, 2003.

Proctor, Jesse Harris. 'The Functional Approach to Political Union: Lessons from the Effort to Federate the British Caribbean Territories.' *International Organization* 10, no. 1 (1956): 35–48.

Rainford, Roderick. 'Awaiting the Dawn of a Greater Unity.' *CARICOM Perspective*, June 1995, 67–70.

———. 'Caribbean Regional Negotiating Machinery. Institutional and Human Resources Review.' Georgetown: CARICOM Secretariat, 2007.

———. 'El Proceso De Adopción De Decisiones Y La Estructura Institucional De La Comunidad Del Caribe.' *Integraciòn Latinoamericana* 91 (1984): 21–30.

———. 'Review of the Achievements and Shortcomings of CARICOM.' In *Paper Prepared for the West Indian Commission*. Black Rock: West Indian Commission, 1991.

———. 'Towards a Commission or Executive Authority for the Community.' In *Caribbean Imperatives: Regional Governance and Integrated Development*, edited by Kenneth Hall and Denis Benn, 78–87. Kingston: Ian Randle Publishers, 2005.

Ramphal, Shridath. 'Careless with CARICOM – Part 1.' *Guyana Chronicle*, Wednesday, 5 May 2010.

———. 'The Caribbean Challenge in the Negotiating Process.' In *The Caribbean Community: Beyond Survival*, edited by Kenneth O. Hall, 665–73. Kinsgton: Ian Randle Publishers, 2001.

———. 'The CARICOM Commission: Towards a Mature Regionalism.' In *Caribbean Imperatives: Regional Governance and Integrated Development*, edited by Kenneth Hall and Denis Benn, 71–77. Kingston: Ian Randle Publishers, 2005.

———. 'Dialogue of Unity. A Search for West Indian Identity.' Paper presented at the Address delivered at the Caribbean Ecumenical Consultation for Development, Chaguaramas, Trinidad, 16 November 1971.

———. 'Progress Report of the Independent West Indian Commission.' In *The Caribbean Community. Beyond Survival*, edited by Kenneth O. Hall, 229–33. Kingston: Ian Randle Publishers, 2001.

———. 'The Prospect for Community in the Caribbean.' Paper presented at the Address to the Royal Commonwealth Society, London, 22 January 1973.

———. 'Remembering to Score.' *CARICOM Perspective*, June 1995, 9–11,17.

———. 'Time to Act.' *Caribbean Quarterly* 39, no. 1 (1993): 1–21.

———. 'To Be a Canoe. Presentation to the 12th Conference of Heads of Government of the Caribbean Community, Basseterre, St Kitts.' In *No Island Is an Island. Selected Speeches of Sir Shridath Ramphal*, edited by David Dabydeen and John Gilmore, 58–68. London: Macmillan Press, 1991.

———. 'To Care for CARICOM. The Need for an Ethos of Community.' Paper presented at the Speech delivered by Secretary-General of the Commonwealth at the Dinner held in his Honour by the CARICOM Council of Ministers, Montego Bay, Jamaica, 5 July 1975 1975.

Ramsaran, Ramesh. 'CARICOM: The Integration Process in Crisis.' *Journal of World Trade Law* 12, no. 3 (1978): 208–17.

———. 'CARICOM's Soft Belly.' In *The Caribbean Community: Beyond Survival*, edited by Kenneth O. Hall, 22–26. Kingston: Ian Randle Publishers, 2001.

Republic of Trinidad and Tobago. *White Paper on CARICOM, 1973–1978*. Port-of-Spain: Government Printery, 1979.

Ridolfi, Roberto. 'The Eu as Integration Model: How Relevant Is the European Experience?' In *Models of Regional Governance for the Pacific: Sovereignty and the Future Architecture of Regionalism*, edited by Kennedy Graham, 50–58. Christchurch: Canterbury University Press, 2008.

Risse, Thomas. 'Neofunctionalism, European Identity, and the Puzzles of European Integration.' *Journal of European Public Policy* 12, no. 2 (2005): 291–309.

Robinson, A.N.R. 'Federation and Tobago. A Speech Delivered in Federal House of Representatives.' Chaguaramas, Trinidad and Tobago, 1960.

Robinson, T. 'A Caribbean Common Law.' *Race & Class* 49, no. 2 (2007): 118–24.

Rosenau, James N. 'Governance and Democracy in a Globalizing World.' In *Re-Imagining Political Community. Studies in Cosmopolitan Democracy*, edited by Daniele Archibugi, David Held and Martin Kohler, 11–27. Cambridge: Polity Press, 1998.

———. 'Governance in the New Global Order.' In *Governing Globalization*, edited by David Held and Anthony McGrew, 70–81. Cambridge: Polity Press, 2002.

———. 'Governance in the Twenty-First Century.' *Global Governance* 1 (1995): 13–43.

————. 'Patterned Chaos in Global Life: Structure and Process in the Two Worlds of World Politics.' *International Political Science Review* 9, no. 4 (1988): 327–64.

Ross-Brewster, Havelock R.H. 'Identity, Space and the West Indian Union.' In *Contending with Destiny: The Caribbean in the 21st Century*, edited by Kenneth Hall and Denis Benn, 37–44. Kingston: Ian Randle Publishers, 2000.

Rudolph, Christopher. 'Sovereignty and Territorial Borders in a Global Age.' *International Studies Review* 7 (2005): 1–20.

Ryan, Selwyn, and Ann Marie Bissessar. 'Overview: Governance.' In *Governance in the Caribbean*, edited by Selwyn Ryan and Ann Marie Bissessar, 3–5. St Augustine: Sir Arthur Lewis Institute for Social and Economic Studies (SALISES), The University of the West Indies, 2002.

Seaga, Edward. 'Integration vs. Cooperation: Rethinking CARICOM.' In *Production Integration in CARICOM: From Theory to Action*, edited by Denis Benn and Kenneth Hall, 235–44. Kingston: Ian Randle Publishers, 2006.

Seales, Iana. 'Immigration Row Heats up at Summit Launch.' *Stabroek News*, 3 July 2009.

Selwyn, Percy. 'Smallness and Islandness.' *World Development* 8 (1980): 945–51.

Sidaway, James D. *Imagined Regional Communities. Integration and Sovereignty in the Global South.* London: Routledge, 2002.

Singh, Rickey. 'CARICOM – Decisions Minus Theatrics.' *Jamaica Observer*, 7 July 2010.

————. 'CARICOM Needs the 'Obama Spirit' – Action , Not Ole' Talk.' *The Sunday Chronicle*, 13 September 2009, 8.

————. 'Changing Leadership in CRNM.' *Trinidad and Tobago Express*, 30 April 2008.

————. 'New Ideas to Push Region Forward.' *The Observer*, Saturday, 4 July 2009.

Slocum-Bradley, Nikki. 'Regional Integration, Identity and Culture.' In *Elements of Regional Integration: A Multidimensional Approach* edited by Ariane Kösler and Martin Zimmek, 241–59. Baden-Baden: Nomos, 2008.

Smouts, Marie-Claude. 'The Proper Use of Governance in International Relations.' *International Social Science Journal* L, no. 155 (1998): 81–89.

Söderbaum, Fredrik. 'The International Political Economy of Regionalism.' In *Globalising International Political Economy*, edited by Nicola Phillips, 221–45. Basingstoke: Palgrave Macmillan, 2005.

————. 'Modes of Regional Governance in Africa: Neo-Liberalism; Sovereignty Boosting, and Shadow Networks.' *Global Governance* 10 (2004): 419–36.

————. 'Regionalisation and Civil Society: The Case of Southern Africa.' *New Political Economy* 12, no. 3 (2007): 319–37.

Solingen, E. 'The Genesis, Design and Effects of Regional Institutions: Lessons from East Asia and the Middle East.' *International Studies Quarterly* 52, no. 2 (2008): 261–94.

Sorenson, Georg. 'Sovereignty: Change and Continuity in a Fundamental Institution.' In *Sovereignty at the Millennium*, edited by Robert Jackson, 168–82. Oxford: Blackwell Publishers, 1999.

Springer, Hugh W. 'Federation in the Caribbean: An Attempt That Failed.' *International Organization* 16, no. 4 (1962): 758–75.

————. *Reflections on the Failure of the First West Indian Federation.* Vol. 4,

Occasional Papers in International Affairs. Cambridge: Centre for International Affairs, Harvard University, 1962.

Spruyt, Hendrik. 'The Origins, Development and Possible Decline of the Modern State.' *Annual Review of Political Science* 5 (2002): 127–49.

Stacey, Jeffrey, and Berthold Rittberger. 'Dynamics of Formal and Informal Institutional Change in the EU.' *Journal of European Public Policy* 10, no. 6 (2003): 858–83.

Stoker, Gerry. 'Governance as Theory: Five Propositions.' *International Social Science Journal* L, no. 155 (1998): 17–28.

Stone, Carl. 'Rethinking Development. The Role of the State in Third World Development.' In *Rethinking Development. From the Lecture Series*, edited by Judith Wedderburn. Kingston: Consortium Graduate School of the Social Sciences, 1991.

Stoneman, Richard, Justice Duke Pollard, and Hugo Inniss. 'Turning around CARICOM: Proposals to Restructure the Secretariat.' Guyana: CARICOM Secretariat, 2012.

Tallberg, Jonas. 'Delegation to Supranational Institutions: Why, How and with What Consequences?' *West European Politics* 25, no. 1 (2002): 23–46.

Teh Cheng Guan, Benny ASEAN's Regional Integration Challenge: The ASEAN Process.' *The Copenhagen Journal of Asian Studies* 20 (2004): 70–94.

Tewarie, Bhoendradatt. 'Redesigning a Strategy for Caribbean Success in the Age of Globalization.' Paper presented at the Sixth Lecture of the Distinguished Lecture Series Celebrating the 30th Anniversary of the Caribbean Community, Belize, 17 September 2003.

Thakur, Ramesh, and Luk Van Langenhove. 'Enhancing Global Governance through Regional Integration.' *Global Governance* 12 (2006): 233–40.

———. 'Enhancing Global Governance through Regional Integration.' In *Regionalisation and Global Governance. The Taming of Globalisation?*, edited by Andrew F. Cooper, Christopher W. Hughes and Philippe De Lombaerde, 17–42. London: Routledge, 2008.

Thomas, Clive Y. 'The Community Is a Big Paper Tiger.' In *The Caribbean Community: Beyond Survival*, edited by Kenneth O. Hall, 27–31. Kingston: Ian Randle Publishers, 2001.

———. 'The Development Glass: Half Empty or Half Full. Perspectives on Caribbean Development.' Paper presented at the Sixth William G. Demas Memorial Lecture, Georgetown, Guyana, 17 May 2005.

———. 'The Interrelationship between Economic and Social Development.' In *Poverty, Empowerment and Social Development in the Caribbean*, edited by Norman Girvan, 20–49. Kingston: Canoe Press, University of the West Indies, 1997.

Tindigarukayo, Jimmy Kazaara. 'Perceptions and Opinions of Jamaicans on CARICOM Single Market Economy.' In *SALISES 5th Annual Conference on the CARICOM Single Market Economy.* St Augustine, Trinidad and Tobago, 2004.

Trinidad and Tobago, Office of the Prime Minister. 'Trinidad and Tobago – Eastern Caribbean States Integration Initiative.' In *Task Force Report* edited by Vaughan Lewis. Port of Spain: Office of the Prime Minister, 2009.

Tripartite Regional Economic Conference. 'The Port of Spain Consensus.' Paper presented at the CARICOM Tripartite Regional Economic Conference, Port of Spain, Trinidad and Tobago, 27 February–March 1 1991.

United Nations General Assembly. 'Declaration on the Establishment of a New International Economic Order – Unga Resolution 3201 (S-Vi).' In *Official Records: Sixth Special Session Supplement No. 1 (A9559)*. New York: United Nations, 1974.

———. 'Programme of Action on the Establishment of a New International Economic Order – Unga Resolution 3202 (S-Vi).' In *Official Records: Sixth Special Session Supplement No.1 (A/9559)*. New York: United Nations, 1974.

UNU-CRIS. 'Regional Integration Knowledge System.' UNU-CRIS, http://www.cris.unu.edu/riks/web/arrangement.

Van Langenhove, Luk, and Daniele Marchesi. 'The Lisbon Treaty and the Emergence of Third Generation Regional Integration.' In *The Jean Monnet/ Robert Schumann Paper Series*. Miami: Miami European Union Centre, 2008.

Venner, Dwight K. 'Sub-Regional Governance: The OECS Experience.' In *Governance in the Age of Globalisation: Caribbean Perspectives*, edited by Kenneth O. Hall and Denis Benn, 527–34. Kingston: Ian Randle Publishers, 2003.

Wallace, Helen. 'Europeanisation and Globalisation: Complementary or Contradictory Trends?' *New Political Economy* 5, no. 3 (2000): 369–82.

Wallace, William. 'The Sharing of Sovereignty: The European Paradox.' In *Sovereignty at the Millennium*, edited by Robert Jackson, 81–99. Oxford: Blackwell Publishers, 1999.

Wedderburn, Judith. 'Organisations and Social Actors in the Regionalization Process.' In *Elements of Regional Integration: The Way Forward*, edited by Peter Wickham, Neville Duncan, Judith Wedderburn, Peggy Antrobus, Andaiye, Andres Serbin, Francine Jacome and Kertist Augustus, 59–69. Kingston: Ian Randle Publishers, 1998.

Weir, Margaret. 'Ideas and the Politics of Bounded Innovation.' In *Structuring Politics. Historical Institutionalism in Comparative Analysis*, edited by Sven Steinmo, Kathleen Thelen and Frank Longstreth, 188–216. Cambridge: Cambridge University Press, 1992.

West Indian Commission. 'Time for Action. The Report of the West Indian Commission.' Blackrock: The West Indian Commission, 1992.

Wickham, Peter. 'More Shadow Than Substance.' In *The Caribbean Community: Beyond Survival*, edited by Kenneth O. Hall, 234–51. Kingston: Ian Randle Publishers, 2001.

Williams, Eric. *Inward Hunger: The Education of a Prime Minister*. Princeton: Nassau Wiener Publishers, 2006.

Wiltshire-Brodber, Rosina. 'The Caribbean Integration Movement: An Alternative Prospective.' *CARICOM Perspective*, 1983, 10.

Wooding, Hugh. 'Lecture on the Failure of the West Indies Federation by Sir Hugh Wooding, C.B.E Chief Justice of Trinidad and Tobago.' Port of Spain, Trinidad, 1964.

# INDEX

ACCP, *see* Association of Caribbean Community Parliamentarians
ALBA, *see* Bolivarian Alternative for Latin America
APEC, *see* Asia-Pacific Economic Cooperation
ASEAN, *see* Association of South East Asian Nations
Adams, Grantley, 42, 46
Adams, Tom, 81, 87
Anglo-American Caribbean Commission, 42
Anthony, Kenny, 165, 185, 208, 209
Archer-Gomes Report, 139–42
Arthur, Owen, 150, 165, 187, 206, 232
Asia-Pacific Economic Cooperation (APEC), 30
Association of Caribbean Community Parliamentarians (ACCP), 101, 104, 107, 114–16, 141, 164, 238
first mention as regional/parliamentary assembly, 88, 94
Association of Caribbean States (ACS), 106
Association of South East Asian Nations (ASEAN), 24–25, 32, 34
"The ASEAN Way", 32
Authority, 22–23, 24, 69, 89, 111, 243–44, 250
Automaticity of financing, 87, 101, 153, 170
Autonomy, 20, 21, 32, 243–44, 250

Barbados Labour Party (BLP), 42
Barrow, Errol, 42, 53, 72, 197, 232
Beckford, George, 56, 68
Benn, Denis, 152, 154, 166, 171, 175, 234
Bernal, Richard, 136, 193
Best, Lloyd, 148

Bird, Lester, 126, 202, 232
Bird, Vere, 54, 61, 197, 206
Bishop, Maurice, 81
Bodin, Jean, 2
Bolivarian Alternative for Latin America (ALBA), 224
Bourne, Compton, 148, 154, 164
Boxill, Ian, 158
Blaize, Herbert, 93
Bradshaw, Robert, 101
Brewster, Havelock, 56, 57, 110, 111, 138, 155
British Caribbean Federation Act (1956), 46
British Development and Welfare Committee, 42
Bureau of Heads of Government, 114, 117, 121, 126, 139, 164, 171, 233, 239
Burnham, Forbes, 53, 54, 57, 68, 72, 232, 238
Bustamante, Alexander, 44, 49, 53
Byers, Bruce, 20

CARICOM, *see* Caribbean Community
CARICOM Secretariat, *see* Caribbean Community Secretariat
CARICOM Commission, 108, 124, 127, 150, 152–53, 159, 161, 168, 171, 194, 239
CARICOM Council, 108, 111, 122
CARICOM Charter of Civil Society, 107, 124–25, 188
CARICOM Single Market (CSM), 185, 213
CARICOM Single Market and Economy (CSME), 92, 120, 181
CARIFTA, *see* Caribbean Free Trade Association
CCJ, *see* Caribbean Court of Justice

CDB, *see* Caribbean Development Bank
CHOG, *see* Conference of Heads of Government of the Caribbean Community
COFAP, *see* Council for Finance and Planning
COFCOR, *see* Council for Foreign and Community Relations
COHSOD, *see* Council for Human and Social Development
CONSLE, *see* Council for National Security and Law Enforcement
COTED, *see* Council for Trade and Economic Development
CRNM, *see* Caribbean Regional Negotiating Machinery
CSM, *see* CARICOM Single Market
CSME, *see* CARICOM Single Market and Economy
Caribbean Association of Industry and Commerce (CAIC), 115, 247
Caribbean Civilisation, 138, 147, 177, 207, 233. *See also* Ideology, of civilisation
Caribbean Community (CARICOM), and Common Market, 65, 228
Organs and Institutions, 76–78, 99–100, 186
membership of, xiv, 251n2
role of Secretary-General, 100, 124
Caribbean Community Secretariat, 74, 78, 116, 140, 150
location, 100, 238
restructuring, 116–17, 160
role in decision-making, 98–99
Caribbean Congress of Labour (CCL), 115, 247. *See also* Congress of Labour Leaders
Caribbean Court of Justice (CCJ), 116, 137, 152, 179–84, 219, 233, 241. *See also* Sovereignty, anomalies
appellate jurisdiction, 180–81
as regional supreme court, 108
first mention as proposal for Regional Court of Appeal, 61, 72

headquarters, 182
Caribbean Development Bank (CDB), 59–60, 77, 123, 20
agreement, 60
Caribbean Examinations Council, 78
Caribbean Free Trade Association (CARIFTA), 56, 58, 185, 199, 228, 237
Caribbean Law Institute, 123
Caribbean Policy Development Centre (CPDC), 116, 193, 247
Caribbean Regional Negotiating Machinery (CRNM), 132–36, 187, 190, 233, 242. *See also* Office of Trade Negotiations (OTN) and Sovereignty, anomalies
legal status, 187
rationalisation, 189–94
restructuring, 134–36
Caribbean political culture, 63, 91, 168, 221, 222, 234, 247
Carnegie, Ralph, 186, 210
Carrington, Edwin, 104, 111, 130, 231, 239
Central American Court of Justice, 31
Central American Integration System (SICA), 31, 224
Charles, Eugenia, 115
Cipriani, AA, 39
Cold War, 8, 12, 68, 81, 93, 236
Common Market of the South (MERCOSUR), 28–29, 30, 31
Common Market Annex, 74
Commonwealth Caribbean Regional Secretariat, 58–59
Community Law, 159, 161, 169–70, 177, 186
Community of Sovereign States, 16, 104, 109, 153, 155, 174, 216
Conference of Heads of Government of the Caribbean Community (CHOG), 70, 73, 230, 236
first meeting, 80
Conference of Heads of Government of the Commonwealth Caribbean Countries, 52, 59

Congress of Labour Leaders (1938), 40–41. *See also* Caribbean Congress of Labour (CCL)

Consultation, 142, 150, 205, 213
with Opposition, 184

Control, 20, 21, 213, 236, 243–44, 250

Council for Foreign and Community Relations (COFCOR), 122, 133

Council for Finance and Planning (COFAP), 122

Council for Human and Social Development (COHSOD), 122, 141

Council for National Security and Law Enforcement (CONSLE), 172

Council for Trade and Economic Development (COTED), 122, 133, 189

Council of Legal Education, 77

Cropper, Angela, 166

Crown Colony, see Government, Crown Colony system of

DeCastro, Steve, 57

Decision-making, 75, 141, 142, 205, 241
compliance, 87
effectiveness, 79
efficiency, 79, 96

Decolonisation, 8

Demas, William, xv, 20, 55, 58, 69, 70, 83–84, 95, 148, 197, 206, 234

Dependent underdevelopment, 67–68

Dickenson Bay Agreement, 56, 74

Dispute settlement, 90, 97

Dominican Republic, 193

ECCB, see Eastern Caribbean Central Bank

ECCM, see Eastern Caribbean Common Market

ECSC, see European Coal and Steel Community

EEC, see European Economic Community

EEZ, see Economic Export Zones

EPA, see EU-CARIFORUM Economic Partnership Agreement

EU, see European Union

EU-CARIFORUM Economic Partnership Agreement (EPA), 191–92

Eastern Caribbean Central Bank (ECCB), 204, 206

Eastern Caribbean Common Market (ECCM), 61, 199, 201

Eastern Caribbean Currency Authority, 199

Eastern Caribbean Supreme Court, 199

Economic Export Zones (EEZ), 23

European Central Bank (ECB), 33

European Coal and Steel Community (ECSC), 13

European Commission, 33, 163

European Council, 30, 31

European Court of Justice, 29

European Economic Community (EEC), 13, 55, 61, 70, 80, 110

European Parliament, 31

European Union (EU), 13, 21, 24, 28–29, 33, 175

Federal Labour Party (FLP), 46

Federal legacy, 62, 73, 118, 147, 165, 174, 184, 230, 231

Federalism, 13, 43

Federation of the Eight, 197

Federations, 43

First World War, 4, 40

Free movement of people/skills, 104, 176

Free Trade Area of the Americas (FTAA), 107, 129

*From CARIFTA to Caribbean Community*, 70–71

Functionalism, 13, 16, 43

Gairy, Eric, 61

Girvan, Norman, 56, 57, 68, 187, 191

Golding, Bruce, 173, 176, 192, 215, 248

Gonsalves, Ralph, 138, 147, 173, 176, 207, 208, 215, 226, 232, 248

Gomes, Albert, 44

Gomes, Patrick, 160

Governance, 7, 16, 17

capacity, 7, 8
global, xiv
good, 8, 84
legitimate, 69. *See also* Legitimacy
regional, *see* Regional governance
subregional, 37, 228
Government, 3, 7, 17
colonial in the West Indies, 39–40
Crown Colony system of, 39
self-government, 39
Globalisation, 8, 14
*Grande Anse Declaration*, 92, 94–95
Greene, Edward, 156–57
Grenada, 80–81, 85, 90
Group of Wise Mean, 85

Haas, Ernst, 14
Haiti, 144, 167
Heads of Government,
as protectors of sovereignty, 63, 235
caucus, 172, 176, 192, 236
Hinsley, F.H., 1
Hoyte, Desmond, 93, 233
Huntley, Earl, 210

ISER, *see* Institute of Social and
Economic Research.
Ideology, 235, 249
of civilisation, 138
of development, 177
of governance, 232, 233
of regional integration, 66–67, 95,
101, 232
ideological conflict, 81
ideological pluralism, 84–86
ideological vacuum, 232
Implementation, 90, 235
capacity, 143
deficit, 184, 241
Independence, 6, 38
Antigua and Barbuda, 201
Barbados, 57, 981
Cyprus, 49
economic, 55
Grenada, 201
Guyana, 57
Jamaica, 49–50

St Kitts and Nevis, 201
St Lucia, 201
St Vincent and the Grenadines,
201
Institute of Social and Economic
Research (ISER), 55. *See also* Sir
Arthur Lewis Institute of
Social and Economic Studies
(SALISES)
Institution(s),
as compliance mechanisms, 26, 27
deliberative, 27
executive, 27
legislative, 27, 28
regional, 26
sovereignty-protecting, 33, 63, 230
Institutional analysis, 35–37
Institutional control, 26
Institutional dysfunctionality, 146, 160
Institutional reform, 117. *See also*
Governance, reform
Institutionalisation, 34
typology of legislative, 28
Intergovernmentalism, 16, 27, 71, 170,
175, 200, 201, 220
legal frameworks, 30
liberal, 12
International law, 6, 27, 28
International legal personality, 6
Islandness, 62–63

Jackson, Robert, 8
Jagan, Cheddi, 52
Jagdeo, Bharat, 145, 171, 176, 192
Jamaica Labour Party (JLP), 180, 231
Joint Consultative Committee, 90, 115,
125
Joint diplomatic representation,
113–14
Joseph, Cuthbert, 154, 159, 166, 171
Juridical hybrid, 73

Krasner, Stephen, 9
dimensions of sovereignty, 9–10

Lamming, George, 161
League of Arab States, 32

League of Nations, 4
Legitimacy, 20–21, 22, 69, 90, 162, 243–44, 250
external, 22
internal, 22
Lewis- Joseph Task Force, 216
report of, 217–22
Lewis, Arthur, 197
Lewis, Patsy, 184
Lewis, Vaughan, 103, 166, 171, 175, 216
Litfin, Karen, 20, 21

MERCOSUR, see Common Market of the South
Manley, Michael, 48, 71–72, 74, 81, 94, 111, 231
Manley, Norman, 41, 44, 47, 68, 74, 231
Manning, Patrick, 111, 145, 150, 165, 173, 215, 232
Marryshow, Albert T, 39
McIntyre, Alister, 55, 56, 57, 81, 83–84, 95, 130, 134, 154
Mills, Gladstone, 99–100
Mitchell, James, 205
Monetary union, 104, 114
Montego Bay Conference on Closer Union, 43–45, 226
Moss-Solomon, James, 166
Munroe, Trevor, 158

North American Free Trade Area (NAFTA), 30
Nation(s), 5
Nationhood, 41
National self-determination, 4
Nationalism, 5, 39–41, 247
island 50–51
regional, 149, 223
territorial, 49, 62
Neo-functionalism, 12, 13, 170
spill-over, 13, 228
Nevis, 85–86, 215. See also
Independence, St Kitts and Nevis
New International Economic Order (NIEO), 68

New World Group, 56, 57, 67–68, 148
Nincic, Djuva, 20

OAS, see Organisation of American States
OAU, see Organisation of African Union
OECS, see Organisation of Eastern Caribbean States
OECS Assembly, 211
OECS Commission, 212
OECS Development Charter, 208–209
OECS Economic Union, 207, 208–14, 237
draft treaty, 211
OECS Secretariat, 204
OECS- Trinidad and Tobago Economic and Political Union, 214
Model 1, 218
Model 2, 221
Office of Trade Negotiations (OTN), 193, 242
Order of the Caribbean Community (OCC), 94, 176
first mention as system of honours, 94
Organisation of African Union (OAU), 12, 32, 53
Organisation of American States (OAS), 12
Organisation of Eastern Caribbean States (OECS), 80, 123, 147, 203, 246
institutions of, 203–204

PNM, see People's National Movement
PNP, see People's National Party
Participation, 69, 101, 164, 205, 238
Patterson, P.J., 101, 104, 111, 131, 134–36, 151, 176, 181, 186, 192, 233, 234
Chairman's Perspective, 152
People's National Movement (PNM), 42, 216
People's National Party (PNP), 41, 180
Personal Sovereignty, 103, 144, 231, 234, 235, 246, 249

Political context analysis, 36–37
Political culture, see Caribbean political culture
Political elites, xv, xvi, 33, 35
Political leadership, 248
Political union, 62, 106, 144, 173, 198, 200, 205, 206, 217, 221. See also West Indian State
Pollard, Duke, 86, 96–99
Prime Ministerial Expert Group on Governance (PMEGG), 151, 159, 179, 211
    report of, 161–64
Prime Ministerial Subcommittee on External Negotiations (PMSCEN), 129–30
Privy Council, see United Kingdom Judicial Committee of the Privy Council
Production Integration, 57
Proportionality, 168, 211

Quasi-Cabinet of Heads of Government, 139, 143, 164, 171, 192, 195, 239

Rainford, Roderick, 86, 91, 95, 102, 154, 166, 190, 239
Ramphal, Shridath, 67, 82, 95, 110, 131, 134, 151, 154, 159, 177, 234
Rawle, Cecil, 39
Referendum, (Jamaica 1962), 49–50, 180
Region(s), 17
Regionness, 14
Regional governance, 140, 146, 170, 227, 229, 231
    definitions, 15, 17
    framework for, 36
    modes of, 26, 27, 246
    models of executive, 126–37
    reform, 170, 174. See also Institutional reform
    subculture of, xviii, 196, 205, 222, 241
Regional governance analysis, 19, 35–37, 230

Regional identity, 14–15, 42, 176, 229
Regional institutions, see Institutions
Regional integration, 12, 13, 227
    economic integration, 12, 55
    ideology, see Ideology, of regional integration
    theories/approaches, 12
    variable geometry, 175, 176
Regional Security System (RSS), 204
Regionalisation, xiv
    Warleigh-Lack's typology of, 27
Regionalism, xvii, 227, 247
    definition, 11
    Fawcett's waves of, 12
    hub and spoke, 30
    mature, 153, 154, 167, 187
    models, 26
    new regionalism, 12, 14, 228
    sub-regionalism, 14
Revised Treaty of Chaguaramas, 108, 119–24, 216, 233, 237, 239
    Protocol I, 119–124
Revised Treaty of Basseterre, 214
Robinson, ANR, 49, 93, 111
Rose Hall Declaration, 152

SALISES, see Sir Arthur Lewis Institute of Social and Economic Studies
SICA, see Central American Integration System
Sandiford, Erskine, 94
Schengen zone, 22
Seaga, Edward, 85, 86, 173, 181
Second World War, xiii, 5, 41, 42
Simpson Miller, Portia, 192
Single CARICOM Act, 161, 170
Single Development Vision (SDV), 187–88, 209
Single European Act, 31
Sir Arthur Lewis Institute of Social and Economic Studies (SALISES), 158. See also Institute of Small size, xiv, xv, 8, 63, 29
Social and Economic Research (ISER)
Sovereignty, xviii,
    absolute, 149

anomalies, 73, 194, 241
attributes, 11, 249
bargains, *see* Sovereignty bargains
Caribbean legal arrangements
which protect sovereignty, 59, 75,
237
claims to, 1, 7, 8
collective, 106, 152, 161, 162, 175,
234
definitions of, 2, 6
disaggregation, *see* Sovereignty,
unbundling
domestic, 10, 24, 71
effective, xv, 20, 55, 56, 64, 66, 69
external, 10
formal, xv, 20, 56, 64, 70
historical stages, 2–7
interdependence, 10, 71
internal, 10
international legal, 9, 24
joint, 209
judicial, 182
novelty of, xv, 9
paradox of, *see* Sovereignty
paradox
personal, *see* Personal sovereignty
pool(ing), 14, 106, 111, 156
popular, 10, 69, 114, 238, 246
re-aggregation, 34, 245
relative, 6
safeguard(ing), xvi, 88, 91, 97,
224, 302, 245
shared, 117, 127, 146, 156, 168,
170, 175
tradition of, *see* Sovereignty
tradition. *See also* Sovereignty,
anomalies
unbundling, 9, 10
Westphalian, 9–10, 22, 24, 26, 71,
148
Sovereignty bargains, 16, 19, 27–28,
174, 195, 224, 243
attributes of, 20–21,22, 24, 243
cocktail, 22–23
definition of, 20, 21
outcomes, 26, 27
scenarios, 25

Sovereignty bargains analysis, 35–37,
243
Sovereignty paradox, xiv, xv, 15, 20,
38, 55, 62–63, 139, 144, 180, 197,
198, 208, 222, 227, 228, 245, 246,
248
Sovereignty-protecting institutions, *see*
Institutions
Sovereignty tradition, xviii, 222, 245
Spill-over, *see* Neo-functionalism
State(s),
capacity, 8–9, 229
independent, 6
modern (democratic), 4, 7
nation-state, 5, 7
new, xv, 51, 229
paradoxes of state power, xiv
quasi-state(s), 8
responsibilities of, 6. *See also*
Statehood
small developing, xiv. *See also*
Small size
*societas*/society of, 2, 6
sovereign, 2
Statehood
legal criteria, 6–7
national independent, 6
sovereign, 6–7
Structural adjustment, 84–85, 87–88
Subsidiarity, 168, 211
Supranationalism, 12, 16, 27, 75, 137,
143, 155, 174–175, 200, 201, 207,
210, 241
supranational legal system, 28
supralegal system, 28
legal system, 28
quasi-supranationalism, 136, 242
Suriname, 95

Technical Working Group on
Governance (TWG), 166–71, 179,
211
The Bahamas, 120–121
*The Economics of Nationhood*, 47–28
Thomas, Clive, 56, 57, 68, 83
Thomas, Tillman, 215
Thompson, David, 177

*Time for Action*, see West Indian
   Commission, report of
Treaty of Asunción, 29
Treaty of Basseterre, 203
   revised, see Revised Treaty of
   Basseterre
Treaty of Chaguaramas, 74
   revised, see Revised Treaty of
   Chaguaramas
Treaty of Lisbon, 28, 31
Treaty of Westphalia, see Westphalia
Transnationalism, 7, 9, 11
Trinidad and Tobago, 61

UN, see United Nations
UNASUR, see Union of South American
   Nations
UWI, see University of the West Indies.
   See also University College of the
   West Indies
Unanimity,
   rule, 31, 87–88, 96–98, 123, 204
   voting, 75, 121, 155, 222, 236, 237
Union of South American Nations
   (UNASUR), 224
United Kingdom Judicial Committee of
   the Privy Council (JCPC), 72, 137,
   182, 184
United Nations (UN), 5, 7, 12, 175
University College of the West Indies,
   42. See also University of the West
   Indies (UWI)
University of Guyana, 78
University of the West Indies (UWI), 52,
   77, 123

Venetiaan, Runaldo, 165
Venner, Dwight, 210

WISA, see West Indies Associated
   States
Westphalia, 26. See also Sovereignty,
   Westphalian
   Treaty of, 2, 3
West Indian Commission, 95, 102,
   104–109, 174, 205, 233
   interim report, 102
   report of, 104–109, 233
West Indian identity, 66–67
West Indian Nationalism, 41–42, 62,
   69, 95, 197, 200, 217, 223, 227,
   228, 232, 245
West Indian State, 61, 66, 198
West Indies Associated States (WISA),
   57, 58, 78, 199
West Indies Federation, 38, 197, 238
   capital of, 48
   constitution of, 46
   membership of, 46
West Indies Shipping Service, 42, 52
Williams, Eric, 42, 45, 47, 51, 53,
   61, 70, 72, 81, 232. See also *The
   Economics of Nationhood*
   famous quote of "10 – 1 = 0", 50
World Trade Organisation (WTO), 129
World War I, see First World War
World War II, see Second World War

www.ingramcontent.com/pod-product-compliance
Lightning Source LLC
Chambersburg PA
CBHW050333270326
41926CB00016B/3440